D1303945

t's YOUR country. Learn it. Love it. Explore it.

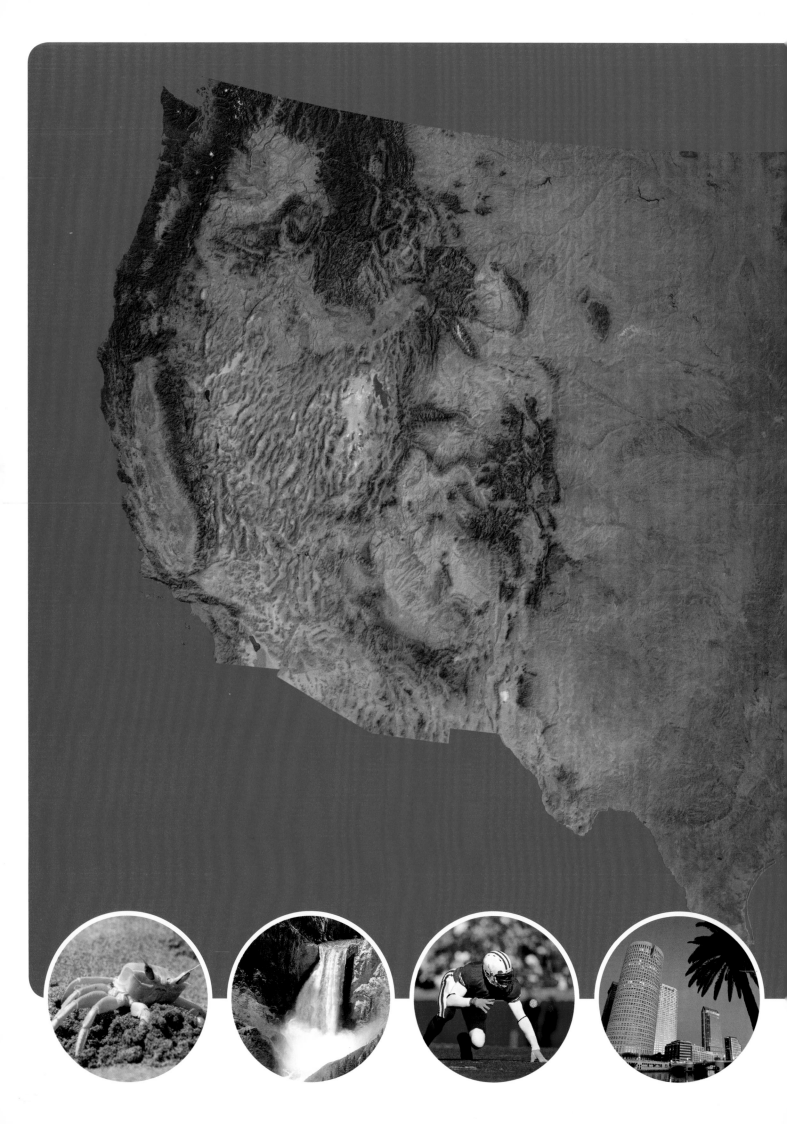

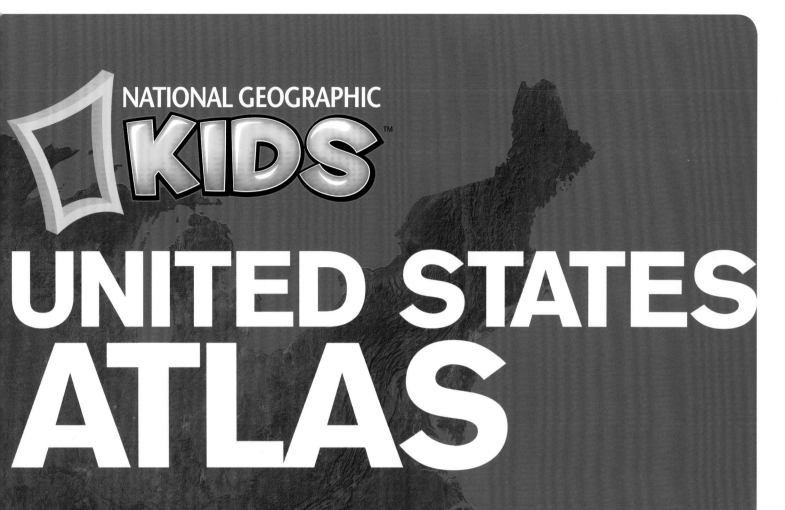

NATIONAL GEOGRAPHIC
KIDS™

UNITED STATES ATLAS

NATIONAL GEOGRAPHIC
WASHINGTON, D.C.

TABLE OF CONTENTS

FRONT OF THE BOOK

GETTING STARTED
How to Use This Atlas 6
How to Use the
  Atlas Web Site 8

THE PHYSICAL UNITED STATES 10
Natural Environment 12
Natural Hazards 14

THE POLITICAL UNITED STATES 16
Population 18
People on the Move 20
Getting Green 22
The National Capital 24

THE NORTHEAST 26

PHYSICAL & POLITICAL MAPS 28
About the Northeast 30
Connecticut 32
Delaware 34
Maine 36
Maryland 38
Massachusetts 40
New Hampshire 42
New Jersey 44
New York 46
Pennsylvania 48
Rhode Island 50
Vermont 52

THE SOUTHEAST 54

PHYSICAL & POLITICAL MAPS 56
About the Southeast 58
Alabama 60
Arkansas 62
Florida 64
Georgia 66
Kentucky 68
Louisiana 70
Mississippi 72
North Carolina 74
South Carolina 76
Tennessee 78
Virginia 80
West Virginia 82

THE MIDWEST 84

PHYSICAL & POLITICAL MAPS 86
About the Midwest 88
Illinois 90
Indiana 92
Iowa 94
Kansas 96
Michigan 98
Minnesota 100
Missouri 102
Nebraska 104
North Dakota 106
Ohio 108
South Dakota 110
Wisconsin 112

Northeast: Maine lighthouse, pp. 36–37

Southeast:
Florida manatee, p. 64

Midwest: Illinois hay field with tractor, pp. 90–91

Title page: Atlantic sand crab; Lower Falls of the Yellowstone, MT; football player; Tampa, FL;
sage grouse; skyline, Seattle, WA; Organ Pipe Cactus National Monument, AZ.

THE SOUTHWEST 114

PHYSICAL & POLITICAL MAPS	116
About the Southwest	118
Arizona	120
New Mexico	122
Oklahoma	124
Texas	126

THE WEST 128

PHYSICAL & POLITICAL MAPS	130
About the West	132
Alaska	134
California	136
Colorado	138
Hawai'i	140
Idaho	142
Montana	144
Nevada	146
Oregon	148
Utah	150
Washington	152
Wyoming	154

THE TERRITORIES 156

POLITICAL MAP & FACT BOXES	156
U.S. Caribbean Territories Puerto Rico, Virgin Islands	
U.S. Pacific Territories American Samoa, Guam, Northern Mariana Islands	
Other U.S. Territories Baker Is., Howland Is., Jarvis Is., Johnston Atoll, Kingman Reef, Midway Islands, Navassa Is., Palmyra Atoll, Wake Is.	
About the Territories	158

BACK OF THE BOOK

U.S. FACTS & FIGURES	160
GLOSSARY	161
OUTSIDE WEB SITES	161
PLACE-NAME INDEX	162
CREDITS	176

Territories: Festival dancers, American Samoa, pp. 158–159

Southwest: Albuquerque balloon festival, p. 122

West: Wyoming ranch, p. 154

HOW TO USE THIS ATLAS

This atlas is much more than just another book of maps about the United States. Of course you'll find all the things you'd expect to find—country, regional, and state maps, essays, photos, flags, graphs, and fact boxes—for the country as a whole as well as for each region and state (even the territories). But there's much more. This atlas, through a specially designed Web site (see pages 8–9), not only leads you to places where you can find more information and keep up-to-date about all kinds of things, it also allows you to go beyond the flat page and experience the sights and sounds of the country through the multimedia archives of National Geographic.

STATE FACT BOX
The fact box has all the key information you need at a glance about a state, its flag and nickname, statistics about area, cities, population, ethnic and racial makeup,* statehood, industry, and agriculture, plus some fun Geo Whiz facts and the state bird and flower.

*The ethnic/racial percentages total more than 100 percent because Hispanics can be included with any race or ethnic group.

WEB LINKS
Throughout the atlas you will find black-and-yellow Web link icons for photos, videos, sounds, games, and more information. You can get to all of these links through one URL: www.nationalgeographic.com/kids-usa-atlas. This link will take you to the Web site specially designed to go with this atlas (see pages 8–9). Bookmark it so you can use it often.

COLOR BARS
Each section of the atlas has its own color to make it easy to move from one to another. Look for the color in the Table of Contents and across the top of the pages in the atlas. The name of the section and the title for each topic or map is in the color bar.

The Northeast
The Southeast
The Midwest
The Southwest
The West
The Territories

WHERE ARE THE PICTURES?
If you want to know where a picture in any of the regional sections in the atlas was taken, check the map in the regional photo essay. Find the label that describes the photograph you are curious about, and follow the line to its location.

CHARTS AND GRAPHS
The photo essay for each state includes a chart or graph that highlights economic, physical, cultural, or some other type of information related to the state.

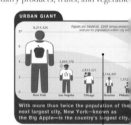

BAR SCALE

Each map has a bar scale in miles and kilometers to help you find out how far it is from one place to another on the map.

"YOU ARE HERE"

Locator maps show you where each region and state within the region is in relation to the rest of the United States. Regions are shown in the regional color; featured states are in yellow.

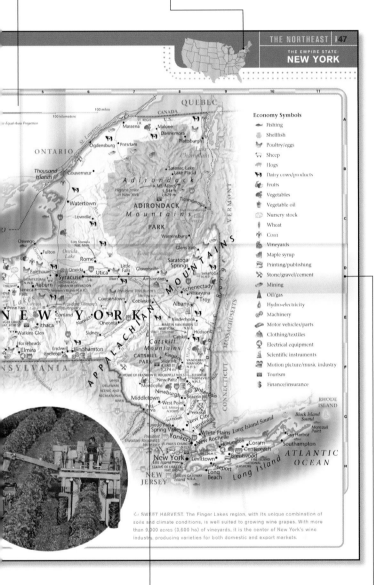

THE NORTHEAST | 47

THE EMPIRE STATE:
NEW YORK

Economy Symbols

- Fishing
- Shellfish
- Poultry/eggs
- Sheep
- Hogs
- Dairy cows/products
- Fruits
- Vegetables
- Vegetable oil
- Nursery stock
- Wheat
- Corn
- Vineyards
- Maple syrup
- Printing/publishing
- Stone/gravel/cement
- Mining
- Oil/gas
- Hydro-electricity
- Machinery
- Motor vehicles/parts
- Clothing/textiles
- Electrical equipment
- Scientific instruments
- Motion picture/music industry
- Tourism
- Finance/insurance

SWEET HARVEST. The Finger Lakes region, with its unique combination of soils and climate conditions, is well suited to growing wine grapes. With more than 9,000 acres (3,600 ha) of vineyards, it is the center of New York's wine industry, producing varieties for both domestic and export markets.

Sycamore, IL **91** B4

Sycan (river), OR **149** F4

Sycan N.W.&S.R., OR **149** F4

Sylacauga, AL **61** D4

Sylvania, OH **109** A3

Syracuse, NY **47** D5

Sysladobsis Lake, ME

INDEX AND GRID

A grid system makes it easy to find places listed in the index. For example, the listing for Syracuse, New York, is followed by **47** D5. The bold type is the page number; D5 tells you the city is near the point where imaginary lines drawn from D and 5 on the grid bars meet.

MAP ICONS

Maps use symbols to stand for many physical, political, and economic features. Below is a complete list of the map symbols used in this atlas. In addition, each state map has its own key featuring symbols for major economic activities. Additional abbreviations used in this atlas as well as metric conversion tables are listed on the endsheets at the back of the book.

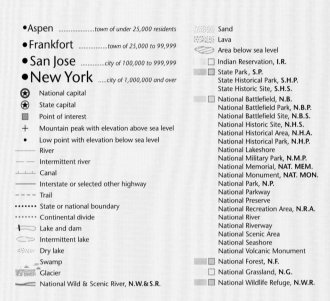

- •Aspen ....town of under 25,000 residents
- •Frankfort ....town of 25,000 to 99,999
- •San Jose ....city of 100,000 to 999,999
- •New York .....city of 1,000,000 and over
- National capital
- State capital
- Point of interest
- Mountain peak with elevation above sea level
- Low point with elevation below sea level
- River
- Intermittent river
- Canal
- Interstate or selected other highway
- Trail
- State or national boundary
- Continental divide
- Lake and dam
- Intermittent lake
- Dry lake
- Swamp
- Glacier
- National Wild & Scenic River, **N.W.&S.R.**

- Sand
- Lava
- Area below sea level
- Indian Reservation, **I.R.**
- State Park, **S.P.**
- State Historical Park, **S.H.P.**
- State Historic Site, **S.H.S.**
- National Battlefield, **N.B.**
- National Battlefield Park, **N.B.P.**
- National Battlefield Site, **N.B.S.**
- National Historic Site, **N.H.S.**
- National Historical Area, **N.H.A.**
- National Historical Park, **N.H.P.**
- National Lakeshore
- National Military Park, **N.M.P.**
- National Memorial, **NAT. MEM.**
- National Monument, **NAT. MON.**
- National Park, **N.P.**
- National Parkway
- National Preserve
- National Recreation Area, **N.R.A.**
- National River
- National Riverway
- National Scenic Area
- National Seashore
- National Volcanic Monument
- National Forest, **N.F.**
- National Grassland, **N.G.**
- National Wildlife Refuge, **N.W.R.**

Economy Symbols

- Fishing
- Lobster fishing
- Shellfish
- Poultry/eggs
- Sheep
- Hogs
- Dairy cows/products
- Beef cattle
- Fruits
- Vegetables
- Vegetable oil
- Peanuts
- Nursery stock
- Wheat
- Corn
- Rice
- Soybeans
- Sugarcane
- Cotton
- Tobacco
- Coffee
- Vineyards
- Maple syrup
- Timber/forest products
- Furniture
- Printing/publishing

- Stone/gravel/cement
- Mining
- Coal
- Oil/gas
- Hydro-electricity
- Machinery
- Metal manufacturing
- Metal products
- Shipbuilding
- Railroad equipment
- Motor vehicles/parts
- Rubber/plastics
- Chemistry
- Food processing
- Clothing/textiles
- Leather products
- Glass/clay products
- Jewelry
- Electrical equipment
- Computers/electronics
- Scientific instruments
- Aircraft/parts
- Aerospace
- Motion picture/music industry
- Tourism
- Finance/insurance

HOW TO USE THE ATLAS WEB SITE

As you can see by flipping through the pages, this atlas is chock full. There are photographs, statistics, quick facts, and—most of all—lots of charts and detailed maps. Plus there is a companion Web site that adds even more. You can watch videos of animals in their natural surroundings or of a volcano erupting; listen to the sounds of people, places, and animals; find lots of state information; download pictures and maps for school reports; and play games that allow you to explore the United States. You can even send e-postcards to your friends. The

Web site provides added value to specific subjects in the atlas and also helps you explore on your own, taking you deep into the resources of National Geographic and beyond. Throughout the atlas you will find these icons.

PHOTOS VIDEO AUDIO GAMES INFO

The icons are placed near pictures, on maps, or next to text. Each icon tells you that you can find more on that subject on the Web site. To follow any icon link, go to www.nationalgeographic.com/kids-usa-atlas.

⇨ **START HERE.**

There are three ways to find what you are looking for from the Home Page:

1. BY ATLAS PAGE NUMBER
2. BY TOPIC
3. BY ICON

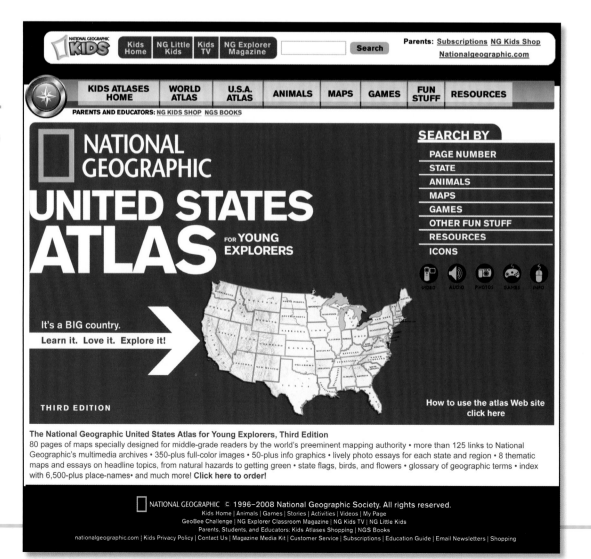

www.nationalgeographic.com/kids-usa-atlas

1. SEARCH BY ATLAS PAGE NUMBER

⇐ **PAGE NUMBER PULL-DOWN MENU.** If you find an icon in the atlas and want to go directly to that link, use the page number pull-down menu. Just drag and click.

2. SEARCH BY TOPIC

⇨ **LIST OF TOPICS.** If you want to explore a specific topic, click on the entry in the topic list. This list is your portal to vast quantities of National Geographic information, photos, videos, games, and more, all arranged by subject. Say you're interested in Animals. One click takes you to the Animals choice page (below).

⇩ **CREATURE FEATURES.** Click to go to the National Geographic Kids' animal site. Click on an animal, and you will find a full feature about it, including photos, video, a range map, and other fun info.

⇩ **CRITTERCAM.** Scientists put video cameras on animals to learn about the animal from its point of view. Click to see those videos, learn about the project, play games such as exploring the virtual world of a seal, and more.

⇐ **ANIMALS A–Z.** This choice takes you to the animal site for adults and older kids. Use the list of animals in the upper right-hand corner of the page. Clicking on an animal name takes you to the profile of that animal.

3. SEARCH BY ICON

⇐ **SELECT ONE OF FIVE ICONS.** If you want to find all the videos referenced in the atlas, or all of the audios, photos, or games, click on one of the icons. A list will drop down. Choose from the list, and you're there! Clicking on Blackbeard takes you to a trailer for a National Geographic Channel film.

THE PHYSICAL UNITED STATES

Stretching from the Atlantic in the east to the Pacific in the west, the United States is the third largest country in area in the world. Its physical diversity ranges from mountains to fertile plains and dry deserts. Shading on the map indicates changes in elevation, while colors suggest different vegetation patterns.

⇨ ALASKA AND HAWAI'I. In addition to the states located on the main landmass, the U.S. has two states—Alaska and Hawai'i—that are not directly connected to the other 48 states. If Alaska and Hawai'i were shown in their correct relative sizes and locations, the map would not fit on the page. The locator globe shows the correct relative size and location of each.

San Francisco

Coast Ranges   **Sierra Nevada**   **Great Basin**   **Rocky Mountains**

0   400 miles

0   400 kilometers

Albers Conic Equal-Area Projection

Lake of the Woods

Red River of the North

Mesabi Ra.

Eagle Mt. 2,301 ft 701 m

Isle Royale

Lake Superior

Keweenaw Peninsula

Source of the Mississippi (Lake Itasca)

Upper Peninsula

Minnesota

James

Mississippi

Wisconsin

Strs. of Mackinac

Lake Huron

Lower Peninsula

Lake Michigan

Lake Winnebago

Lake St. Clair

Lake Erie

Lake Ontario

Niagara Falls

Lake Champlain

Adirondack Mts.

Green Mts.

Mt. Washington 6,288 ft 1,917 m

Gulf of Maine

Connecticut

Catskill Mts.

Hudson

Cape Cod

Delaware

Long Island

Cedar

CENTRAL

Des Moines

Illinois

Platte

Geographical Center of the 48 Contiguous United States

Hills

Missouri

Wabash

Great Miami

Ohio

LOWLAND

Allegheny

Allegheny Plateau

Susquehanna

Potomac

Delaware Bay

Washington, D.C.

James

Chesapeake Bay

Lake of the Ozarks

Harry S. Truman Res.

Ozark Plateau

Ohio

Kentucky Lake

Lake Barkley

Tennessee

Cumberland

Appalachian Plateau

Cumberland Plateau

APPALACHIAN MOUNTAINS

Mt. Mitchell 6,684 ft, 2,037 m

Roanoke

James

Cape Fear

Great Pee Dee

Cape Hatteras

Magazine Mt. 2,753 ft 839 m

Ouachita Mts.

Arkansas

Mississippi

Black

Chattahoochee

Savannah

Cape Fear

Red

Ouachita

Alabama Belt

Altamaha

Trinity

Sabine

Red

COASTAL

Okefenokee Swamp

Suwannee

PLAIN

Colorado

Mississippi River Delta

Cape Canaveral

Lake Okeechobee

The Everglades

Florida Keys

NATURAL VEGETATION

	NEEDLELEAF FOREST
	BROADLEAF FOREST
	MIXED FOREST
	GRASSLAND
	TROPICAL VEGETATION
	DESERT
	TUNDRA

⇩ CROSS SECTION. Trace a line from Washington, D.C., to San Francisco. Locate the features shown in the cross-section below.

Washington, D.C.

Great Plains   **Ozark Plateau**   **Appalachian Mountains**

NATURAL ENVIRONMENT

A big part of the natural environment of the United States is the climate. With humid areas near the coasts, dry interior regions far from any major water body, and land areas that extend from northern Alaska to southern Florida and Hawai'i, the country experiences great variation in climate. Location is the key. Distance from the Equator, nearness to water, wind patterns, temperature of nearby water bodies, and elevation are things that influence temperature and precipitation. Climate affects the types of vegetation that grow in a particular place and plays a part in soil formation.

CHANGING CLIMATE

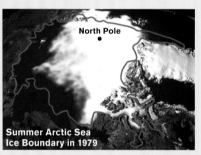

North Pole

Summer Arctic Sea Ice Boundary in 1979

Scientists are concerned that a recent warming trend may be more than a natural cycle and that human activity may be a contributing factor. An increase in average temperatures could result in more severe storms, changes in precipitation patterns, and the spread of deserts. Rising temperatures may also play a part in the melting of glaciers, which could lead to a rise in ocean levels and the shrinking of the Arctic ice cover. NASA satellite images indicate that Arctic ice is shrinking as much as 9 percent each decade. Many believe that this puts polar bears at risk, since they normally hunt and raise their young on ice floes.

0   400 miles
0   400 kilometers

ALASKA

HAWAI'I

0   150 miles
0   150 kilometers

Missouri

Lake Superior

0   400 miles
0   400 kilometers
Albers Conic Equal-Area Projection

Lake Huron

Lake Michigan

Lake Ontario

Lake Erie

Hudson

Mississippi

Missouri

Platte

Ohio

Arkansas

Savannah

Red

Rio Grande

Pecos

Brazos

Red

Mississippi

Lake Okeechobee

⇧ **CLIMATE MOSAIC.** The United States includes every major climate type, shown in different colors on the map above.

CLIMATE ZONES

Tropical
- Tropical wet
- Tropical wet and dry

Dry
- Semiarid
- Arid

Mild
- Marine west coast
- Mediterranean
- Humid subtropical

Continental
- Hot summer
- Warm summer
- Subarctic

Polar
- Tundra and ice

High Elevations
- Highlands

WARMING UP

Temperatures normally fluctuate from year to year, but evidence indicates that Earth is experiencing a warming pattern unlike any in recorded history. Data for major U.S. cities show a clear trend of rising average temperatures. The increase could be as much as 3 to 9 degrees Fahrenheit (1.7° to 5°C) by the end of the 21st century.

°F	°C	
75	24	
72	22	Orlando, FL*
68	20	
64	18	
61	16	
57	14	Albuquerque, NM
54	12	
50	10	Boise, ID
46	8	Syracuse, NY
43	6	Minneapolis - St. Paul, MN

1900   1910   1920   1930   1940   1950   1960   1970   1980   1990   2000

* Data for Orlando and Syracuse is not available before the dates shown.

NATURAL HAZARDS

The natural environment of the United States provides much diversity, but it also poses many dangers, especially when people locate homes and businesses in places at risk of natural disasters. Tornadoes bring destructive winds, and hurricanes bring strong winds, rain, and more; shifting of Earth's crust along fault lines rattles buildings; flood waters and wildfires threaten lives and property. More than one-third of the U.S. population lives in hazard-prone areas. Compare this natural disasters map to the population map on pages 18–19.

ALASKA

Alaska has about 80 major volcanic centers.
More earthquakes occur in Alaska than in the other 49 states combined.

Prince William Sound, 1964

Novarupta, 1912

Tsunami, 1964

Tsunami, 1958

Tsunami, 1946, 1957

0   400 miles
0   400 kilometers

HAWAI'I

Iniki, 1992

Tsunami, 1946

Tsunami, 1868, 1946

Haleakala

Hualalai

Mauna Loa

Kilauea

Kau District, 1868

Loihi

0   150 miles
0   150 kilometers

NATURAL HAZARDS

BLIZZARD. Severe storm with bitter cold temperatures and wind-whipped snow and ice particles that reduce visibility to less than 650 feet (198 m), paralyzing transportation systems

FLOOD. Inundation of buildings or roadways caused by overflow of a river or stream swollen by heavy rainfall or rapid snowmelt; may involve displacement of people

DROUGHT. Long and continuous period of abnormally low precipitation, resulting in water shortages that negatively impact people, animals, and plant life; may result in crop loss

HURRICANE. Tropical storm in the Atlantic, Caribbean, Gulf of Mexico, or eastern Pacific with a minimum sustained wind speed of 74 miles per hour (119 kmph)

ICE STORM. Damaging accumulations of ice associated with freezing rain; may pull down trees or utility lines, causing extensive damage and creating dangerous travel conditions

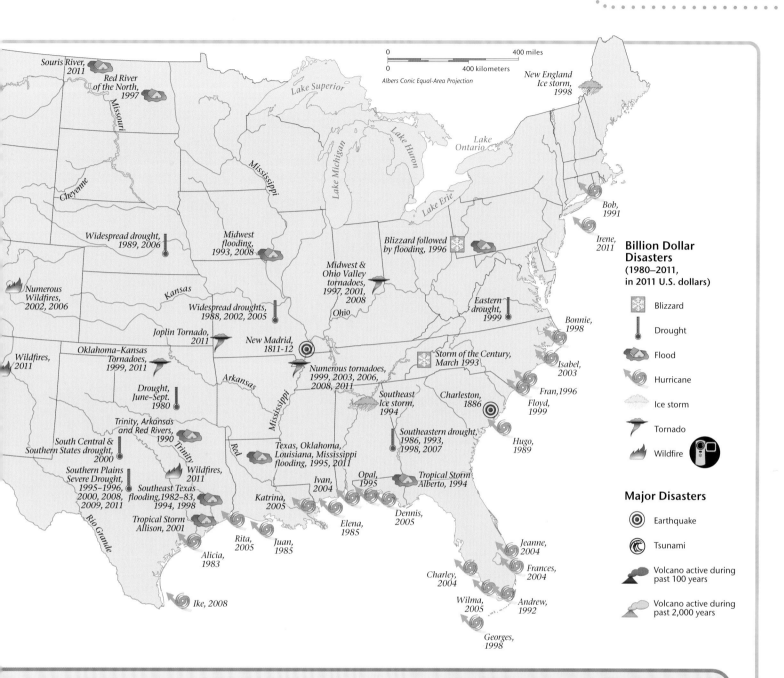

Souris River,
2011

Red River
of the North,
1997

Missouri

Cheyenne

Widespread drought,
1989, 2006

Lake Superior

Lake Michigan

Lake Huron

Lake
Ontario

Lake Erie

New England
Ice storm,
1998

Bob,
1991

Irene,
2011

Midwest
flooding,
1993, 2008

Blizzard followed
by flooding, 1996

Midwest &
Ohio Valley
tornadoes,
1997, 2001,
2008

Kansas

Numerous
Wildfires,
2002, 2006

Widespread droughts,
1988, 2002, 2005

Ohio

Eastern
drought,
1999

Bonnie,
1998

Joplin Tornado,
2011

New Madrid,
1811-12

Isabel,
2003

Wildfires,
2011

Oklahoma-Kansas
Tornadoes,
1999, 2011

Arkansas

Numerous tornadoes,
1999, 2003, 2006,
2008, 2011

Storm of the Century,
March 1993

Southeast
Ice storm,
1994

Charleston,
1886

Fran,1996

Floyd,
1999

Drought,
June–Sept.
1980

Mississippi

Trinity, Arkansas
and Red Rivers,
1990

South Central &
Southern States drought,
2000

Trinity

Red

Texas, Oklahoma,
Louisiana, Mississippi
flooding, 1995, 2011

Southeastern drought,
1986, 1993,
1998, 2007

Hugo,
1989

Southern Plains
Severe Drought,
1995–1996,
2000, 2008,
2009, 2011

Wildfires,
2011

Southeast Texas
flooding,1982–83,
1994, 1998

Ivan,
2004

Opal,
1995

Tropical Storm
Alberto, 1994

Tropical Storm
Allison, 2001

Katrina,
2005

Elena,
1985

Dennis,
2005

Rio Grande

Rita,
2005

Juan,
1985

Alicia,
1983

Charley,
2004

Jeanne,
2004

Frances,
2004

Ike, 2008

Wilma,
2005

Andrew,
1992

Georges,
1998

0   400 miles
0   400 kilometers
Albers Conic Equal-Area Projection

**Billion Dollar
Disasters**
(1980–2011,
in 2011 U.S. dollars)

- Blizzard
- Drought
- Flood
- Hurricane
- Ice storm
- Tornado
- Wildfire

Major Disasters

- Earthquake
- Tsunami
- Volcano active during
  past 100 years
- Volcano active during
  past 2,000 years

TORNADO. Violently
rotating column of air
that, when it reaches the
ground, is the most dam-
aging of all atmospheric
phenomena; most com-
mon in the central U.S.

WILDFIRE. Free-burning,
uncontained fire in a forest
or grassland; may result
from lightning strikes or
accidental or deliberate
human activity in areas
where conditions are dry

EARTHQUAKE. Shaking
or vibration created by
the energy released by
movement of Earth's crust
along plate boundaries;
can cause structural
damage and loss of life

TSUNAMI. Series of
unusually large ocean
waves caused by an
underwater earthquake,
landslide, or volcanic
eruption; very destructive
in coastal areas

VOLCANO. Vent or
opening in Earth's surface
through which molten
rock called lava, ash, and
gases are released; often
associated with tectonic
plate boundaries

POLITICAL MAP

THE POLITICAL UNITED STATES

Like a giant patchwork quilt, the United States is made up of 50 states, each uniquely different but together making a national fabric held together by a Constitution and a federal government. State boundaries, outlined in various colors on the map, set apart internal political units within the country. The national capital—Washington, D.C.—is marked by a star in a double circle on the map. The capital of each state is marked by a star in a single circle.

9:00 AM — PACIFIC TIME
10:00 AM — MOUNTAIN TIME

Cape Flattery

Seattle
Olympia • Tacoma
WASHINGTON
• Spokane
• Yakima
Portland
• Lewiston
Great Falls
Missouri
Salem
IDAHO
• Butte
Helena
MONTANA
Eugene
OREGON
• Billings
• Medford
• Boise
Klamath Falls
Idaho Falls
Cody
Yellowstone L.
Snake
• Eureka
• Pocatello
WYOMING
• Redding
Great Salt Lake
Casper
Reno • Ogden
Cheyenne
Sacramento • Carson City
Great Basin
Salt Lake City
Laramie
Lake Tahoe
• Provo
Fort Collins
San Francisco • Oakland
NEVADA
UTAH
Grand Junction
Denver
San Jose
Salinas
COLORADO
Fresno
Lake Powell
Colorado
Mojave
St. George
Colorado Springs
Bakersfield
Las Vegas
Lake Mead
Point Conception
Desert
Grand Canyon
Flagstaff
Santa Fe
Los Angeles
Long Beach • Riverside
ARIZONA
Albuquerque
Salton Sea
NEW MEXICO
San Diego
Phoenix • Mesa
• Yuma
• Tucson
Ros
Las Cruces
Rio Grande
El Paso

0 — 400 miles
0 — 400 kilometers

7:00 AM
HAWAI'I-ALEUTIAN TIME

North Slope
Brooks Range
ALASKA
Yukon
Alaska Range
Juneau
• Anchorage
Alaska Peninsula
ALEUTIAN ISLANDS

8:00 AM
ALASKA TIME

7:00 AM
HAWAI'I-ALEUTIAN TIME

Kaua'i
Ni'ihau O'ahu HAWAI'I
Honolulu Moloka'i
Lana'i Maui
Kaho'olawe
Hilo
Hawai'i

0 — 150 mi
0 — 150 km

⬆ TIME ZONES. Earth is divided into 24 time zones, each about 15 degrees of longitude wide, reflecting the distance Earth turns from west to east each hour. The U.S. is divided into six time zones, indicated by red dotted lines on the maps. When it is noon in Boston, what is the time in Seattle?

11:00 AM
CENTRAL TIME

12:00 PM
EASTERN TIME

0   300 miles
0   300 kilometers
Albers Conic Equal-Area Projection

Lake of the Woods

Isle Royale

Lake Superior

MAINE

Minot
Grand Forks
International Falls
Duluth
Marquette
Bangor
Augusta

NORTH DAKOTA
Bismarck Fargo
MINNESOTA Superior
MICHIGAN
Lake Champlain
Burlington
VT.
N.H.
Portland
Concord

Aberdeen
SOUTH DAKOTA
Minneapolis
St. Paul
WISCONSIN
Green Bay
Montpelier
Lake Ontario
Rochester
Syracuse Albany
MASS.
Boston
Cape Cod
Providence

Pierre
Sioux Falls
Madison
Grand Rapids
Lansing
NEW YORK
Buffalo
Hartford
CONN. RHODE ISLAND

rapid
Missouri
IOWA
Milwaukee
Rockford
Detroit
Erie
Lake Erie
PENNSYLVANIA
Newark
Long Island
New York
Trenton
NEW JERSEY

NEBRASKA
Omaha
Grand Island
Des Moines
Davenport
Chicago
Gary
Fort Wayne
Toledo Cleveland
OHIO
Columbus
Harrisburg
Pittsburgh
Philadelphia
Baltimore
DELAWARE
Dover

Platte
Lincoln
ILLINOIS
INDIANA
Dayton
Cincinnati
WEST VIRGINIA
Washington
D.C.
Annapolis
MARYLAND
Chesapeake Bay

Kansas City
Jefferson City
Springfield
Indianapolis
Louisville
Frankfort
Charleston
Richmond
VIRGINIA

Topeka
St. Louis
Evansville
Lexington
Roanoke
Norfolk
Virginia Beach

KANSAS
Dodge City
Wichita
MISSOURI
Springfield
Paducah
KENTUCKY
Greensboro
Raleigh
Cape Hatteras

Arkansas
Knoxville
Nashville
NORTH CAROLINA
Charlotte

Tulsa
OKLAHOMA
Fort Smith
ARKANSAS
Memphis
Chattanooga
Greenville
Columbia
SOUTH CAROLINA

Amarillo
Oklahoma City
Lawton
Little Rock
Huntsville
TENNESSEE
Atlanta
Charleston

Lubbock
Wichita Falls
MISSISSIPPI
Birmingham
GEORGIA
Macon
Savannah

Fort Worth
Abilene
Red
Shreveport
Jackson
ALABAMA
Columbus

midland
Dallas
Montgomery
Savannah

ssa
Waco
LOUISIANA
Natchez
Mobile
Jacksonville

TEXAS
Austin
Beaumont
Lafayette
Baton Rouge
Biloxi
Tallahassee
Gainesville
FLORIDA

Houston
New Orleans
Mobile Bay
Apalachee Bay
Orlando
Cape Canaveral

San Antonio
Mississippi River Delta
Tampa
St. Petersburg
Lake Okeechobee

Laredo
Corpus Christi
Fort Lauderdale
Miami
The Everglades

Rio Grande
Brownsville
Florida Keys

Red River basin ceded by Great Britain, 1818
Ceded by Great Britain, 1842
Ceded by Great Britain, 1842

Oregon Country ceded by Great Britain, 1846

Louisiana Purchase from France, 1803

Ceded by Mexico, 1848

United States, 1783

Western boundary of original 13 colonies, 1775

Texas annexed by U.S., 1845

Alaska purchased from Russia, 1867

Gadsden Purchase from Mexico, 1853

Florida ceded by Spain, 1819

Hawai'i annexed in 1898

⇐ **WESTWARD EXPANSION.** The United States had its origins in 13 British colonies established along the Atlantic coast. After gaining independence in 1783, the young country began adding new territories—some by treaty, others by purchase or by war. The map traces the country's expansion and shows the date each territory was acquired.

POPULATION

More than 312 million and growing! The population of the United States topped the 300 million mark in 2006, and it continues to grow by more than 600,000 people each year. Before the arrival of European settlers, the population consisted of Native Americans living in tribal groups scattered across the country. In the 16th and 17th centuries, Europeans, some with slaves from Africa, settled first along the eastern seaboard and later moved westward. In 1790 the U.S. population was not quite 4 million people. Today, New York City alone has a population more than double that number. The country's population is unevenly distributed. The map shows the number of people per square mile for each county in every state. Greatest densities are in the East and along the West Coast, especially around major cities. The most rapid growth is occurring in the South and the West—an area referred to as the Sunbelt—as well as in suburban areas around cities.

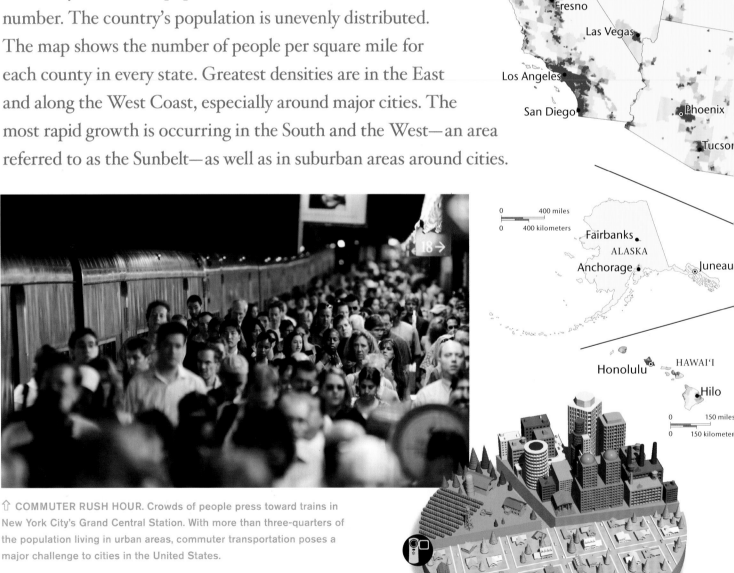

⇧ **COMMUTER RUSH HOUR.** Crowds of people press toward trains in New York City's Grand Central Station. With more than three-quarters of the population living in urban areas, commuter transportation poses a major challenge to cities in the United States.

⇨ **WHERE WE LIVE.** The first U.S. census in 1790 revealed that only 5 percent of people lived in towns. As industry has grown and agriculture has become increasingly mechanized, people have left farms (green), moving to urban places (blue) and their surrounding suburbs (orange).

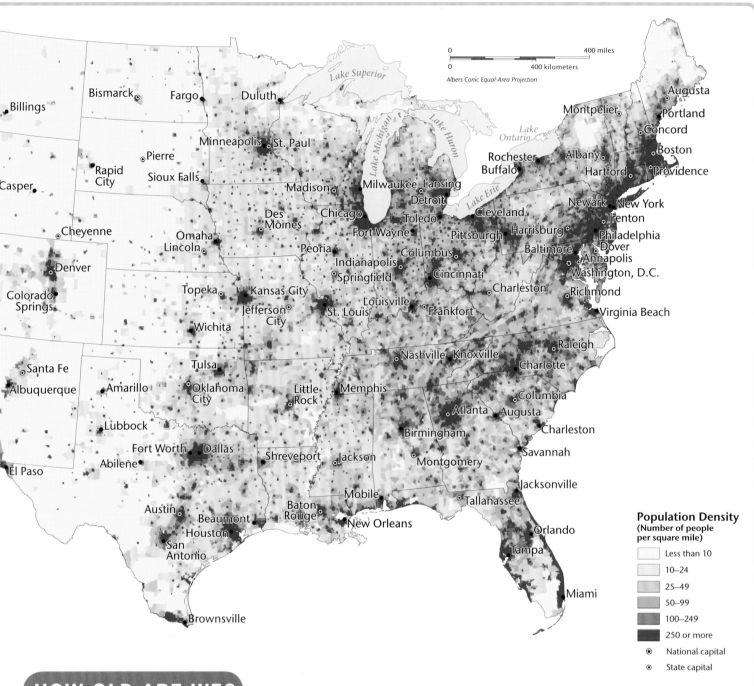

Population Density
(Number of people per square mile)

- Less than 10
- 10–24
- 25–49
- 50–99
- 100–249
- 250 or more

✴ National capital
◉ State capital

HOW OLD ARE WE?

Population pyramids show the distribution of population by sex and age groups, called cohorts. In 1960 the largest cohorts, born after World War II and known as Baby Boomers, were under 15 years of age. By 2000 Baby Boomers had become middle-age. By 2040 they will reach the top of the pyramid.

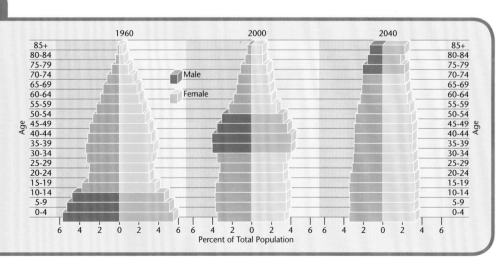

PEOPLE ON THE MOVE

From earliest human history, the land of the United States has been a focus of migration. Native peoples arrived thousands of years ago. The first European settlers came in the 16th and 17th centuries, and slave ships brought people from Africa. Today, people are still on the move. Since the mid-20th century, most international migrants have come from Latin America—especially Mexico and countries of Central America and the Caribbean—and Asia, particularly China, the Philippines, and India. While most of the population is still of European descent, certain regions have large minority concentrations, as shown on the map, that influence local cultural landscapes.

⇧ BRIDGE OF HOPE. Many Mexicans enter the U.S. (foreground) by bridges across the Rio Grande, such as this one between Nuevo Laredo, Mexico, and Laredo, Texas.

⇧ IMMIGRANT INFLUENCE. With Hispanics making up over 16 percent of the population, signs in Spanish are popping up everywhere—even at voting areas.

⇧ SUNBELT SPRAWL. Spreading suburbs are becoming a common feature of the desert Southwest as people flock to the Sunbelt.

San Francisco
San Jose

Los Angeles

San Diego

Phoeni

| 0 | 400 miles |
| 0 | 400 kilometers |

| 0 | 150 m |
| 0 | 150 kilome |

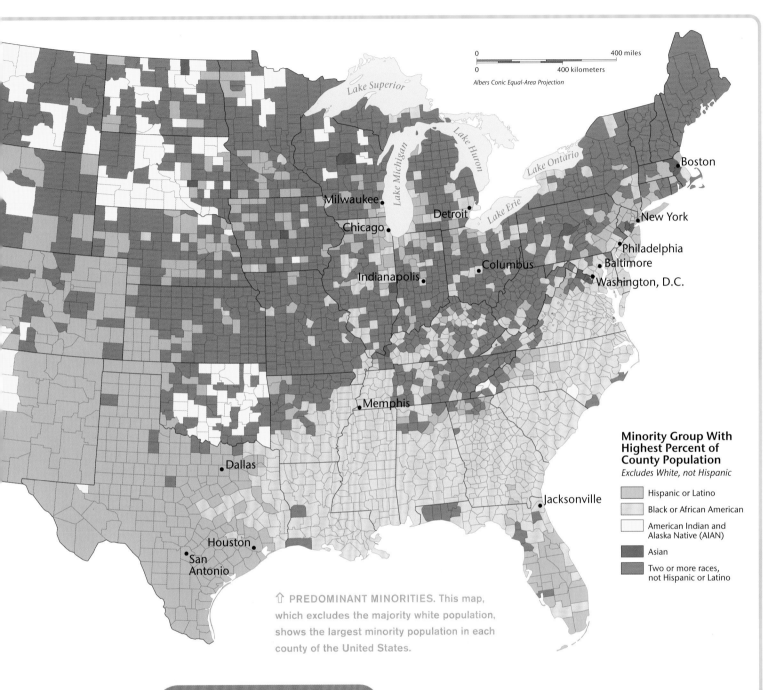

Milwaukee
Chicago
Detroit
Columbus
Indianapolis
Boston
New York
Philadelphia
Baltimore
Washington, D.C.
Memphis
Dallas
Jacksonville
Houston
San Antonio

Lake Superior
Lake Michigan
Lake Huron
Lake Ontario
Lake Erie

0   400 miles
0   400 kilometers
Albers Conic Equal-Area Projection

**Minority Group With
Highest Percent of
County Population**
Excludes White, not Hispanic

☐ Hispanic or Latino
☐ Black or African American
☐ American Indian and
   Alaska Native (AIAN)
☐ Asian
☐ Two or more races,
   not Hispanic or Latino

⇧ PREDOMINANT MINORITIES. This map,
which excludes the majority white population,
shows the largest minority population in each
county of the United States.

POPULATION SHIFT

In the last half century, people have begun moving from the historical industrial and agricultural regions of the Northeast and Midwest toward the South and West, attracted by the promise of jobs, generally lower living costs, and a more relaxed way of life. This trend can be seen in the population growth patterns shown in the map at right.

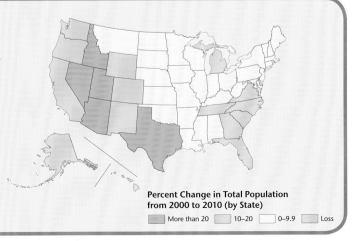

**Percent Change in Total Population
from 2000 to 2010 (by State)**
☐ More than 20   ☐ 10–20   ☐ 0–9.9   ☐ Loss

GETTING GREEN

Every day the media are filled with stories about global warming, pollution, and dwindling resources. Headlines warn of environmental risks that may threaten our way of life. The United States is the source of a quarter of the world's greenhouse gas emissions, and Americans generate more than 250 million tons of trash each year. The average American also uses 32 times more resources than a person in the African country of Kenya. But there's a bright side to these grim statistics: We can make a positive difference to the environment by making simple lifestyle changes. Scientists and engineers have developed energy-efficient appliances, cars that run on alternative fuels, and products made from recycled paper and plastics. But it is up to each of us to make changes that take advantage of these environment-friendly developments.

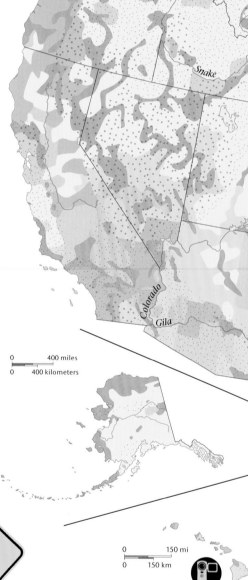

THINGS YOU CAN DO

Each year the average American household generates more than 80 tons of carbon dioxide gases, uses 102,000 gallons (386,111 l) of water, and creates 3.3 tons of landfill waste. Improving the health of our environment begins with you. You can make a difference if you practice the 3 R's of "getting green."

• REDUCE resource consumption by turning off lights, the TV, computers, and other electronic devices when you leave the room. Close the faucet when you are not using the water. Avoid buying things you do not need.

• REUSE items whenever possible, rather than throwing things away. Consider whether a container can be used again or a pair of shoes repaired.

• RECYCLE paper, plastic, glass, and aluminum cans. Recycling makes for less landfill trash, plus it preserves resources by reusing old products to make new ones.

Visit the library or go online to learn what your community is doing to protect the environment.

⇧ GREEN STREETS. Biking to work or school reduces use of gasoline, a source of greenhouse gases, and it is healthy, too.

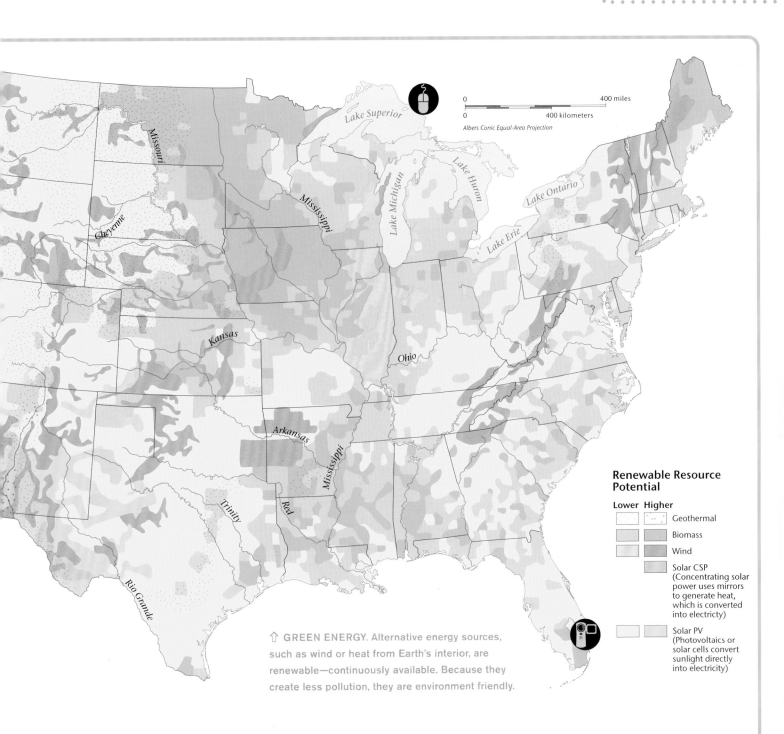

Missouri

Cheyenne

Mississippi

Lake Superior

Lake Michigan

Lake Huron

Lake Ontario

Lake Erie

Kansas

Ohio

Arkansas

Mississippi

Trinity

Red

Rio Grande

0   400 miles

0   400 kilometers

Albers Conic Equal-Area Projection

Renewable Resource Potential

Lower   Higher

- Geothermal
- Biomass
- Wind
- Solar CSP (Concentrating solar power uses mirrors to generate heat, which is converted into electricity)
- Solar PV (Photovoltaics or solar cells convert sunlight directly into electricity)

⬆ GREEN ENERGY. Alternative energy sources, such as wind or heat from Earth's interior, are renewable—continuously available. Because they create less pollution, they are environment friendly.

⬅ GREEN GARDENING. An organic farmer turns a compost pile with a pitchfork. Compost is a natural fertilizer made from decayed plant material. It is good for the environment because it reuses natural materials and avoids the use of chemicals that can pollute soil and water.

⬅ RECYCLE. Bright blue trash collectors overflow with plastic containers waiting to go to a recycling center. Citizen participation is an important step toward reducing landfill waste and restoring the health of the environment.

THE NATIONAL CAPITAL

THE BASICS

STATS

Area
68 sq mi (177 sq km)

Population
601,723

Ethnic/racial groups
50.7% African American; 38.5% white;
3.5% Asian; .3% Native American.
Hispanic (any race) 9.1%

Industry
Government, services, tourism

Founded
1790–91

GEO WHIZ

License plates in the District of
Columbia bear the slogan "Taxation
Without Representation," reflecting the
fact that residents of the District have
no voting representative in either house
of the U.S. Congress.

The flag of the District of Columbia,
with its three red stars and two red
stripes, is based on the shield in George
Washington's family coat of arms.

In 1790 Benjamin Banneker, a free
black, helped survey the land that
would become the capital city. The
40 stones that were placed at one-mile
intervals to mark the boundaries
were set according to his
celestial measurements.

WOOD THRUSH
AMERICAN
BEAUTY ROSE

THE NATIONAL CAPITAL

Chosen as a compromise location between Northern and Southern interests and built on land ceded by Virginia and Maryland in the late 1700s, Washington, D.C., sits on a bank of the Potomac River. It is the seat of U.S. government and symbol of the country's history. Pierre L'Enfant, a French architect, was appointed by President George Washington to design the city, which is distinguished by a grid pattern cut by diagonal avenues. At the city's core is the National Mall, a broad park lined by monuments, museums, and stately government buildings.

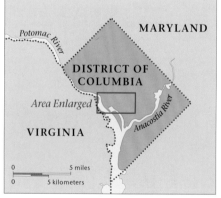

⇦ **DISTRICT OF COLUMBIA.**
Originally on both sides of
the Potomac River, the city
returned land to Virginia
in 1846.

⇦ **GREAT LEADER.** Abraham Lincoln,
who was president during the Civil War
and a strong opponent of slavery,
is remembered in a monument
that houses this seated
statue at the west end
of the National Mall.

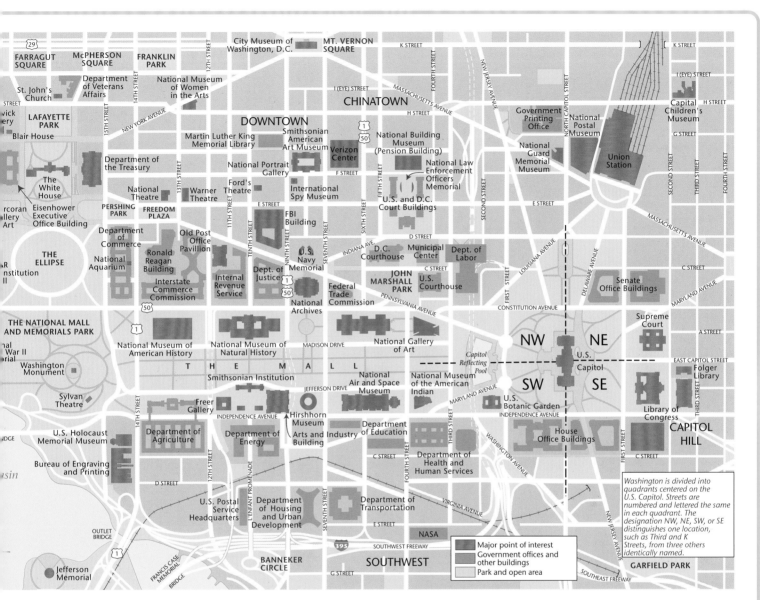

FARRAGUT SQUARE

McPHERSON SQUARE

FRANKLIN PARK

City Museum of Washington, D.C.

MT. VERNON SQUARE

K STREET

29

St. John's Church

Department of Veterans Affairs

National Museum of Women in the Arts

I (EYE) STREET

CHINATOWN

K STREET

I (EYE) STREET

Capital Children's Museum

H STREET

LAFAYETTE PARK

Blair House

DOWNTOWN

Martin Luther King Memorial Library

Smithsonian American Art Museum

Verizon Center

National Building Museum (Pension Building)

Government Printing Office

National Postal Museum

H STREET

G STREET

The White House

Department of the Treasury

National Portrait Gallery

Ford's Theatre

F STREET

National Law Enforcement Officers Memorial

National Guard Memorial Museum

Union Station

Eisenhower Executive Office Building

National Theatre

Warner Theatre

International Spy Museum

U.S. and D.C. Court Buildings

E STREET

PERSHING PARK

FREEDOM PLAZA

Department of Commerce

Old Post Office Pavilion

FBI Building

D STREET

THE ELLIPSE

National Aquarium

Ronald Reagan Building

U.S. Navy Memorial

D.C. Courthouse

Municipal Center

Dept. of Labor

C STREET

Interstate Commerce Commission

Internal Revenue Service

Dept. of Justice

JOHN MARSHALL PARK

U.S. Courthouse

Senate Office Buildings

C STREET

Federal Trade Commission

National Archives

CONSTITUTION AVENUE

THE NATIONAL MALL AND MEMORIALS PARK

National Museum of American History

National Museum of Natural History

MADISON DRIVE

National Gallery of Art

Supreme Court

A STREET

Washington Monument

THE MALL

Capitol Reflecting Pool

NW

NE

U.S. Capitol

EAST CAPITOL STREET

Folger Library

Sylvan Theatre

Smithsonian Institution

JEFFERSON DRIVE

National Air and Space Museum

National Museum of the American Indian

SW

SE

Library of Congress

CAPITOL HILL

Freer Gallery

INDEPENDENCE AVENUE

Hirshhorn Museum

U.S. Botanic Garden

INDEPENDENCE AVENUE

U.S. Holocaust Memorial Museum

Department of Agriculture

Department of Energy

Arts and Industry Building

Department of Education

House Office Buildings

Bureau of Engraving and Printing

D STREET

C STREET

Department of Health and Human Services

Washington is divided into quadrants centered on the U.S. Capitol. Streets are numbered and lettered the same in each quadrant. The designation NW, NE, SW, or SE distinguishes one location, such as Third and K Streets, from three others identically named.

U.S. Postal Service Headquarters

Department of Housing and Urban Development

Department of Transportation

E STREET

GARFIELD PARK

OUTLET BRIDGE

NASA

SOUTHWEST FREEWAY

Major point of interest

Jefferson Memorial

FRANCIS CASE MEMORIAL BRIDGE

BANNEKER CIRCLE

395

SOUTHWEST

G STREET

Government offices and other buildings

Park and open area

SOUTHEAST FREEWAY

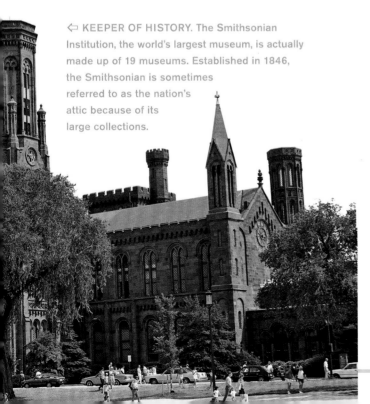

⇐ KEEPER OF HISTORY. The Smithsonian Institution, the world's largest museum, is actually made up of 19 museums. Established in 1846, the Smithsonian is sometimes referred to as the nation's attic because of its large collections.

⇧ NATIONAL ICON. The gleaming dome of the U.S. Capitol, home to the Senate and House of Representatives, is a familiar symbol of Washington's main business—the running of the country's government.

THE REGION

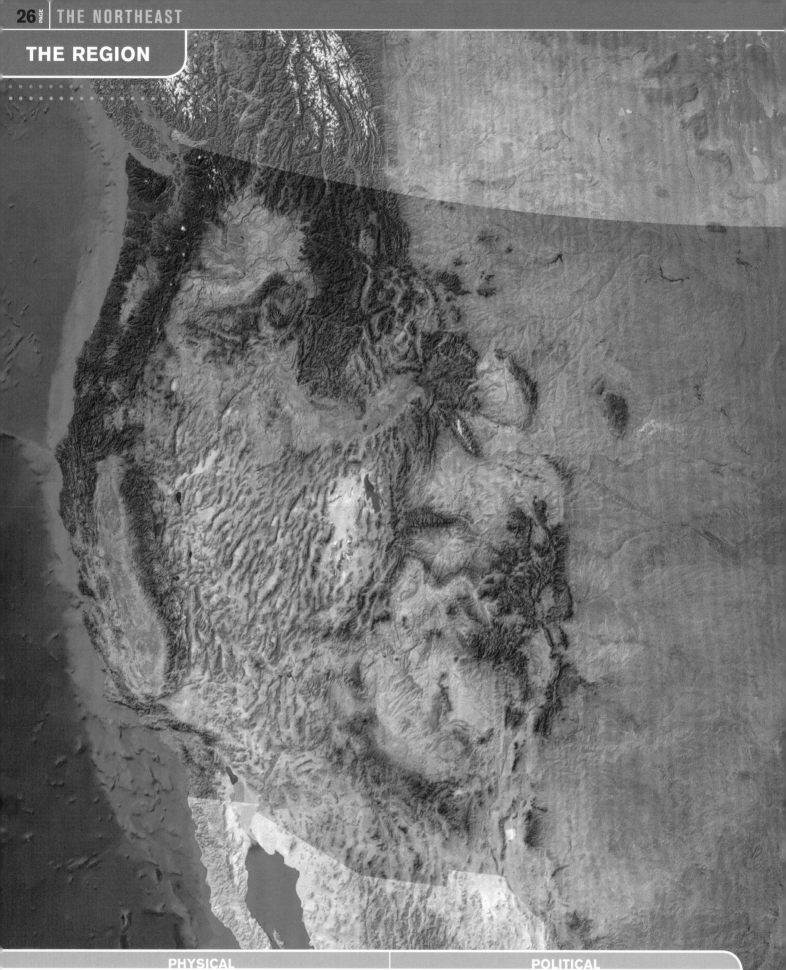

PHYSICAL			POLITICAL	
Total area 196,220 sq mi (508,209 sq km)	**Lowest point** Sea level, shores of the Atlantic Ocean	**Vegetation** Needleleaf, broadleaf, and mixed forest	**Total population** 61,988,726	**Smallest state** Rhode Island: 1,545 sq mi (4,002 sq km)
Highest point Mount Washington, NH 6,288 ft (1,917 m)	**Longest rivers** St. Lawrence, Susquehanna, Connecticut, Hudson	**Climate** Continental to mild, with cool to warm summers, cold winters, and moderate precipitation throughout the year	**States (11):** Connecticut, Delaware, Maine, Maryland, Massachusetts, New Hampshire, New Jersey, New York, Pennsylvania, Rhode Island, Vermont	**Most populous state** New York: 19,378,102
	Largest lakes Erie, Ontario, Champlain			**Least populous state** Vermont: 625,741
			Largest state New York: 54,556 sq mi (141,300 sq km)	**Largest city proper** New York, NY: 8,175,133

The Northeast

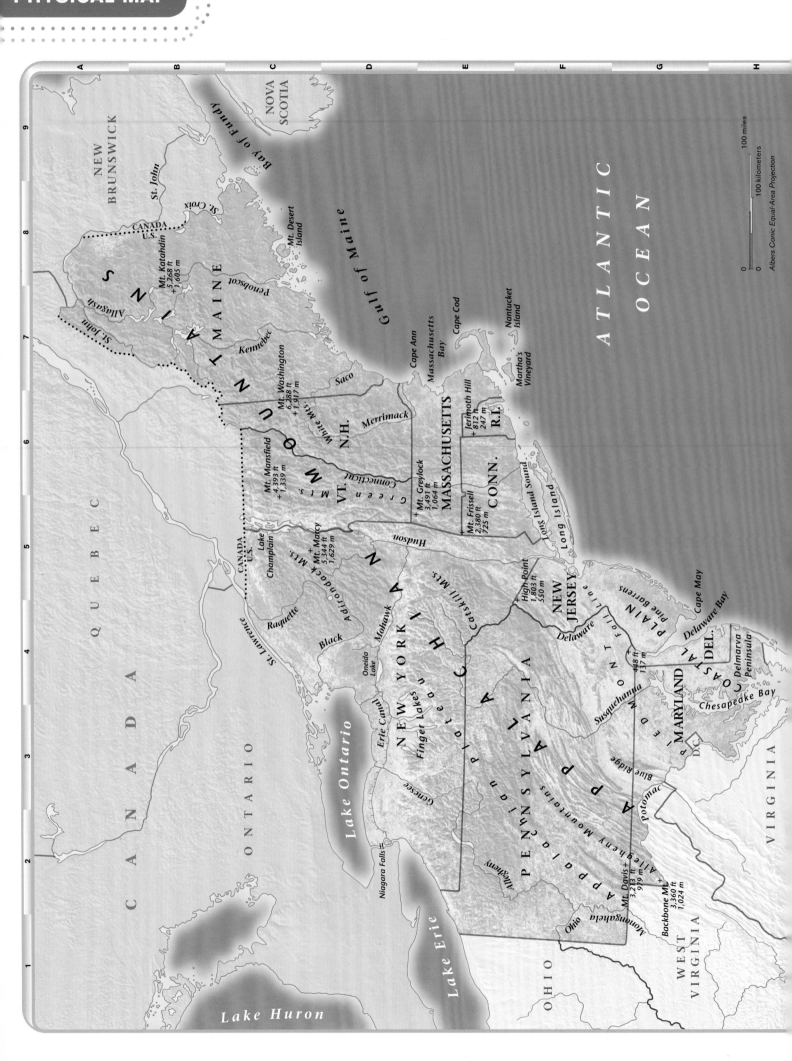

ATLANTIC OCEAN

100 miles

100 kilometers

Albers Conic Equal-Area Projection

NEW BRUNSWICK

NOVA SCOTIA

CANADA
U.S.

Bay of Fundy

St. John

St. Croix

Mt. Desert Island

Gulf of Maine

MAINE

Mt. Katahdin
+5,268 ft
1,605 m

Allagash

St. John

Penobscot

Kennebec

Saco

Cape Ann

Massachusetts Bay

Cape Cod

Nantucket Island

Martha's Vineyard

Mt. Washington
6,288 ft
+1,917 m

White Mts.

N.H.

Merrimack

Jerimoth Hill
+ 812 ft
247 m

R.I.

Mt. Mansfield
+4,393 ft
1,339 m

Green Mts.

VT.

Connecticut

Mt. Greylock
3,491 ft
+1,064 m

MASSACHUSETTS

CONN.

Mt. Frissell
2,380 ft
725 m

Long Island Sound

Long Island

QUEBEC

CANADA
U.S.

Lake Champlain

Mt. Marcy
+5,344 ft
1,629 m

Adirondack Mts.

Hudson

Catskill Mts.

High Point
+1,803 ft
550 m

NEW JERSEY

Cape May

Delaware Bay

DEL.

Delmarva Peninsula

CANADA

Raquette

Black

Mohawk

Oneida Lake

NEW YORK

Finger Lakes

Plateau

Pine Barrens

Fall Line

COASTAL

448 ft
+ 137 m

MARYLAND

Chesapeake Bay

St. Lawrence

ONTARIO

Erie Canal

Genesee

Appalachian

Delaware

PLAIN

Susquehanna

Blue Ridge

D.C.

Piedmont

Niagara Falls

Lake Ontario

PENNSYLVANIA

Allegheny

Allegheny Mountains

Mt. Davis +
3,213 ft
979 m

Backbone Mt. +
3,360 ft
1,024 m

Potomac

VIRGINIA

Lake Erie

OHIO

Monongahela

Ohio

WEST VIRGINIA

Lake Huron

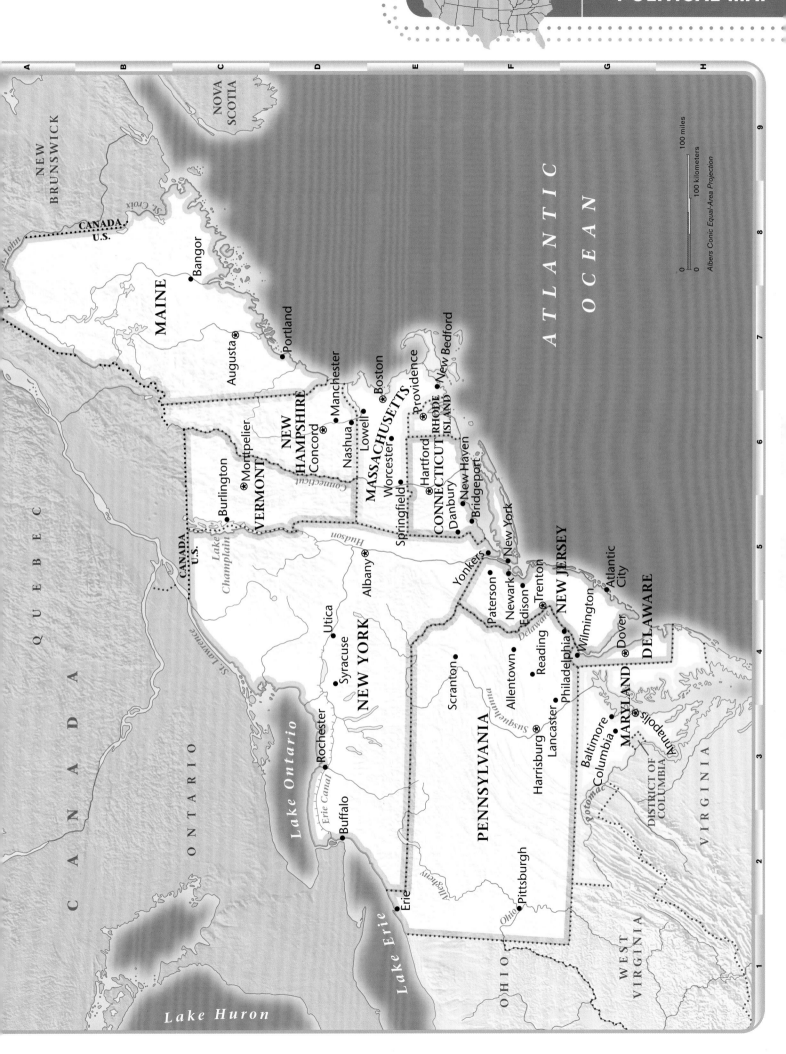

NEW BRUNSWICK

NOVA SCOTIA

St. Croix

CANADA
U.S.

St. John

MAINE

Bangor

Portland

Augusta ✪

Manchester

Boston

Providence

New Bedford

New Hampshire

Concord ✪

Nashua

Lowell

Worcester ✪

MASSACHUSETTS

Montpelier ✪

VERMONT

Burlington

Springfield

Hartford ✪

CONNECTICUT

New Haven

Danbury

Bridgeport

RHODE ISLAND

Connecticut

Lake Champlain

Albany ✪

Hudson

Yonkers

New York

Newark

Paterson

Trenton ✪

Edison

NEW JERSEY

Atlantic City

Delaware

Wilmington

Dover ✪

DELAWARE

Annapolis ✪

QUEBEC

CANADA

ONTARIO

St. Lawrence

Utica

Syracuse

NEW YORK

Rochester

Erie Canal

Buffalo

Lake Ontario

Scranton

Allentown

Reading

Philadelphia

Lancaster

Harrisburg ✪

PENNSYLVANIA

Susquehanna

Susquehanna

Baltimore

Columbia

MARYLAND

DISTRICT OF COLUMBIA

Potomac

VIRGINIA

WEST VIRGINIA

OHIO

Erie

Lake Erie

Lake Huron

Pittsburgh

Ohio

Allegheny

ATLANTIC OCEAN

100 miles
100 kilometers
Albers Conic Equal-Area Projection

CANADA
U.S.

⇨ DINNER DELICACY. Lobsters, a favorite food for many people, turn bright red when cooked. These crustaceans live in the cold waters of the Atlantic Ocean and are caught using baited traps.

The Northeast
BIRTHPLACE OF A NATION

The United States had its beginnings in the Northeast region. Early European traders and settlers were quickly followed by immigrants from around the globe, making the region's population the most diverse in the country. The region includes the country's financial center, New York City, and its political capital, Washington, D.C. While the region boasts tranquil mountains, lakes, and rivers, its teeming cities have always been the heart of the Northeast.

⬇ MELTING POT. From colonial times, the Northeast has been a gateway for immigration. These young girls, dressed in traditional saris and performing in an India Cultural Festival in New Jersey, reflect the rich diversity of the region.

⇨ DEFENDER OF FREEDOM. Rising 548 feet (167 m) above Penn Square, Philadelphia's City Hall, with its statue of William Penn, is the country's largest municipal building. Penn was founder of the Pennsylvania colony and defender of equal rights for men and women.

⇧ DAWN'S EARLY LIGHT. The lights of New York City's skyline sparkle against the early morning sky. The tall buildings of Lower Manhattan, reflected in the dark waters of the East River, are home to companies whose influence reaches around the world.

⇧ STILL WATERS. A father and son enjoy a quiet day of fishing on the smooth-as-glass waters of Lake Chocurua in New Hampshire's White Mountains. Deciduous trees turning red and gold will soon shed their leaves, and the hillsides will turn white with winter's snow, attracting skiers to the valley.

WHERE THE PICTURES ARE

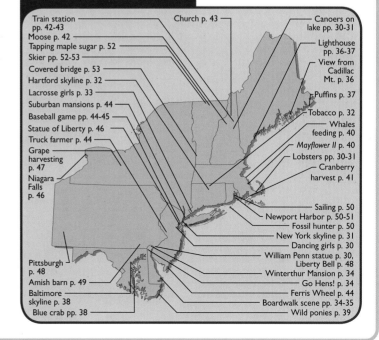

Train station pp. 42-43
Moose p. 42
Tapping maple sugar p. 52
Skier pp. 52-53
Covered bridge p. 53
Hartford skyline p. 32
Lacrosse girls p. 33
Suburban mansions p. 44
Baseball game pp. 44-45
Statue of Liberty p. 46
Truck farmer p. 44
Grape harvesting p. 47
Niagara Falls p. 46

Church p. 43

Canoers on lake pp. 30-31
Lighthouse pp. 36-37
View from Cadillac Mt. p. 36
Puffins p. 37
Tobacco p. 32
Whales feeding p. 40
Mayflower II p. 40
Lobsters pp. 30-31
Cranberry harvest p. 41
Sailing p. 50
Newport Harbor pp. 50-51
Fossil hunter p. 50
New York skyline p. 31
Dancing girls p. 30
William Penn statue p. 30, Liberty Bell p. 48
Winterthur Mansion p. 34
Go Hens! p. 34
Ferris Wheel p. 44
Boardwalk scene pp. 34-35
Wild ponies p. 39

Pittsburgh p. 48
Amish barn p. 49
Baltimore skyline p. 38
Blue crab pp. 38

CONNECTICUT

As early as 1614, Dutch explorers founded trading posts along the coast of Connecticut, but the first permanent European settlements were established in 1635 by English Puritans from nearby Massachusetts. The Connecticut Fundamental Orders, which in 1639 established a democratic system of government in the colony, were an important model for the writing of the U.S. Constitution in 1787. This earned the state its nickname—Constitution State. Even in colonial times, Connecticut was an important industrial center, producing goods that competed with factories in England. During the Revolutionary War, Connecticut produced military goods for the colonial army. Today, Connecticut industries produce jet aircraft engines, helicopters, and nuclear submarines. Connecticut is home to many international corporations, but it is best known as the "insurance state." Following independence, businessmen offered to insure ship cargoes in exchange for a share of the profits. Soon after, other types of insurance were offered. Today, Connecticut is home to more than 100 insurance companies.

THE BASICS

STATS

Area
5,543 sq mi (14,357 sq km)

Population
3,574,097

Capital
Hartford
Population 124,775

Largest city
Bridgeport
Population 144,229

Ethnic/racial groups
77.6% white; 10.1% African American; 3.8% Asian; .3% Native American. Hispanic (any race) 13.4%.

Industry
Transportation equipment, metal products, machinery, electrical equipment, printing and publishing, scientific instruments, insurance

Agriculture
Nursery stock, dairy products, poultry, eggs, shellfish

Statehood
January 9, 1788; 5th state

GEO WHIZ

The sperm whale, Connecticut's state animal, is known for its massive head. Its brain is larger than that of any other creature known to have lived on Earth.

The first hamburgers in U.S. history were served by Louis Lassen at his New Haven lunch wagon in 1895. He didn't like to waste the excess beef left after the daily noon rush, so he ground it up, grilled it, and served it between two slices of bread.

The nuclear-powered U.S.S. *Virginia*, the first of a class of technologically advanced submarines, was built at Groton, home of the U.S. Naval Submarine Base.

ROBIN
MOUNTAIN LAUREL

⇧ LEAFY HARVEST. The Connecticut River Valley is a major source of world-class premium cigar tobacco in the United States. Most of the harvest is used for cigar wrappers.

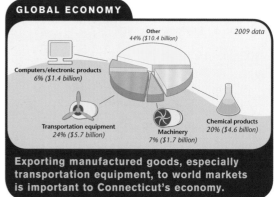

⇦ BRIGHT CITY LIGHTS. Established as a fort in the early 1600s, Hartford was one of the earliest cities of colonial America. Today, this modern state capital is a center of economic growth and cultural diversity.

GLOBAL ECONOMY

2009 data

Other
44% ($10.4 billion)

Computers/electronic products
6% ($1.4 billion)

Transportation equipment
24% ($5.7 billion)

Machinery
7% ($1.7 billion)

Chemical products
20% ($4.6 billion)

Exporting manufactured goods, especially transportation equipment, to world markets is important to Connecticut's economy.

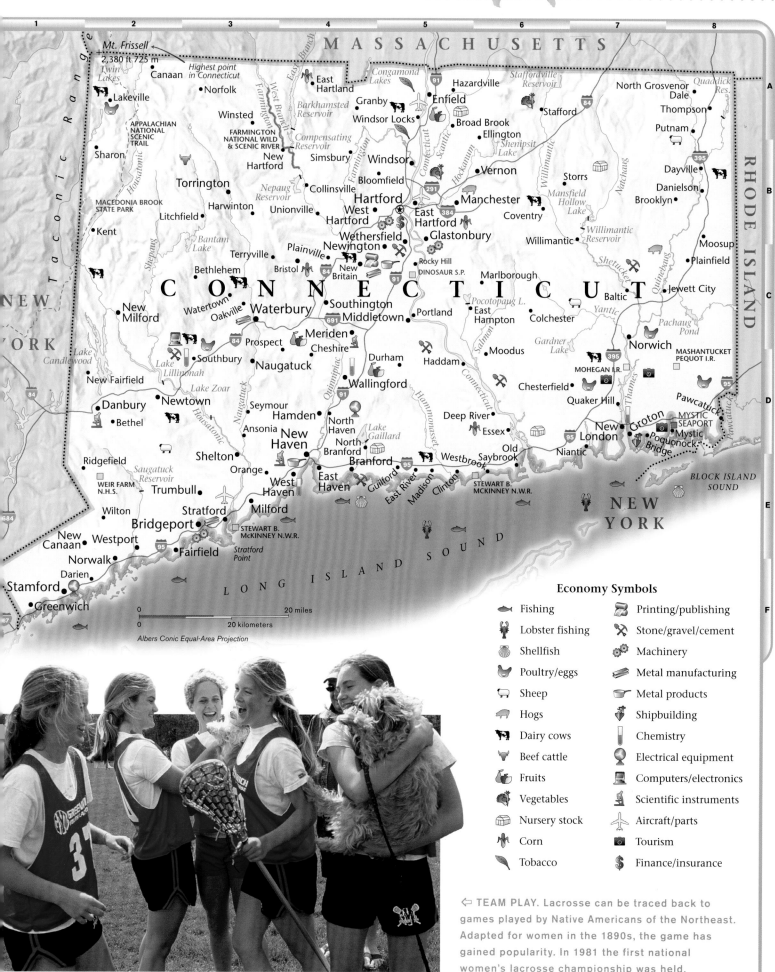

M A S S A C H U S E T T S

Mt. Frissell
2,380 ft 725 m
Highest point
in Connecticut

Twin
Lakes
Canaan

Lakeville

Norfolk

East
Hartland

Congamond
Lakes

Hazardville

Staffordville
Reservoir

North Grosvenor
Dale

Quaddick
Res.

TACONIC RANGE

APPALACHIAN
NATIONAL
SCENIC
TRAIL

Sharon

Winsted

FARMINGTON
NATIONAL WILD
& SCENIC RIVER

New
Hartford

Barkhamsted
Reservoir

Compensating
Reservoir

Granby

Windsor Locks

Enfield

Broad Brook

Ellington

Stafford

Thompson

Putnam

Dayville

RHODE ISLAND

Torrington

Nepaug
Reservoir

Collinsville

Simsbury

Windsor

Vernon

Storrs

Danielson

MACEDONIA BROOK
STATE PARK

Harwinton

Unionville

Bloomfield

Hartford

Manchester

Mansfield
Hollow
Lake

Brooklyn

Litchfield

West
Hartford

East
Hartford

Coventry

Willimantic
Reservoir

Moosup

Kent

Bantam
Lake

Terryville

Plainville

Wethersfield
Newington

Glastonbury

Willimantic

Plainfield

C O N N E C T I C U T

Bethlehem

Bristol

New
Britain

Rocky Hill

DINOSAUR S.P.

Marlborough

Baltic

Jewett City

New
Milford

Watertown

Oakville

Waterbury

Southington

Middletown

Portland

East
Hampton

Pocotopaug L.

Colchester

Pachaug
Pond

Prospect

Meriden

Cheshire

Durham

Haddam

Moodus

Gardner
Lake

Norwich

MASHANTUCKET
PEQUOT I.R.

Lake
Candlewood

Southbury

Naugatuck

Wallingford

Chesterfield

MOHEGAN I.R.

New Fairfield

Lake
Lillinonah

Lake Zoar

Quaker Hill

Pawcatuck

Danbury

Newtown

Seymour

Hamden

North
Haven

Lake
Gaillard

Deep River

Essex

New
London

Groton

MYSTIC
SEAPORT

Mystic

Bethel

Ansonia

New
Haven

North
Branford

Branford

Westbrook

Old
Saybrook

Niantic

Poquonock
Bridge

Ridgefield

Saugatuck
Reservoir

Shelton

Orange

Guilford

East River

Madison

Clinton

STEWART B.
McKINNEY N.W.R.

BLOCK ISLAND
SOUND

WEIR FARM
N.H.S.

Trumbull

West
Haven

East
Haven

Milford

Wilton

Stratford

STEWART B.
McKINNEY N.W.R.

N E W
Y O R K

New
Canaan

Westport

Bridgeport

Stratford
Point

Norwalk

Fairfield

Darien

Stamford

0   20 miles

0   20 kilometers

L O N G   I S L A N D   S O U N D

Greenwich

Albers Conic Equal-Area Projection

Economy Symbols

Fishing		Printing/publishing	
Lobster fishing		Stone/gravel/cement	
Shellfish		Machinery	
Poultry/eggs		Metal manufacturing	
Sheep		Metal products	
Hogs		Shipbuilding	
Dairy cows		Chemistry	
Beef cattle		Electrical equipment	
Fruits		Computers/electronics	
Vegetables		Scientific instruments	
Nursery stock		Aircraft/parts	
Corn		Tourism	
Tobacco		Finance/insurance	

⇐ TEAM PLAY. Lacrosse can be traced back to
games played by Native Americans of the Northeast.
Adapted for women in the 1890s, the game has
gained popularity. In 1981 the first national
women's lacrosse championship was held.

DECEMBER 7, 1787

THE BASICS

STATS

Area
2,489 sq mi (6,447 sq km)

Population
897,934

Capital
Dover
Population 36,047

Largest city
Wilmington
Population 70,851

Ethnic/racial groups
68.9% white; 21.4% African American;
3.2% Asian; .5% Native American.
Hispanic (any race) 8.2%.

Industry
Food processing, chemicals, rubber
and plastic products, scientific
instruments, printing and publishing,
financial services

Agriculture
Poultry, soybeans, nursery stock, corn,
vegetables, dairy products

Statehood
December 7, 1787; 1st state

GEO WHIZ

Each year contestants bring their pumpkins and launching machines to the
Punkin Chunkin World Championship in
Bridgeville to see who can catapult their
big, orange squash the farthest.

The Delaware Estuary is one of the four
most important shorebird migration
sites in the world and has the second
highest concentration of shorebirds in
North America. The estuary
also provides wintering
and migratory habitat to
many species of songbirds
and raptors.

The first steam railroad to
provide regular service
began operations in
New Castle in 1831.

BLUE HEN CHICKEN
PEACH BLOSSOM

DELAWARE

Second smallest among the states in
area, Delaware has played a big role in
the history of the U.S. Explored at various times by the Spanish, Portuguese,
and Dutch, it was Swedes who established the first permanent European
settlement in 1638 in the Delaware
River Valley. In 1655 the colony fell
under Dutch authority, but in 1682 the
land was annexed by William Penn
and the Pennsylvania colony. In 1787
Delaware was the first state to ratify the new U.S. Constitution. Delaware's
Atlantic coast beaches are popular with tourists. Its fertile farmland, mainly
in the south, produces soybeans, corn, dairy products, and poultry. But the
state's real economic power is located in the north, around Wilmington,
where factories employ thousands of workers to process food products and
produce machinery and chemicals. Industry has been a source of wealth,
but it also poses a danger to the environment. Protecting the
environment is a high priority for Delaware.

⇩ TEAM SPIRIT. Enthusiastic fans
and the University of Delaware
band support the "Fightin' Blue
Hens." Located in Newark, the
university was founded in 1743.

⇧ PAST GRANDEUR. Built in 1837 in the fashion of a British
country house, Winterthur was expanded from 12 to 196
rooms by the du Ponts, chemical industry tycoons. In 1951
the house was opened to the public as a museum for the
family's extensive collection of antiques and Americana.

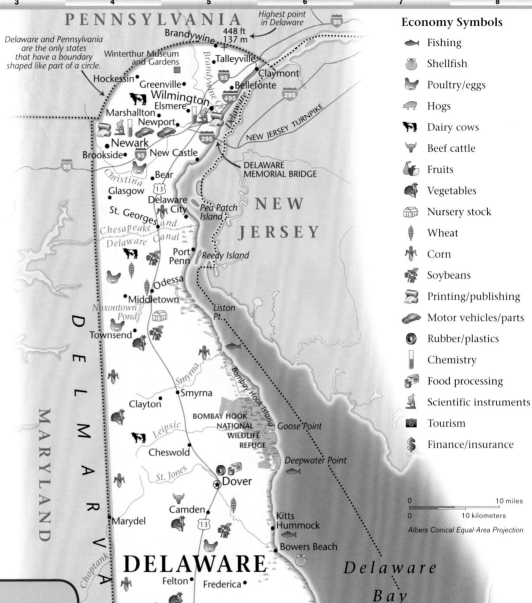

PENNSYLVANIA

Delaware and Pennsylvania are the only states that have a boundary shaped like part of a circle.

Highest point in Delaware
448 ft
137 m

Brandywine
Talleyville
Claymont
Winterthur Museum and Gardens
Bellefonte
Hockessin
Greenville
Wilmington
Elsmere
Marshallton
Newport
Newark
Brookside
New Castle
Christina
Bear
Glasgow
Delaware City
St. Georges
Chesapeake and Delaware Canal
Pea Patch Island
Port Penn
Reedy Island
Odessa
Middletown
Noxontown Pond
Townsend
Smyrna
Smyrna
Clayton
Bombay Hook Island
Leipsic
BOMBAY HOOK NATIONAL WILDLIFE REFUGE
Goose Point
Cheswold
Deepwater Point
St. Jones
Dover
Camden
Kitts Hummock
Marydel
Bowers Beach
Choptank
DELAWARE
Felton
Frederica
Delaware Bay
Harrington
Houston
Milford
Lincoln
Slaughter Beach
PRIME HOOK NATIONAL WILDLIFE REFUGE
Broadkill Beach
Greenwood
Ellendale
Lewes
Cape Henlopen
Milton
Bridgeville
Lewes & Rehoboth Canal
ATLANTIC
Harbeson
Midway
Rehoboth Beach
Georgetown
Dewey Beach
Rehoboth Bay
Seaford
Blades
OCEAN
Oak Orchard
Laurel
Indian River Bay
Indian River Inlet
Millsboro
Ocean View
Dagsboro
Bethany Beach
Frankford
Assawoman Canal
Cypress Swamp
Delmar
Selbyville
Fenwick Island

NEW JERSEY
NEW JERSEY TURNPIKE
DELAWARE MEMORIAL BRIDGE
Liston Pt.

MARYLAND

D E L M A R V A   P E N I N S U L A

Marshyhope Creek
Nanticoke

Economy Symbols

- Fishing
- Shellfish
- Poultry/eggs
- Hogs
- Dairy cows
- Beef cattle
- Fruits
- Vegetables
- Nursery stock
- Wheat
- Corn
- Soybeans
- Printing/publishing
- Motor vehicles/parts
- Rubber/plastics
- Chemistry
- Food processing
- Scientific instruments
- Tourism
- Finance/insurance

0   10 miles
0   10 kilometers
Albers Conical Equal-Area Projection

⇧ SEASIDE RETREAT. Originally established in 1873 as a church campground, Rehoboth Beach is still a popular getaway destination on Delaware's Atlantic coastline. A concrete dolphin overlooks the town's boardwalk, a popular promenade that separates shops and restaurants from the beach. The boardwalk has been destroyed on several occasions by storms.

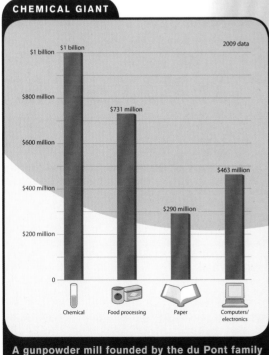

CHEMICAL GIANT

2009 data

$1 billion	$1 billion
$800 million	$731 million
$600 million	
$400 million	$463 million
$200 million	$290 million
0	

Chemical | Food processing | Paper | Computers/electronics

A gunpowder mill founded by the du Pont family in 1802 gave rise to a chemical industry that is now the state's leading industry and employer.

MAINE

Maine's story begins long before the arrival of European settlers in the 1600s. Evidence of native people dates back to at least 3000 B.C., and Leif Erikson and his Viking sailors may have explored Maine's coastline 500 years before Columbus crossed the Atlantic. English settlements were established along the southern coast in the 1620s, and in 1677 the territory of Maine came under control of Massachusetts.

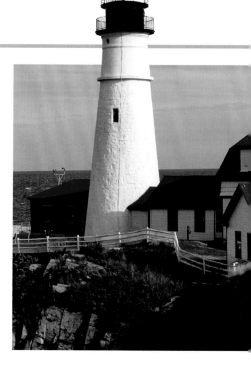

Following the Revolutionary War, the people of Maine pressed for separation from Massachusetts, and in 1820 Maine entered the Union as a non-slave state under the terms of the Missouri Compromise. Most of Maine's population is concentrated in towns along the coast. Famous for its rugged beauty, it is the focus of the tourist industry. Cold offshore waters contribute to a lively fishing industry, while timber from the state's mountainous interior supports wood product and paper businesses. Maine, a leader in environmental awareness, seeks a balance between economic growth and environmental protection.

⇩ACADIA NATIONAL PARK, established in 1929, attracts thousands of tourists each year. The park includes Cadillac Mountain, the highest point along the North Atlantic coast and the site from which the earliest sunrises in the United States can be viewed from October 7 through March 6.

THE BASICS

STATS

Area
35,385 sq mi (91,646 sq km)

Population
1,328,361

Capital
Augusta
Population 19,136

Largest city
Portland
Population 66,194

Ethnic/racial groups
95.2% white; 1.2% African American; 1.0% Asian; .6% Native American. Hispanic (any race) 1.3%.

Industry
Health services, tourism, forest products, leather products, electrical equipment, food processing, textiles

Agriculture
Seafood, potatoes, dairy products, poultry and eggs, livestock, apples, blueberries, vegetables

Statehood
March 15, 1820; 23rd state

GEO WHIZ

With world shark populations declining, some conservation-minded deep-sea fishermen in Maine have turned the idea of a shark tournament upside-down. They still compete to see who can catch the biggest fish, but then they tag and release the sharks.

Eartha, a scale model of our planet, holds the Guinness World Record as the World's Largest Revolving/Rotating Globe. It is on display in a three-story glass building in Yarmouth.

Forests cover nearly 90 percent of Maine. No wonder it is called the Pine Tree State.

Until the last ice age, Maine's coast was relatively straight. Glaciers carved hundreds of bays and inlets out of its shoreline and created some 2,000 islands off the coast.

CHICKADEE

WHITE PINE CONE AND TASSEL

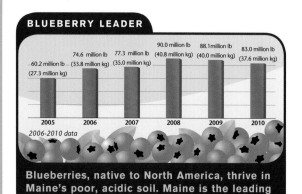

BLUEBERRY LEADER

60.2 million lb (27.3 million kg) — 2005
74.6 million lb (33.8 million kg) — 2006
77.3 million lb (35.0 million kg) — 2007
90.0 million lb (40.8 million kg) — 2008
88.1 million lb (40.0 million kg) — 2009
83.0 million lb (37.6 million kg) — 2010

2006-2010 data

Blueberries, native to North America, thrive in Maine's poor, acidic soil. Maine is the leading harvester of wild blueberries in the U.S.

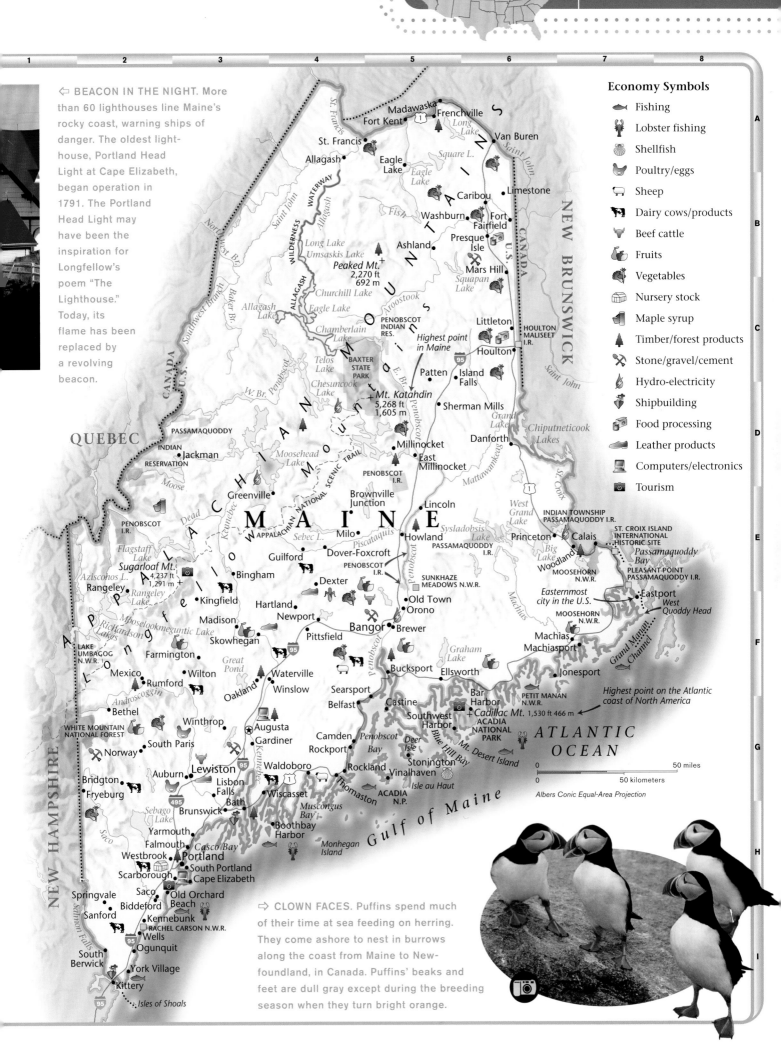

⇦ BEACON IN THE NIGHT. More than 60 lighthouses line Maine's rocky coast, warning ships of danger. The oldest lighthouse, Portland Head Light at Cape Elizabeth, began operation in 1791. The Portland Head Light may have been the inspiration for Longfellow's poem "The Lighthouse." Today, its flame has been replaced by a revolving beacon.

Economy Symbols

- Fishing
- Lobster fishing
- Shellfish
- Poultry/eggs
- Sheep
- Dairy cows/products
- Beef cattle
- Fruits
- Vegetables
- Nursery stock
- Maple syrup
- Timber/forest products
- Stone/gravel/cement
- Hydro-electricity
- Shipbuilding
- Food processing
- Leather products
- Computers/electronics
- Tourism

QUEBEC

NEW BRUNSWICK

CANADA
U.S.

Madawaska
Fort Kent
Frenchville
St. Francis
Allagash
Van Buren
Eagle Lake
Square L.
Long Lake
Eagle Lake
Caribou
Limestone
Washburn
Fort Fairfield
Ashland
Presque Isle
Peaked Mt.
2,270 ft
692 m
Mars Hill
Squapan Lake
Churchill Lake
Eagle Lake
Aroostook
Chamberlain Lake
PENOBSCOT INDIAN RES.
Littleton
HOULTON MALISEET I.R.
Highest point in Maine
Houlton
Telos Lake
BAXTER STATE PARK
Patten
Island Falls
Chesuncook Lake
Mt. Katahdin
5,268 ft
1,605 m
Sherman Mills
Grand Lake
Danforth
Chiputneticook Lakes
Millinocket
East Millinocket
PENOBSCOT I.R.
Mattawamkeag
St. Croix
Jackman
PASSAMAQUODDY INDIAN RESERVATION
Moosehead Lake
Greenville
Brownville Junction
Lincoln
Sysladobsis Lake
West Grand Lake
INDIAN TOWNSHIP PASSAMAQUODDY I.R.
Howland
Princeton
Calais
ST. CROIX ISLAND INTERNATIONAL HISTORIC SITE
PENOBSCOT I.R.
Milo
Sebec L.
Dover-Foxcroft
PENOBSCOT I.R.
PASSAMAQUODDY I.R.
Big Lake
Woodland
Passamaquoddy Bay
PENOBSCOT I.R.
Guilford
SUNKHAZE MEADOWS N.W.R.
MOOSEHORN N.W.R.
PLEASANT POINT PASSAMAQUODDY I.R.
Sugarloaf Mt.
4,237 ft
1,291 m
Bingham
Dexter
Old Town
Orono
Easternmost city in the U.S.
Eastport
West Quoddy Head
Rangeley
Rangeley Lake
Kingfield
Hartland
Newport
Bangor
Brewer
MOOSEHORN N.W.R.
Machias
Machiasport
Madison
Pittsfield
Graham Lake
Moselookmeguntic Lake
Richardson Lakes
Skowhegan
Grand Manan Channel
LAKE UMBAGOG N.W.R.
Farmington
Great Pond
Bucksport
Ellsworth
Jonesport
Mexico
Wilton
Waterville
Searsport
PETIT MANAN N.W.R.
Rumford
Oakland
Winslow
Belfast
Castine
Bar Harbor
Highest point on the Atlantic coast of North America
Bethel
Androscoggin
Southwest Harbor
Cadillac Mt. 1,530 ft 466 m
WHITE MOUNTAIN NATIONAL FOREST
Winthrop
Augusta
Camden
Penobscot Bay
Deer Isle
Blue Hill Bay
ACADIA NATIONAL PARK
ATLANTIC OCEAN
Norway
South Paris
Gardiner
Rockport
Mt. Desert Island
Bridgton
Fryeburg
Auburn
Lewiston
Lisbon Falls
Waldoboro
Rockland
Stonington
Vinalhaven
Isle au Haut
Sebago Lake
Brunswick
Bath
Wiscasset
Thomaston
ACADIA N.P.
Yarmouth
Muscongus Bay
Falmouth
Casco Bay
Boothbay Harbor
Monhegan Island
Gulf of Maine
Westbrook
Portland
South Portland
Cape Elizabeth
Springvale
Scarborough
Saco
Old Orchard Beach
Sanford
Biddeford
Kennebunk
RACHEL CARSON N.W.R.
Wells
South Berwick
Ogunquit
York Village
Kittery
Isles of Shoals

NEW HAMPSHIRE

50 miles
50 kilometers
Albers Conic Equal-Area Projection

⇨ CLOWN FACES. Puffins spend much of their time at sea feeding on herring. They come ashore to nest in burrows along the coast from Maine to Newfoundland, in Canada. Puffins' beaks and feet are dull gray except during the breeding season when they turn bright orange.

THE BASICS

STATS

Area
12,407 sq mi (32,133 sq km)

Population
5,773,552

Capital
Annapolis
Population 38,394

Largest city
Baltimore
Population 620,961

Ethnic/racial groups
58.2% white; 29.4% African American;
5.5% Asian; .4% Native American.
Hispanic (any race) 8.2%.

Industry
Real estate, federal government, health
services, business services, engineering services, electrical and gas services,
communications, banking, insurance

Agriculture
Poultry and eggs, dairy products,
nursery stock, soybeans, corn, seafood,
cattle, vegetables

Statehood
April 28, 1788; 7th state

GEO WHIZ

The Captain John Smith Chesapeake
National Historic Water Trail, which
traces some 3,000 miles (4,800 km)
of Smith's 1607–1608 explorations
of the bay, is the first national
water trail in the United States.

The Naval Support Facility Thurmont,
better known as Camp David, the
mountain retreat of American presidents, is part of Catoctin Mountain
Park in north-central Maryland.

Residents on Smith Island, in the lower
Chesapeake Bay, are being robbed of
their land by rising sea levels and of
their traditional livelihood by dwindling
blue crab harvests. They fear a major
Atlantic hurricane could wipe out their
island home.

The name of Baltimore's professional
football team—the Ravens—may
have been inspired by the title
of a poem written by noted
American author Edgar Allan
Poe, who lived in Baltimore
in the mid-1800s and whose
grave is in that city.

NORTHERN
(BALTIMORE)
ORIOLE

BLACK-EYED
SUSAN

MARYLAND

Native Americans, who raised crops and harvested oysters from the nearby waters of Chesapeake Bay, lived on the land that would become Maryland long before early European settlers arrived. In 1608 Captain John Smith explored the waters of the bay, and in 1634 English settlers established the colony of Maryland. In 1788 Maryland became the 7th state to ratify the new U.S. Constitution. Chesapeake Bay, the largest estuary in the U.S., almost splits Maryland into two parts. East of

⇧ GATEWAY CITY. Since the early 1700s, Baltimore, near the upper Chesapeake Bay, has been a major seaport and focus of trade, industry, and immigration. Today, the Inner Harbor is not only a modern working port, but also the city's vibrant cultural center.

the bay lies the flat coastal plain, while to the west the land rises through the hilly piedmont and mountainous panhandle. Chesapeake Bay, the state's economic and environmental focal point, supports a busy seafood industry. It is also a major transportation artery, linking Baltimore and other Maryland ports to the Atlantic Ocean. Most of the people of Maryland live in an urban corridor between Baltimore and Washington, D.C., where jobs in government, research, and high-tech businesses provide employment.

⇦ COLORFUL CRUSTACEAN. Blue crabs, found in Maryland's Chesapeake Bay waters, were a staple in the diet of Native Americans. They have been harvested commercially since the mid-1800s, and the tasty meat is a popular menu item—especially crab cakes—in seafood restaurants throughout the area.

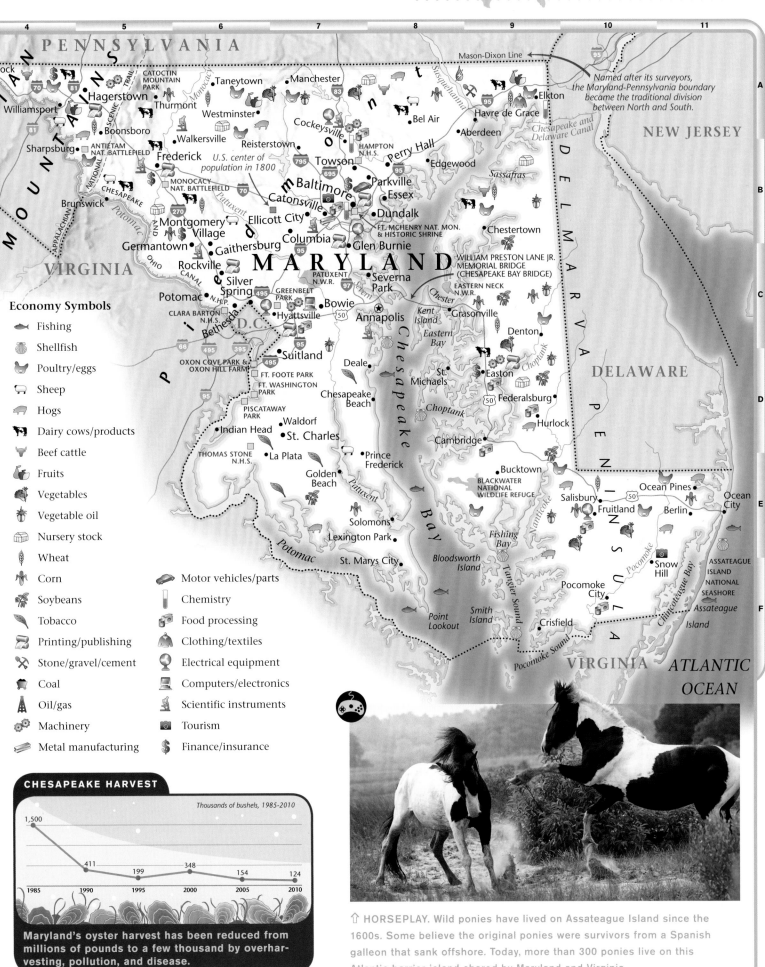

PENNSYLVANIA

Mason-Dixon Line

Named after its surveyors, the Maryland-Pennsylvania boundary became the traditional division between North and South.

NEW JERSEY

VIRGINIA

Williamsport
Hagerstown
Thurmont
Taneytown
Manchester
Boonsboro
Westminster
Walkersville
Sharpsburg
ANTIETAM NAT. BATTLEFIELD
Frederick
Reisterstown
Cockeysville
HAMPTON N.H.S.
Bel Air
Havre de Grace
Aberdeen
Elkton

Chesapeake and Delaware Canal

Sassafras

CATOCTIN MOUNTAIN PARK

U.S. center of population in 1800

MONOCACY NAT. BATTLEFIELD

Towson
Perry Hall
Edgewood

Baltimore
Parkville
Essex
Dundalk
FT. MCHENRY NAT. MON. & HISTORIC SHRINE

Chestertown

Brunswick
Montgomery Village
Germantown
Rockville
Gaithersburg
Ellicott City
Catonsville
Columbia
Glen Burnie

MARYLAND

WILLIAM PRESTON LANE JR. MEMORIAL BRIDGE (CHESAPEAKE BAY BRIDGE)

EASTERN NECK N.W.R.

Silver Spring
Potomac
CLARA BARTON N.H.S.
Bethesda
D.C.
Hyattsville
GREENBELT PARK
Bowie
PATUXENT N.W.R.
Severna Park
Annapolis
Kent Island
Grasonville
Denton

Eastern Bay

Chester

Suitland
OXON COVE PARK & OXON HILL FARM
FT. FOOTE PARK
FT. WASHINGTON PARK
Deale
St. Michaels
Easton
Federalsburg
Hurlock

Choptank

DELAWARE

PISCATAWAY PARK
Indian Head
Waldorf
St. Charles
Chesapeake Beach
Cambridge

THOMAS STONE N.H.S.
La Plata
Prince Frederick
Bucktown

Golden Beach
BLACKWATER NATIONAL WILDLIFE REFUGE
Ocean Pines

Salisbury
Fruitland
Berlin
Ocean City

Solomons
Lexington Park

Fishing Bay

Snow Hill

St. Marys City
Bloodsworth Island
Pocomoke City

ASSATEAGUE ISLAND NATIONAL SEASHORE

Assateague Island

Point Lookout
Smith Island
Crisfield

VIRGINIA

ATLANTIC OCEAN

Chesapeake Bay
Potomac
Patuxent
Nanticoke
Pocomoke
Tangier Sound
Pocomoke Sound
Chincoteague Bay

PENINSULA

Economy Symbols

- Fishing
- Shellfish
- Poultry/eggs
- Sheep
- Hogs
- Dairy cows/products
- Beef cattle
- Fruits
- Vegetables
- Vegetable oil
- Nursery stock
- Wheat
- Corn
- Soybeans
- Tobacco
- Printing/publishing
- Stone/gravel/cement
- Coal
- Oil/gas
- Machinery
- Metal manufacturing

- Motor vehicles/parts
- Chemistry
- Food processing
- Clothing/textiles
- Electrical equipment
- Computers/electronics
- Scientific instruments
- Tourism
- Finance/insurance

CHESAPEAKE HARVEST

Thousands of bushels, 1985-2010

1985	1990	1995	2000	2005	2010
1,500	411	199	348	154	124

Maryland's oyster harvest has been reduced from millions of pounds to a few thousand by overharvesting, pollution, and disease.

⇧ HORSEPLAY. Wild ponies have lived on Assateague Island since the 1600s. Some believe the original ponies were survivors from a Spanish galleon that sank offshore. Today, more than 300 ponies live on this Atlantic barrier island shared by Maryland and Virginia.

THE BASICS

STATS

Area
10,555 sq mi (27,336 sq km)

Population
6,547,629

Capital
Boston
Population 617,594

Largest city
Boston
Population 617,594

Major ethnic/racial groups
80.4% white; 6.6% African
American; 5.3% Asian;
.3% Native American.
Hispanic (any race) 9.6%.

Industry
Electrical equipment,
machinery, metal products,
scientific instruments, printing
and publishing, tourism

Agriculture
Fruits, nuts, berries, nursery
stock, dairy products

Statehood
February 6, 1788; 6th state

GEO WHIZ

In 1717 the pirate ship *Whydah*,
under the command of Captain
Samuel Bellamy (also known
as Black Sam), went down in a
storm off Cape Cod. Treasure and
artifacts recovered from the ship are
on display at the Whydah Museum, in
Provincetown, and are also part of a
National Geographic traveling exhibit.

Massachusetts is the birthplace of
several famous inventors, including Eli
Whitney, Samuel Morse, and Benjamin
Franklin.

The country's first lighthouse was built
on Little Brewster Island in Boston
Harbor in 1716. It is the last manned
lighthouse in the United States. Use the
online link to see what it's like to be a
lighthouse keeper for Boston Light.

Cape Cod is considered one of the
world's best spots for whale
watching, thanks to Stellwagen Bank,
a protected area at the mouth of
Massachusetts Bay.

CHICKADEE
MAYFLOWER

⇨ LEVIATHANS OF THE DEEP. In the
19th century, Massachusetts was an
important center for the whaling industry,
with more than 300 registered whaling
ships. Today, humpback whales swim
in the protected waters of a marine
sanctuary in Massachusetts Bay.

MASSACHUSETTS

Earliest human inhabitants of Massachusetts were
Native Americans who arrived more than 10,000
years ago. The first Europeans
to visit Massachusetts may
have been Norsemen
around A.D. 1000,
and later fishermen
from France and
Spain. But the
first permanent
European settlement
was established in
1620 when people
aboard the sailing ship
Mayflower landed near Plymouth on the coast
of Massachusetts. The Puritans arrived soon after, and by 1630 they had
established settlements at Salem and Boston. By 1640 more than 16,000
people, most seeking religious freedom, had settled in Massachusetts.
In the early days, the economy of Massachusetts was based on shipping,
fishing, and whaling. By the 19th century, industry, taking advantage
of abundant water power, had a firm foothold. Factory jobs attracted
thousands of immigrants, mainly from Europe. In the late 20th century,
Massachusetts experienced a boom in high-tech jobs, drawing on the
state's skilled labor force and its more than 80 colleges and universities.

⇧ REMINDER OF TIMES PAST.
Shrouded in morning mist, this
replica of the *Mayflower* docked
in Plymouth Harbor is a reminder
of Massachusetts's early history.

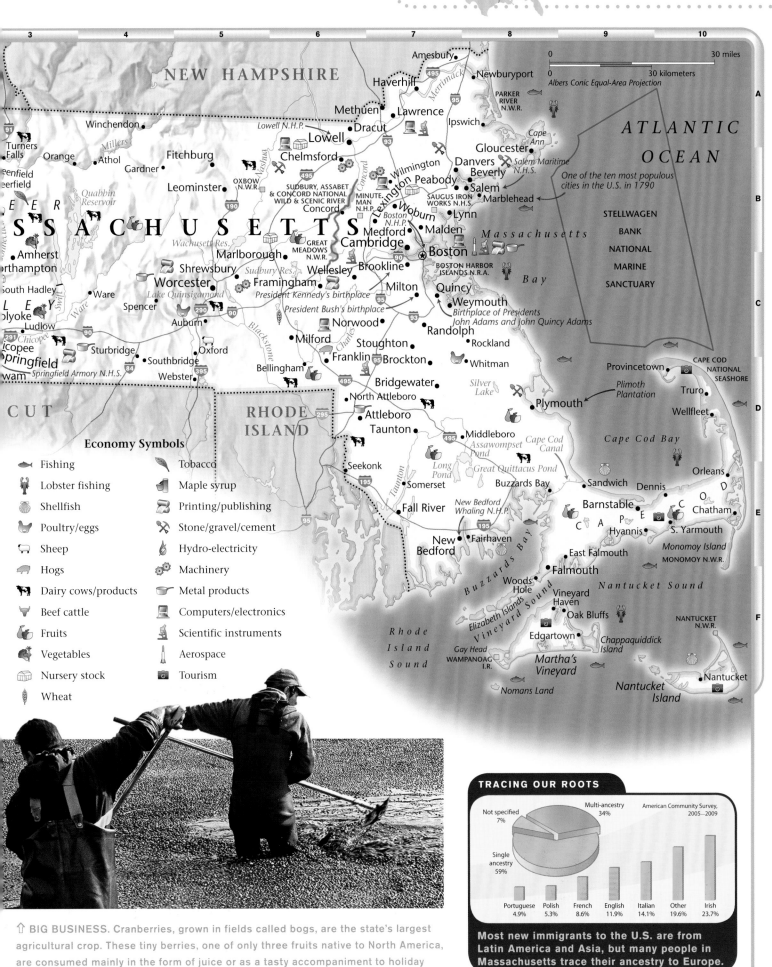

Map Labels

NEW HAMPSHIRE

Amesbury
Haverhill
Methuen
Newburyport
Lawrence
Ipswich
Dracut
Lowell N.H.P.
Lowell
PARKER RIVER N.W.R.
Winchendon
Fitchburg
Chelmsford
Cape Ann
Turners Falls
Orange
Athol
Gardner
Gloucester
Danvers
Beverly
Salem Maritime N.H.S.
Greenfield
Deerfield
Leominster
OXBOW N.W.R.
SUDBURY, ASSABET & CONCORD NATIONAL WILD & SCENIC RIVER
Peabody
Salem
Marblehead

MASSACHUSETTS

Quabbin Reservoir
Concord
MINUTE MAN N.H.P.
Lexington
Woburn
SAUGUS IRON WORKS N.H.S.
Lynn
Amherst
Northampton
Wachusett Res.
Marlborough
GREAT MEADOWS N.W.R.
Medford
Cambridge
Malden
Boston N.H.P.
Massachusetts
Shrewsbury
Sudbury Res.
Wellesley
Brookline
Boston
BOSTON HARBOR ISLANDS N.R.A.
Bay
South Hadley
Worcester
Framingham
Milton
Bay
Ware
Lake Quinsigamond
President Kennedy's birthplace
Quincy
Holyoke
Spencer
Auburn
President Bush's birthplace
Weymouth
Birthplace of Presidents John Adams and John Quincy Adams
STELLWAGEN BANK NATIONAL MARINE SANCTUARY
Ludlow
Norwood
Chicopee
Milford
Stoughton
Randolph
Springfield
Sturbridge
Oxford
Franklin
Brockton
Rockland
Agawam
Springfield Armory N.H.S.
Southbridge
Bellingham
Whitman
Webster
Bridgewater
Silver Lake
Provincetown
CAPE COD NATIONAL SEASHORE
North Attleboro
Plymouth
Plimoth Plantation
Truro

RHODE ISLAND

Attleboro
Taunton
Middleboro
Assawompset Pond
Cape Cod Canal
Cape Cod Bay
Wellfleet

CONNECTICUT

Seekonk
Long Pond
Great Quittacus Pond
Sandwich
Orleans
Somerset
Buzzards Bay
Dennis
Fall River
New Bedford Whaling N.H.P.
Barnstable
Chatham
C A P E C O D
New Bedford
Fairhaven
Hyannis
S. Yarmouth
East Falmouth
Monomoy Island
MONOMOY N.W.R.
Woods Hole
Falmouth
Nantucket Sound
Buzzards Bay
Vineyard Haven
Oak Bluffs
NANTUCKET N.W.R.
Rhode Island Sound
Elizabeth Islands
Vineyard Sound
Edgartown
Chappaquiddick Island
Gay Head
WAMPANOAG I.R.
Martha's Vineyard
Nantucket
Nantucket Island
Nomans Land

ATLANTIC OCEAN

One of the ten most populous cities in the U.S. in 1790

0 _____ 30 miles
0 _____ 30 kilometers
Albers Conic Equal-Area Projection

Economy Symbols

- Fishing
- Lobster fishing
- Shellfish
- Poultry/eggs
- Sheep
- Hogs
- Dairy cows/products
- Beef cattle
- Fruits
- Vegetables
- Nursery stock
- Wheat
- Tobacco
- Maple syrup
- Printing/publishing
- Stone/gravel/cement
- Hydro-electricity
- Machinery
- Metal products
- Computers/electronics
- Scientific instruments
- Aerospace
- Tourism

⇧ BIG BUSINESS. Cranberries, grown in fields called bogs, are the state's largest agricultural crop. These tiny berries, one of only three fruits native to North America, are consumed mainly in the form of juice or as a tasty accompaniment to holiday dishes. Workers flood fields to make harvesting the floating berries easier.

TRACING OUR ROOTS

American Community Survey, 2005–2009

Pie chart:
- Multi-ancestry 34%
- Single ancestry 59%
- Not specified 7%

Bar chart:
Portuguese	Polish	French	English	Italian	Other	Irish
4.9%	5.3%	8.6%	11.9%	14.1%	19.6%	23.7%

Most new immigrants to the U.S. are from Latin America and Asia, but many people in Massachusetts trace their ancestry to Europe.

NEW HAMPSHIRE

The territory that would become the state of New Hampshire, the 9th state to approve the U.S. Constitution in 1788, began as a fishing colony established along the short 18-mile-long coastline (29 km) in 1623. New Hampshire was named a royal colony in 1679, but as the Revolutionary War approached, it was the first colony to declare its independence from English rule.

In the early 19th century, life in New Hampshire followed two very different paths. Near the coast, villages and towns grew up around sawmills, shipyards, and warehouses. But in the forested, mountainous interior, people lived on small, isolated farms, and towns provided only basic services. Today, New Hampshire is one of the fastest growing states in the Northeast. Modern industries, such as computers and electronics, and high-tech companies have brought prosperity to the state. Its natural beauty attracts tourists year-round to hike on forest trails, swim in pristine lakes, and ski on snow-covered mountain slopes.

⇧ LUMBERING GIANT. Averaging 6 feet (2 m) tall at the shoulders, moose are the largest of North America's deer. Moose are found throughout New Hampshire.

THE BASICS

STATS

Area
9,350 sq mi (24,216 sq km)

Population
1,316,470

Capital
Concord
Population 42,695

Largest city
Manchester
Population 109,565

Ethnic/racial groups
93.9% white; 2.2% Asian; 1.1% African American; .2% Native American. Hispanic (any race) 2.8%.

Industry
Machinery, electronics, metal products

Agriculture
Nursery stock, poultry and eggs, fruits and nuts, vegetables

Statehood
June 21, 1788; 9th state

GEO WHIZ

About ten million tourists visit New Hampshire each year, nearly ten times the number of people who live in the state.

The Granite State boasts more than 200 different kinds of rocks and minerals. Use the icon to play Rock Stars and test your knowledge.

The first potato grown in the United States was planted in 1719 in Londonderry on the Common Field, now known simply as the Commons.

Ben Kilham's unique ways of rehabilitating abandoned black bear cubs he finds in the New Hampshire woods has earned him the nickname Bear Man by residents of Lyme. He has been working with orphaned, sick, and injured cubs for more than nine years.

PURPLE FINCH
PURPLE LILAC

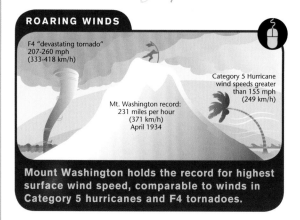

ROARING WINDS

F4 "devastating tornado"
207-260 mph
(333-418 km/h)

Category 5 Hurricane
wind speeds greater
than 155 mph
(249 km/h)

Mt. Washington record:
231 miles per hour
(371 km/h)
April 1934

Mount Washington holds the record for highest surface wind speed, comparable to winds in Category 5 hurricanes and F4 tornadoes.

⇨ ALL ABOARD. Tourists traveling by train through the White Mountains enjoy the cool autumn weather and the colorful fall foliage of deciduous trees that cover the mountains.

⇧ AUTUMN PEACE. A white steepled church sits nestled among trees in a village near New Hampshire's White Mountains. Such traditional churches, common in the New England landscape, are a reminder of early settlers' search for religious freedom.

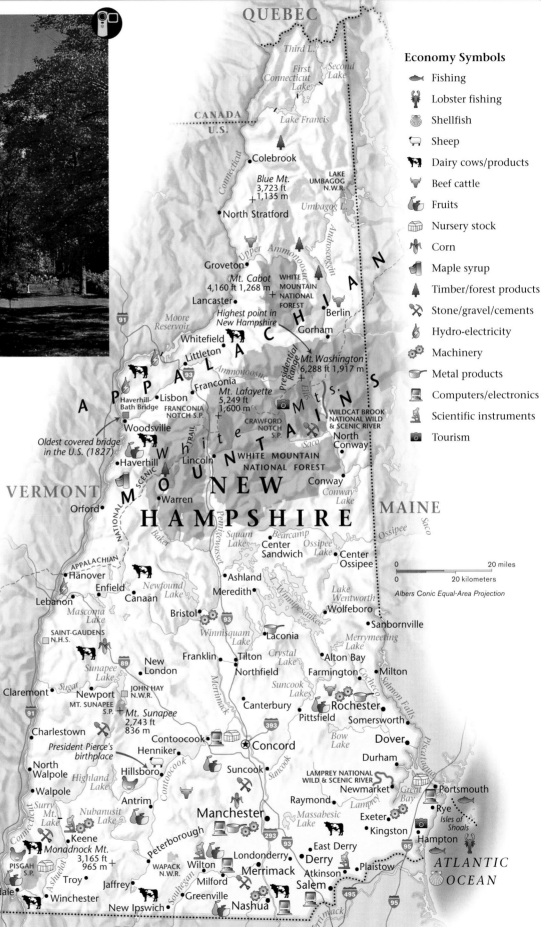

Economy Symbols

- 🐟 Fishing
- 🦞 Lobster fishing
- 🐚 Shellfish
- 🐑 Sheep
- 🐄 Dairy cows/products
- 🐂 Beef cattle
- 🍏 Fruits
- 🏭 Nursery stock
- 🌽 Corn
- 🍁 Maple syrup
- 🌲 Timber/forest products
- ⚒ Stone/gravel/cements
- 💧 Hydro-electricity
- ⚙ Machinery
- 🍳 Metal products
- 💻 Computers/electronics
- 🔬 Scientific instruments
- 📷 Tourism

QUEBEC

Third L.

First
Connecticut
Lakes

Second
Lake

Lake Francis

CANADA
U.S.

Lake Umbagog N.W.R.

LAKE UMBAGOG N.W.R.

Colebrook

Blue Mt.
3,723 ft
1,135 m

Umbagog L.

North Stratford

Connecticut

Upper Ammonoosuc

Androscoggin

Groveton

WHITE MOUNTAIN NATIONAL FOREST

Mt. Cabot
4,160 ft 1,268 m
Highest point in New Hampshire

Lancaster

Berlin

Gorham

Moore Reservoir

Whitefield

Ammonoosuc

Presidential Range

Mt. Washington
6,288 ft 1,917 m

Littleton

Franconia

Mt. Lafayette
5,249 ft
1,600 m

Haverhill
Bath Bridge

Lisbon

FRANCONIA NOTCH S.P.

CRAWFORD NOTCH S.P.

WILDCAT BROOK NATIONAL WILD & SCENIC RIVER

Ellis

Saco

Woodsville

Oldest covered bridge in the U.S. (1827)

White

Lincoln

WHITE MOUNTAIN NATIONAL FOREST

North Conway

Haverhill

VERMONT

Orford

Warren

Baker

NEW HAMPSHIRE

Conway

Conway Lake

MAINE

Saco

Ossipee

Squam Lake

Bearcamp

Ossipee Lake

Center Sandwich

Center Ossipee

Hanover

Newfound Lake

Ashland

Winnipesaukee

Lake Wentworth

Wolfeboro

20 miles

20 kilometers

Albers Conic Equal-Area Projection

Enfield

Canaan

Meredith

Lebanon

Mascoma Lake

Bristol

Winnisquam Lake

Laconia

Sanbornville

Merrymeeting Lake

SAINT-GAUDENS N.H.S.

Franklin

Tilton

Crystal Lake

Alton Bay

Milton

Claremont

Sunapee Lake

New London

Northfield

Farmington

Cochecco

Sugar

Newport

JOHN HAY N.W.R.

Suncook Lakes

Rochester

Salmon Falls

MT. SUNAPEE S.P.

Mt. Sunapee
2,743 ft
836 m

Canterbury

Pittsfield

Somersworth

Charlestown

President Pierce's birthplace

Contoocook

Concord

Bow Lake

Dover

North Walpole

Henniker

Suncook

Durham

Walpole

Highland Lake

Hillsboro

Contoocook

LAMPREY NATIONAL WILD & SCENIC RIVER

Newmarket

Great Bay

Portsmouth

Antrim

Raymond

Lamprey

Rye

Isles of Shoals

Surry Mt. Lake

Nubanusit Lake

Massabesic Lake

Exeter

Kingston

Hampton

Keene

Manchester

Peterborough

East Derry

Londonderry

Derry

Plaistow

ATLANTIC OCEAN

PISGAH S.P.

Monadnock Mt.
3,165 ft
965 m

WAPACK N.W.R.

Wilton

Atkinson

Hinsdale

Troy

Jaffrey

Milford

Salem

Winchester

New Ipswich

Greenville

Nashua

Merrimack

Southegan

Merrimack

MASSACHUSETTS

THE BASICS

STATS

Area
8,721 sq mi (22,588 sq km)

Population
8,791,894

Capital
Trenton
Population 84,913

Largest city
Newark
Population 277,140

Ethnic/racial groups
68.6% white; 13.7% African American; 8.3% Asian; .3% Native American. Hispanic (any race) 17.1%.

Industry
Machinery, electronics, metal products, chemicals

Agriculture
Nursery stock, poultry and eggs, fruits and nuts, vegetables

Statehood
December 18, 1787; 3rd state

GEO WHIZ

Site of a one-time trash heap, the Meadowlands, a swampy lowland on either side of the Hackensack River, is now home to a major sports complex, bustling suburban neighborhoods, and congested roadways. Parts of it are isolated enough to allow days of quiet canoeing.

In 1930 New Jerseyite Charles Darrow developed the game Monopoly. He named Boardwalk and other streets in the game after those in Atlantic City.

The first dinosaur skeleton found in North America was excavated at Haddonfield in 1858. It was named *Hadrosaurus* in honor of its discovery site.

AMERICAN GOLDFINCH
VIOLET

NEW JERSEY

Long before Europeans settled in New Jersey, the region was home to hunting and farming communities of Delaware Indians. The Dutch set up a trading post in northern New Jersey in 1618, calling it New Netherland, but yielded the land in 1664 to the English, who named it New Jersey after the English Channel Isle of Jersey. New Jersey saw more than 90 battles during the Revolutionary War. It became the 3rd U.S. state in 1787 and the first to sign the Bill of Rights. In the 19th century southern New Jersey remained largely agricultural, while the northern part of the state rapidly industrialize. Today highways and railroads link the state to urban centers along the Atlantic seaboard. More than 10,000 farms grow fruits and vegetables for nearby urban markets. Industries as well as services and trade are thriving. Beaches along the Atlantic coast attract thousands of tourists each year.

⇧ HOLD ON! New Jersey's Atlantic coast is lined with sandy beaches that attract vacationers from near and far. Amusement parks, such as this one in Wildwood, add to the fun.

⇨ HEADED TO MARKET. New Jersey is a leading producer of fresh fruits and vegetables. These organic vegetables are headed for urban markets in the Northeast.

⇦ SUBURBAN SPRAWL. With more than 90 percent of the state's population living in urban areas, housing developments, with close-set, look-alike houses, are a common characteristic of the suburban landscape. Residents commute to jobs in the city.

⇧ PLAY BALL! Fans pack the seats at Newark's Bear and Eagles Riverfront Stadium to watch a minor league baseball game. Built in 1999, the stadium is a part of Newark's plan to revitalize the downtown area, drawing people into the city.

Economy Symbols

⚓	Fishing	🌽	Corn
🦪	Shellfish	🌿	Soybeans
🦃	Poultry/eggs	📰	Printing/publishing
🐑	Sheep	⚒	Stone/gravel/cement
🐖	Hogs	⚙	Machinery
🐄	Dairy cows/products	🧪	Chemistry
🐂	Beef cattle	📷	Food processing
🍓	Fruits	💻	Computers/electronics
🥬	Vegetables	🚀	Aerospace
🏠	Nursery stock	📷	Tourism
🌾	Wheat		

CROWDED

Average number of people per square mile of land, 2010 data

New Jersey	Massachusetts	New York	Vermont	Maine	U.S. average
1,195.5	839.4	411.2	67.9	43.1	87.4

Although it ranks 47th among the states in area, New Jersey has the highest population density—people per square mile—in the country.

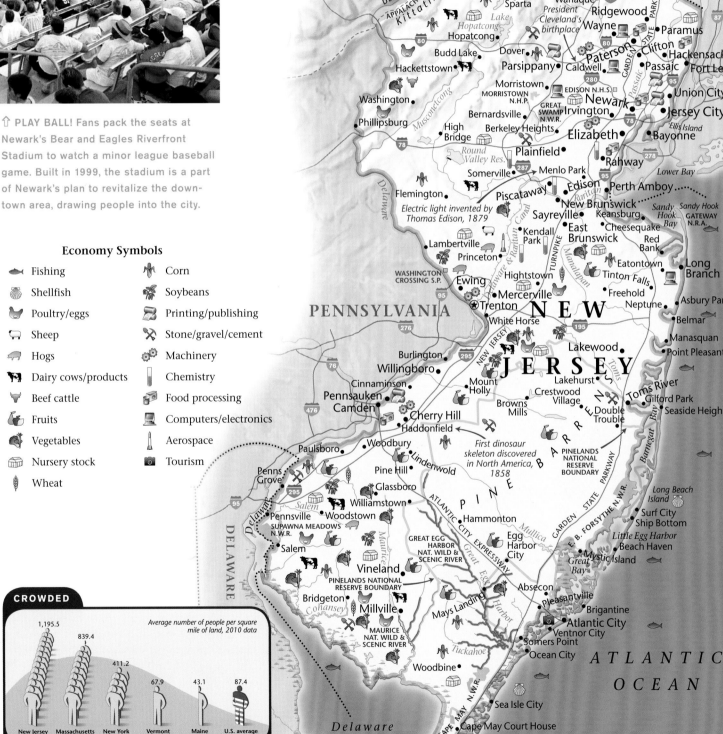

NEW YORK

High Point
1,803 ft
550 m

Highest point in New Jersey

WALLKILL RIVER N.W.R.

Highland Lakes
West Milford
Ringwood
Franklin
Ramsey
Newton
Wanaque Reservoir
Sparta
Wanaque
President Cleveland's birthplace
Ridgewood
Paramus
Hopatcong
Wayne
Clifton
Hackensack
Budd Lake
Dover
Paterson
Passaic
Fort Lee
Hackettstown
Parsippany
Caldwell
Union City
Washington
Morristown
MORRISTOWN N.H.P.
EDISON N.H.S.
Newark
Jersey City
Bernardsville
GREAT SWAMP N.W.R.
Irvington
Ellis Island
Phillipsburg
Berkeley Heights
Elizabeth
Bayonne
High Bridge
Plainfield
Rahway
Round Valley Res.
Somerville
Menlo Park
Lower Bay
Flemington
Piscataway
Edison
Perth Amboy
Electric light invented by Thomas Edison, 1879
New Brunswick
Sandy Hook Bay
Sandy Hook GATEWAY N.R.A.
Sayreville
Keansburg
Lambertville
Kendall Park
East Brunswick
Cheesequake
Red Bank
Princeton
Eatontown
Long Branch
WASHINGTON CROSSING S.P.
Ewing
Hightstown
Tinton Falls
Mercerville
Freehold
Neptune
Asbury Park
Trenton
White Horse
NEW JERSEY
Belmar
Burlington
Manasquan
Willingboro
Lakewood
Point Pleasant
Cinnaminson
Mount Holly
Lakehurst
Toms River
Pennsauken
Crestwood Village
Gilford Park
Camden
Browns Mills
Double Trouble
Seaside Heights
Cherry Hill
Haddonfield
PINELANDS NATIONAL RESERVE BOUNDARY
Woodbury
First dinosaur skeleton discovered in North America, 1858
Paulsboro
Lindenwold
Pine Hill
Long Beach Island
Penns Grove
Glassboro
Surf City
Ship Bottom
Williamstown
Little Egg Harbor
Beach Haven
Pennsville
Woodstown
Hammonton
Mystic Island
SUPAWNA MEADOWS N.W.R.
Egg Harbor City
Great Bay
Salem
GREAT EGG HARBOR NAT. WILD & SCENIC RIVER
Absecon
Vineland
Pleasantville
PINELANDS NATIONAL RESERVE BOUNDARY
Brigantine
Bridgeton
Mays Landing
Atlantic City
Millville
Ventnor City
Somers Point
Ocean City
MAURICE NAT. WILD & SCENIC RIVER
Woodbine

PENNSYLVANIA

DELAWARE

ATLANTIC OCEAN

Delaware Bay
Villas
Cape May Court House
North Wildwood
Wildwood
Cape May
Cape May Canal

0 20 miles
0 20 kilometers
Albers Conic Equal-Area Projection

THE EMPIRE STATE:
NEW YORK

STATS

Area
54,556 sq mi (141,300 sq km)

Population
19,378,102

Capital
Albany
Population 97,856

Largest city
New York City
Population 8,175,133

Ethnic/racial groups
65.7% white; 15.9% African American;
7.3% Asian; .6% Native American.
Hispanic (any race) 17.6%.

Industry
Printing and publishing, machinery,
computer products, finance, tourism

Agriculture
Dairy products, cattle and other livestock, vegetables, nursery stock, apples

Statehood
July 26, 1788; 11th state

GEO WHIZ

Each year at Halloween the Headless
Horseman rides again through the coun-
tryside of Sleepy Hollow as residents
reenact Washington Irving's *The Legend
of Sleepy Hollow.*

The Erie Canal, built in the 1820s
between Albany and Buffalo, helped
New York City become a worldwide
trading center and opened the Midwest
to development by linking the Hudson
River and the Great Lakes.

Cooperstown, New York, home of the
National Baseball Hall of
Fame, takes its name
from a town estab-
lished in the late 1700s
by the father of James
Fenimore Cooper, author of
such American classics as
The Last of the Mohicans and
The Deerslayer.

EASTERN
BLUEBIRD

ROSE

⬆ LADY LIBERTY.
Standing in New York
Harbor, the Statue of
Liberty, a gift from the
people of France, is
a symbol of freedom
and democracy.

NEW YORK

1   2   3

When Englishman Henry Hudson explored New York's
Hudson River Valley in 1609, the territory was already
inhabited by large tribes of Native Americans, including
the powerful Iroquois. In 1624 a Dutch trading company
established the New Netherland colony, but after just
40 years the colony was taken over by the English and
renamed for England's Duke of York. In 1788 New
York became the 11th state. The state can be
divided into two parts. The powerful
port city of New York, center of
trade and commerce and gateway to immigrants, is the
largest city in the U.S. Its
metropolitan area has
more than 18 million
people. Everything
north of the city
is simply referred
to as "Upstate."
Cities such as Buffalo
and Rochester are industrial centers, while
Ithaca and Syracuse boast major universities. Agriculture is also
important in New York. With almost 5 million acres in cropland,
the state is a major producer of dairy products, fruits, and vegetables.

⬅ NATURAL WONDER.
As many as 12 million
tourists annually visit
Niagara Falls on the
U.S.-Canada border.
Visitors in rain slickers
trek through the mists
below Bridal Veil Falls
on the American side.

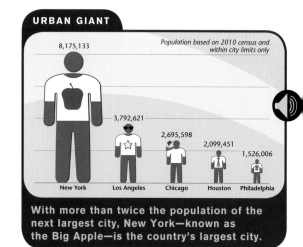

URBAN GIANT

8,175,133

*Population based on 2010 census and
within city limits only*

3,792,621

2,695,598

2,099,451

1,526,006

New York   Los Angeles   Chicago   Houston   Philadelphia

**With more than twice the population of the
next largest city, New York—known as
the Big Apple—is the country's largest city.**

Scale

100 miles

100 kilometers

Albers Conic Equal-Area Projection

4 · 5 · 6 · 7 · 8 · 9 · 10 · 11

Economy Symbols

- Fishing
- Shellfish
- Poultry/eggs
- Sheep
- Hogs
- Dairy cows/products
- Fruits
- Vegetables
- Vegetable oil
- Nursery stock
- Wheat
- Corn
- Vineyards
- Maple syrup
- Printing/publishing
- Stone/gravel/cement
- Mining
- Oil/gas
- Hydro-electricity
- Machinery
- Motor vehicles/parts
- Clothing/textiles
- Electrical equipment
- Scientific instruments
- Motion picture/music industry
- Tourism
- Finance/insurance

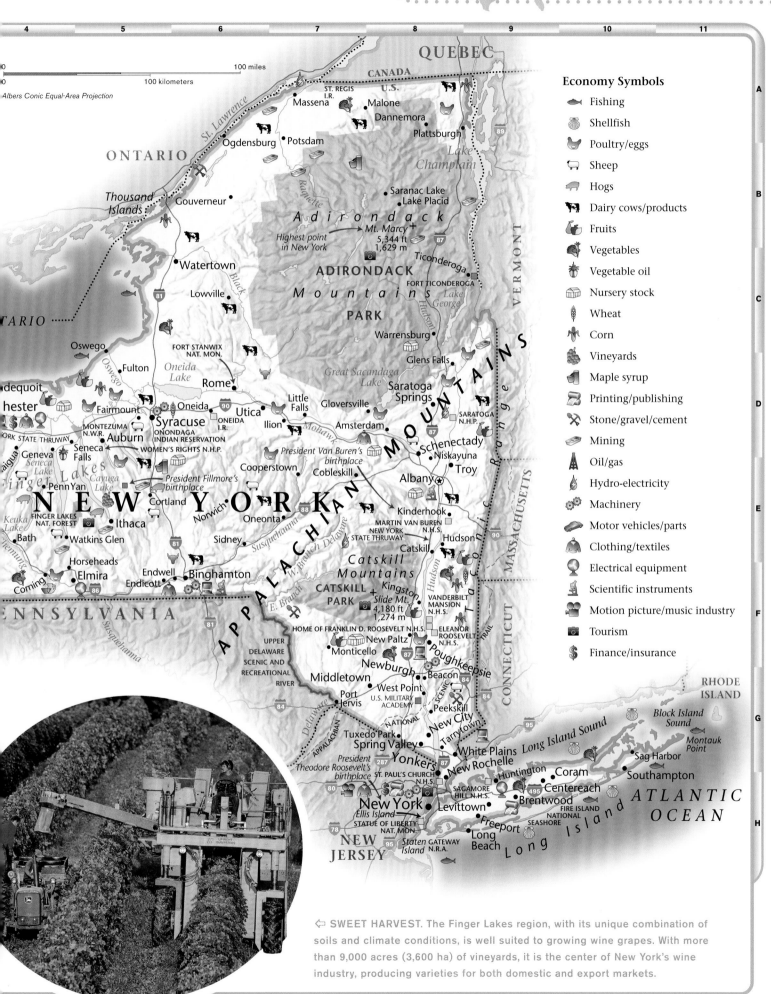

QUEBEC

CANADA
U.S.

ONTARIO

Thousand
Islands

Massena
Malone
Dannemora
Plattsburgh
ST. REGIS
I.R.
Ogdensburg
Potsdam
Gouverneur
Lake
Champlain

A d i r o n d a c k

Saranac Lake
Lake Placid

Highest point
in New York
Mt. Marcy
5,344 ft
1,629 m

Watertown

Ticonderoga

ADIRONDACK
M o u n t a i n s
PARK
FORT TICONDEROGA
Lake
George

Lowville

VERMONT

Warrensburg

Oswego
Fulton
FORT STANWIX
NAT. MON.
Great Sacandaga
Lake
Glens Falls

Oneida
Lake
Rome

Saratoga
Springs

equoit
hester
Fairmount
Syracuse
Oneida
Utica
Little
Falls
Gloversville
SARATOGA
N.H.P.

ONTARIO

ORK STATE THRUWAY
MONTEZUMA
N.W.R.
ONONDAGA
INDIAN RESERVATION
ONEIDA
I.R.
Ilion
Amsterdam
Mohawk

Geneva
Seneca
Falls
Auburn
WOMEN'S RIGHTS N.H.P.
Schenectady
Niskayuna

*President Van Buren's
birthplace*

aigua
Seneca
Lake
Cayuga
Lake
Cooperstown
Cobleskill
Troy

Finger Lakes
PennYan

N E W   Y O R K

Albany

Kinderhook

Keuka
Lake
FINGER LAKES
NAT. FOREST
Cortland
Norwich
Oneonta
MARTIN VAN BUREN
N.H.S.
MASSACHUSETTS
Taconic Range

Bath
Ithaca
Watkins Glen
NEW YORK
STATE THRUWAY
Hudson

Susquehanna
Sidney
Catskill
W. Branch Delaware

Horseheads
Elmira
Endwell
Endicott
Binghamton
*Catskill
Mountains*

Corning

A P P A L A C H I A N   M O U N T A I N S

E. Branch
CATSKILL
PARK
Slide Mt.
4,180 ft
1,274 m
Kingston
VANDERBILT
MANSION
N.H.S.

P E N N S Y L V A N I A

Susquehanna

HOME OF FRANKLIN D. ROOSEVELT N.H.S.
ELEANOR
ROOSEVELT
N.H.S.

UPPER
DELAWARE
SCENIC AND
RECREATIONAL
RIVER

New Paltz
Monticello
Newburgh
Poughkeepsie
Beacon

Delaware

Middletown
West Point
Port
Jervis
U.S. MILITARY
ACADEMY
Peekskill

CONNECTICUT

NATIONAL
APPALACHIAN
New City
Tarrytown

RHODE
ISLAND

Tuxedo Park
Spring Valley
Yonkers
White Plains
New Rochelle

Block Island
Sound
Long Island Sound

Montauk
Point

*President
Theodore Roosevelt's
birthplace*
ST. PAUL'S CHURCH
N.H.S.

Sag Harbor

Huntington
Coram
Southampton

Centereach
Brentwood

A T L A N T I C

SAGAMORE
HILL N.H.S.

New York
Levittown
FIRE ISLAND
NATIONAL
SEASHORE

O C E A N

Ellis Island
STATUE OF LIBERTY
NAT. MON.

Freeport

Long
Beach

Long Island

NEW
JERSEY

Staten
Island
GATEWAY
N.R.A.

⬅ **SWEET HARVEST.** The Finger Lakes region, with its unique combination of soils and climate conditions, is well suited to growing wine grapes. With more than 9,000 acres (3,600 ha) of vineyards, it is the center of New York's wine industry, producing varieties for both domestic and export markets.

PENNSYLVANIA

Pennsylvania, the 12th of England's 13 American colonies, was established in 1682 by Quaker William Penn and 360 settlers seeking religious freedom and fair government. The colony enjoyed abundant natural resources—dense woodlands, fertile soils, industrial minerals, and water power—that soon attracted Germans, Scotch-Irish, and other immigrants. Pennsylvania played a central role in the move for independence from Britain, and Philadelphia served as the new country's capital from 1790 to 1800. In the 19th century Philadelphia, in the east, and Pittsburgh, in the west, became booming centers of industrial growth. Philadelphia produced ships, locomotives, and textiles, while the iron and steel industry fueled Pittsburgh's growth. Jobs in industry as well as agriculture attracted immigrants from around the world. Today, Pennsylvania's economy has shifted toward information technology, health care, financial services, and tourism, but the state remains a leader in coal and steel production.

⇧ LET FREEDOM RING. The Liberty Bell, cast in 1753 by Pennsylvania craftsmen, hangs silent in Philadelphia. Because of a crack, it is no longer rung.

THE BASICS

STATS

Area
46,055 sq mi (119,283 sq km)

Population
12,702,379

Capital
Harrisburg
Population 49,528

Largest city
Philadelphia
Population 1,526,006

Ethnic/racial groups
81.9% white; 10.8% African American; 2.7% Asian; .2% Native American. Hispanic (any race) 5.7%.

Industry
Machinery, printing and publishing, forest products, metal products

Agriculture
Dairy products, poultry and eggs, mushrooms, cattle, hogs, grains

Statehood
December 12, 1787; 2nd state

GEO WHIZ

If you are into guitars or other acoustic instruments, you will want to put the Martin Guitar Company, in Nazareth, on your list of places to visit. It has been handcrafting these instruments for musicians all over the world for more than 150 years.

For more than a century, the streets of Philadelphia have been transformed on New Year's Day as some 15,000 revelers dressed in sequined and feathered costumes "strut their stuff" to the sound of string-band music in the Mummers Parade past millions of onlookers.

RUFFED GROUSE

MOUNTAIN LAUREL

1 2

LAKE ERIE

Erie
Millcreek

ERIE NATION WILDLIF REFUGE

Meadville
Pymatuning Reservoir

Titus

Greenville
Oil C

Sharon

Grove City

New Castle

But

Beaver Falls

Aliquippa
McCand

Pittsburgh

McKeesport

Jear

Washington
Mo

Connell

Waynesburg
Uniontown

FRIENDSHIP HILL N.H.S.
FT. NECE NATI BATTLE

WEST VIRGINI

OHIO

⇨ RIVER TOWN. Pittsburgh, one of the largest inland ports in the U.S., was established in 1758 where the Monongahela and Allegheny Rivers meet to form the Ohio River. Once a booming steel town, Pittsburgh is now a center of finance, medicine, and education.

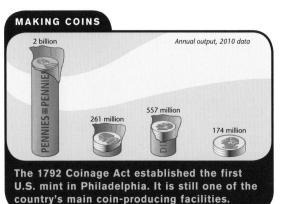

MAKING COINS

2 billion

Annual output, 2010 data

261 million

557 million

174 million

The 1792 Coinage Act established the first U.S. mint in Philadelphia. It is still one of the country's main coin-producing facilities.

3   4   5   6   7   8   9   10

0 ——— 50 miles
0 ——— 50 kilometers
Albers Conic Equal-Area Projection

NEW YORK

Chemung

A

Susquehanna

Warren
Allegheny Reservoir
Bradford
HENY
NAL &
ALLEGHENY
NATIONAL
FOREST
Coudersport
Mansfield
Wellsboro
Towanda
Sayre
Tioga

B

Upper Delaware Scenic & Recreational River

Emporium
St. Marys
Ridgway
Clarion
CLARION NATIONAL WILD & SCENIC RIVER
Pine Creek Gorge
Carbondale
Archbald
Scranton   Dunmore
STEAMTOWN N.H.S.
Lake Wallenpaupack

Du Bois
Clearfield
West Branch Susquehanna
Jersey Shore
Lock Haven
Williamsport
Wilkes-Barre
Kingston
Pocono Mts.
DELAWARE WATER GAP NATIONAL RECREATION AREA

C

unxsutawney
PENNSYLVANIA
Lewisburg
Bloomsburg
Hazleton
Stroudsburg
Delaware Water Gap

nning
State College
Selinsgrove
Sunbury
Shamokin
Mt. Carmel
Tamaqua
Pottsville
Nazareth
Bangor
Easton

Indiana
Tyrone
Lewistown
APPALACHIAN
Juniata
Mt.
SCENIC TRAIL
Allentown
Bethlehem
Quakertown

D

NEW JERSEY

ALLEGHENY PORTAGE RAILROAD N.H.S.
Altoona
Huntingdon
Blue
Reading
Doylestown

maugh
JOHNSTOWN FLOOD NAT. MEM.
Hollidaysburg
Raystown Lake
Mechanicsburg
Harrisburg
Lebanon
Pottstown
HOPEWELL FURNACE N.H.S.
Norristown
Levittown

sburg
Johnstown
Windber
President Buchanan's birthplace
Carlisle
Hershey
PENNSYLVANIA
TURNPIKE
Ephrata
VALLEY FORGE N.H.P.

E

YLVANIA TURNPIKE
Bedford
Three Mile Island
Elizabethtown
Lancaster
Coatesville
Upper Darby
Philadelphia

omerset
Shippensburg
Columbia
West Chester
Chester
JOHN HEINZ N.W.R.

Mt. Davis
3,213 ft 979 m
Highest point in Pennsylvania
Chambersburg
York
Red Lion
Kennett Square

asselman
Mercersburg
EISENHOWER N.H.S.
Gettysburg
GETTYSBURG N.M.P.
Hanover
Mason-Dixon Line
DEL.

F

Waynesboro

W.VA.   MARYLAND

Named after its surveyors, the Pennsylvania-Maryland boundary became the traditional division between North and South.

Busiest freshwater port in the U.S., Independence N.H.P. (includes Independence Hall, Liberty Bell, Christ Church, Franklin Court), Betsy Ross House, Edgar Allan Poe N.H.S., Deshler-Morris House, Gloria Dei Church N.H.S.

Economy Symbols

- Poultry/eggs
- Sheep
- Hogs
- Dairy cows/products
- Beef cattle
- Fruits
- Vegetables
- Nursery stock
- Corn
- Soybeans
- Tobacco
- Vineyards
- Timber/forest products
- Printing/publishing
- Stone/gravel/cement

- Mining
- Coal
- Oil/gas
- Hydro-electricity
- Machinery
- Metal manufacturing
- Railroad equipment
- Motor vehicles/parts
- Rubber/plastics
- Chemistry
- Food processing
- Glass/clay products
- Computers/electronics
- Tourism
- Finance/insurance

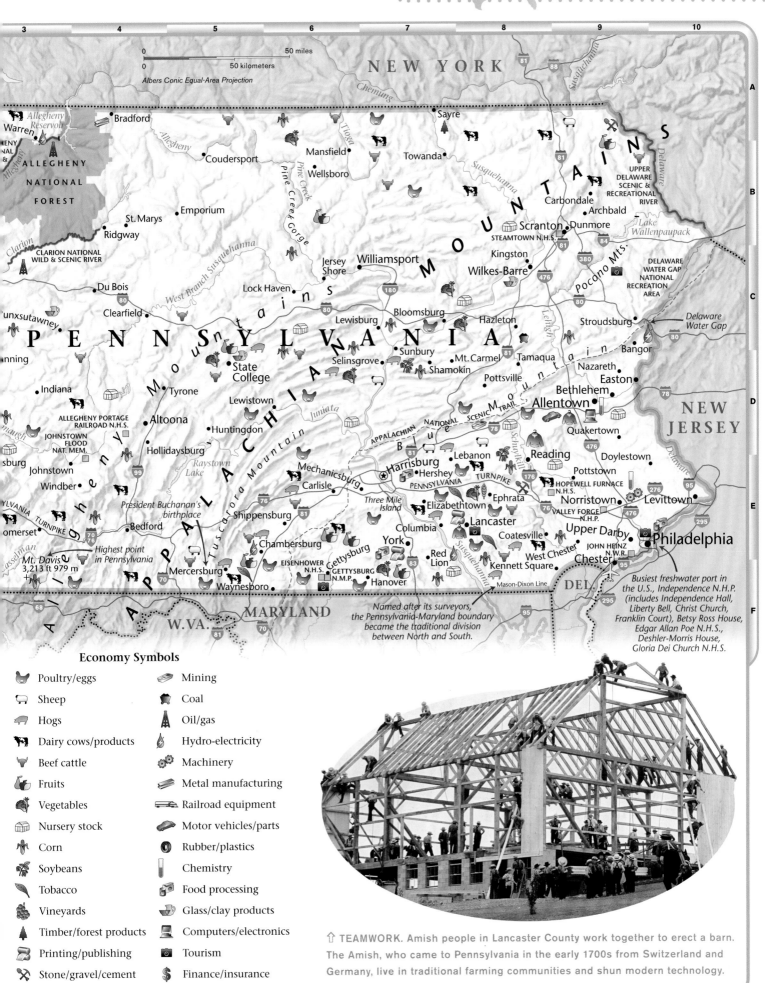

⇧ TEAMWORK. Amish people in Lancaster County work together to erect a barn. The Amish, who came to Pennsylvania in the early 1700s from Switzerland and Germany, live in traditional farming communities and shun modern technology.

RHODE ISLAND

THE BASICS

STATS

Area
1,545 sq mi (4,002 sq km)

Population
1,052,567

Capital
Providence
Population 178,042

Largest city
Providence
Population 178,042

Ethnic/racial groups
81.4% white; 5.7% African American;
2.9% Asian; .6% Native American.
Hispanic (any race) 12.4%.

Industry
Health services, business services,
silver and jewelry products,
metal products

Agriculture
Nursery stock, vegetables, dairy
products, eggs

Statehood
May 29, 1790; 13th state

GEO WHIZ

Pawtucket is one of several communities in Rhode Island that have become home to a growing number of people from Cape Verde. Drought has forced people from this African country to find a new place to live. Massachusetts and North Dakota are the only other states with measurable Cape Verdean populations.

Wild coyotes are living and thriving on islands in Narragansett Bay. Researchers have outfitted some of the animals with radio collars so that their numbers and whereabouts can be tracked online—even by schoolkids.

RHODE ISLAND RED
VIOLET

⇧ CLUES TO THE PAST.
Fossils embedded in rocks
left behind 10,000 years
ago by retreating glaciers
tell of Block Island's past.

In 1524 Italian navigator Giovanni Verrazzano was the first European explorer to visit Rhode Island, but place-names such as Quonochontaug and Narragansett tell of an earlier Native American population. In 1636 Roger Williams, seeking greater religious freedom, left Massachusetts and established the first European settlement in what was to become the colony of Rhode Island. In the years following the Revolutionary War, Rhode Island pressed for fairness in trade, taxes, and representation in Congress, as well as greater freedom of worship, before becoming the 13th state. By the 19th century, Rhode Island had become an important center of trade and textile factories, attracting many immigrants from Europe. In addition to commercial activities, Rhode Island's coastline became a popular vacation retreat for the wealthy. Today, Rhode Island, like many other states, has seen its economy shift toward high-tech jobs and service industries. It is also promoting its coastline and bays, as well as its rich history, to attract tourists.

⇦ SETTING SAIL. Newport Harbor invites sailors of all ages. From 1930 to 1983, the prestigious America's Cup Yacht Race took place in the waters off Newport. Today, the town provides 900 moorings for boats of all types.

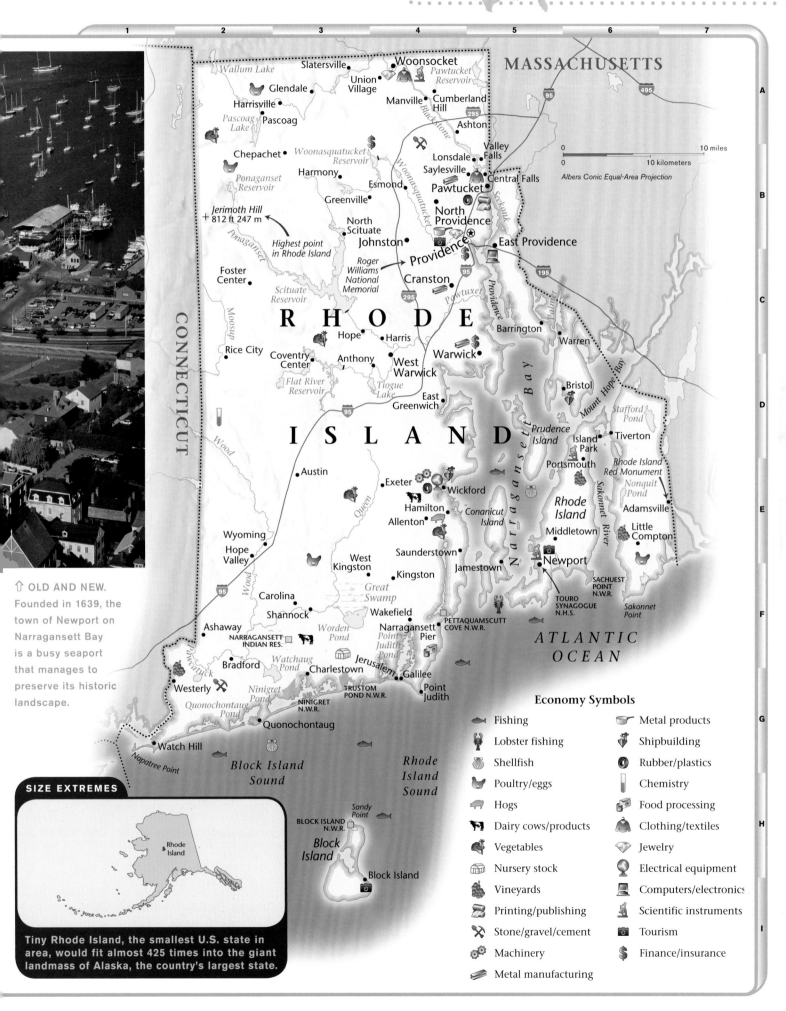

MASSACHUSETTS

1 2 3 4 5 6 7

Wallum Lake
Slatersville
Woonsocket
Pawtucket Reservoir
Union Village
Glendale
Manville
Cumberland Hill
Harrisville
Ashton
Pascoag Lake
Pascoag
Valley Falls
Chepachet
Lonsdale
Woonasquatucket Reservoir
Saylesville
Central Falls
Harmony
Pawtucket
Esmond
Greenville
North Providence
Ponaganset Reservoir
North Scituate
Jerimoth Hill
+ 812 ft 247 m
Highest point
in Rhode Island
Johnston
Providence
East Providence
Foster Center
Roger Williams National Memorial
Cranston
Scituate Reservoir

R H O D E

Moosup
Hope
Harris
Barrington
Warren
Rice City
Coventry Center
Anthony
West Warwick
Warwick
Bristol
Flat River Reservoir
Tiogue Lake
East Greenwich
Mount Hope Bay
Stafford Pond

I S L A N D

Wood
Prudence Island
Island Park
Tiverton
Austin
Rhode Island Red Monument
Nonquit Pond
Queen
Exeter
Wickford
Hamilton
Conanicut Island
Portsmouth
Adamsville
Allenton
Rhode Island
Wyoming
Saunderstown
Middletown
Little Compton
Hope Valley
West Kingston
Newport
Jamestown
Wood
Kingston
SACHUEST POINT N.W.R.
Carolina
Great Swamp
TOURO SYNAGOGUE N.H.S.
Sakonnet Point
Shannock
Wakefield
Ashaway
NARRAGANSETT INDIAN RES.
Worden Pond
Narragansett Pier
PETTAQUAMSCUTT COVE N.W.R.

ATLANTIC OCEAN

Bradford
Watchaug Pond
Jerusalem
Point Judith Pond
Galilee
Westerly
Charlestown
Point Judith
NINIGRET N.W.R.
Ninigret Pond
TRUSTOM POND N.W.R.
Quonochontaug Pond
Quonochontaug
Watch Hill
Napatree Point

Block Island Sound

Rhode Island Sound

Sandy Point
BLOCK ISLAND N.W.R.

Block Island

Block Island

0   10 miles
0   10 kilometers
Albers Conic Equal-Area Projection

CONNECTICUT

⇧ OLD AND NEW.
Founded in 1639, the town of Newport on Narragansett Bay is a busy seaport that manages to preserve its historic landscape.

Economy Symbols

Fishing		Metal products	
Lobster fishing		Shipbuilding	
Shellfish		Rubber/plastics	
Poultry/eggs		Chemistry	
Hogs		Food processing	
Dairy cows/products		Clothing/textiles	
Vegetables		Jewelry	
Nursery stock		Electrical equipment	
Vineyards		Computers/electronics	
Printing/publishing		Scientific instruments	
Stone/gravel/cement		Tourism	
Machinery		Finance/insurance	
Metal manufacturing			

SIZE EXTREMES

Rhode Island

Tiny Rhode Island, the smallest U.S. state in area, would fit almost 425 times into the giant landmass of Alaska, the country's largest state.

THE GREEN MOUNTAIN STATE:
VERMONT

VERMONT

When French explorer Jacques Cartier arrived in Vermont in 1535, Native Americans living in woodland villages had been there for hundreds of years. Settled first by the French in 1666 and then by the English in 1724, the territory of Vermont became an area of conflict between these colonial powers. The French finally withdrew, but conflict continued between New York and New Hampshire, both of which wanted to take over Vermont. The people of Vermont declared their independence in 1777, and Vermont became the 14th U.S. state in 1791. Vermont's name, which means "Green Mountain," comes from the extensive forests that cover much of the state and provide the basis for furniture and pulp industries. Vermont also boasts the world's largest granite quarry and the largest underground marble quarry, both of which produce valuable building materials. Tourism and recreation are also important in Vermont. Lakes, rivers, and mountain trails are popular summer attractions, while snow-covered mountains attract skiers throughout the winter.

⇑ LIQUID GOLD. In spring, sap from maple trees is collected in buckets by drilling a hole in the tree trunk—called "tapping." The sap is boiled to remove water, then filtered, and finally bottled.

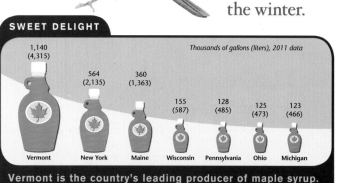

SWEET DELIGHT

Thousands of gallons (liters), 2011 data

1,140 (4,315) **Vermont**
564 (2,135) **New York**
360 (1,363) **Maine**
155 (587) **Wisconsin**
128 (485) **Pennsylvania**
125 (473) **Ohio**
123 (466) **Michigan**

Vermont is the country's leading producer of maple syrup. The syrup is all natural, with no added ingredients or preservatives, just boiled sap collected from maple trees.

⇑ WINTER WONDERLAND. One of the snowiest places in the Northeast, Jay Peak averages 355 inches (900 cm) of snow each year. With 76 trails, the mountain, near Vermont's border with Canada, attracts beginner and expert skiers from near and far.

Economy Symbols

- Poultry/eggs
- Sheep
- Dairy cows/products
- Beef cattle
- Fruits
- Vegetables
- Nursery stock
- Corn
- Maple syrup
- Timber/forest products
- Printing/publishing
- Stone/gravel/cement
- Hydro-electricity
- Metal products
- Food processing
- Computers/electronics
- Tourism

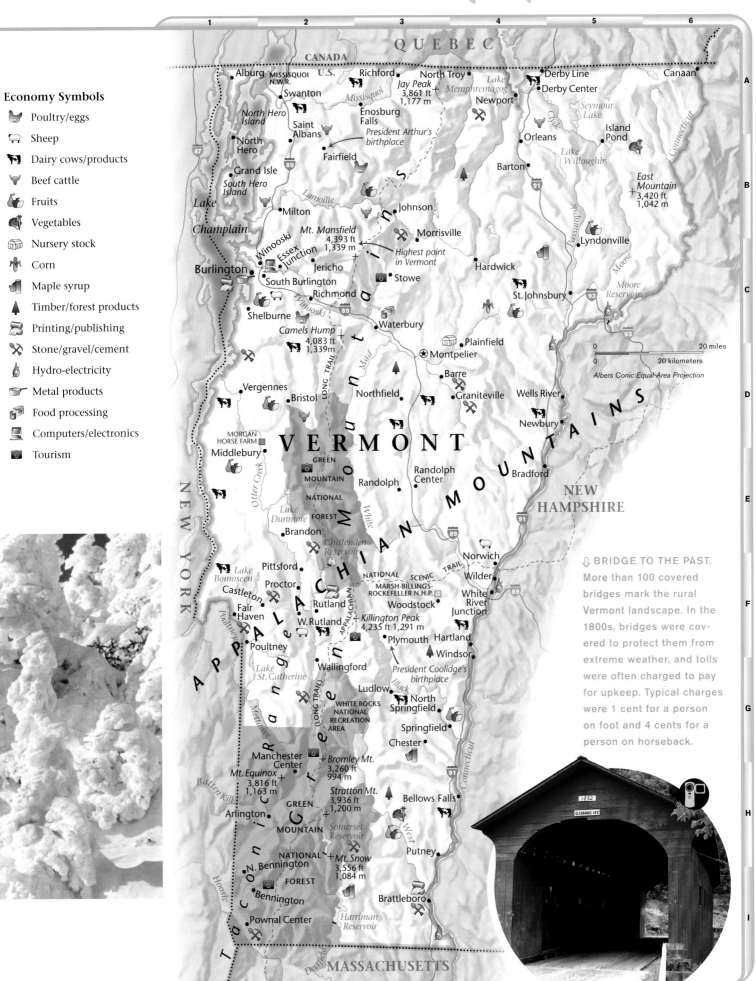

CANADA
U.S.
QUEBEC

Alburg MISSISQUOI N.W.R. Richford North Troy Derby Line Canaan
Swanton Jay Peak Derby Center
3,861 ft Lake
1,177 m Memphremagog
North Hero Island Enosburg Falls Newport
Saint Albans President Arthur's birthplace Orleans Seymour Lake
North Hero Fairfield Island Pond
Grand Isle Barton East Mountain
South Hero Island Lake Willoughby +3,420 ft 1,042 m
Lake Champlain Milton Lamoille Johnson Lyndonville
Mt. Mansfield Morrisville
4,393 ft Passumpsic
Winooski 1,339 m Highest point Hardwick
Essex Junction in Vermont Moose
Burlington Jericho Moore Reservoir
South Burlington Stowe St. Johnsbury
Richmond Waterbury
Shelburne Winooski Camels Hump Plainfield
4,083 ft Montpelier
1,339 m Barre
Vergennes Northfield Graniteville Wells River
Bristol Newbury
VERMONT
MORGAN HORSE FARM
Middlebury GREEN MOUNTAIN Randolph Bradford
NATIONAL Center NEW HAMPSHIRE
Otter Creek FOREST Randolph
Lake Dunmore White
Brandon
Chittenden Reservoir Norwich
Lake Bomoseen Pittsford Wilder
Proctor MARSH-BILLINGS- White River Junction
Castleton ROCKEFELLER N.H.P.
Fair Haven Rutland Woodstock
W. Rutland Killington Peak Hartland
Poultney 4,235 ft 1,291 m Plymouth Windsor
Lake St. Catherine Wallingford President Coolidge's birthplace
Ludlow Black
WHITE ROCKS North Springfield
NATIONAL RECREATION AREA Springfield
Manchester Center Chester
Mt. Equinox Bromley Mt.
3,816 ft 3,260 ft
1,163 m 994 m
Battenkill Stratton Mt. Bellows Falls
GREEN 3,936 ft
MOUNTAIN 1,200 m
Arlington Somerset Reservoir West Putney
N. Bennington NATIONAL Mt. Snow
FOREST 3,556 ft
Bennington 1,084 m Brattleboro
Pownal Center Harriman Reservoir
Deerfield
MASSACHUSETTS

0 20 miles
0 20 kilometers
Albers Conic Equal-Area Projection

⬇ BRIDGE TO THE PAST.
More than 100 covered
bridges mark the rural
Vermont landscape. In the
1800s, bridges were cov-
ered to protect them from
extreme weather, and tolls
were often charged to pay
for upkeep. Typical charges
were 1 cent for a person
on foot and 4 cents for a
person on horseback.

THE REGION

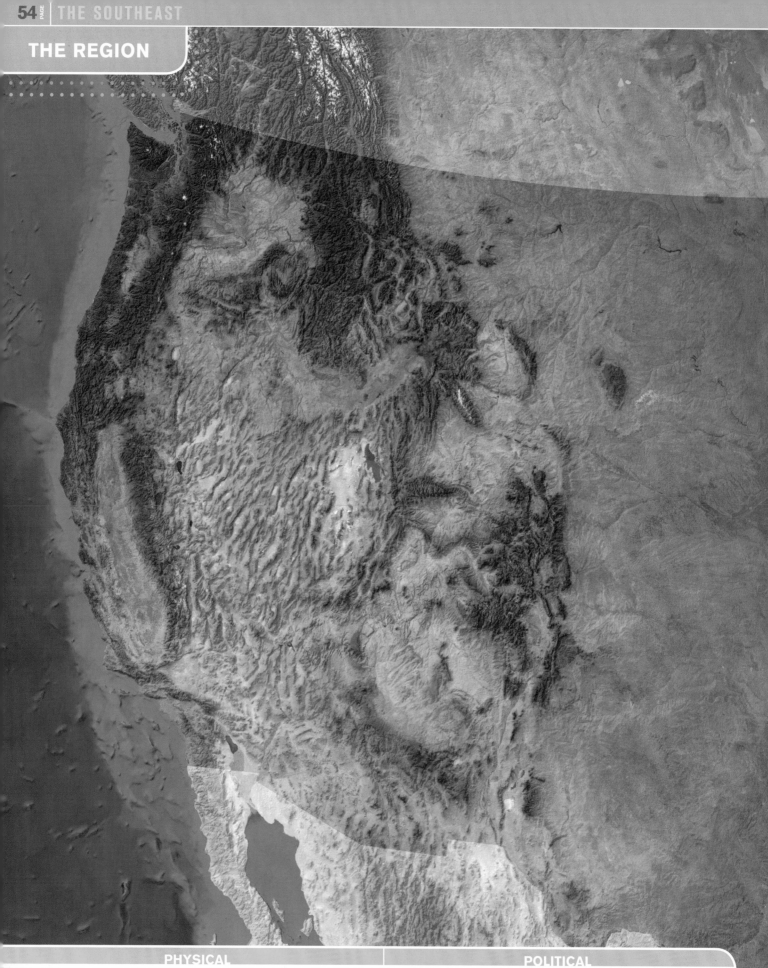

PHYSICAL

Total area
566,443 sq mi
(1,467,082 sq km)

Highest point
Mount Mitchell, NC
6,684 ft (2,037 m)

Lowest point
New Orleans, LA
8 ft (2 m) below sea level

Longest rivers
Mississippi, Arkansas,
Red, Ohio

Largest lakes
Okeechobee, Pontchartrain,
Kentucky (reservoir)

Vegetation
Needleleaf, broadleaf, and
mixed forest

Climate
Continental to mild, ranging
from cool summers in the
north to humid, subtropical
conditions in the south

POLITICAL

Total population
78,385,623

States (12):
Alabama, Arkansas, Florida, Georgia,
Kentucky, Louisiana, Mississippi, North
Carolina, South Carolina, Tennessee,
Virginia, West Virginia

Largest state
Florida: 65,755 sq mi (170,304 sq km)

Smallest state
West Virginia: 24,230 sq mi (62,755 sq km)

Most populous state
Florida: 18,801,310

Least populous state
West Virginia: 1,852,994

Largest city proper
Jacksonville, FL: 821,784

The Southeast

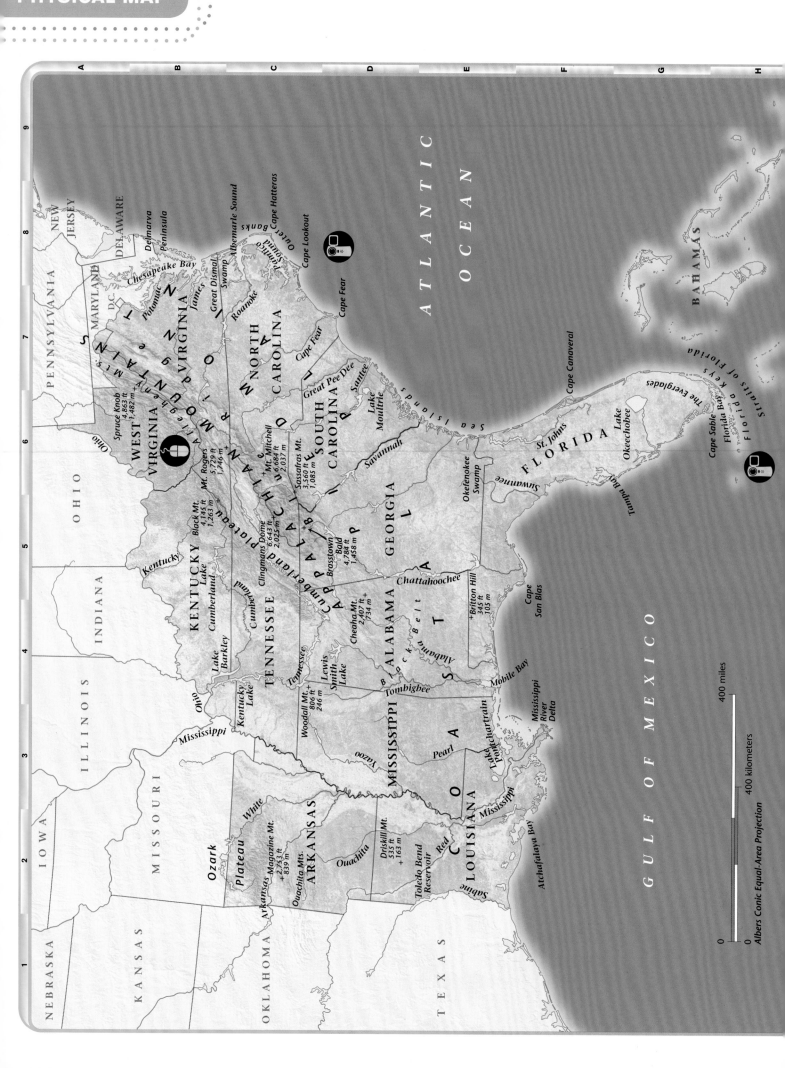

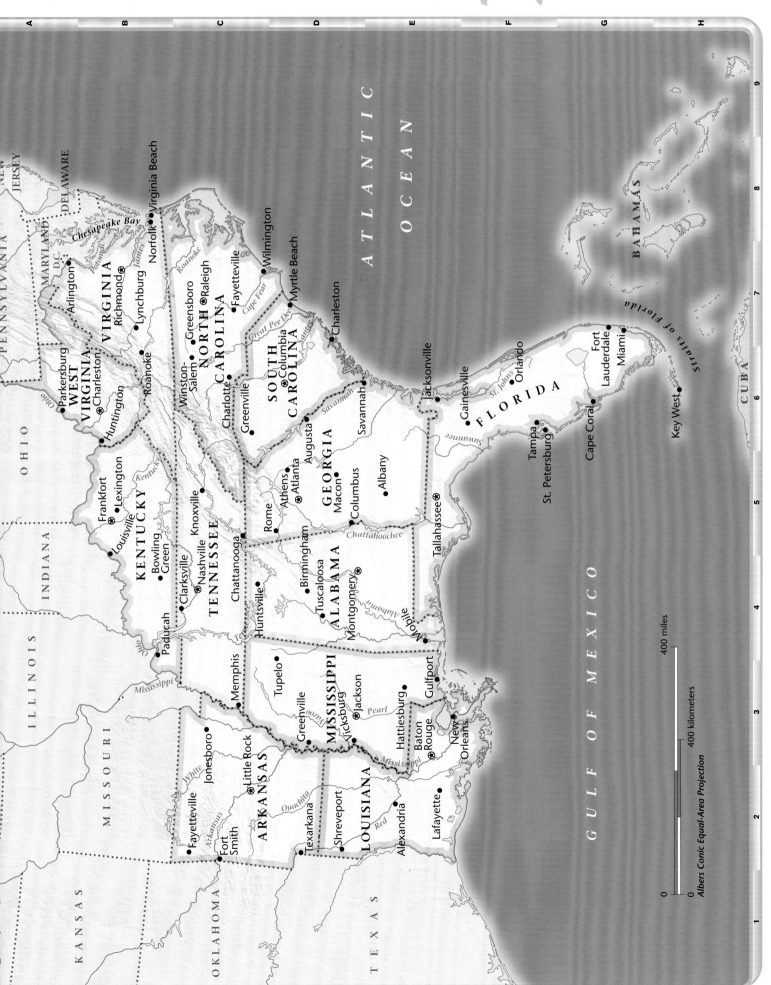

A B C D E F G H

9

ATLANTIC

OCEAN

8

BAHAMAS

NEW JERSEY

DELAWARE

PENNSYLVANIA

MARYLAND

Chesapeake Bay

D.C.

Arlington

Norfolk ● Virginia Beach

Potomac

James

VIRGINIA

Richmond ✪

Lynchburg

Roanoke

Greensboro

NORTH ✪ Raleigh

CAROLINA

Fayetteville

Wilmington

Cape Fear

Myrtle Beach

7

WEST

VIRGINIA

Parkersburg

Charleston ✪

Huntington

Roanoke

Winston-Salem

Charlotte

Great Pee Dee

Santee

SOUTH

✪ Columbia

CAROLINA

Charleston

STRAITS OF FLORIDA

CUBA

6

OHIO

Frankfort ● Lexington

Kentucky

Greenville

Savannah

Jacksonville

Gainesville

St. Johns

Orlando

FLORIDA

Fort Lauderdale

Miami

Key West

INDIANA

Louisville

KENTUCKY

Bowling Green

Clarksville

Knoxville

Nashville ✪

Chattanooga

Rome

Athens

Atlanta ✪

GEORGIA

Macon

Columbus

Albany

Tallahassee ✪

Suwannee

Tampa

St. Petersburg

Cape Coral

5

ILLINOIS

MISSOURI

Paducah

Ohio

TENNESSEE

Memphis

Tennessee

Huntsville

Birmingham

Tuscaloosa

ALABAMA

Montgomery ✪

Chattahoochee

Alabama

Mobile

GULF OF MEXICO

4

Tupelo

MISSISSIPPI

Greenville

Yazoo

Vicksburg ● Jackson

Pearl

Hattiesburg

Baton Rouge

Gulfport

New Orleans

3

Mississippi

KANSAS

Jonesboro

Little Rock ✪

ARKANSAS

White

Arkansas

Fayetteville

Fort Smith

Texarkana

Ouachita

Shreveport

LOUISIANA

Alexandria

Red

Mississippi

Lafayette

2

OKLAHOMA

TEXAS

400 miles

400 kilometers

Albers Conic Equal-Area Projection

0

1

⇨ OPEN WIDE. An American alligator in Florida's Big Cypress Swamp shows off sharp teeth. These large reptiles live mainly in fresh-water swamps and marshes in coastal areas of the Southeast. Adult males average 14 feet (4 m) in length.

The Southeast

TRADITION MEETS TECHNOLOGY

From deeply weathered mountains in West Virginia to warm, humid wetlands in south Florida and the Mississippi River's sprawling delta in southern Louisiana, the Southeast is marked by great physical diversity. The region's historical roots are in agriculture—especially cotton and tobacco. The Civil War brought economic and political upheaval in the mid-19th century, but today the Southeast is part of the Sunbelt, where 6 of the top 20 metropolitan areas of the U.S. are found and where high-tech industries are redefining the way people earn a living and the way the region is connected to the global economy.

⇨ ENCHANTED KINGDOM. Fireworks light up the night sky above Cinderella's Castle at Walt Disney World near Orlando, Florida. The park, which accounts for 6 percent of all jobs in central Florida, attracts millions of tourists from around the world each year.

⇧ SOCIAL CONSCIENCE. Members of the Big Nine Social Aid and Pleasure Club of New Orleans's Lower Ninth Ward march in a parade through a neighborhood devastated by Hurricane Katrina. Such clubs, which date back to late-19th-century benevolent societies, bring support and hope to communities in need.

WHERE THE PICTURES ARE

Banjo playing p. 69
River rafting p. 83
Coal miner p. 82
Horse race p. 68
Cyclists on outcrop pp. 58-59
Black bear family p. 78
Harpers Ferry p. 82
Motorboats p. 79
Luray Caverns p. 80
Grand Ole Opry p. 79
Cyclists pp. 80-81
Indian Woman p. 75
Dice p. 80
Space camp p. 60
Race car p. 59
Rockclimber p. 62
Wright Brothers Memorial p. 74
Bird-watchers p. 62
Blackbeard's cannon p. 59
Boys playing basketball p. 74
Beach scene p. 76
Diamond hunter p. 63
Wild turkey p. 77
Paddleboat p. 72
Historic Charleston pp. 76-77
Blues guitarist p. 72
Atlanta p. 66
Catfish p. 73
Oil rig p. 60
Aerial of Sea Islands p. 66
Oak Alley Plantation p. 70
Peanuts p. 66
Manatee p. 64
Shuttle launch pp. 64-65
Katrina parade p. 58
Cinderella's Castle p. 58, Girl in parade p. 64
Shrimp fisherman p. 70
Alligator p. 58

⇧ VIEW FROM ABOVE. Cyclists look out from a rocky ledge across West Virginia's Germany Valley. The area took its name from German immigrants who moved there in the mid-1700s from North Carolina and Pennsylvania and established farming villages.

⇨ CAR STARS. For more than 50 years, auto racing has been a leading sport in the U.S., especially in the Southeast. The International Motorsports Hall of Fame, located adjacent to the Talledega Superspeedway in Alabama, features racing cars, motorcycles, and vintage cars.

⇦ PIRATE'S DEFENSE. This 4.5-foot (1.4-m) cast-iron cannon was recovered from the wreck of the *Queen Anne's Revenge* off North Carolina's coast. The vessel, which probably belonged to the notorious pirate Blackbeard, grounded on a sandbar and sank in 1718 near Cape Lookout.

THE HEART OF DIXIE STATE:
ALABAMA

THE BASICS

STATS

Area
52,419 sq mi (135,765 sq km)

Population
4,779,736

Capital
Montgomery
Population 205,764

Largest city
Birmingham
Population 212,237

Ethnic/racial groups
68.5% white; 26.2% African American;
1.1% Asian; .6% Native American.
Hispanic (any race) 3.9%.

Industry
Retail and wholesale trade, services,
government, finance, insurance, real
estate, transportation, construction,
communication

Agriculture
Fruits and vegetables, dairy products,
cattle, forest products, commercial
fishing

Statehood
December 14, 1819; 22nd state

GEO WHIZ

Condoleezza Rice, the first African-
American woman to serve as U.S.
Secretary of State, and Rosa Parks,
whose refusal to give up her seat on
a Montgomery bus earned her the
title "mother of the modern-day civil
rights movement," were both born in
Alabama: Rice in Birmingham and
Parks in Tuskegee.

Russell Cave, near Bridgeport, was home
to prehistoric peoples for more than
10,000 years. In 1961 a national monument was established on land donated
by the National Geographic Society.
Today, visitors can take guided tours of
the cave and see the kinds of tools and
weapons its early inhabitants used.

In 2004 Hurricane Ivan, one of
the worst storms to batter
Alabama's gulf coast
since 1900, struck
Orange Beach.

NORTHERN
FLICKER
CAMELLIA

ALABAMA

Alabama has a colorful story.
The French established the
first permanent European settlement at Mobile Bay in 1702,
but different groups—British,
Native Americans, and U.S.
settlers—struggled over control of
the land for more than 100 years. In
1819 Alabama became the 22nd state,
but in 1861 it joined the Confederacy.
During the Civil War, Montgomery
was the capital of the secessionist

⇧ UNDERWATER RESOURCE. A massive drill
descends from an offshore oil rig to tap petroleum
deposits beneath the water of the Gulf of Mexico
off Alabama's shore.

South for a time. After the war Alabama struggled to rebuild its agriculture-
based economy. By 1900 the state was producing more than one million
bales of cotton annually. In the mid-20th century, Alabama was at the center
of the civil rights movement, which pressed for equal rights for all people
regardless of race or social status. Key players included Martin Luther King,
Jr., and Rosa Parks. Modern industries, including the NASA space program,
have given the state's economy a big boost. In 2002 assembly plants built by
automakers from Asia
created thousands
of new jobs.

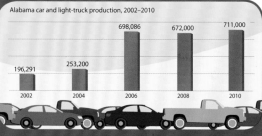

ON THE ROAD

Alabama car and light-truck production, 2002–2010

2002	2004	2006	2008	2010
196,291	253,200	698,086	672,000	711,000

Since the first vehicles rolled off the assembly
line in 1993, Alabama has risen to number 5 in
national car and light-truck production.

⇧ ROCKET POWER. Students inspect giant booster rockets during Space
Camp at Marshall Space Flight Center, in Huntsville, Alabama. The center
is one of NASA's largest installations, providing support to space shuttle
missions and the International Space Station.

Economy Symbols

- 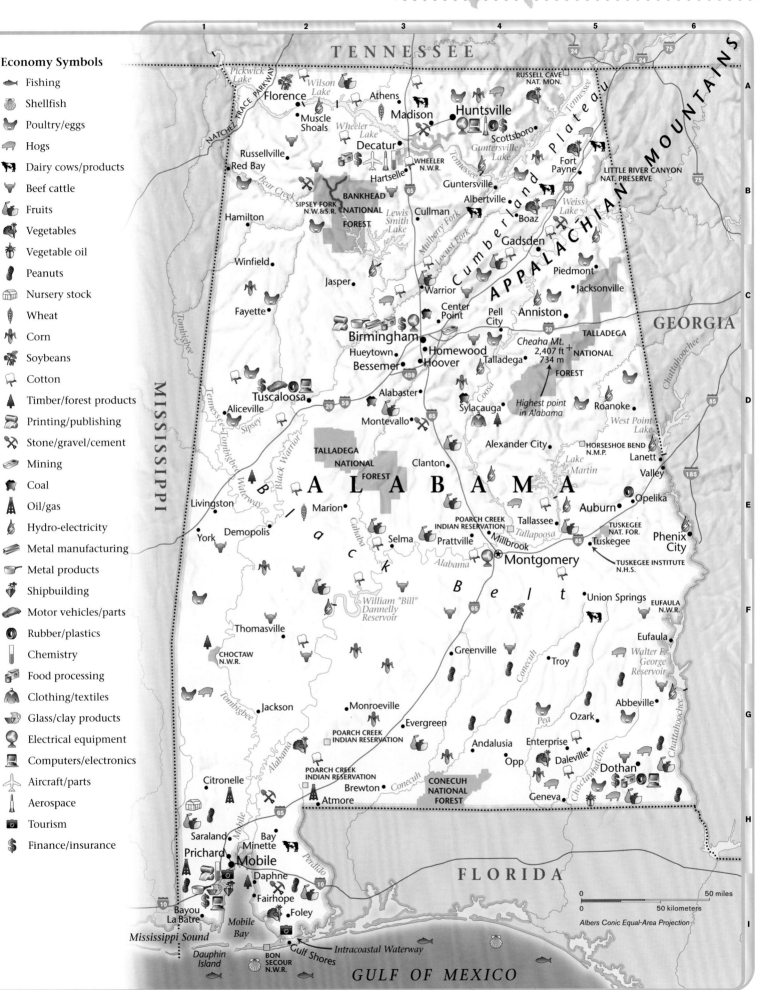 Fishing
- Shellfish
- Poultry/eggs
- Hogs
- Dairy cows/products
- Beef cattle
- Fruits
- Vegetables
- Vegetable oil
- Peanuts
- Nursery stock
- Wheat
- Corn
- Soybeans
- Cotton
- Timber/forest products
- Printing/publishing
- Stone/gravel/cement
- Mining
- Coal
- Oil/gas
- Hydro-electricity
- Metal manufacturing
- Metal products
- Shipbuilding
- Motor vehicles/parts
- Rubber/plastics
- Chemistry
- Food processing
- Clothing/textiles
- Glass/clay products
- Electrical equipment
- Computers/electronics
- Aircraft/parts
- Aerospace
- Tourism
- Finance/insurance

Map Labels

TENNESSEE

Pickwick Lake
Wilson Lake
Florence
Muscle Shoals
Russellville
Red Bay
Athens
Madison
Huntsville
Scottsboro
Wheeler Lake
RUSSELL CAVE NAT. MON.
Decatur
WHEELER N.W.R.
Hartselle
Guntersville Lake
Guntersville
Fort Payne
LITTLE RIVER CANYON NAT. PRESERVE
BANKHEAD NATIONAL FOREST
SIPSEY FORK N.W.&S.R.
Lewis Smith Lake
Cullman
Albertville
Boaz
Weiss Lake
Hamilton
Winfield
Jasper
Warrior
Gadsden
Piedmont
Jacksonville
Fayette
Center Point
Anniston
Birmingham
Hueytown
Homewood
Hoover
Bessemer
Pell City
Talladega
Cheaha Mt. 2,407 ft 734 m
TALLADEGA NATIONAL FOREST
Highest point in Alabama
Roanoke
Tuscaloosa
Aliceville
Alabaster
Montevallo
Sylacauga
West Point Lake
Lanett
Valley
Livingston
York
Demopolis
Marion
Clanton
Alexander City
HORSESHOE BEND N.M.P.
Lake Martin
Opelika
Auburn
TALLADEGA NATIONAL FOREST
Selma
Prattville
Tallassee
POORCH CREEK INDIAN RESERVATION
Tallapoosa
Millbrook
Montgomery
Tuskegee
TUSKEGEE NAT. FOR.
Phenix City
TUSKEGEE INSTITUTE N.H.S.
Thomasville
William "Bill" Dannelly Reservoir
Union Springs
EUFAULA N.W.R.
CHOCTAW N.W.R.
Greenville
Troy
Eufaula
Walter F. George Reservoir
Jackson
Monroeville
Ozark
Abbeville
POORCH CREEK INDIAN RESERVATION
Evergreen
Andalusia
Enterprise
Daleville
Dothan
Opp
Citronelle
POORCH CREEK INDIAN RESERVATION
Brewton
CONECUH NATIONAL FOREST
Geneva
Saraland
Bay Minette
Prichard
Mobile
Daphne
Bayou La Batre
Fairhope
Foley
Mobile Bay
Mississippi Sound
Dauphin Island
BON SECOUR N.W.R.
Gulf Shores
Intracoastal Waterway
FLORIDA
GULF OF MEXICO

MISSISSIPPI

GEORGIA

ALABAMA

Black Warrior

Tombigbee

Natchez Trace Parkway

Cumberland Plateau

APPALACHIAN MOUNTAINS

0   50 miles
0   50 kilometers
Albers Conic Equal-Area Projection

THE NATURAL STATE:
ARKANSAS

THE BASICS

STATS

Area
53,179 sq mi (137,732 sq km)

Population
2,915,918

Capital
Little Rock
Population 193,524

Largest city
Little Rock
Population 193,524

Ethnic/racial groups
77.0% white; 15.4% African American; 1.2% Asian; .8% Native American. Hispanic (any race) 6.4%.

Industry
Services, food processing, paper products, transportation, metal products, machinery, electronics

Agriculture
Poultry and eggs, rice, soybeans, cotton, wheat

Statehood
June 15, 1836; 25th state

GEO WHIZ

In 1924 Arkansas's Crater of Diamonds State Park yielded the largest natural diamond ever found in the United States—a 40.23-carat whopper named "Uncle Sam." A 13-year-old girl from Missouri found a 2.93-carat diamond there in 2007.

Since 1936 Stuttgart has been the site of the annual World Championship Duck Calling Contest. The first winner took home a grand total of $6.60. Today, the prize package is worth more than $15,000.

The city of Texarkana is divided by the Arkansas-Texas border. It has two governments, one for each state.

MOCKINGBIRD
APPLE BLOSSOM

ARKANSAS

The land that is Arkansas was explored by the Spanish in 1541 and later by the French, but it came under U.S. control with the Louisiana Purchase in 1803. As settlers arrived, Native Americans were pushed out, and cotton fields spread across the fertile valleys of the Arkansas and Mississippi Rivers. Arkansas became the 25th state in 1836, but joined the Confederacy in 1861. Following the war, Arkansas faced hard times, and many people moved away in search of jobs. Today, agriculture remains an important part of the economy. Rice has replaced cotton as the state's main crop, and poultry and grain production are also important. Natural gas, in the northwestern part of the state, and petroleum, along the southern border with Louisiana, are key mining products in Arkansas. The state is headquarters for Wal-Mart, the world's largest retail chain, and tourism is growing as visitors are attracted to the natural beauty of the Ozark and Ouachita Mountains.

⇧ HOLD ON! A rock climber clings to a sandstone cliff in northwest Arkansas, where the Ozark and Ouachita Mountains make up the Interior Highlands of the United States. The Ouachita are folded mountains, but the Ozarks are really a deeply eroded plateau.

SUPERSTORE

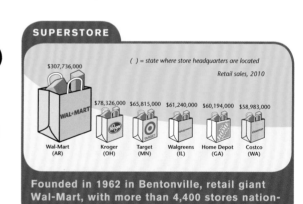

( ) = state where store headquarters are located
Retail sales, 2010

$307,736,000 — Wal-Mart (AR)
$78,326,000 — Kroger (OH)
$65,815,000 — Target (MN)
$61,240,000 — Walgreens (IL)
$60,194,000 — Home Depot (GA)
$58,983,000 — Costco (WA)

Founded in 1962 in Bentonville, retail giant Wal-Mart, with more than 4,400 stores nationwide, leads the country in annual revenues.

⇦ BIRDWATCHERS. Biologists and volunteers scan the treetops for a rare ivory-billed woodpecker in the White River National Wildlife Refuge. Established in 1935 along the White River near where it joins the Mississippi, the refuge provides a protected habitat for migratory birds.

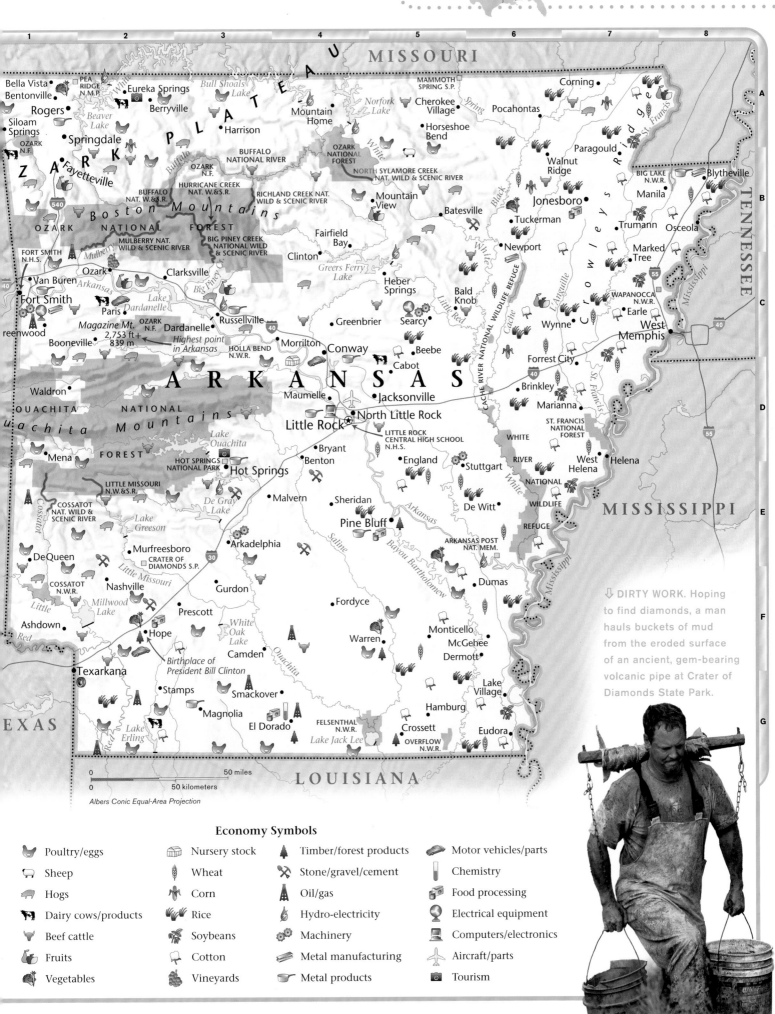

MISSOURI

A
B
C
D
E
F
G

1 2 3 4 5 6 7 8

Bella Vista
Bentonville
Rogers
Siloam Springs
Springdale
Fayetteville
OZARK N.F.
Z ARK PLATEAU
PEA RIDGE N.M.P.
White
Beaver Lake
Eureka Springs
Berryville
Harrison
Bull Shoals Lake
Mountain Home
Norfork Lake
Buffalo
BUFFALO NATIONAL RIVER
OZARK N.F.
HURRICANE CREEK NAT. W.&S.R.
BUFFALO NAT. W.&S.R.
Boston Mountains
OZARK NATIONAL FOREST
RICHLAND CREEK NAT. WILD & SCENIC RIVER
MULBERRY NAT. WILD & SCENIC RIVER
BIG PINEY CREEK NATIONAL WILD & SCENIC RIVER
OZARK NATIONAL FOREST
NORTH SYLAMORE CREEK NAT. WILD & SCENIC RIVER
MAMMOTH SPRING S.P.
Cherokee Village
Horseshoe Bend
Spring
Corning
Pocahontas
Paragould
Walnut Ridge
Jonesboro
Tuckerman
Trumann
BIG LAKE N.W.R.
Manila
Blytheville
Osceola
Crowleys Ridge
St. Francis
Mountain View
Batesville
Fairfield Bay
Clinton
Newport
Marked Tree
WAPANOCCA N.W.R.
Earle
West Memphis
Helena
West Helena
Black
White
Little Red
L'Anguille
Cache
St. Francis
Mississippi
TENNESSEE
MISSISSIPPI
FORT SMITH N.H.S.
Ozark
Clarksville
Van Buren
Mulberry
Arkansas
Fort Smith
Paris
Lake Dardanelle
reenwood
Booneville
Magazine Mt. 2,753 ft + 839 m
Highest point in Arkansas
OZARK N.F.
Dardanelle
Russellville
HOLLA BEND N.W.R.
Big Piney
Greers Ferry Lake
Heber Springs
Greenbrier
Searcy
Bald Knob
CACHE RIVER NATIONAL WILDLIFE REFUGE
Forrest City
Brinkley
Marianna
ST. FRANCIS NATIONAL FOREST
WHITE
RIVER
NATIONAL
WILDLIFE
REFUGE
A R K A N S A S
Morrilton
Conway
Beebe
Cabot
Maumelle
Jacksonville
North Little Rock
Little Rock
LITTLE ROCK CENTRAL HIGH SCHOOL N.H.S.
Bryant
Benton
England
Stuttgart
De Witt
Waldron
OUACHITA
NATIONAL
Ouachita Mountains
FOREST
Mena
Lake Ouachita
HOT SPRINGS NATIONAL PARK
Hot Springs
LITTLE MISSOURI N.W.&S.R.
De Gray Lake
Cossatot
COSSATOT NAT. WILD & SCENIC RIVER
Lake Greeson
Malvern
Sheridan
Arkansas
Pine Bluff
Arkansas
Bayou Bartholomew
ARKANSAS POST NAT. MEM.
Saline
DeQueen
COSSATOT N.W.R.
Nashville
Murfreesboro
CRATER OF DIAMONDS S.P.
Arkadelphia
Little Missouri
Gurdon
Fordyce
Monticello
Dumas
McGehee
Dermott
Lake Village
Little
Red
Millwood Lake
Ashdown
Prescott
White Oak Lake
Camden
Warren
Ouachita
Hope
Birthplace of President Bill Clinton
Texarkana
Stamps
Smackover
Magnolia
El Dorado
FELSENTHAL N.W.R.
Lake Jack Lee
Crossett
OVERFLOW N.W.R.
Hamburg
Eudora
Mississippi
EXAS
Lake Erling
Red

0   50 miles
0   50 kilometers

Albers Conic Equal-Area Projection

LOUISIANA

⇩ DIRTY WORK. Hoping to find diamonds, a man hauls buckets of mud from the eroded surface of an ancient, gem-bearing volcanic pipe at Crater of Diamonds State Park.

Economy Symbols

Poultry/eggs	Nursery stock	Timber/forest products
Sheep	Wheat	Stone/gravel/cement
Hogs	Corn	Oil/gas
Dairy cows/products	Rice	Hydro-electricity
Beef cattle	Soybeans	Machinery
Fruits	Cotton	Metal manufacturing
Vegetables	Vineyards	Metal products

Motor vehicles/parts
Chemistry
Food processing
Electrical equipment
Computers/electronics
Aircraft/parts
Tourism

FLORIDA

Florida is home to St. Augustine, the country's oldest permanent European settlement, established by the Spanish in 1565. But native peoples had called Florida home long before then. Florida became a U.S. territory in 1821 and a state in 1845. The state's turbulent early history included the Civil War and three wars with Native Americans over control of the land. Railroads opened Florida to migration from the northern states as early as the 1890s. The mild climate and sandy beaches attracted people seeking to escape cold winters in the north. This trend continues today and includes both tourists and retirees. South Florida has a large Hispanic population that has migrated from all over Latin America—especially from nearby Cuba. Florida is working to solve many challenges: competition between city-dwellers and farmers for limited water resources; the annual risk of tropical storms; and the need to preserve its natural environment, including the vast Everglades wetland.

THE BASICS

STATS

Area
65,755 sq mi (170,304 sq km)

Population
18,801,310

Capital
Tallahassee
Population 181,376

Largest city
Jacksonville
Population 821,784

Ethnic/racial groups
75.0% white; 16.0% African American; 2.4% Asian; .4% Native American. Hispanic (any race) 22.5%.

Industry
Tourism, health services, business services, communications, banking, electronic equipment, insurance

Agriculture
Citrus fruits, vegetables, field crops, nursery stock, cattle, dairy products

Statehood
March 3, 1845; 27th state

GEO WHIZ

Key West, the southernmost point in the continental U.S., is just 90 miles (145 km) from Cuba.

In 1937 Amelia Earhart and her navigator took off from Miami with the goal of making an around-the-world flight, but disappeared over the Pacific Ocean and were never seen again. You can read all about this famous flying ace in our children's book *Sky Pioneer*, by Corine Szabo.

Everglades National Park, the largest subtropical wilderness in the United States, is home to rare and endangered species such as the American crocodile, Florida panther, and West Indian manatee.

Britton Hill, Florida's highest point, is only 345 feet (105 m) above sea level.

Lightning strikes occur more often in Florida than in any other U.S. state.

MOCKINGBIRD
ORANGE BLOSSOM

⇧ CULTURAL PRIDE. A young girl marches in Orlando's Puerto Rican Parade, a celebration of the music, dance, and culture of this U.S. island territory.

⇨ LIFTOFF! A NASA rocket rises amid clouds of steam from Cape Canaveral Space Center on Florida's Atlantic coast. The center has been the launch site for many U.S. space exploration projects.

ALABAMA

POARCH CREEK I.R.

Highest point in Florida
Britto 345 ft 105 m
Crestview ●

Pensacola ●

Niceville ●
Fort Walton Beach

FORT PICKENS
GULF ISLANDS NATIONAL SEASHORE

Intraco Water

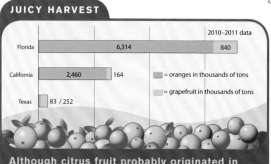

JUICY HARVEST

2010–2011 data

	oranges	grapefruit
Florida	6,314	840
California	2,460	164
Texas	83	252

■ = oranges in thousands of tons
■ = grapefruit in thousands of tons

Although citrus fruit probably originated in Southeast Asia, perfect growing conditions have made Florida the leading producer in the U.S.

⇨ GENTLE GIANT. The manatee, which is closely related to the elephant, is Florida's state marine mammal. Averaging 10 feet (3 m) in length and 1,000 pounds (453 kg), these endangered animals live on a diet of sea grasses.

3 4 5 6 7 8 9 10

G E O R G I A

OKEFENOKEE
NATIONAL
WILDLIFE
REFUGE

0   100 miles
0   100 kilometers
Albers Conic Equal-Area Projection

A T L A N T I C

O C E A N

rianna

Lake
Seminole

Ochlockonee

Tallahassee

St. Marys

Fernandina Beach

TIMUCUAN ECOLOGICAL
AND HISTORIC PRESERVE

FORT CAROLINE NAT. MEM.

Jacksonville   Jacksonville Beach

Live
Oak
Lake City

Apalachicola

nama
ty

APALACHICOLA
NATIONAL
FOREST

ST. MARKS
N.W.R.

Perry

OSCEOLA
NAT. FOREST

St. Johns

CASTILLO DE SAN
MARCOS NAT. MON.

St. Augustine

Oldest permanent European
settlement on the continent,
est. 1565

F L O R I D A

Suwannee

Gainesville

Palatka

FORT MATANZAS
NAT. MON.

Palm Coast

ST. VINCENT
N.W.R.

LOWER
SUWANNEE
NATIONAL
WILDLIFE
REFUGE

Ocala

OCALA
NATIONAL
FOREST

Lake
George

LAKE WOODRUFF
N.W.R.

Daytona Beach

New Smyrna Beach

CEDAR KEYS
N.W.R.

CRYSTAL RIVER
N.W.R.

Homosassa Springs

Leesburg

De Land
Deltona

Sanford

St. Johns

CANAVERAL
NATIONAL
SEASHORE

Titusville

MERRITT ISLAND N.W.R.

CHASSAHOWITZKA
N.W.R.

Spring Hill

Walt Disney World
& EPCOT Center

Orlando

John F. Kennedy Space Center

Cape Canaveral

Bayonet Point

Kissimmee

Merritt Island

Tarpon Springs

Lakeland

Haines
City

Melbourne

Palm Bay

Clearwater

TAMPA
I.R.

Winter
Haven

FLORIDA'S TURNPIKE

PELICAN ISLAND N.W.R.

St. Petersburg

Tampa

Tampa
Bay

Vero Beach

PINELLAS N.W.R.

EGMONT KEY N.W.R.

Sebring

Kissimmee

Fort Pierce

FORT PIERCE I.R.

Port St. Lucie

DE SOTO NAT. MEM.

Bradenton

Sarasota

Arcadia

BRIGHTON
SEMINOLE
I.R.

St. Lucie

Lake
Okeechobee

HOBE SOUND N.W.R.

LOXAHATCHEE NAT.
WILD & SCENIC RIVER

Jupiter

Venice

Port Charlotte

Punta Gorda

Peace

Caloosahatchee

West Palm Beach

Charlotte Harbor

Cape Coral

Fort Myers

J. N. "DING" DARLING N.W.R.

Sanibel
Island

Immokalee

IMMOKALEE
I.R.

Belle
Glade

ARTHUR R.
MARSHALL
LOXAHATCHEE
N.W.R.

Delray Beach

Boca Raton

BIG CYPRESS
SEMINOLE I.R.

COCONUT CREEK I.R.

Coral Springs

Fort Lauderdale

Naples

Big Cypress
Swamp

BIG
CYPRESS
NATIONAL
PRESERVE

MICCOSUKEE
INDIAN
RES.

HOLLYWOOD

SEMINOLE I.R.

Hollywood

G U L F   O F

Ten
Thousand
Islands

The Everglades

Hialeah

Miami

Kendall

Miami Beach

M E X I C O

EVERGLADES

NATIONAL

Biscayne Bay

BISCAYNE
N.P.

Largest subtropical wilderness
in the 48 contiguous states

PARK

Cape
Sable

Key Largo

Florida Bay

FLORIDA KEYS

FLORIDA KEYS NATIONAL MARINE SANCTUARY

NAT. KEY DEER
REFUGE

GREAT WHITE HERON
N.W.R.

Marathon

DRY TORTUGAS
NATIONAL PARK

KEY WEST
N.W.R.

STRAITS OF FLORIDA

Key West

Southernmost point in the
continental United States

Economy Symbols

- Fishing
- Lobster fishing
- Shellfish
- Poultry/eggs
- Hogs
- Dairy cows
- Beef cattle
- Fruits
- Vegetables
- Peanuts
- Nursery stock
- Corn
- Rice
- Sugarcane
- Cotton

- Tobacco
- Timber/forest products
- Printing/publishing
- Hydro-electricity
- Metal products
- Shipbuilding
- Chemistry
- Food processing
- Electrical equipment
- Computers/electronics
- Scientific instruments
- Aerospace
- Tourism
- Finance/insurance

THE EMPIRE STATE OF THE SOUTH:
GEORGIA

GEORGIA

When Spanish explorers arrived in the mid-1500s in what would become Georgia, they found the land already occupied by Cherokees, Creeks, and other native peoples. Georgia was the frontier separating Spanish Florida and English South Carolina, but in 1733 James Oglethorpe founded a new colony on the site of present-day Savannah. Georgia became the 4th state in 1788 and built an economy based on agriculture and slave labor. The state suffered widespread destruction during the Civil War and endured a long period of poverty in the years that followed. Modern-day Georgia is part of the fast-changing Sunbelt region. Agriculture—especially poultry, cotton, and forest products—remains important. Atlanta has emerged as a regional center of banking, telecommunications, and transportation, and Savannah is a major container port near the Atlantic coast, linking the state to the global economy. Historic sites, sports, and beaches draw thousands of tourists to the state every year.

THE BASICS

STATS

Area
59,425 sq mi (153,910 sq km)

Population
9,687,653

Capital
Atlanta
Population 420,003

Largest city
Atlanta
Population 420,003

Ethnic/racial groups
59.7% white; 30.5% African American; 3.2% Asian; .3% Native American. Hispanic (any race) 8.8%.

Industry
Textiles and clothing, transportation equipment, food processing, paper products, chemicals, electrical equipment, tourism

Agriculture
Poultry and eggs, cotton, peanuts, vegetables, sweet corn, melons, cattle

Statehood
January 2, 1788; 4th state

GEO WHIZ

The Okefenokee Swamp, the largest swamp in North America, is home to many meat-eating plants, which capture animals for food. The swamp was also the setting for the adventures of Pogo the Possum, Albert the Alligator, and other characters created by cartoonist Walt Kelly.

The Georgia Aquarium in Atlanta, the world's largest, features more than 100,000 animals in more than 8 million gallons (30.3 million liters) of water.

Stone Mountain near Atlanta is famous for its enormous carving of three historic figures from the Confederate States of America: Stonewall Jackson, Robert E. Lee, and Jefferson Davis. It is one of the largest single masses of exposed granite in the world.

BROWN THRASHER
CHEROKEE ROSE

⇧ CASH CROP. Peanuts are a big moneymaker in Georgia, where almost half the U.S. crop is grown—about half of which is used to make peanut butter.

⇧ LIGHT SHOW. Busy Interstate traffic appears as ribbons of light below Atlanta's nighttime skyline. Atlanta is a center of economic growth, leading all cities in the region with 10 Fortune 500 companies. Its metropolitan area leads the country in population growth, adding almost one million people since 2000.

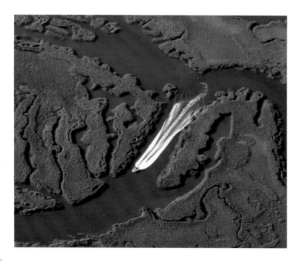

⇦ PAST MEETS PRESENT. Georgia's 100-mile (160-km) coastline is laced with barrier islands, wetlands, and winding streams. In the 19th century plantations grew Sea Island cotton here. Today, tourists are attracted to the area's natural beauty and beaches.

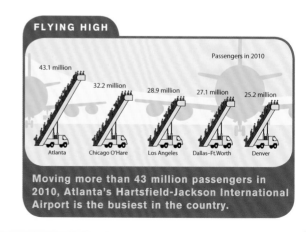

FLYING HIGH

Passengers in 2010

43.1 million — Atlanta
32.2 million — Chicago O'Hare
28.9 million — Los Angeles
27.1 million — Dallas–Ft.Worth
25.2 million — Denver

Moving more than 43 million passengers in 2010, Atlanta's Hartsfield-Jackson International Airport is the busiest in the country.

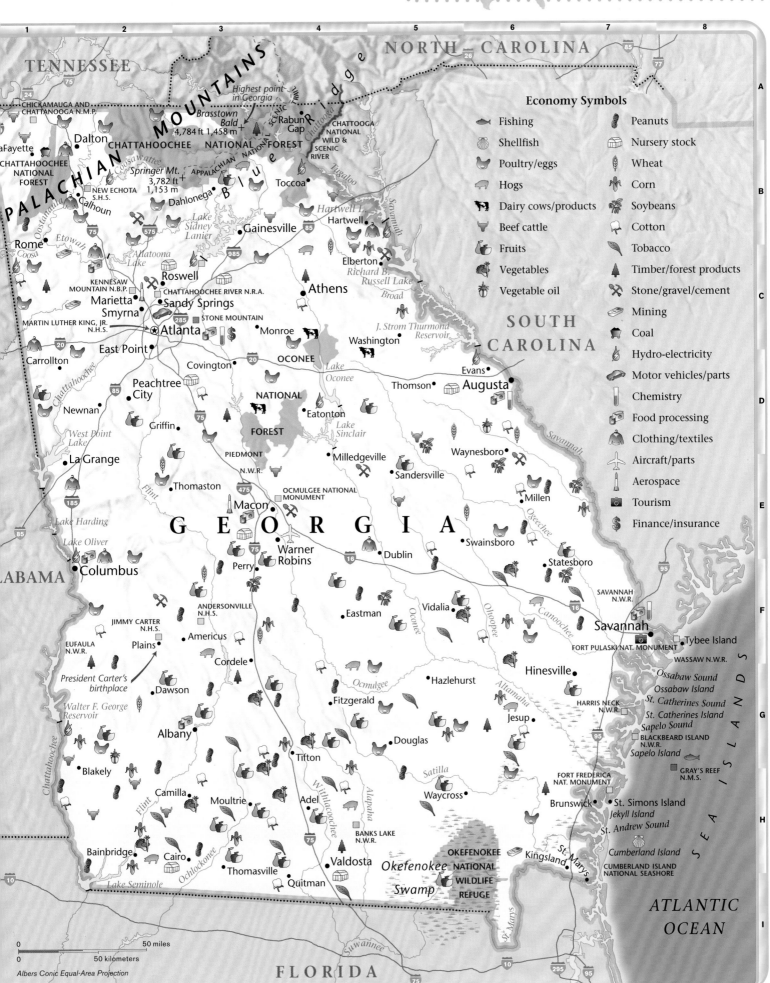

Economy Symbols

- Fishing
- Shellfish
- Poultry/eggs
- Hogs
- Dairy cows/products
- Beef cattle
- Fruits
- Vegetables
- Vegetable oil
- Peanuts
- Nursery stock
- Wheat
- Corn
- Soybeans
- Cotton
- Tobacco
- Timber/forest products
- Stone/gravel/cement
- Mining
- Coal
- Hydro-electricity
- Motor vehicles/parts
- Chemistry
- Food processing
- Clothing/textiles
- Aircraft/parts
- Aerospace
- Tourism
- Finance/insurance

TENNESSEE

NORTH CAROLINA

SOUTH CAROLINA

ALABAMA

FLORIDA

ATLANTIC OCEAN

SEA ISLANDS

APPALACHIAN MOUNTAINS

Blue Ridge

CHATTAHOOGA NATIONAL WILD & SCENIC RIVER

CHICKAMAUGA AND CHATTANOOGA N.M.P.

CHATTAHOOCHEE NATIONAL FOREST

LaFayette
Dalton
Rome
Calhoun
NEW ECHOTA S.H.S.
Dahlonega
Brasstown Bald 4,784 ft 1,458 m
Highest point in Georgia
Springer Mt. 3,782 ft 1,153 m
Rabun Gap
Toccoa
Lake Sidney Lanier
Gainesville
Hartwell L.
Hartwell
Elberton
Richard B. Russell Lake
Broad

Coosawattee
Oostanaula
Etowah
Coosa

KENNESAW MOUNTAIN N.B.P.
Roswell
Allatoona Lake
CHATTAHOOCHEE RIVER N.R.A.
Marietta
Smyrna
Sandy Springs
MARTIN LUTHER KING, JR. N.H.S.
Atlanta
STONE MOUNTAIN
Monroe
Washington
Athens
OCONEE
J. Strom Thurmond Reservoir

East Point
Carrollton
Covington
Lake Oconee
Evans
Thomson
Augusta

Newnan
Peachtree City
Griffin
NATIONAL FOREST
Eatonton
Lake Sinclair
Waynesboro

La Grange
Thomaston
PIEDMONT N.W.R.
Milledgeville
Sandersville
Millen

Chattahoochee
West Point Lake
Flint

Lake Harding
Lake Oliver
Columbus

OCMULGEE NATIONAL MONUMENT
Macon
Warner Robins
Perry
Dublin
Swainsboro
Statesboro

SAVANNAH N.W.R.
Savannah
FORT PULASKI NAT. MONUMENT
Tybee Island
WASSAW N.W.R.

ANDERSONVILLE N.H.S.
Eastman
Vidalia
Hinesville
HARRIS NECK N.W.R.

JIMMY CARTER N.H.S.
EUFAULA N.W.R.
Plains
Americus
Hazlehurst
Jesup
Ossabaw Sound
Ossabaw Island
St. Catherines Sound
St. Catherines Island
Sapelo Sound

President Carter's birthplace
Cordele
Fitzgerald
Douglas
BLACKBEARD ISLAND N.W.R.
Sapelo Island
GRAY'S REEF N.M.S.

Walter F. George Reservoir
Dawson
Ocmulgee
FORT FREDERICA NAT. MONUMENT

Albany
Tifton
Waycross
Brunswick
St. Simons Island
Jekyll Island
St. Andrew Sound

Blakely
Satilla
Camilla
Moultrie
Adel
Cumberland Island

Bainbridge
Cairo
BANKS LAKE N.W.R.
Kingsland
CUMBERLAND ISLAND NATIONAL SEASHORE

Thomasville
Valdosta
Quitman
Okefenokee Swamp
OKEFENOKEE NATIONAL WILDLIFE REFUGE
St. Marys

Lake Seminole
Ochlockonee
Withlacoochee
Alapaha
Suwannee

G E O R G I A

Flint
Oconee
Ohoopee
Canoochee
Ogeechee
Altamaha
Savannah

THE BASICS

STATS

Area
40,409 sq mi (104,659 sq km)

Population
4,339,367

Capital
Frankfort
Population 25,527

Largest city
Louisville/Jefferson County
Population 597,337

Ethnic/racial groups
87.8% white; 7.8% African American; 1.1% Asian; .2% Native American. Hispanic (any race) 3.1%.

Industry
Manufacturing, services, government, finance, insurance, real estate, retail trade, transportation, wholesale trade, construction, mining

Agriculture
Horses, tobacco, cattle, corn, dairy products

Statehood
June 1, 1792; 15th state

GEO WHIZ

A favorite Kentucky dessert is Derby Pie, a rich chocolate-and-walnut pastry that was first created by George Kern, manager of the Melrose Inn, in Prospect, in the 1950s. It became so popular that the name was registered with the U.S. Patent Office and the Commonwealth of Kentucky.

Pleasant Hill, near Lexington, was the site of a Shaker religious community. It is now a National Historic Site where visitors can tour the living history museum.

The song "Happy Birthday to You," one of the most popular songs in the English language, was the creation of two Louisville sisters in 1893.

Post-it notes are manufactured exclusively in Cynthiana. Millions of self-stick notes in 27 sizes and 57 colors are produced each year.

CARDINAL
GOLDENROD

KENTUCKY

1   2   3

The original inhabitants of the area known today as Kentucky were Native Americans, but a treaty with the Cherokees, signed in 1775, opened the territory to settlers—including the legendary Daniel Boone—from the soon-to-be-independent eastern colonies. In 1776 Kentucky became a western county of the state of Virginia. In 1792 it became the 15th state of the young U.S. Eastern Kentucky is a part of Appalachia, a region rich in soft bituminous coal but burdened with environmental problems that often accompany the mining industry. The region is known for crafts and music that can be traced back to Scotch-Irish immigrants who settled there. In central Kentucky, the Bluegrass region produces some of the finest Thoroughbred horses in the world, and the Kentucky Derby, held in Louisville, is a part of racing's coveted Triple Crown. In western Kentucky, coal found near the surface is strip mined, leaving scars on the landscape, but federal laws now require that the land be restored.

BENEATH THE SURFACE

Cave	Length
Mammoth Cave System, KY	367 miles/591 km
Jewel Cave, SD	140 miles/225 km
Wind Cave, SD	125 miles/201 km
Lechuguilla Cave, NM	121 miles/195 km
Fisher Ridge Cave System, KY	110 miles/177 km

Caves, natural openings in Earth's surface extending beyond the reach of sunlight, are often created by water dissolving limestone.

⬆ THEY'RE OFF! Riders and horses press for the finish line at Churchill Downs, in Louisville. Kentucky is a major breeder of Thoroughbred race horses, and horses are the leading source of farm income in the state.

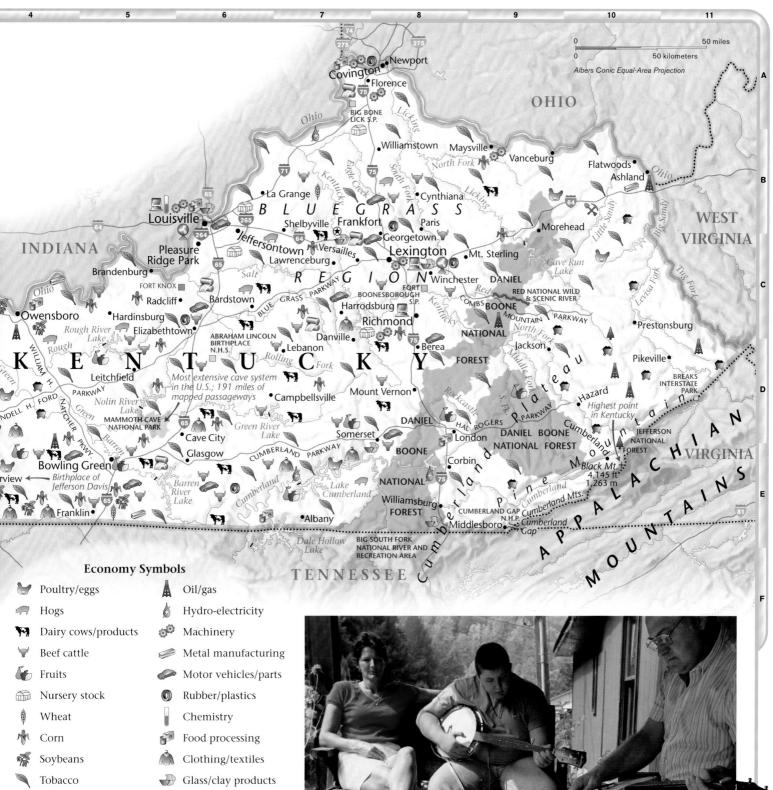

OHIO

INDIANA

WEST VIRGINIA

KENTUCKY

VIRGINIA

TENNESSEE

APPALACHIAN MOUNTAINS

Newport
Covington
Florence
BIG BONE LICK S.P.
Williamstown
Maysville
Vanceburg
Flatwoods
Ashland
La Grange
B L U E G R A S S
Shelbyville
Frankfort
Paris
Cynthiana
Morehead
Louisville
Jeffersontown
Versailles
Georgetown
Lexington
Mt. Sterling
Pleasure Ridge Park
Lawrenceburg
Winchester
DANIEL
Brandenburg
R E G I O N
Cave Run Lake
RED NATIONAL WILD & SCENIC RIVER
FORT KNOX
FORT BOONESBOROUGH S.P.
BOONE
Prestonsburg
Radcliff
Bardstown
Harrodsburg
MOUNTAIN PARKWAY
Owensboro
Hardinsburg
Richmond
NATIONAL
Pikeville
Elizabethtown
ABRAHAM LINCOLN BIRTHPLACE N.H.S.
Danville
Berea
FOREST
Jackson
BREAKS INTERSTATE PARK
K E N T U C K Y
Lebanon
Hazard
Leitchfield
Mount Vernon
Highest point in Kentucky
JEFFERSON NATIONAL FOREST
Most extensive cave system in the U.S.; 191 miles of mapped passageways
Campbellsville
DANIEL
DANIEL BOONE
Cumberland Mountain
MAMMOTH CAVE NATIONAL PARK
BOONE
NATIONAL FOREST
Cave City
Somerset
London
Glasgow
Black Mt. 4,145 ft 1,263 m
Bowling Green
NATIONAL
Corbin
Birthplace of Jefferson Davis
Franklin
FOREST
Williamsburg
CUMBERLAND GAP N.H.P.
Cumberland Mts.
Middlesboro
Cumberland Gap
Albany
BIG SOUTH FORK NATIONAL RIVER AND RECREATION AREA
Dale Hollow Lake

Economy Symbols

- Poultry/eggs
- Hogs
- Dairy cows/products
- Beef cattle
- Fruits
- Nursery stock
- Wheat
- Corn
- Soybeans
- Tobacco
- Timber/forest products
- Printing/publishing
- Stone/gravel/cement
- Coal
- Oil/gas
- Hydro-electricity
- Machinery
- Metal manufacturing
- Motor vehicles/parts
- Rubber/plastics
- Chemistry
- Food processing
- Clothing/textiles
- Glass/clay products
- Electrical equipment
- Computers/electronics
- Aerospace

⇨ STRUMMING A TUNE. Music is an important part of Kentucky's cultural heritage, especially in remote mountain areas where a banjo can become the focus of a family gathering.

LOUISIANA

Louisiana's Native American heritage is evident in place-names such as Natchitoches and Opelousas. Spanish sailors explored the area in 1528, but the French, traveling down the Mississippi River, established permanent settlements in the mid-17th century and named the region for King Louis XIV. The U.S. gained possession of the territory as part of the Louisiana Purchase in 1803, and Louisiana became the 18th state in 1812. New Orleans and the Port of South Louisiana, located near the delta of the Mississippi River, are Louisiana's main ports. Trade from the interior of the U.S. moves through these ports and out to world markets. Oil and gas are drilled in the Mississippi Delta area, and coastal waters are an important source of seafood. Louisiana is vulnerable to tropical storms. In late August 2005 Hurricane Katrina roared in off the Gulf of Mexico, flooding towns, breaking through levees, and changing forever the lives of everyone in southern Louisiana.

⇧ TASTY HARVEST. Louisiana produces more than half of all shrimp caught in the U.S. Most of this harvest comes from the Barataria-Terrebonne region, an estuary at the mouth of the Mississippi River that supports shrimp, oysters, crabs, and fish.

THE BASICS

STATS

Area
51,840 sq mi (134,265 sq km)

Population
4,533,372

Capital
Baton Rouge
Population 229,493

Largest city
New Orleans
Population 343,829

Ethnic/racial groups
62.6% white; 32.0% African American; 1.5% Asian; .7% Native American. Hispanic (any race) 4.2%.

Industry
Chemicals, petroleum products, food processing, health services, tourism, oil and natural gas extraction, paper products

Agriculture
Forest products, poultry, marine fisheries, sugarcane, rice, dairy products, cotton, cattle, aquaculture

Statehood
April 30, 1812; 18th state

GEO WHIZ

The brown pelican, the state bird of Louisiana, was placed on the endangered species list in 1970. The species has made a remarkable recovery in the Atlantic coastal states, but it is still considered endangered in the Gulf Coast area.

The magnolia, Louisiana's state flower, is the oldest flowering plant in the world. Some species are believed to be 100 million years old.

Cajuns, people whose French-speaking ancestors were exiled by the British from Acadia, in what is now Canada, live primarily in the bayou region of Louisiana. Their distinctive music and spicy food have become popular throughout the country.

BROWN PELICAN
MAGNOLIA

⇦ AVENUE TO THE PAST. Stately live oaks, believed to be 300 years old, frame Oak Alley Plantation on the banks of the Mississippi River west of New Orleans. Built in 1839, the house has been restored to its former grandeur and is open to the public for tours and private events.

Springhill
Vivian
KISA
NATIO
Caddo
Lake
FORES
Shreveport • Bossier
City
Lake
Bistine
Mansfield
Red
Natchito
CANE RIVER CREOLE
AND HERITAGE
Many
Toledo
Bend
Reservoir
Leesville
TEXAS
Rosepine
De Ridder
De Quincy
Sulphur
La
Ch
Intracoastal
CAM
P
Calcasieu
Lake
Sabine
Lake SABINE NAT. WILDLIFE REFUGE

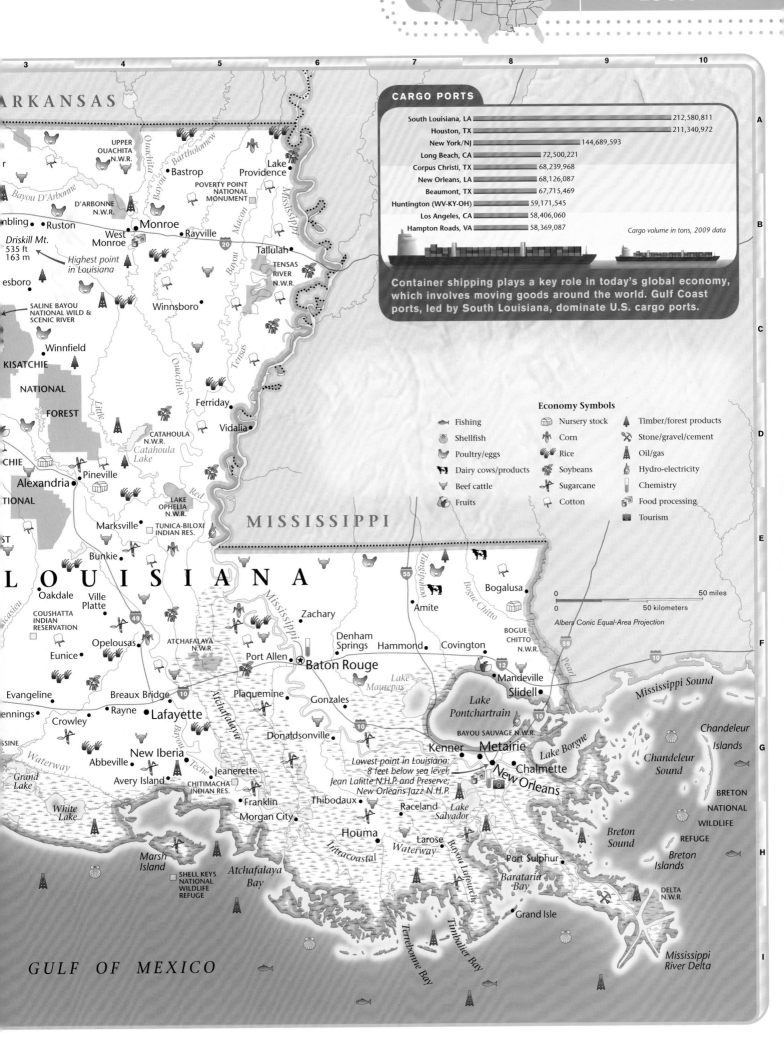

CARGO PORTS

South Louisiana, LA	212,580,811
Houston, TX	211,340,972
New York/NJ	144,689,593
Long Beach, CA	72,500,221
Corpus Christi, TX	68,239,968
New Orleans, LA	68,126,087
Beaumont, TX	67,715,469
Huntington (WV-KY-OH)	59,171,545
Los Angeles, CA	58,406,060
Hampton Roads, VA	58,369,087

Cargo volume in tons, 2009 data

Container shipping plays a key role in today's global economy, which involves moving goods around the world. Gulf Coast ports, led by **South Louisiana**, dominate U.S. cargo ports.

Economy Symbols

- Fishing
- Shellfish
- Poultry/eggs
- Dairy cows/products
- Beef cattle
- Fruits
- Nursery stock
- Corn
- Rice
- Soybeans
- Sugarcane
- Cotton
- Timber/forest products
- Stone/gravel/cement
- Oil/gas
- Hydro-electricity
- Chemistry
- Food processing
- Tourism

ARKANSAS

UPPER OUACHITA N.W.R.
Bastrop
Lake Providence
POVERTY POINT NATIONAL MONUMENT
Bayou D'Arbonne
D'ARBONNE N.W.R.
nbling · Ruston
Monroe
Rayville
West Monroe
Driskill Mt. 535 ft 163 m
Highest point in Louisiana
Tallulah
TENSAS RIVER N.W.R.
esboro
SALINE BAYOU NATIONAL WILD & SCENIC RIVER
Winnsboro
Winnfield
KISATCHIE
NATIONAL
FOREST
Ferriday
Vidalia
CATAHOULA N.W.R.
Catahoula Lake
CHIE
Pineville
Alexandria
NATIONAL
LAKE OPHELIA N.W.R.
Marksville
TUNICA-BILOXI INDIAN RES.
ST
Bunkie

MISSISSIPPI

LOUISIANA

Oakdale
Ville Platte
COUSHATTA INDIAN RESERVATION
Opelousas
Eunice
Evangeline
Breaux Bridge
ennings · Rayne
Crowley
Lafayette
New Iberia
Abbeville
Avery Island
CHITIMACHA INDIAN RES.
Franklin
Morgan City
Houma

Zachary
Denham Springs
Hammond
Port Allen
Baton Rouge
Plaquemine
Gonzales
ATCHAFALAYA N.W.R.
Donaldsonville
Thibodaux
Raceland
Larose

Amite
Bogalusa
BOGUE CHITTO N.W.R.
Covington
Lake Maurepas
Mandeville
Slidell
Lake Pontchartrain
BAYOU SAUVAGE N.W.R.
Kenner
Metairie
Chalmette
New Orleans
Lake Borgne
Lake Salvador

Lowest point in Louisiana: 8 feet below sea level; Jean Lafitte N.H.P. and Preserve; New Orleans Jazz N.H.P.

Mississippi Sound
Chandeleur Islands
Chandeleur Sound
BRETON NATIONAL WILDLIFE REFUGE
Breton Sound
Breton Islands

Port Sulphur
Barataria Bay
Grand Isle
DELTA N.W.R.
Mississippi River Delta

Marsh Island
SHELL KEYS NATIONAL WILDLIFE REFUGE
Atchafalaya Bay
White Lake
Grand Lake
Waterway
ssine
Intracoastal Waterway
Terrebonne Bay
Timbalier Bay
Bayou Lafourche

GULF OF MEXICO

0   50 miles
0   50 kilometers
Albers Conic Equal-Area Projection

THE MAGNOLIA STATE:
MISSISSIPPI

THE BASICS

STATS

Area
48,430 sq mi (125,434 sq km)

Population
2,967,297

Capital
Jackson
Population 173,514

Largest city
Jackson
Population 173,514

Ethnic/racial groups
59.1% white; 37.0% African American;
.9% Asian; .5% Native American.
Hispanic (any race) 2.7%.

Industry
Petroleum products, health services,
electronic equipment, transportation, banking, forest products,
communications

Agriculture
Poultry and eggs, cotton, catfish,
soybeans, cattle, rice, dairy products

Statehood
December 10, 1817; 20th state

GEO WHIZ

The Windsor Ruins, located near Port
Gibson, are 23 monolithic columns that
once made up the largest antebellum
mansion in the state. The mansion
survived the Civil War but was destroyed
by a fire in 1890.

The Marine Life Oceanarium in Gulfport
was almost completely destroyed
by Hurricane Katrina in 2005. Eight
of its 14 bottlenose dolphins were
swept into the Gulf of Mexico by a
40-foot (12-m) wave. These animals
and two sea lions named Splash and
Elliot were eventually rescued.
Others were not so lucky.

Greenville is the birthplace of
Jim Henson, creator of Kermit
the Frog, Miss Piggy, Big Bird,
and other famous Muppets.

MOCKINGBIRD

MAGNOLIA

MISSISSIPPI

Mississippi is named for the river that forms its western boundary. The name comes from the Chippewa words *mici zibi,* meaning "great river." Indeed it is a great river, draining much of the interior U.S. and providing a trade artery to the world. Explored by the Spanish in 1540 and claimed by the French in 1699, the territory of Mississippi passed to the U.S. in 1783 and became the 20th state in 1817. For more than a hundred years following statehood, Mississippi was the center of U.S. cotton production and trade. The

⇧ SINGING THE BLUES. B. B. King
sings the soulful sounds of the blues,
a music form that traces its roots to
Mississippi's cotton fields and the
sorrows of West Africans traveling
on slave ships to the Americas.

fertile soils and mild climate of the delta region in northwestern Mississippi provided a perfect environment for cotton, a crop that depended on slave labor. When the Civil War broke out, it took a heavy toll on the state. Today, poverty, especially in rural areas, is a major challenge for the state where agriculture—poultry, cotton, soybeans, and rice—is still the base of the economy.

GONE FISHIN'

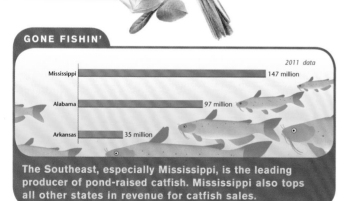

2011 data

Mississippi	147 million
Alabama	97 million
Arkansas	35 million

The Southeast, especially Mississippi, is the leading
producer of pond-raised catfish. Mississippi also tops
all other states in revenue for catfish sales.

⇨ BIG WHEEL TURNING. Now popular with tourists,
paddlewheel boats made the Mississippi River a
major artery for trade and travel in the 19th century.

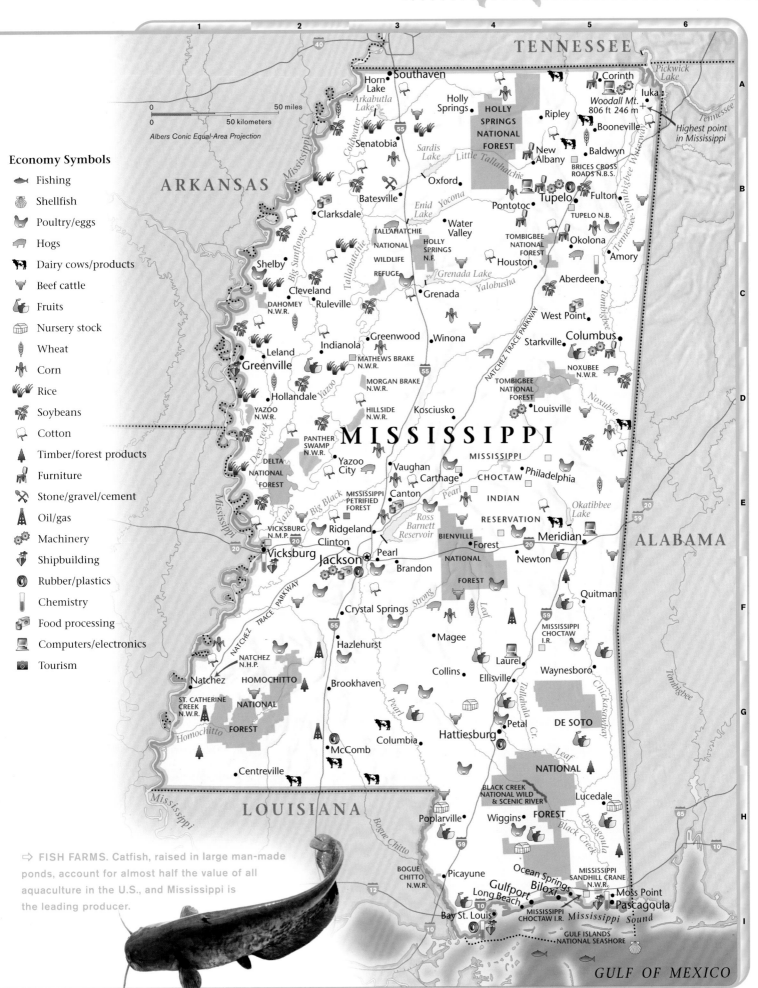

Economy Symbols

- Fishing
- Shellfish
- Poultry/eggs
- Hogs
- Dairy cows/products
- Beef cattle
- Fruits
- Nursery stock
- Wheat
- Corn
- Rice
- Soybeans
- Cotton
- Timber/forest products
- Furniture
- Stone/gravel/cement
- Oil/gas
- Machinery
- Shipbuilding
- Rubber/plastics
- Chemistry
- Food processing
- Computers/electronics
- Tourism

⇨ FISH FARMS. Catfish, raised in large man-made ponds, account for almost half the value of all aquaculture in the U.S., and Mississippi is the leading producer.

TENNESSEE

ARKANSAS

LOUISIANA

ALABAMA

MISSISSIPPI

MISSISSIPPI CHOCTAW INDIAN RESERVATION

Southaven
Horn Lake
Arkabutla Lake
Holly Springs
HOLLY SPRINGS NATIONAL FOREST
Corinth
Iuka
Woodall Mt. 806 ft 246 m — Highest point in Mississippi
Ripley
Booneville
Baldwyn
New Albany
Senatobia
Sardis Lake
Little Tallahatchie
BRICES CROSS ROADS N.B.S.
Oxford
Batesville
Yocona
Pontotoc
Tupelo
Fulton
Clarksdale
TALLAHATCHIE
Enid Lake
Water Valley
TUPELO N.B.
TALLAHATCHIE NATIONAL WILDLIFE REFUGE
HOLLY SPRINGS N.F.
TOMBIGBEE NATIONAL FOREST
Houston
Okolona
Amory
Shelby
Grenada Lake
Yalobusha
Aberdeen
Cleveland
Ruleville
DAHOMEY N.W.R.
Grenada
West Point
Greenwood
Winona
Columbus
Indianola
Starkville
Leland
MATHEWS BRAKE N.W.R.
Kosciusko
NOXUBEE N.W.R.
Greenville
MORGAN BRAKE N.W.R.
Louisville
Hollandale
HILLSIDE N.W.R.
TOMBIGBEE NATIONAL FOREST
YAZOO N.W.R.
PANTHER SWAMP N.W.R.
Vaughan
Carthage
Philadelphia
CHOCTAW INDIAN RESERVATION
Yazoo City
DELTA NATIONAL FOREST
MISSISSIPPI PETRIFIED FOREST
Canton
Ridgeland
Ross Barnett Reservoir
Okatibbee Lake
VICKSBURG N.M.P.
Clinton
BIENVILLE NATIONAL FOREST
Meridian
Vicksburg
Jackson
Pearl
Forest
Newton
Brandon
Quitman
Crystal Springs
MISSISSIPPI CHOCTAW I.R.
NATCHEZ TRACE PARKWAY
Hazlehurst
Magee
Laurel
NATCHEZ N.H.P.
Collins
Ellisville
Waynesboro
Natchez
HOMOCHITTO
Brookhaven
ST. CATHERINE CREEK N.W.R.
NATIONAL FOREST
DE SOTO
Columbia
Hattiesburg
Petal
McComb
NATIONAL
Centreville
BLACK CREEK NATIONAL WILD & SCENIC RIVER
Lucedale
FOREST
Poplarville
Wiggins
BOGUE CHITTO N.W.R.
MISSISSIPPI SANDHILL CRANE N.W.R.
Picayune
Ocean Springs
Biloxi
Moss Point
Gulfport
Long Beach
Pascagoula
Bay St. Louis
MISSISSIPPI CHOCTAW I.R.
Mississippi Sound
GULF ISLANDS NATIONAL SEASHORE

GULF OF MEXICO

THE TAR HEEL STATE:
NORTH CAROLINA

NORTH CAROLINA

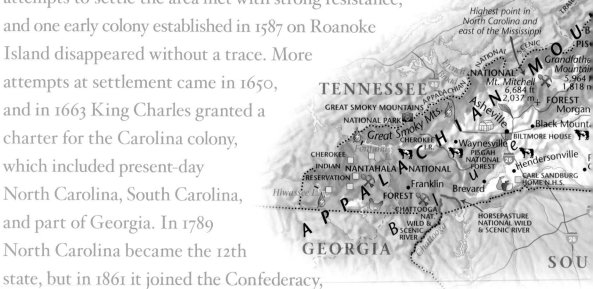

1   2   3

Before European contact, the land that became North Carolina was inhabited by numerous Native American groups. Early attempts to settle the area met with strong resistance, and one early colony established in 1587 on Roanoke Island disappeared without a trace. More attempts at settlement came in 1650, and in 1663 King Charles granted a charter for the Carolina colony, which included present-day North Carolina, South Carolina, and part of Georgia. In 1789 North Carolina became the 12th state, but in 1861 it joined the Confederacy, supplying more men and equipment to the Southern cause than any other state. In 1903 the Wright brothers piloted the first successful airplane near Kitty Hawk, foreshadowing the change and growth coming to the Tar Heel State. Traditional industries included agriculture, textiles, and furniture making. Today, these, plus high-tech industries and education in the Raleigh-Durham Research Triangle area, as well as banking and finance in Charlotte, are important to the economy.

THE BASICS

STATS

Area
53,819 sq mi (139,390 sq km)

Population
9,535,483

Capital
Raleigh
Population 403,892

Largest city
Charlotte
Population 731,424

Ethnic/racial groups
68.5% white; 21.5% African American; 2.2% Asian; 1.3% Native American. Hispanic (any race) 8.4%.

Industry
Real estate, health services, chemicals, tobacco products, finance, textiles

Agriculture
Poultry, hogs, tobacco, nursery stock, cotton, soybeans

Statehood
November 21, 1789; 12th state

GEO WHIZ

The University of North Carolina at Chapel Hill, which opened its doors in 1795, is the oldest state university in the United States.

The Biltmore estate in Asheville is the largest private residence in the United States. Built to resemble a French chateau, the mansion is still owned by descendants of Cornelius Vanderbilt, who made the family's original fortune in the late 1800s.

Standing 208 feet (63 m) high, Cape Hatteras Light is the tallest lighthouse in the U.S. Its beacon can be seen some 20 miles (32 km) out to sea and has warned sailors for more than a century about the shallow waters around a group of treacherous sandbars called Diamond Shoals.

CARDINAL

FLOWERING DOGWOOD

⇨ **FAVORITE PASTIME.** With four of the state's major schools represented in the powerful Atlantic Coast Conference, it is not surprising that basketball is a popular sport among all ages, whether on the court or in the backyard.

⇦ **TAKING FLIGHT.** The Wright Brothers Memorial on Kill Devil Hill, near Kitty Hawk on North Carolina's Outer Banks, marks the site of the first successful airplane flight in 1903.

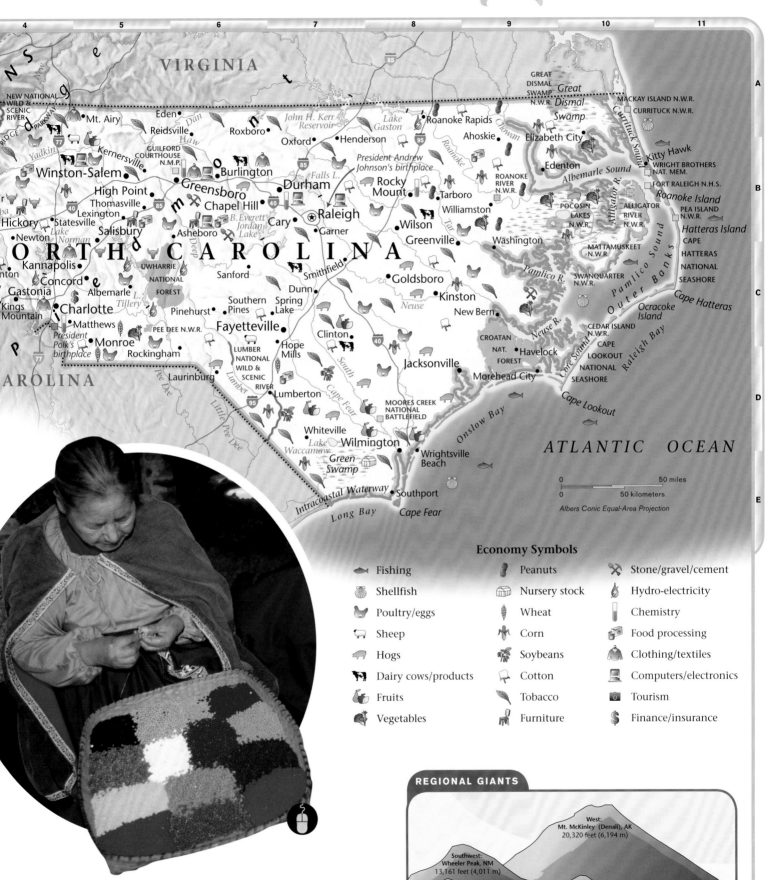

VIRGINIA

NEW NATIONAL
WILD &
SCENIC
RIVER

Mt. Airy
Eden
Reidsville
Roxboro
Oxford
Henderson
Roanoke Rapids
Ahoskie
Elizabeth City

GREAT
DISMAL
SWAMP
N.W.R.
Great Dismal Swamp

MACKAY ISLAND N.W.R.
CURRITUCK N.W.R.

Kernersville
GUILFORD
COURTHOUSE
N.M.P.
John H. Kerr Reservoir
Lake Gaston
Edenton
Kitty Hawk
WRIGHT BROTHERS
NAT. MEM.

Winston-Salem
Burlington
President Andrew
Johnson's birthplace
Rocky Mount
ROANOKE
RIVER
N.W.R.
Albemarle Sound
FORT RALEIGH N.H.S.
Roanoke Island

High Point
Greensboro
Durham
Falls L.
Tarboro
POCOSIN
LAKES
ALLIGATOR
RIVER
N.W.R.
PEA ISLAND
N.W.R.

Thomasville
Chapel Hill
Cary
Raleigh
Williamston
Hatteras Island
CAPE

Hickory
Lexington
Asheboro
B. Everett
Jordan
Lake
Garner
Wilson
Greenville
Washington
MATTAMUSKEET
N.W.R.
HATTERAS

Statesville
Salisbury

NORTH CAROLINA

Newton
Lake
Norman
UWHARRIE
NATIONAL
FOREST
Sanford
Smithfield
Goldsboro
SWANQUARTER
N.W.R.
NATIONAL
SEASHORE

Kannapolis
Concord
Albemarle
L. Tillery
Dunn
Kinston
New Bern
Ocracoke
Island
Cape Hatteras

Gastonia
Charlotte
Pinehurst
Southern
Pines
Spring
Lake
Neuse
CROATAN
NAT.
FOREST
CEDAR ISLAND
N.W.R.

Kings
Mountain
Matthews
President
Polk's
birthplace
Fayetteville
Clinton
Havelock
CAPE
LOOKOUT
NATIONAL
SEASHORE

Monroe
Rockingham
LUMBER
NATIONAL
WILD &
SCENIC
RIVER
Hope
Mills
Jacksonville
Morehead City
Cape Lookout

CAROLINA
Laurinburg
Lumberton
South
MOORES CREEK
NATIONAL
BATTLEFIELD
Onslow Bay
ATLANTIC OCEAN

PEE DEE N.W.R.
Little Pee Dee
Whiteville
Lake
Waccamaw
Green
Swamp
Wilmington
Wrightsville
Beach

Pee Dee
Intracoastal Waterway
Southport
Long Bay
Cape Fear

0   50 miles
0   50 kilometers
Albers Conic Equal-Area Projection

Economy Symbols

Fishing		Peanuts		Stone/gravel/cement	
Shellfish		Nursery stock		Hydro-electricity	
Poultry/eggs		Wheat		Chemistry	
Sheep		Corn		Food processing	
Hogs		Soybeans		Clothing/textiles	
Dairy cows/products		Cotton		Computers/electronics	
Fruits		Tobacco		Tourism	
Vegetables		Furniture		Finance/insurance	

⬆ SKILLED ARTISAN. A Cherokee woman sews a beaded belt in Oconaluftee Indian Village in western North Carolina. Cherokees in this mountainous region are descendants of Indians who hid in the hills to avoid the forced migration known as the Trail of Tears. The village preserves traditional 18th-century crafts, customs, and lifestyles.

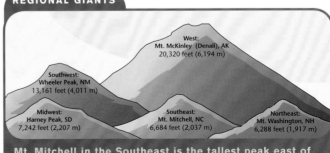

REGIONAL GIANTS

West:
Mt. McKinley (Denali), AK
20,320 feet (6,194 m)

Southwest:
Wheeler Peak, NM
13,161 feet (4,011 m)

Midwest:
Harney Peak, SD
7,242 feet (2,207 m)

Southeast:
Mt. Mitchell, NC
6,684 feet (2,037 m)

Northeast:
Mt. Washington, NH
6,288 feet (1,917 m)

Mt. Mitchell in the Southeast is the tallest peak east of the Mississippi, but young mountains in the West and Southwest tower above older eastern peaks.

THE BASICS

STATS

Area
32,020 sq mi (82,932 sq km)

Population
4,625,364

Capital
Columbia
Population 129,272

Largest city
Columbia
Population 129,272

Ethnic/racial groups
66.2% white; 27.9% African American; 1.3% Asian; .4% Native American. Hispanic (any race) 5.1%.

Industry
Service industries, tourism, chemicals, textiles, machinery, forest products

Agriculture
Chickens, tobacco, nursery stock, beef cattle, dairy products, cotton

Statehood
May 23, 1788; 8th state

GEO WHIZ

The loggerhead sea turtle, South Carolina's state reptile, is threatened throughout its range. These turtles weigh between 200–450 pounds (90–204 kg).

North America's largest remnant of old-growth bottomland hardwood forest towers above the Congaree River and is protected as a 22,000-acre (8,903-ha) refuge called Congaree National Park.

Sweetgrass basketmaking, a traditional art form of African origin, has been a part of the Mount Pleasant community for more than 300 years. The baskets were originally used by slaves in the planting and processing of rice in coastal lowland regions.

Bobcats are thriving on Kiawah Island, a resort community southeast of Charleston. The elusive, nocturnal cats, which are about twice the size of an average house cat, play an important role in controlling the island's deer population.

CAROLINA WREN
YELLOW JESSAMINE

SOUTH CAROLINA

Attempts in the 16th century by the Spanish and the French to colonize the area that would become South Carolina met fierce resistance from local Native American groups, but in 1670 the English were the first to establish a permanent European settlement at present-day Charleston. The colony prospered by relying on slave labor to produce first cotton, then rice and indigo. South Carolina became the 8th state in 1788 and the first to leave the Union just months before the first shots of the Civil War were fired on Fort Sumter in 1861. After the war, South Carolina struggled to rebuild its economy. Early in the 20th century, textile mills introduced new jobs. Today, agriculture remains important, manufacturing and high-tech industries are expanding along interstate highway corridors, and tourists and retirees are drawn to the state's Atlantic coastline. But these coastal areas are not without risk. In 1989 Hurricane Hugo's 135-mile-per-hour (217-kmph) winds left a trail of destruction.

⇧ GLOW OF DAWN. The rising sun reflects off the water along the Atlantic coast. Beaches attract visitors year-round, contributing to tourism, the state's largest industry.

⇩ SOUTHERN CHARM. Twilight settles over antebellum homes in the historic district of Charleston. The city, established in 1670, is an important port located where the Ashley and Cooper Rivers merge before flowing to the Atlantic Ocean.

TRADE PARTNERS

Kuwait 2.7%
India 2.4%
Japan 2.2%
Brazil 2.8%
Canada 15.7%
2010 data
Australia 3.0%
United Kingdom 5.5%
Mexico 6.5%
China 10.6%
Germany 14.5%

With more than $20 billion in export goods in 2010, export industries supported more than 28% of all manufacturing jobs in South Carolina. Transportation equipment is the leading manufactured export.

[Map labels:] Highest point South Carolina · CHATTOOGA NATIONAL WILD & SCENIC RIVER · SUMTER · Lake Keowee · Green · Easley · Ga · Sassafras M 3,560 ft 1,085 m · Blue Ridge · Chattooga · NATIONAL FOREST · Tugaloo · Seneca · Clemson · 85 · Belto · Ande · Hartwell Lake · Savannah · Richard B. Russell Lake · Abbe · P · J. Strom Thu Re · 1 · 2

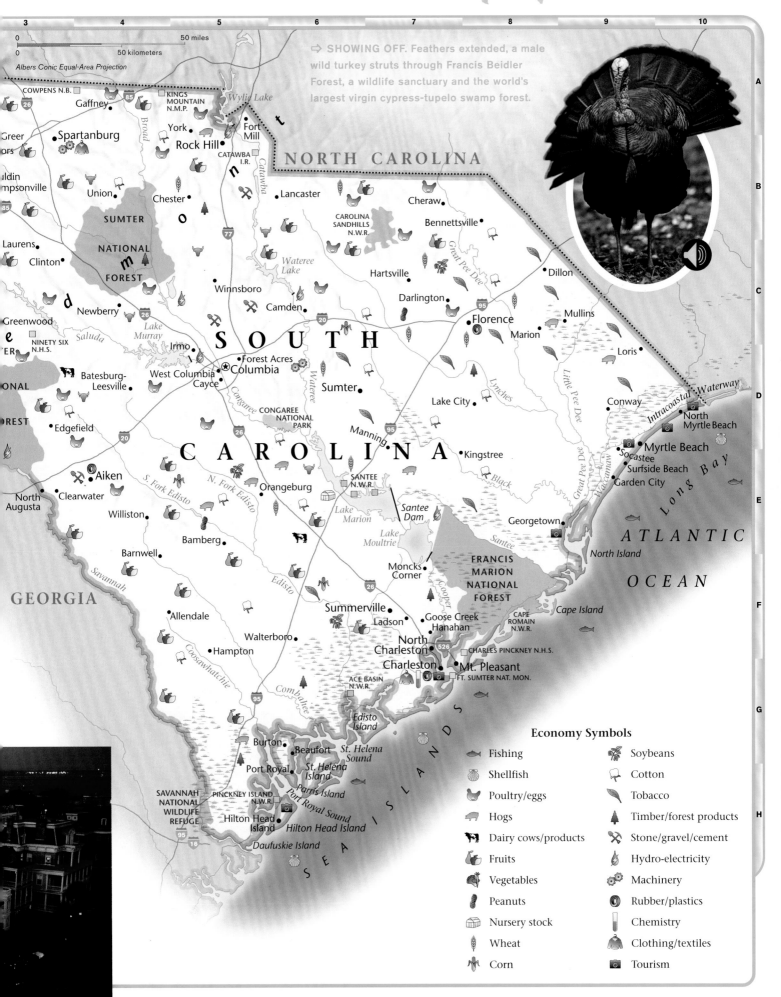

⇨ SHOWING OFF. Feathers extended, a male wild turkey struts through Francis Beidler Forest, a wildlife sanctuary and the world's largest virgin cypress-tupelo swamp forest.

0 — 50 miles
0 — 50 kilometers
Albers Conic Equal-Area Projection

NORTH CAROLINA

COWPENS N.B.
Gaffney
KINGS MOUNTAIN N.M.P.
Wylie Lake
Greer
ors
Spartanburg
York
Fort Mill
CATAWBA I.R.
uldin
mpsonville
Union
Rock Hill
Chester
Lancaster
Cheraw
Laurens
Clinton
SUMTER
NATIONAL
FOREST
Newberry
CAROLINA SANDHILLS N.W.R.
Bennettsville
Greenwood
NINETY SIX N.H.S.
Winnsboro
Lake Murray
Saluda
Camden
Hartsville
Darlington
Dillon
Florence
Mullins

SOUTH

ER
Batesburg-Leesville
Irmo
Forest Acres
Columbia
West Columbia
Cayce
Sumter
Lake City
Marion
Loris
Conway
Waterway
Intracoastal
North Myrtle Beach

CAROLINA

ONAL
REST
Edgefield
CONGAREE NATIONAL PARK
Manning
Kingstree
Myrtle Beach
Socastee
Surfside Beach
Garden City

Aiken
Clearwater
North Augusta
S. Fork Edisto
N. Fork Edisto
Orangeburg
SANTEE N.W.R.
Georgetown
North Island
Long Bay

Williston
Bamberg
Lake Marion
Santee Dam
Lake Moultrie
Moncks Corner
ATLANTIC

Barnwell
Savannah
Edisto
FRANCIS MARION NATIONAL FOREST
OCEAN

GEORGIA
Allendale
Coosawhatchie
Summerville
Ladson
Goose Creek
Hanahan
CAPE ROMAIN N.W.R.
Cape Island

Walterboro
Hampton
North Charleston
CHARLES PINCKNEY N.H.S.
Charleston
Mt. Pleasant
FT. SUMTER NAT. MON.

Combahee
ACE BASIN N.W.R.

Edisto Island
Burton
Beaufort
St. Helena Sound
Port Royal
St. Helena Island
Parris Island

SAVANNAH NATIONAL WILDLIFE REFUGE
PINCKNEY ISLAND N.W.R.
Port Royal Sound
Hilton Head Island
Hilton Head Island
Daufuskie Island

SEA ISLANDS

Economy Symbols

Fishing		Soybeans	
Shellfish		Cotton	
Poultry/eggs		Tobacco	
Hogs		Timber/forest products	
Dairy cows/products		Stone/gravel/cement	
Fruits		Hydro-electricity	
Vegetables		Machinery	
Peanuts		Rubber/plastics	
Nursery stock		Chemistry	
Wheat		Clothing/textiles	
Corn		Tourism	

THE BASICS

STATS

Area
42,143 sq mi (109,151 sq km)

Population
6,346,105

Capital
Nashville-Davidson
Population 601,222

Largest city
Memphis
Population 646,889

Ethnic/racial groups
77.6% white; 16.7% African American; 1.4% Asian; .3% Native American. Hispanic (any race) 4.6%.

Industry
Service industries, chemicals, transportation equipment, processed foods, machinery

Agriculture
Cattle, cotton, dairy products, hogs, poultry, nursery stock

Statehood
June 1, 1796; 16th state

GEO WHIZ

Twenty-seven species of salamanders live in Great Smoky Mountains National Park, earning it the nickname Salamander Capital of the World. Among the species are the spotted; the Jordans, which is found nowhere else; and the five-foot-long hellbender (1.5 m).

The New Madrid Earthquakes of 1811–1812, some of the largest earthquakes in the history of the U.S., created Reelfoot Lake in northwestern Tennessee. It is the state's only large, natural lake; others were created by damming waterways.

The Tennessee-Tombigbee Waterway is a 234-mile (376-km) artificial waterway that connects the Tennessee and Tombigbee Rivers. This water transportation route provides inland ports with an outlet to the Gulf of Mexico.

MOCKINGBIRD

IRIS

TENNESSEE

Following the last ice age, Native Americans moved onto the fertile lands of Tennessee. The earliest Europeans in Tennessee were Spanish explorers who passed through in 1541. In 1673 both the English and French made claims on the land, hoping to develop trade with the powerful Cherokees, whose town, called *Tanasi,* gave the state its name. Originally part of North Carolina, Tennessee was ceded to the federal government and became the 16th state in 1796. Tennessee was the last state to join the Confederacy and endured years of hardship after the war. Beginning in the 1930s, the federally funded Tennessee Valley Authority (TVA) set a high standard in water management in the state, and the hydropower it generated supported major industrial development. Tennessee played a key role in the civil rights movement of the 1960s. Today, visitors to Tennessee are drawn to national parks, Nashville's country music, and the mournful sound of the blues in Memphis.

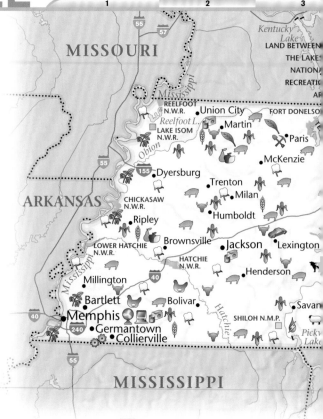

⇦ OUT FOR A STROLL. Black bear cubs are usually born in January and remain with their mother for about 18 months. The Great Smoky Mountains National Park is one of the few remaining natural habitats for black bears in the eastern U.S.

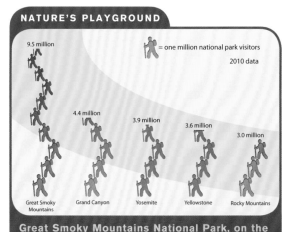

NATURE'S PLAYGROUND

9.5 million

👤 = one million national park visitors
2010 data

4.4 million

3.9 million

3.6 million

3.0 million

Great Smoky Mountains

Grand Canyon

Yosemite

Yellowstone

Rocky Mountains

Great Smoky Mountains National Park, on the Tennessee–North Carolina border, attracts more visitors than any other U.S. national park.

4 5 6 7 8 9 10 11

KENTUCKY

VIRGINIA

A

S CREEKS
R.
Red
Cumberland
Clarksville
Portland
Springfield
Gallatin
Goodlettsville
Hendersonville
THE HERMITAGE
ome of
esident
ackson
Nashville ★
Lebanon
Old Hickory L.
Cookeville
Dale Hollow
Lake
BIG SOUTH FORK
NATIONAL RIVER AND
RECREATION AREA
La
Follette
CUMBERLAND
GAP N.H.P.
Powell
Clinch
Cherokee
Lake
Holston
Church Hill
Johnson City
Bristol
Kingsport
Elizabethton
CHEROKEE
ANDREW JOHNSON N.H.S.
Morristown
Greeneville
Erwin
DAVY CROCKETT
BIRTHPLACE
S.P.
kson
J. Percy Priest
Lake
Brentwood
Franklin
Smyrna
STONES RIVER
N.B.
Center Hill
Lake
Crossville
Sparta
Obed
OBED NATIONAL
WILD & SCENIC
RIVER
Oak Ridge
Harriman
Clinton
Norris L.
Knoxville
Farragut
Jefferson
City
Newport
Douglas
Lake
FOREST
SCENIC
NATIONAL
Roan Mt.
6,285 ft
1,916 m
Highest point
in Tennessee
B
T E N N E S S E E
Spring Hill
Columbia
Murfreesboro
McMinnville
Lenoir City
Alcoa
Sevierville
Fort Loudoun
L. Gatlinburg
Maryville
Watts
Bar L.
APPALACHIAN
French
Broad
Nolichucky
NORTH
CAROLINA
Shelbyville
Lewisburg
Tullahoma
Manchester
Caney
Sequatchie
Dayton
Tellico L.
Sweetwater
Athens
CHEROKEE
Great
Smoky MTS.
Clingmans Dome
6,643 ft 2,025 m
GREAT
SMOKY MOUNTAINS
NATIONAL PARK
C
Lawrenceburg
Pulaski
Fayetteville
Lynchburg
Winchester
Tims Ford
L.
Elk
Chickamauga
Lake
Soddy-Daisy
Red Bank
Cleveland
Chattanooga
Harrison
East Ridge
NATIONAL
FOREST
Hiwassee
Tennessee
0   50 miles
0   50 kilometers
Albers Conic Equal-Area Projection
TRACE PARKWAY
Cumberland
APPALACHIAN
SOUTH
CAROLINA
D
ALABAMA
CHICKAMAUGA &
CHATTANOOGA
N.M.P.
Tennessee
GEORGIA

Economy Symbols

Poultry/eggs		Printing/publishing	
Sheep		Stone/gravel/cement	
Hogs		Mining	
Dairy cows/products		Coal	
Beef cattle		Hydro-electricity	
Fruits		Machinery	
Vegetables		Metal manufacturing	
Nursery stock		Motor vehicles/parts	
Wheat		Chemistry	
Corn		Food processing	
Soybeans		Electrical equipment	
Cotton		Computers/electronics	
Tobacco		Aerospace	
Furniture		Motion picture/music industry	

⬆ WATTS BAR DAM is one of nine TVA dams built on
the Tennessee River to aid navigation and flood control
and to supply power. The large reservoir behind the
dam provides a recreation area that attracts millions
of vacationers each year. Without the dam, cities such
as Chattanooga would face devastating floods.

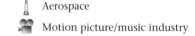

⇨ SOUTHERN TRADITION. Nashville's Grand Ole Opry
is the home of country music. Originally a 1925 radio show
called "Barn Dance," the Opry now occupies a theater with
a seating capacity of 4,400 and the largest broadcasting
studio in the world. Country music, using mainly stringed
instruments, evolved from traditional folk tunes of the Appalachians.

THE OLD DOMINION STATE:
VIRGINIA

VIRGINIA

1   2   3   4

Long before Europeans arrived in present-day Virginia, Native Americans populated the area. Early Spanish attempts to establish a colony failed, but in 1607 merchants established the first permanent English settlement in North America at Jamestown. Virginia became a prosperous colony, growing tobacco using slave labor. Virginia played a key role in the drive for independence, and the final battle of the Revolutionary War was at Yorktown, near Jamestown. In 1861 Virginia joined the Confederacy and became a major battleground of the Civil War, which left the state in financial ruin. Today, Virginia has a diversified economy. Farmers still grow tobacco, along with other crops. The Hampton Roads area, near the mouth of Chesapeake Bay, is a center for shipbuilding and home to major naval bases. Northern Virginia, across the Potomac River from Washington, D.C., boasts federal government offices and high-tech businesses. And the state's natural beauty and many historic sites attract tourists from around the world.

⬆ EARLY ENTER-
TAINMENT. Dating
back to ancient
Greece and Rome,
dice made of bone,
ivory, or lead were
popular during
colonial times.

THE BASICS

STATS

Area
42,774 sq mi (110,785 sq km)

Population
8,001,024

Capital
Richmond
Population 204,214

Largest city
Virginia Beach
Population 437,994

Ethnic/racial groups
68.6% white; 19.4% African American; 5.5% Asian; .4% Native American. Hispanic (any race) 7.9%.

Industry
Food processing, communication and electronic equipment, transportation equipment, printing, shipbuilding, textiles

Agriculture
Tobacco, poultry, dairy products, beef cattle, soybeans, hogs

Statehood
June 25, 1788; 10th state

GEO WHIZ

In the early 1700s the bustling port of Hampton was a major target for pirates, including the notorious Blackbeard. Today, each spring the city hosts the Blackbeard Festival, complete with pirate re-enactors, live music, games, and fireworks.

Virginia is the birthplace of eight U.S. presidents—more than any other state. They are: George Washington, Thomas Jefferson, James Madison, James Monroe, William Harrison, John Tyler, Zachary Taylor, and Woodrow Wilson. Learn about them and more in our book *Our Country's Presidents*.

During the Battle of Hampton Roads in 1862, the USS *Monitor* and the CSS *Virginia* (a rebuilt version of the USS *Merrimac*) met in one of the most famous naval engagements in U.S. history. It marked the dawn of a new era of naval warfare.

More than 200,000 telephone calls are made each day at the Pentagon, the headquarters for the U.S. Department of Defense, through phones connected by 100,000 miles (160,000 km) of telephone cable. It is one of the largest office buildings in the world.

CARDINAL
FLOWERING
DOGWOOD

⇨ NATURAL WONDER.
Winding under the Appalachian Mountains, Luray Caverns formed as water dissolved limestone rocks and precipitated calcium deposits to form stalactites and stalagmites.

KENTUCKY

Bluefield
Tazewell
Richlands   APPAL
Norton   Lebanon   Clinch   Mountain   Wythe
CUMBERLAND   Big   JEFFERSON   NATIONAL   FORES
GAP   Stone   Clinch   MT.
N.H.P.   Powell   Gap   North Fork Marion   RECR
                              Abingdon   AP
                   Bristol   A   Mt. Roge
                   Holston   +5,729 ft
TENNESSEE   S. Fork   A P   1,746 m
                                         Highest po
                                         in Virginia

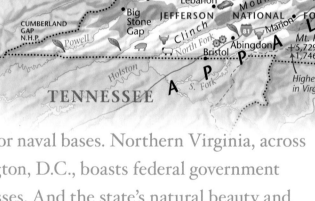

⇓ PAST AND PRESENT. Cyclists speed past a statue of Confederate General Robert E. Lee on Richmond's Monument Avenue. The street has drawn criticism for recognizing leaders of the Confederacy.

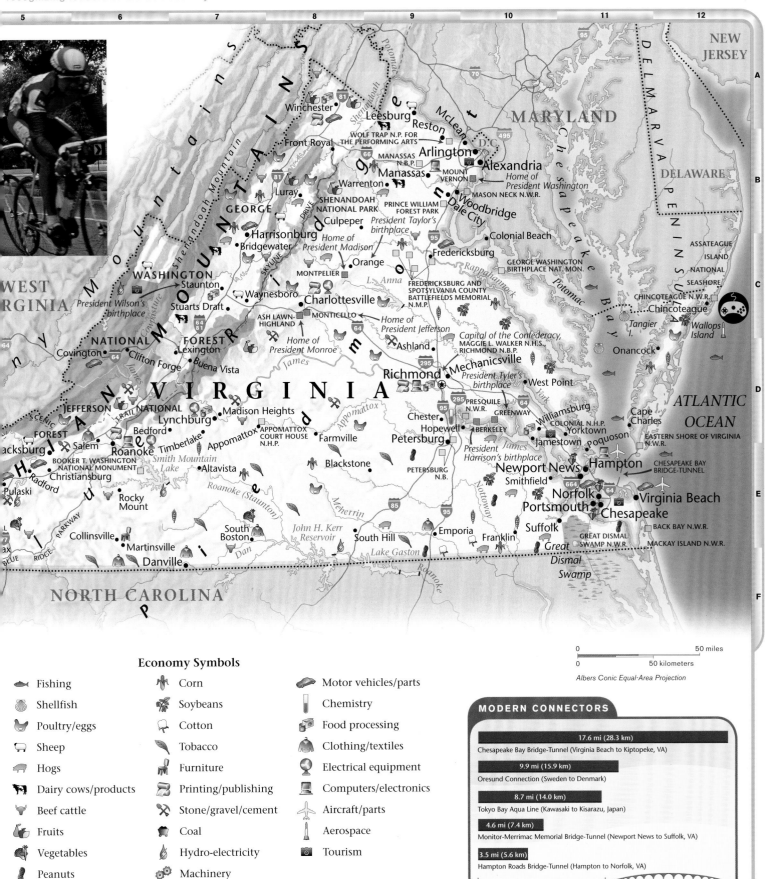

Economy Symbols

- Fishing
- Shellfish
- Poultry/eggs
- Sheep
- Hogs
- Dairy cows/products
- Beef cattle
- Fruits
- Vegetables
- Peanuts
- Wheat

- Corn
- Soybeans
- Cotton
- Tobacco
- Furniture
- Printing/publishing
- Stone/gravel/cement
- Coal
- Hydro-electricity
- Machinery
- Ship Building

- Motor vehicles/parts
- Chemistry
- Food processing
- Clothing/textiles
- Electrical equipment
- Computers/electronics
- Aircraft/parts
- Aerospace
- Tourism

0 ____ 50 miles
0 ____ 50 kilometers
Albers Conic Equal-Area Projection

MODERN CONNECTORS

17.6 mi (28.3 km)	Chesapeake Bay Bridge-Tunnel (Virginia Beach to Kiptopeke, VA)
9.9 mi (15.9 km)	Oresund Connection (Sweden to Denmark)
8.7 mi (14.0 km)	Tokyo Bay Aqua Line (Kawasaki to Kisarazu, Japan)
4.6 mi (7.4 km)	Monitor-Merrimac Memorial Bridge-Tunnel (Newport News to Suffolk, VA)
3.5 mi (5.6 km)	Hampton Roads Bridge-Tunnel (Hampton to Norfolk, VA)

Advanced engineering has made it possible to span wide expanses of water. Three of the world's longest bridge-tunnels are in Virginia.

THE MOUNTAIN STATE:
WEST VIRGINIA

WEST VIRGINIA

1   2

Mountainous West Virginia was first settled by Native Americans who favored the wooded region for hunting. The first Europeans to settle in what originally was an extension of Virginia were Germans and Scotch-Irish, who came through mountain valleys of Pennsylvania in the early 1700s. Because farms in West Virginia did not depend upon slaves, residents opposed secession during the Civil War and broke away from Virginia, becoming the 35th state in 1863. In the early 1800s West Virginia harvested forest products and mined salt, but it was the exploitation of vast coal deposits that brought industrialization to the state. Coal fueled steel mills, steamboats, and trains, and jobs in the mines attracted immigrants from far and near. However, poor work conditions resulted in a legacy of poverty, illness, and environmental degradation— problems the state continues to face. Today, the state is working to build a tourist industry based on its natural beauty and mountain crafts and culture.

⇧ HARD LABOR. Coal miners work under difficult conditions. In 2010 West Virginia mined more than 178 million tons of coal, or 12.5 percent of U.S. production.

O H

Point Pleas

Hurricane

Huntington   64

Kenova   St.

Big Sandy   Ohio   Kanu

M

Guyandotte

Tug Fork

Williamson

KENTUCKY

⇐ STRATEGIC LOCATION. Founded in 1751 by Robert Harper, who built a ferry to cross the Shenandoah River, Harpers Ferry was a departure point for pioneers heading West as well as the site of many battles during the Civil War.

A

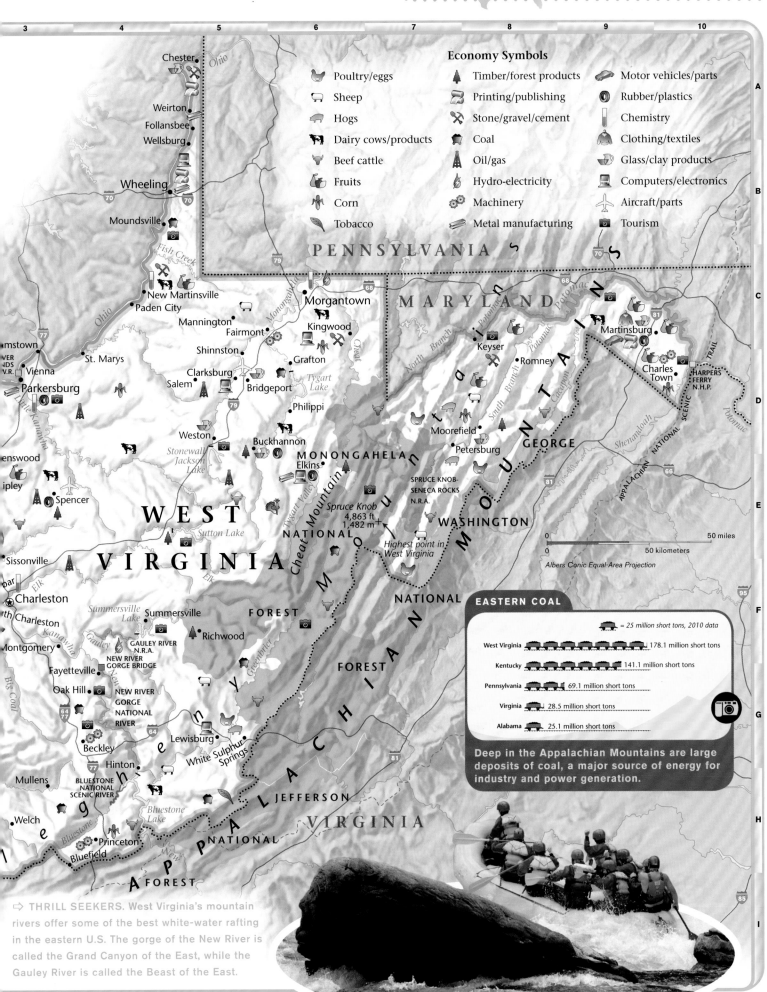

Economy Symbols

- Poultry/eggs
- Sheep
- Hogs
- Dairy cows/products
- Beef cattle
- Fruits
- Corn
- Tobacco
- Timber/forest products
- Printing/publishing
- Stone/gravel/cement
- Coal
- Oil/gas
- Hydro-electricity
- Machinery
- Metal manufacturing
- Motor vehicles/parts
- Rubber/plastics
- Chemistry
- Clothing/textiles
- Glass/clay products
- Computers/electronics
- Aircraft/parts
- Tourism

PENNSYLVANIA

MARYLAND

WEST VIRGINIA

VIRGINIA

Chester, Weirton, Follansbee, Wellsburg, Wheeling, Moundsville, New Martinsville, Paden City, Mannington, Fairmont, Shinnston, Clarksburg, Salem, Bridgeport, Grafton, Philippi, Morgantown, Kingwood, St. Marys, Vienna, Parkersburg, Weston, Buckhannon, Elkins, Moorefield, Petersburg, Keyser, Romney, Martinsburg, Charles Town, HARPERS FERRY N.H.P., Spencer, Ripley, Sissonville, Charleston, South Charleston, Montgomery, Summersville, Richwood, Fayetteville, Oak Hill, Beckley, Lewisburg, White Sulphur Springs, Hinton, Mullens, Welch, Princeton, Bluefield

MONONGAHELA NATIONAL FOREST

GEORGE WASHINGTON NATIONAL FOREST

JEFFERSON NATIONAL FOREST

APPALACHIAN MOUNTAINS

Spruce Knob 4,863 ft 1,482 m
Highest point in West Virginia

SPRUCE KNOB-SENECA ROCKS N.R.A.

Cheat Mountain

Tygart Valley

Stonewall Jackson Lake

Sutton Lake

Summersville Lake

Tygart Lake

Bluestone Lake

GAULEY RIVER N.R.A.

NEW RIVER GORGE BRIDGE

NEW RIVER GORGE NATIONAL RIVER

BLUESTONE NATIONAL SCENIC RIVER

Ohio, Monongahela, Cheat, North Branch Potomac, South Branch Potomac, Cacapon, Potomac, Shenandoah, Appalachian National Scenic Trail, Gauley, Greenbrier, Elk, Kanawha, Little Kanawha, Big Coal, New, Bluestone

EASTERN COAL

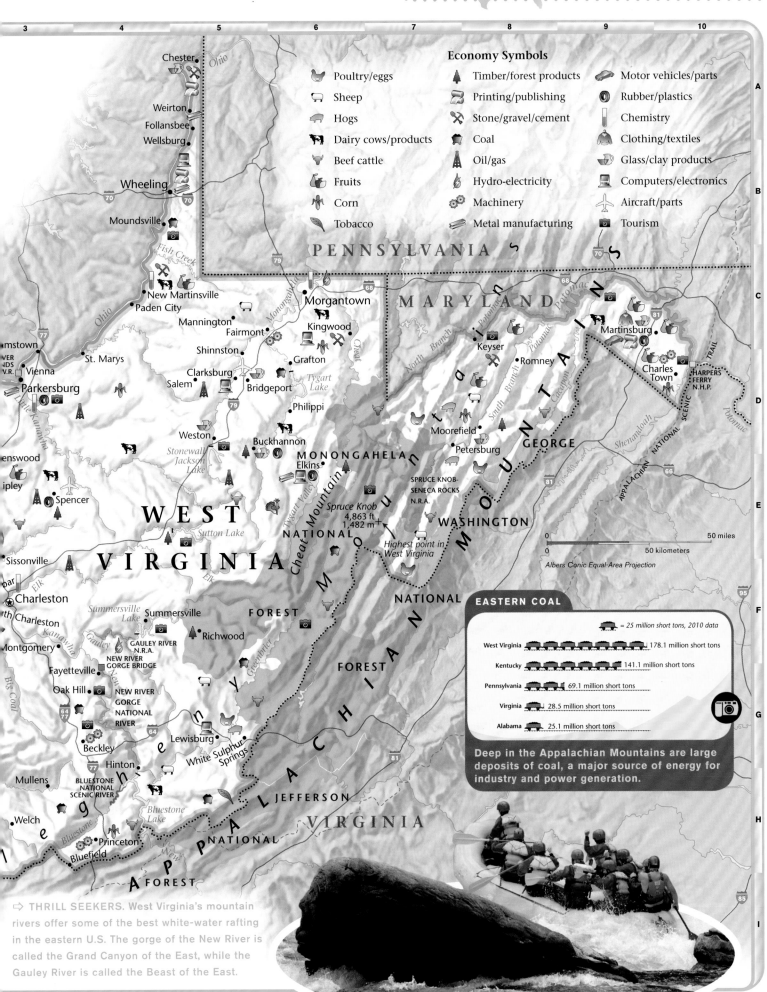

= 25 million short tons, 2010 data

West Virginia		178.1 million short tons
Kentucky		141.1 million short tons
Pennsylvania		69.1 million short tons
Virginia		28.5 million short tons
Alabama		25.1 million short tons

Deep in the Appalachian Mountains are large deposits of coal, a major source of energy for industry and power generation.

0   50 miles
0   50 kilometers
Albers Conic Equal-Area Projection

⇨ THRILL SEEKERS. West Virginia's mountain rivers offer some of the best white-water rafting in the eastern U.S. The gorge of the New River is called the Grand Canyon of the East, while the Gauley River is called the Beast of the East.

THE REGION

PHYSICAL

Total area
821,739 sq mi
(2,128,287 sq km)

Highest point
Harney Peak, SD
7,242 ft (2,207 m)

Lowest point
St. Francis River, MO
230 ft (70 m)

Longest rivers
Mississippi, Missouri,
Arkansas, Ohio

Largest lakes
Superior, Michigan,
Huron, Erie

Vegetation
Grassland; broadleaf, needleleaf,
and mixed forest

Climate
Continental to mild, ranging
from cold winters and cool
summers in the north to mild
winters and humid summers
in the south

POLITICAL

Total population
66,927,001

States (12):
Illinois, Indiana, Iowa, Kansas, Michigan,
Minnesota, Missouri, Nebraska, North
Dakota, Ohio, South Dakota, Wisconsin

Largest state
Michigan: 96,716 sq mi (250,495 sq km)

Smallest state
Indiana: 36,418 sq mi (94,322 sq km)

Most populous state
Illinois: 12,830,632

Least populous state
North Dakota: 672,591

Largest city proper
Chicago, IL: 2,695,598

The Midwest

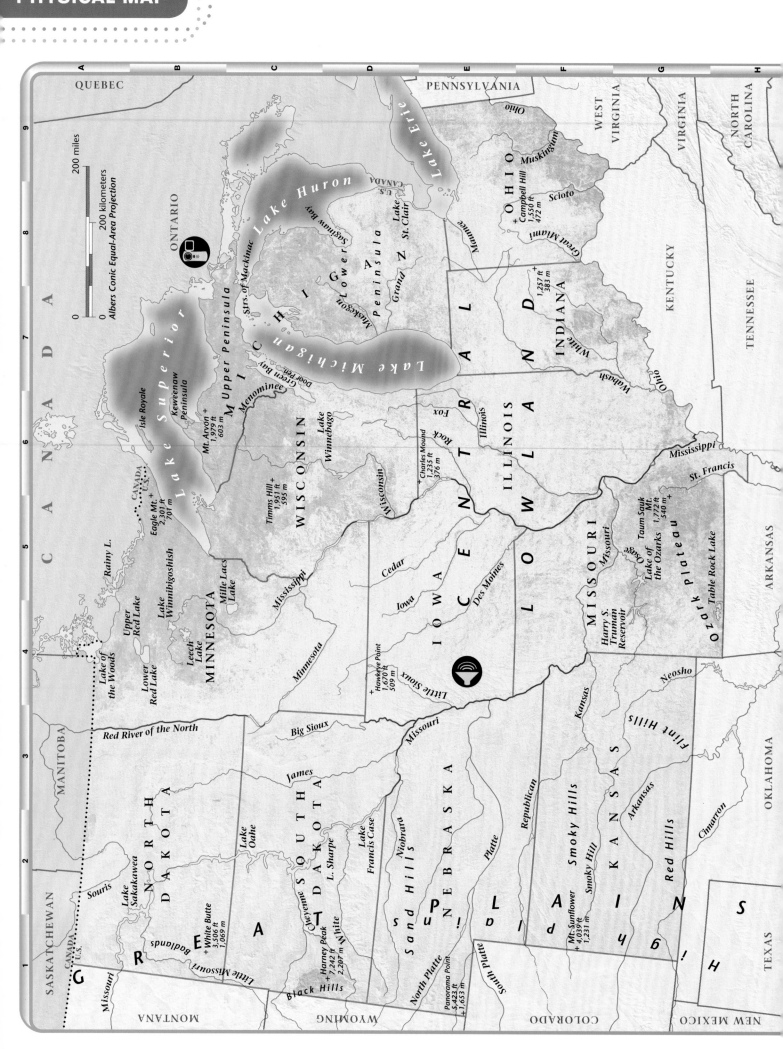

QUEBEC

PENNSYLVANIA

A B C D E F G H

9 8 7 6 5 4 3 2 1

ONTARIO

CANADA

200 miles

200 kilometers

Albers Conic Equal-Area Projection

Lake Superior

Isle Royale

Keweenaw Peninsula

Upper Peninsula

MICHIGAN

Lake Huron

Strs. of Mackinac

Saginaw Bay

CANADA U.S.

Lake Michigan

Lower Peninsula

Grand

Muskegon

Lake St. Clair

Lake Erie

WEST VIRGINIA

OHIO

Muskingum

Campbell Hill 1,550 ft 472 m

Scioto

Maumee

Great Miami

INDIANA

1,257 ft 383 m

White

Wabash

Ohio

VIRGINIA

KENTUCKY

NORTH CAROLINA

TENNESSEE

CANADA U.S.

Eagle Mt. + 2,301 ft 701 m

Mt. Arvon + 1,979 ft 603 m

Menominee

Green Bay

Door Pen.

Lake Winnebago

WISCONSIN

Wisconsin

Timms Hill + 1,951 ft 595 m

Rainy L.

Lake Winnibigoshish

Mille Lacs Lake

Mississippi

Charles Mound 1,235 ft 376 m

Rock

Fox

Illinois

ILLINOIS

IOWA

LOWLAND

CENTRAL

Mississippi

St. Francis

Taum Sauk Mt. 1,772 ft 540 m +

Ozark Plateau

Lake of the Ozarks

Osage

Table Rock Lake

Upper Red Lake

Lower Red Lake

Leech Lake

MINNESOTA

Minnesota

Cedar

Iowa

Des Moines

Missouri

MISSOURI

Harry S. Truman Reservoir

Neosho

ARKANSAS

Lake of the Woods

CANADA U.S.

MANITOBA

SASKATCHEWAN

Red River of the North

Big Sioux

Hawkeye Point 1,670 ft 509 m

Little Sioux

Missouri

Kansas

Flint Hills

OKLAHOMA

Souris

Lake Sakakawea

NORTH DAKOTA

James

Cheyenne

SOUTH DAKOTA

L. Sharpe

Lake Oahe

Lake Francis Case

White

Niobrara

NEBRASKA

Platte

Republican

Smoky Hills

Smoky Hill

KANSAS

Arkansas

Red Hills

GREAT

Little Missouri

Badlands

White Butte + 3,506 ft 1,069 m

Harney Peak + 7,242 ft 2,207 m

Black Hills

Panorama Point 5,423 ft 1,653 m

North Platte

Sand Hills

South Platte

Mt. Sunflower 4,039 ft 1,231 m

Cimarron

P L A I N S

Missouri

MONTANA

WYOMING

COLORADO

NEW MEXICO

TEXAS

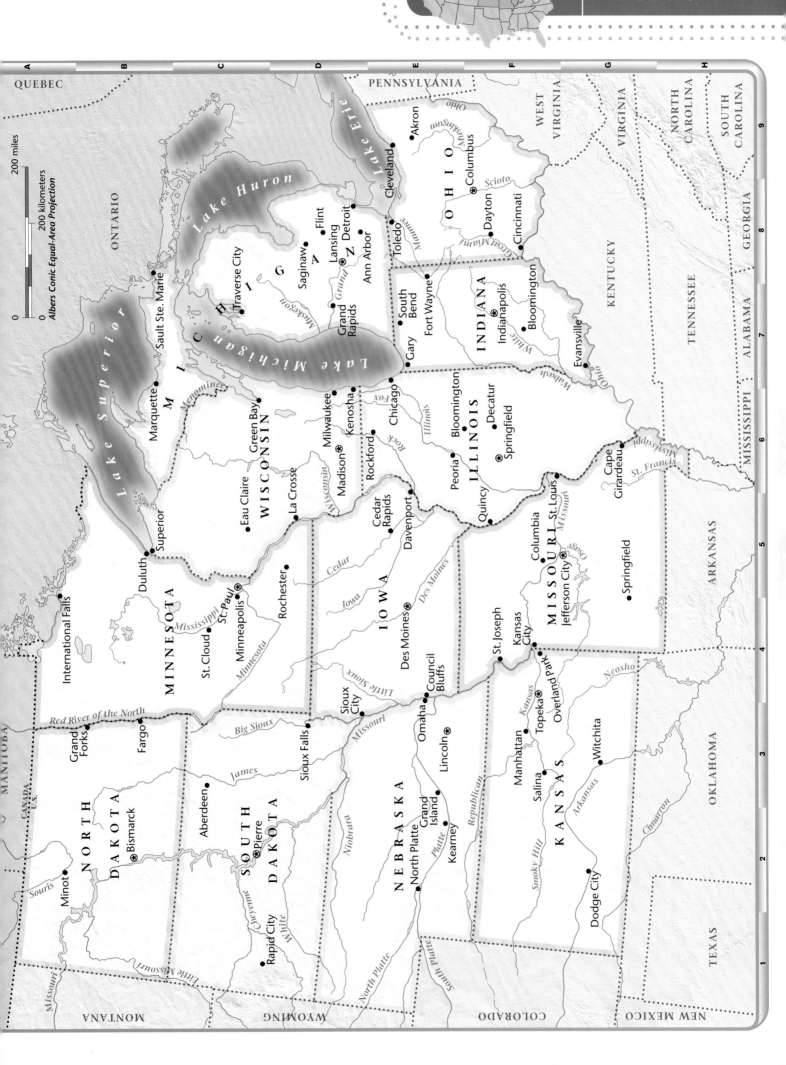

⇨ FIERCE GIANT. Students in Chicago's Field Museum eye the skeleton of *Tyrannosaurus rex*, a dinosaur that roamed North America's plains 65 million years ago.

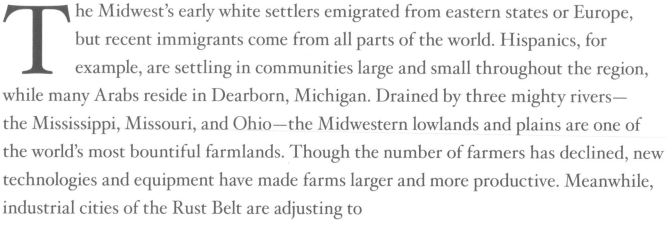

The Midwest
GREAT LAKES, GREAT RIVERS

The Midwest's early white settlers emigrated from eastern states or Europe, but recent immigrants come from all parts of the world. Hispanics, for example, are settling in communities large and small throughout the region, while many Arabs reside in Dearborn, Michigan. Drained by three mighty rivers—the Mississippi, Missouri, and Ohio—the Midwestern lowlands and plains are one of the world's most bountiful farmlands. Though the number of farmers has declined, new technologies and equipment have made farms larger and more productive. Meanwhile, industrial cities of the Rust Belt are adjusting to an economy focused more on information and services than on manufacturing.

⇩ CROP CIRCLES. Much of the western part of the region receives less than 20 inches (50 cm) of rain yearly—not enough to support agriculture. Large, circular center-pivot irrigation systems draw water from underground reserves called aquifers to provide life-giving water to crops.

⇩ DAIRY HEARTLAND. Dairy cows, such as these in Wisconsin, are sometimes treated with growth hormones to increase milk production. These animals play an important role in the economy of the Midwest, which supplies much of the country's milk, butter, and cheese.

⬇ MIDWEST URBAN HUB. Chicago, the third largest urban area in the U.S., with almost 10 million people, is the economic and cultural core of the Midwest and a major transportation hub.

⇨ PRESERVING THE PAST. A young Cherokee man, dressed in beaded costume and feathered headband, dances at a powwow in Milwaukee. Such gatherings provide Indians from across the country with a chance to share their traditions.

⬆ NATURE'S MOST VIOLENT STORMS. Parts of the midwestern U.S. have earned the nickname Tornado Alley because these destructive, swirling storms, which develop in association with thunderstorms along eastward-moving cold fronts, occur here more than any other place on Earth.

WHERE THE PICTURES ARE

- Ice house p. 101
- Great Lakes shipping p. 100
- Girls swinging p. 100
- Crop-duster & sunflowers p. 107
- Wild mustang p. 106
- Prairie dog p. 106
- Crazy Horse Memorial p. 111
- Chimney Rock p. 105
- Corn Palace p. 110
- Sandhill crane p. 104
- Cowboys p. 97
- Rodeo p. 104
- Center-pivot irrigation pp. 88-89
- Stormy sky p. 96
- Cyclists and farm p. 95
- Pig p. 94
- Stetson hats p. 102
- Tornado p. 89
- St. Louis skyline pp. 102-103
- Bison p. 103
- Wolf p. 99
- Indian boys p. 94
- Farm scene p. 112
- Cows p. 88
- Cow p. 112
- Indian dancer p. 89, Milwaukee skyline pp. 112-113
- Lakeside town p. 98
- Car assembly line p. 98
- Rock and Roll Hall of Fame p. 108
- Amish horse & buggy p. 108
- Cincinnati skyline p. 108
- Corn harvest pp. 92-93
- Race cars p. 92
- Dinosaur skeleton p. 88, Chicago skyline pp. 88-89, Wrigley Field p. 90
- Lincoln's tomb p. 90
- John Deere tractor pp. 90-91

THE LAND OF LINCOLN STATE:
ILLINOIS

ILLINOIS

THE BASICS

STATS

Area
57,914 sq mi (149,998 sq km)

Population
12,830,632

Capital
Springfield
Population 116,250

Largest city
Chicago
Population 2,695,598

Ethnic/racial groups
71.5% white; 14.5% African American;
4.6% Asian; .3% Native American.
Hispanic (any race) 15.8%.

Industry
Industrial machinery, electronic
equipment, food processing, chemicals,
metals, printing and publishing, rubber
and plastics, motor vehicles

Agriculture
Corn, soybeans, hogs, cattle, dairy
products, nursery stock

Statehood
December 3, 1818; 21st state

GEO WHIZ

A giant fossilized rain forest has
been unearthed in an eastern
Illinois coal mine near the town
of Danville. Scientists believe an
earthquake buried the entire forest
300 million years ago.

The Great Chicago fire of 1871
destroyed the city's
waterworks, so fire-
men had to drag
water in buckets from
Lake Michigan and the
Chicago River. The fire
burned out of control for two
days until rain finally put it out.

CARDINAL
VIOLET

ILLINOIS

Two rivers that now form the borders of
Illinois aided the state's early white settlement.
Frenchmen first explored the area in 1673 by traveling down the Mississippi, and the Ohio brought
many 19th-century settlers to southern Illinois.
Most Indians were forced out by the 1830s, more
than a decade after Illinois became the 21st state.
Ethnically diverse Chicago, the most populous
city in the Midwest, is an economic giant and
one of the country's busiest rail, highway, and air
transit hubs. Barges from its port reach the Gulf
of Mexico via rivers and canals, while ships reach
the Atlantic Ocean via the Great Lakes and St.
Lawrence Seaway. Flat terrain and fertile prairie
soils in the northern and central regions help make the state a top producer
of corn and soybeans. The more rugged, forested south has deposits of
bituminous coal. Springfield, capital
of the Land of Lincoln,
welcomes tourists visiting
the home and tomb of the
country's 16th president.

⇧ REMEMBERING A PRESIDENT.
Dedicated in 1874, the National
Lincoln Monument in Springfield
honors Abraham Lincoln, who was
assassinated in 1865. A special
vault holds the remains of the
slain president, who led the
country during the Civil War.

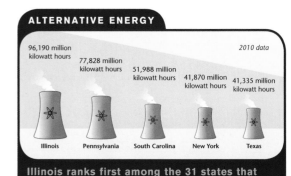

ALTERNATIVE ENERGY

2010 data

96,190 million
kilowatt hours

77,828 million
kilowatt hours

51,988 million
kilowatt hours

41,870 million
kilowatt hours

41,335 million
kilowatt hours

Illinois   Pennsylvania   South Carolina   New York   Texas

Illinois ranks first among the 31 states that
produce nuclear power. The state has 6
nuclear power plants with 11 reactors.

⇧ PLAY BALL! Wrigley Field, home to the Chicago Cubs baseball
team, is affected by wind conditions more than any other major
league park due to its location near Lake Michigan.

⇧ FIELDS OF GRAIN. Illinois has long been a major grain
producer, but farming today is highly mechanized. Above,
a tractor moves bales of rolled hay.

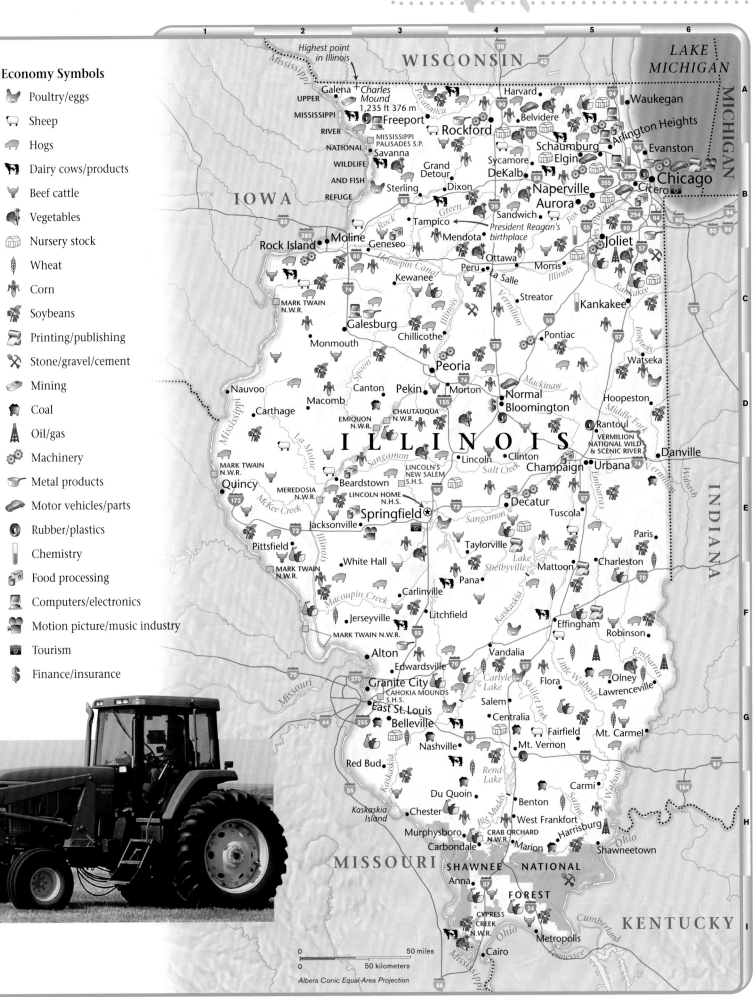

Economy Symbols

- Poultry/eggs
- Sheep
- Hogs
- Dairy cows/products
- Beef cattle
- Vegetables
- Nursery stock
- Wheat
- Corn
- Soybeans
- Printing/publishing
- Stone/gravel/cement
- Mining
- Coal
- Oil/gas
- Machinery
- Metal products
- Motor vehicles/parts
- Rubber/plastics
- Chemistry
- Food processing
- Computers/electronics
- Motion picture/music industry
- Tourism
- Finance/insurance

WISCONSIN

LAKE MICHIGAN

IOWA

MICHIGAN

INDIANA

MISSOURI

KENTUCKY

ILLINOIS

Highest point in Illinois

UPPER MISSISSIPPI RIVER NATIONAL WILDLIFE AND FISH REFUGE

Galena
Charles Mound 1,235 ft 376 m
Freeport
Harvard
Waukegan
Belvidere
Rockford
Schaumburg
Arlington Heights
Savanna
Sycamore
Elgin
Evanston
MISSISSIPPI PALISADES S.P.
Grand Detour
DeKalb
Naperville
Chicago
Sterling
Dixon
Aurora
Cicero
Sandwich
Rock Island
Moline
Geneseo
Mendota
Tampico
Joliet
Kewanee
Ottawa
Morris
Peru
La Salle
Streator
Galesburg
Chillicothe
Kankakee
Monmouth
Pontiac
Watseka
Peoria
Canton
Pekin
Morton
Normal
Hoopeston
Nauvoo
Macomb
Bloomington
Rantoul
Carthage
EMIQUON N.W.R.
CHAUTAUQUA N.W.R.
VERMILION NATIONAL WILD & SCENIC RIVER
Danville
MARK TWAIN N.W.R.
Lincoln
Clinton
Champaign
Urbana
Beardstown
LINCOLN'S NEW SALEM S.H.S.
Quincy
MEREDOSIA N.W.R.
LINCOLN HOME N.H.S.
Decatur
Tuscola
Springfield
Jacksonville
Taylorville
Paris
Pittsfield
Charleston
White Hall
Pana
Mattoon
MARK TWAIN N.W.R.
Carlinville
Jerseyville
Litchfield
Effingham
Robinson
MARK TWAIN N.W.R.
Alton
Vandalia
Edwardsville
Flora
Olney
Granite City
CAHOKIA MOUNDS S.H.S.
Lawrenceville
East St. Louis
Salem
Centralia
Fairfield
Mt. Carmel
Belleville
Nashville
Mt. Vernon
Red Bud
Carmi
Du Quoin
Benton
West Frankfort
Chester
Harrisburg
Kaskaskia Island
Murphysboro
CRAB ORCHARD N.W.R.
Marion
Shawneetown
Carbondale
SHAWNEE NATIONAL FOREST
Anna
CYPRESS CREEK N.W.R.
Metropolis
Cairo

Mississippi
Pecatonica
Rock
Green
Fox
Des Plaines
Illinois
Kankakee
Iroquois
Spoon
Sangamon
Salt Creek
Mackinaw
Middle Fork
Embarras
Vermilion
Wabash
La Moine
McKee Creek
Macoupin Creek
Kaskaskia
Lake Shelbyville
Little Wabash
Skillet Fork
Carlyle Lake
Rend Lake
Big Muddy
Saline
Ohio
Cumberland
Tennessee
Hennepin Canal

President Reagan's birthplace

0   50 miles
0   50 kilometers
Albers Conic Equal-Area Projection

THE HOOSIER STATE:
INDIANA

THE BASICS

STATS

Area
36,418 sq mi (94,322 sq km)

Population
6,483,802

Capital
Indianapolis
Population 820,445

Largest city
Indianapolis
Population 820,445

Ethnic/racial groups
84.3% white; 9.1% African American;
1.6% Asian; .3% Native American.
Hispanic (any race) 6.0%.

Industry
Transportation equipment, steel,
pharmaceutical and chemical products,
machinery, petroleum, coal

Agriculture
Corn, soybeans, hogs, poultry and eggs,
cattle, dairy products

Statehood
December 11, 1816; 19th state

GEO WHIZ

Every July during Circus Festival,
in Peru, a couple hundred local
kids and a couple thousand
volunteers put on a three-ring
circus complete with clowns, snow
cones, and standing ovations from
sellout crowds. The city is home to the
International Circus Hall of Fame.

Every year Fort Wayne hosts the
Johnny Appleseed Festival to honor
John Chapman, the man who planted
apple orchards from Pennsylvania
to Illinois.

The Indianapolis Children's
Museum, in partner-
ship with National
Geographic and
the Environmental
Research Systems
Institute, has created
an international traveling
exhibit to teach children
and parents that maps are
tools of adventure.

CARDINAL
PEONY

INDIANA

Indiana's name, meaning "Land of the Indians," honors the tribes who lived in the region before the arrival of Europeans. The first permanent white settlement was Vincennes, established by the French in the early 1700s. Following statehood in 1816, most Indians were forced out to make way for white settlement. Lake Michigan, in the state's northwest corner, brings economic and recreational opportunities. The lakefront city of Gary anchors a major industrial region. Nearby, the natural beauty and shifting sands of the Indiana Dunes National Lakeshore attract many visitors. Corn, soybeans, and hogs are the most important products from Indiana's many farms. True to the state motto, "The Crossroads of America," highways from all directions converge at Indianapolis. Traveling at a much higher speed are cars on that city's famed Motor Speedway, home to the Indy 500 auto race since 1911. Cheering for a favorite high school or college team is a favorite pastime for many Hoosiers who catch basketball fever.

⇧ START YOUR ENGINES. The Indianapolis Motor Speedway seats 250,000 sports fans. Nicknamed the Brickyard, its track was once paved with 3.2 million bricks.

⇨ FUEL FARMING. Indiana farming is undergoing dramatic changes as corn is used in the production of ethanol, a non-fossil fuel energy source that is increasingly popular.

HEAVY INDUSTRY

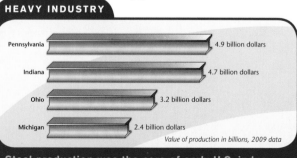

Pennsylvania	4.9 billion dollars
Indiana	4.7 billion dollars
Ohio	3.2 billion dollars
Michigan	2.4 billion dollars

Value of production in billions, 2009 data

Steel production was the core of early U.S. industrialization. Pennsylvania and Indiana lead in steel
production, but the U.S. also imports much of the
steel it uses.

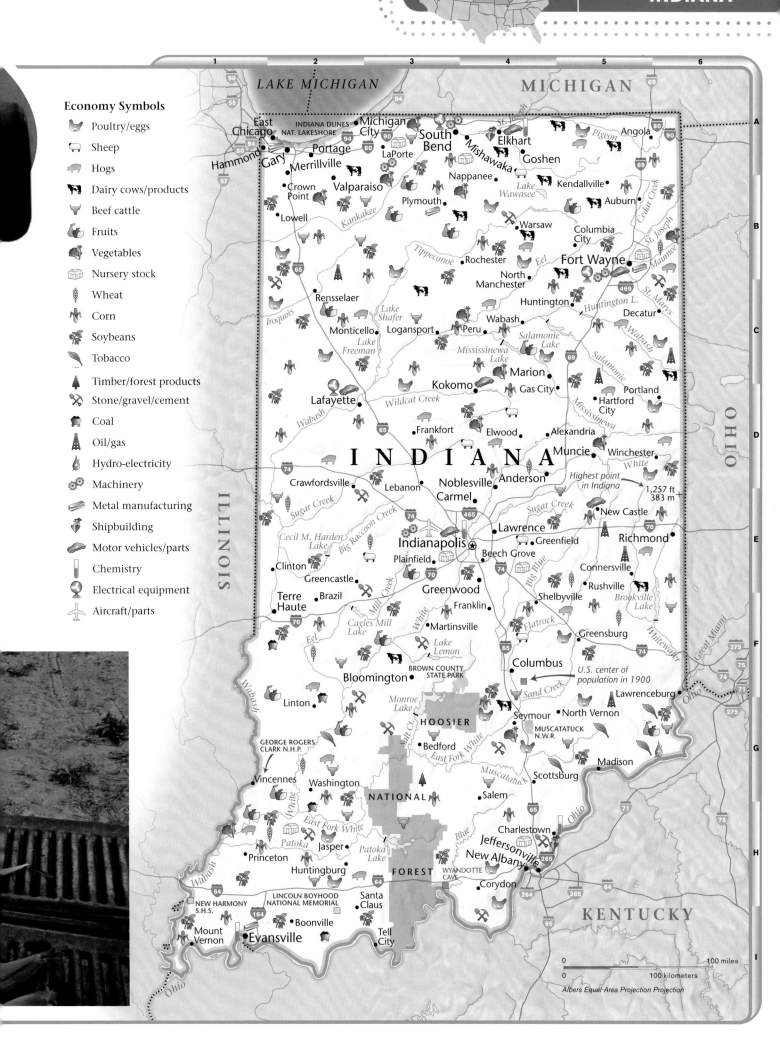

Economy Symbols

- Poultry/eggs
- Sheep
- Hogs
- Dairy cows/products
- Beef cattle
- Fruits
- Vegetables
- Nursery stock
- Wheat
- Corn
- Soybeans
- Tobacco
- Timber/forest products
- Stone/gravel/cement
- Coal
- Oil/gas
- Hydro-electricity
- Machinery
- Metal manufacturing
- Shipbuilding
- Motor vehicles/parts
- Chemistry
- Electrical equipment
- Aircraft/parts

LAKE MICHIGAN

MICHIGAN

ILLINOIS

OHIO

KENTUCKY

East Chicago
INDIANA DUNES NAT. LAKESHORE
Michigan City
South Bend
Elkhart
Angola
Hammond
Gary
Portage
LaPorte
Mishawaka
Goshen
Merrillville
Nappanee
Kendallville
Crown Point
Valparaiso
Plymouth
Lake Wawasee
Auburn
Lowell
Warsaw
Columbia City
Kankakee
Rochester
North Manchester
Fort Wayne
Rensselaer
Tippecanoe
Huntington
Decatur
Wabash
Huntington L.
Monticello
Logansport
Peru
Salamonie Lake
Lake Shafer
Lake Freeman
Mississinewa Lake
Marion
Gas City
Portland
Lafayette
Kokomo
Hartford City
Wildcat Creek
Wabash
Frankfort
Elwood
Alexandria
Muncie
Winchester
White
INDIANA
Crawfordsville
Lebanon
Noblesville
Anderson
Highest point in Indiana
1,257 ft 383 m
Carmel
Sugar Creek
New Castle
Sugar Creek
Cecil M. Harden Lake
Big Raccoon Creek
Lawrence
Richmond
Clinton
Indianapolis
Greenfield
Greencastle
Plainfield
Beech Grove
Connersville
Terre Haute
Brazil
Greenwood
Shelbyville
Rushville
Brookville Lake
Mill Creek
Franklin
Eel
Cagles Mill Lake
Martinsville
Flatrock
Greensburg
Whitewater
White
Lake Lemon
Columbus
U.S. center of population in 1900
Lawrenceburg
Bloomington
BROWN COUNTY STATE PARK
Sand Creek
Wabash
Linton
Monroe Lake
Seymour
North Vernon
HOOSIER
MUSCATATUCK N.W.R.
GEORGE ROGERS CLARK N.H.P.
Bedford
Salt Cr.
East Fork White
Madison
Vincennes
Washington
NATIONAL
Salem
Scottsburg
Muscatatuck
White
East Fork White
Blue
Charlestown
Patoka
Jasper
Patoka Lake
FOREST
Jeffersonville
New Albany
Princeton
Huntingburg
WYANDOTTE CAVE
Corydon
Wabash
NEW HARMONY S.H.S.
LINCOLN BOYHOOD NATIONAL MEMORIAL
Santa Claus
KENTUCKY
Mount Vernon
Boonville
Tell City
Evansville
Ohio

0   100 miles
0   100 kilometers
Albers Equal-Area Projection Projection

THE HAWKEYE STATE:
IOWA

IOWA

IOWA

Iowa's prehistoric inhabitants built earthen mounds—some shaped like birds and bears—that are visible in the state's northeast. Nineteenth-century white settlers found rolling prairies covered by a sea of tall grasses that soon yielded to the plow. A decade after statehood in 1846, a group of religious German immigrants established the Amana Colonies, a communal society that still draws visitors. Blessed with ample precipitation and rich soils, Iowa is the heart of one of the world's most productive farming regions. The state is the country's top producer of corn, soybeans, hogs, and eggs. Food processing and manufacturing machinery are two of the biggest industries. Much of the grain crop feeds livestock destined to reach dinner plates in the U.S. and around the world. An increasing amount of corn is used to make ethanol, which is mixed with gasoline to fuel cars and trucks. Des Moines, the capital and largest city, is a center of insurance and publishing.

⇧ PIG BUSINESS. Hogs outnumber people more than six to one in Iowa. The state raises 30 percent of the nation's hogs, making it the leading producer.

THE BASICS

STATS

Area
56,272 sq mi (145,743 sq km)

Population
3,046,355

Capital
Des Moines
Population 203,433

Largest city
Des Moines
Population 203,433

Ethnic/racial groups
91.3% white; 2.9% African American; 1.7% Asian; .4% Native American. Hispanic (any race) 5.0%.

Industry
Real estate, health services, industrial machinery, food processing, construction

Agriculture
Hogs, corn, soybeans, oats, cattle, dairy products

Statehood
December 28, 1846; 29th state

GEO WHIZ

The most famous house in Iowa and one of the most famous houses in America is in Eldon. It was immortalized in Grant Wood's famous painting "American Gothic." The stern-faced, pitchfork-holding farmer and his wife shown in the art were not farmers at all. Wood's sister and his dentist posed for the painting.

Effigy Mounds National Monument, in the northeast corner of Iowa, is the only place in the country with such a large collection of mounds in the shapes of mammals, birds, and reptiles. Of the 191 mounds, 29 are shaped like animals. Eastern Woodland Indians built these mounds from about 500 B.C. to 1300 A.D.

Iowa ranks number 7 among leading U.S. wind energy producers, which are led by Texas and Kansas.

AMERICAN GOLDFINCH

WILD ROSE

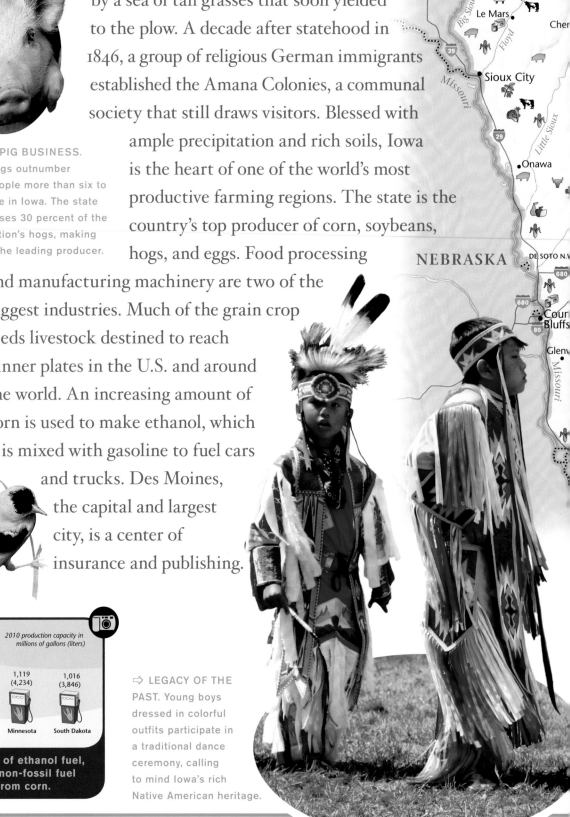

SOUTH DAKOTA

Hawkeye Poi
1,670
509

Highest point in Iowa

Sioux Center

Sh

Orange City

Big Sioux

Le Mars

Floyd

Cher

Missouri

Sioux City

Little Sioux

Onawa

NEBRASKA

DE SOTO N.V

680

680

Cour Bluffs

Glenv

Missouri

⇨ LEGACY OF THE PAST. Young boys dressed in colorful outfits participate in a traditional dance ceremony, calling to mind Iowa's rich Native American heritage.

GREEN ENERGY

2010 production capacity in millions of gallons (liters)

Iowa	Nebraska	Illinois	Minnesota	South Dakota
3,595 (13,609)	1,839 (6,961)	1,480 (5,602)	1,119 (4,234)	1,016 (3,846)

Iowa is the leading producer of ethanol fuel, a clean-burning, renewable, non-fossil fuel energy source made mainly from corn.

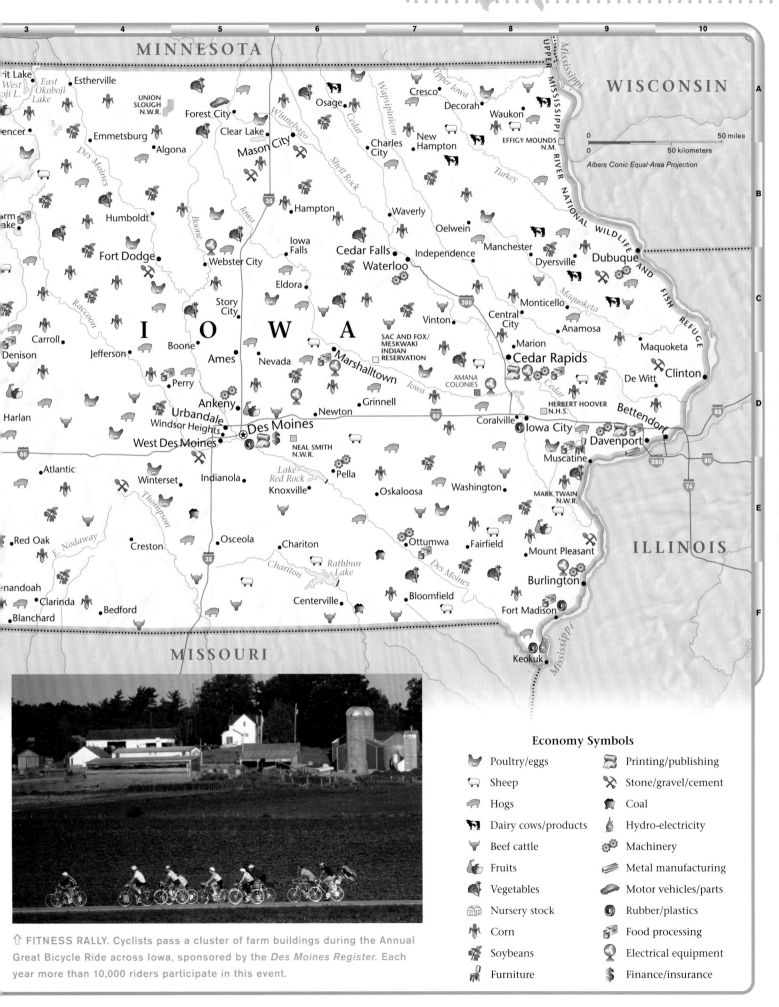

MINNESOTA

WISCONSIN

ILLINOIS

MISSOURI

0   50 miles
0   50 kilometers
Albers Conic Equal-Area Projection

Spirit Lake
West
Okoboji L.
East
Okoboji Lake
Estherville
Spencer
Storm Lake
Snake L.
Emmetsburg
Algona
Forest City
Clear Lake
Mason City
UNION SLOUGH N.W.R.
Cresco
Osage
Decorah
Waukon
New Hampton
Charles City
Waverly
EFFIGY MOUNDS N.M.
Humboldt
Hampton
Fort Dodge
Iowa Falls
Webster City
Oelwein
Manchester
Dubuque
Eldora
Cedar Falls
Waterloo
Independence
Dyersville
Story City
Vinton
Monticello
Central City
Anamosa
Carroll
Boone
Nevada
Marshalltown
Marion
Maquoketa
Denison
Jefferson
Ames
SAC AND FOX/ MESKWAKI INDIAN RESERVATION
Cedar Rapids
De Witt
Clinton
Perry
Grinnell
AMANA COLONIES
Harlan
Ankeny
Urbandale
Windsor Heights
Newton
HERBERT HOOVER N.H.S.
Bettendorf
West Des Moines
Des Moines
NEAL SMITH N.W.R.
Coralville
Iowa City
Davenport
Atlantic
Winterset
Indianola
Muscatine
Red Oak
Creston
Osceola
Knoxville
Pella
Oskaloosa
Washington
MARK TWAIN N.W.R.
Shenandoah
Clarinda
Blanchard
Bedford
Chariton
Lake Red Rock
Rathbun Lake
Ottumwa
Fairfield
Mount Pleasant
Centerville
Bloomfield
Burlington
Fort Madison
Keokuk

Des Moines *Boone* *Raccoon* *Iowa* *Shell Rock* *Cedar* *Winnebago* *Wapsipinicon* *Upper Iowa* *Turkey* *Maquoketa* *Mississippi RIVER NATIONAL WILDLIFE AND FISH REFUGE* *Thompson* *E. Nodaway* *Chariton* *Des Moines*

⬆ **FITNESS RALLY.** Cyclists pass a cluster of farm buildings during the Annual Great Bicycle Ride across Iowa, sponsored by the *Des Moines Register*. Each year more than 10,000 riders participate in this event.

Economy Symbols

Poultry/eggs		Printing/publishing	
Sheep		Stone/gravel/cement	
Hogs		Coal	
Dairy cows/products		Hydro-electricity	
Beef cattle		Machinery	
Fruits		Metal manufacturing	
Vegetables		Motor vehicles/parts	
Nursery stock		Rubber/plastics	
Corn		Food processing	
Soybeans		Electrical equipment	
Furniture		Finance/insurance	

KANSAS

THE BASICS

STATS

Area
82,277 sq mi (213,097 sq km)

Population
2,853,118

Capital
Topeka
Population 127,473

Largest city
Wichita
Population 382,368

Ethnic/racial groups
83.8% white; 5.9% African American; 4.8% Asian; 1.0% Native American. Hispanic (any race) 10.5%.

Industry
Aircraft manufacturing, transportation equipment, construction, food processing, printing and publishing, health care

Agriculture
Cattle, wheat, sorghum, soybeans, hogs, corn

Statehood
January 29, 1861; 34th state

GEO WHIZ

Plesiosaur skeletons and many other marine reptile fossils have been unearthed in Kansas. In 2007 National Geographic released the IMAX film *Sea Monsters,* which explores the kinds of animals that lived in the prehistoric sea that covered Kansas and much of North America 82 million years ago.

The Tallgrass Prairie National Preserve, the nation's last great expanse of tallgrass prairie, anchors a world renewed by fire. It is in the Flint Hills of Kansas.

Lindsborg is proud of its Swedish heritage and the fact that it is home to the Anatoly Karpov International School of Chess. The school is named for the Russian player who succeeded American Bobby Fischer as world champion in 1975.

WESTERN MEADOWLARK

SUNFLOWER

KANSAS

Considered by whites to be unsuitable for settlement, Kansas was made part of Indian Territory—a vast tract of land between Missouri and the Rockies—in the 1830s. By the 1850s whites were fighting Indians for more land and among themselves over the issue of slavery. In 1861 Kansas entered the Union as a free state. After the Civil War, cowboys drove Texas cattle to railheads in the Wild West towns of Abilene and Dodge City, where waiting trains hauled cattle to slaughterhouses in the East. Today, the state remains a major beef producer and the country's top wheat grower. Oil and natural gas wells dot the landscape, while factories in Wichita, the largest city, make aircraft equipment. A preserve in the Flint Hills boasts one of the few tallgrass prairies to escape farmers' plows. Heading west toward the Rockies, elevations climb slowly, and the climate gets drier. Threats of fierce thunderstorms accompanied by tornados have many Kansans keeping an eye on the sky.

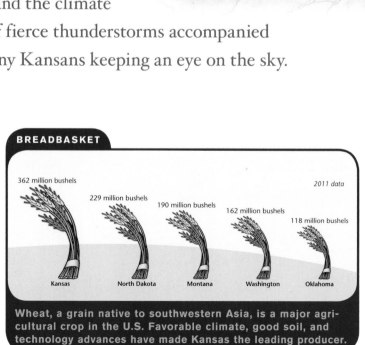

⇧ **OMINOUS SKY.** Lightning splits the sky as black clouds of a thunderstorm roll across a field of wheat. Such storms bring heavy rain and often spawn dangerous tornadoes.

BREADBASKET

362 million bushels

229 million bushels

190 million bushels

162 million bushels

118 million bushels

2011 data

Kansas | North Dakota | Montana | Washington | Oklahoma

Wheat, a grain native to southwestern Asia, is a major agricultural crop in the U.S. Favorable climate, good soil, and technology advances have made Kansas the leading producer.

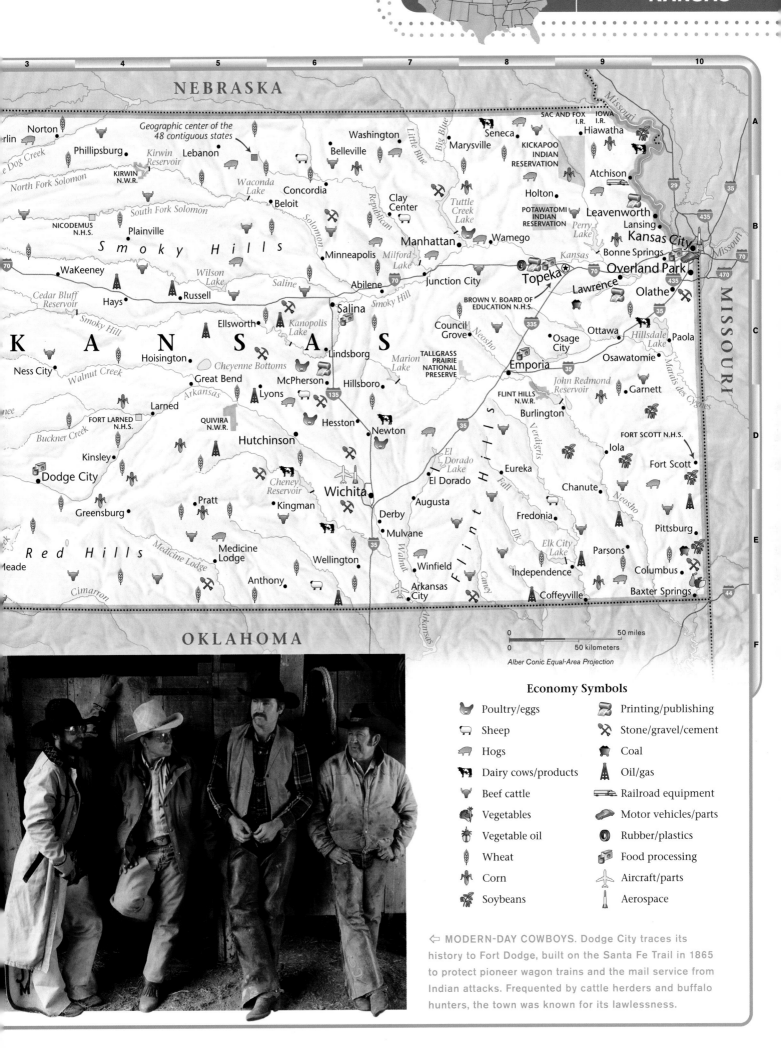

NEBRASKA

3   4   5   6   7   8   9   10

Norton
rlin
Phillipsburg
e Dog Creek
Kirwin Reservoir
Lebanon
Geographic center of the 48 contiguous states
Washington
Belleville
Seneca
Marysville
SAC AND FOX I.R.
IOWA I.R.
Hiawatha
KICKAPOO INDIAN RESERVATION
KIRWIN N.W.R.
North Fork Solomon
Waconda Lake
Concordia
Atchison
Beloit
Holton
NICODEMUS N.H.S.
Plainville
South Fork Solomon
Clay Center
Tuttle Creek Lake
POTAWATOMI INDIAN RESERVATION
Leavenworth
Lansing
S m o k y   H i l l s
Minneapolis
Milford Lake
Manhattan
Wamego
Perry Lake
Kansas City
WaKeeney
Wilson Lake
Saline
Abilene
Junction City
Kansas
Topeka
Bonne Springs
Overland Park
Cedar Bluff Reservoir
Hays
Russell
Smoky Hill
BROWN V. BOARD OF EDUCATION N.H.S.
Lawrence
Olathe
Smoky Hill
K A N S A S
Ellsworth
Kanopolis Lake
Salina
Council Grove
Neosho
Osage City
Ottawa
Hillsdale Lake
Paola
Ness City
Hoisington
Lindsborg
Marion Lake
TALLGRASS PRAIRIE NATIONAL PRESERVE
Emporia
Osawatomie
Walnut Creek
Cheyenne Bottoms
Great Bend
McPherson
Hillsboro
John Redmond Reservoir
Garnett
Arkansas
Lyons
FLINT HILLS N.W.R.
FORT LARNED N.H.S.
Larned
Hesston
Newton
Burlington
FORT SCOTT N.H.S.
QUIVIRA N.W.R.
Hutchinson
El Dorado Lake
Iola
Fort Scott
Buckner Creek
Kinsley
Cheney Reservoir
Eureka
Chanute
Neosho
Dodge City
Wichita
El Dorado
Greensburg
Pratt
Augusta
Fredonia
Pittsburg
R e d   H i l l s
Kingman
Derby
Elk City Lake
Parsons
Meade
Medicine Lodge
Medicine Lodge
Mulvane
Independence
Columbus
Cimarron
Anthony
Wellington
Winfield
Coffeyville
Baxter Springs
Arkansas City

MISSOURI

OKLAHOMA

0 — 50 miles
0 — 50 kilometers
Alber Conic Equal-Area Projection

Economy Symbols

Poultry/eggs		Printing/publishing
Sheep		Stone/gravel/cement
Hogs		Coal
Dairy cows/products		Oil/gas
Beef cattle		Railroad equipment
Vegetables		Motor vehicles/parts
Vegetable oil		Rubber/plastics
Wheat		Food processing
Corn		Aircraft/parts
Soybeans		Aerospace

⇐ MODERN-DAY COWBOYS. Dodge City traces its history to Fort Dodge, built on the Santa Fe Trail in 1865 to protect pioneer wagon trains and the mail service from Indian attacks. Frequented by cattle herders and buffalo hunters, the town was known for its lawlessness.

THE GREAT LAKE STATE:
MICHIGAN

THE BASICS

STATS

Area
96,716 sq mi (250,495 sq km)

Population
9,883,640

Capital
Lansing
Population 114,297

Largest city
Detroit
Population 713,777

Ethnic/racial groups
78.9% white; 14.2% African American;
2.4% Asian; .6% Native American.
Hispanic (any race) 4.4%.

Industry
Motor vehicles and parts, machinery,
metal products, office furniture,
tourism, chemicals

Agriculture
Dairy products, cattle, vegetables,
hogs, corn, nursery stock, soybeans,
hay, fruit

Statehood
January 26, 1837; 26th state

GEO WHIZ

Researchers at the Seney National
Wildlife Refuge near Seney, Michigan,
have discovered that male loons change
the sound of their call when they move
to a new territory. The reason is still a
mystery, but it does explain why people
say that loons sound different on different lakes.

The Keweenaw Peninsula is an adven-
turer's paradise. There's a 100-mile
(161-km) water trail for canoers, scores
of wrecks for divers, 14 miles (23 km)
of forested bike paths, and more than
150 miles (240 km) of hiking trails on
nearby Isle Royale National Park.

Climate change is causing Lake
Michigan and the other Great
Lakes to shrink, a fact that is
very costly to shipping. For every
inch (2.5 cm) of draft that a ship
loses, a freighter must lighten
its cargo by as much as 270 tons
to keep from running aground. The
collective annual cost can be in the
billions of dollars.

ROBIN
APPLE BLOSSOM

MICHIGAN

Indians had friendly relations with early French fur traders who came to what is now Michigan, but they waged battles with the British who later assumed control. Completion of New York's Erie Canal in 1825 made it easier for settlers to reach the area, and statehood came in 1837. Michigan consists of two large peninsulas that border four of the five Great Lakes— Erie, Huron, Michigan, and Superior.

⇧ ROLLING OFF THE ASSEMBLY LINE. Motor vehicle production is one of the largest manu-facturing sectors in the U.S., and Michigan is the center of the industry. At Chrysler's Sterling Heights assembly plant, almost 800 robots speed production by making it possible to build different car models on the same assembly line.

Most of the population is on the state's Lower Peninsula, while the Upper Peninsula, once a productive mining area, now is popular among vacation-ing nature lovers. The five-mile-long Mackinac Bridge (8 km) has linked the peninsulas since 1957. In the 20th century, Michigan became the center of the American auto industry, and the state's fortunes have risen and fallen with those of the Big Three car companies. Though it remains a big producer of cars and trucks, the state is working to diversify its economy. Michigan's farms grow crops ranging from grains to fruits and vegetables.

WINTER SPORT

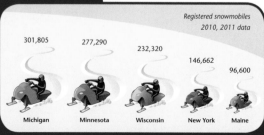

Registered snowmobiles
2010, 2011 data

301,805 — Michigan
277,290 — Minnesota
232,320 — Wisconsin
146,662 — New York
96,600 — Maine

Snowmobiling has become a popular winter sport.
Michigan and other states of the upper Midwest
lead in number of registered snowmobiles.

⇧ REFLECTION OF THE PAST. Victorian-style summer homes, built on Mackinac Island in the late 19th century by wealthy railroad families, now welcome vacationers to the island. To protect the environment, cars are not allowed.

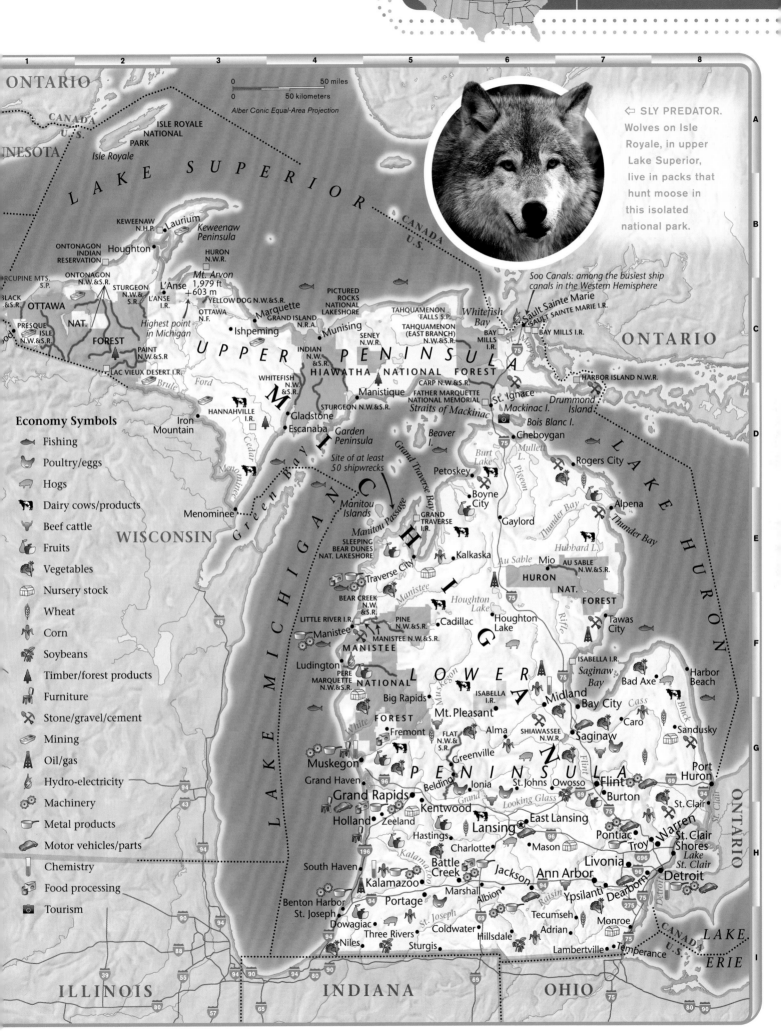

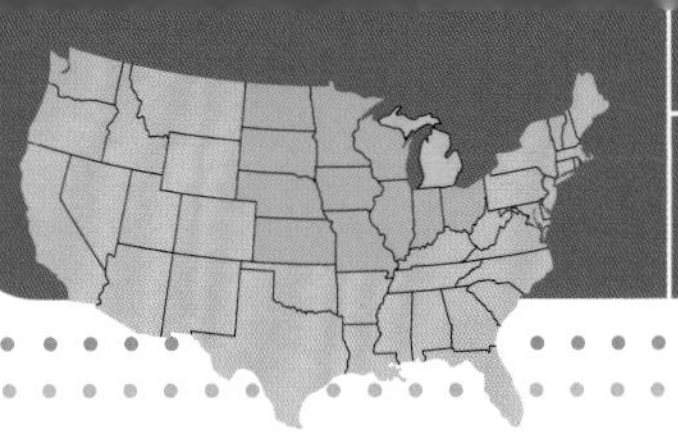

⇦ SLY PREDATOR.
Wolves on Isle
Royale, in upper
Lake Superior,
live in packs that
hunt moose in
this isolated
national park.

Soo Canals: among the busiest ship
canals in the Western Hemisphere

Economy Symbols

- ⟋ Fishing
- 🦃 Poultry/eggs
- 🐗 Hogs
- 🐄 Dairy cows/products
- 🐄 Beef cattle
- 🍎 Fruits
- 🥬 Vegetables
- 🪴 Nursery stock
- 🌾 Wheat
- 🌽 Corn
- 🌱 Soybeans
- 🌲 Timber/forest products
- 🪑 Furniture
- ✒ Stone/gravel/cement
- ⛏ Mining
- 🛢 Oil/gas
- 💧 Hydro-electricity
- ⚙ Machinery
- 🍳 Metal products
- �car Motor vehicles/parts
- 🧪 Chemistry
- 🥫 Food processing
- 📷 Tourism

ONTARIO

CANADA
U.S.

MINESOTA

Isle Royale

ISLE ROYALE
NATIONAL
PARK

LAKE SUPERIOR

KEWEENAW
N.H.P. · Laurium
Keweenaw
Peninsula

ONTONAGON
INDIAN
RESERVATION · Houghton
ONTONAGON
N.W.&S.R.

PORCUPINE MTS.
S.P.

L'Anse
L'ANSE
I.R.

BLACK
&S.R.

OTTAWA

HURON
N.W.R.

Mt. Arvon
1,979 ft
+603 m
Highest point
in Michigan

PRESQUE
ISLE
N.W.&S.R.

NAT.

FOREST

PAINT
N.W.&S.R.

LAC VIEUX DESERT I.R.

STURGEON
N.W.&
S.R.

Ford

Brule

YELLOW DOG N.W.&S.R.
OTTAWA
N.F.

Marquette
· Ishpeming

GRAND ISLAND
N.R.A.

PICTURED
ROCKS
NATIONAL
LAKESHORE

· Munising

SENEY
N.W.R.

TAHQUAMENON
FALLS S.P.

TAHQUAMENON
(EAST BRANCH)
S.P.

Whitefish
Bay

Sault Sainte Marie
SAULT SAINTE MARIE I.R.
St. Mary's

BAY
MILLS
I.R.

BAY MILLS I.R.

75

UPPER · PENINSULA

INDIAN
N.W.
&S.R.

HIAWATHA NATIONAL FOREST

ONTARIO

WHITEFISH
N.W.
&S.R.

HANNAHVILLE
I.R.

Iron
Mountain

Gladstone
Escanaba

STURGEON N.W.&S.R.

· Manistique

FATHER MARQUETTE
NATIONAL MEMORIAL
Straits of Mackinac

CARP N.W.&S.R.

St. Ignace

Mackinac I.

HARBOR ISLAND N.W.R.

Drummond
Island

Garden
Peninsula

Bois Blanc I.

· Cheboygan

Beaver
I.

Burt
Lake

Mullett
L.

75

LAKE HURON

WISCONSIN

Menominee

Green Bay

Cedar

Menominee

Site of at least
50 shipwrecks

Manitou
Islands

Manitou Passage

Grand Traverse Bay

Petoskey

· Boyne
City

Pigeon

Rogers City

Alpena

Thunder Bay

Thunder Bay

GRAND
TRAVERSE
I.R.

Gaylord

Hubbard L.

SLEEPING
BEAR DUNES
NAT. LAKESHORE

· Kalkaska

Au Sable

Mio

AU SABLE
N.W.&S.R.

HURON

NAT.

FOREST

Traverse City

BEAR CREEK
N.W.
&S.R.

LITTLE RIVER I.R.

PINE
N.W.&S.R.

Manistee

Houghton
Lake

· Cadillac

Houghton
Lake

Rifle

Tawas
City

MANISTEE

MANISTEE N.W.&S.R.

Ludington

PERE
MARQUETTE
N.W.&S.R.

NATIONAL

ISABELLA I.R.

Saginaw
Bay

Bad Axe

Harbor
Beach

LOWER

FOREST

Muskegon

White

Big Rapids

Mt. Pleasant

ISABELLA
I.R.

· Alma

Midland

Bay City

Cass

Caro

Sandusky

Fremont

FLAT
N.W.&
S.R.

SHIAWASSEE
N.W.R.

Saginaw

Black

Greenville

SHIAWASSEE N.W.R.

PENINSULA

Grand Haven

Beiding

Ionia

St. Johns

Owosso

Flint

Burton

Port
Huron

Grand Rapids

96

Kentwood

Grand

Looking Glass

East Lansing

69

St. Clair

ONTARIO

Holland

Zeeland

Hastings

Lansing ☆

Mason

Pontiac

Troy

Warren

St. Clair
Shores

Charlotte

Livonia

696

Lake
St. Clair

South Haven

196

Kalamazoo

Battle
Creek

Jackson

Ann Arbor

94

Dearborn

75

Detroit

Benton Harbor
St. Joseph

Portage

Marshall

Albion

Raisin

Ypsilanti

275

Dowagiac

Three Rivers

St. Joseph

Coldwater

Hillsdale

Tecumseh

Adrian

Monroe

LAKE

Niles

Sturgis

Lambertville

Temperance

ERIE

ILLINOIS

39

80

88

90

94

55

94

90

94

80

90

57

65

69

INDIANA

OHIO

75

94

THE GOPHER STATE:
MINNESOTA

MINNESOTA

MINNESOTA

THE BASICS

STATS

Area
86,939 sq mi (225,172 sq km)

Population
5,303,925

Capital
St. Paul
Population 285,068

Largest city
Minneapolis
Population 382,578

Ethnic/racial groups
85.3% white; 5.2% African American; 4.0% Asian; 1.1% Native American. Hispanic (any race) 4.7%.

Industry
Health services, tourism, real estate, banking and insurance, industrial machinery, printing and publishing, food processing, scientific equipment

Agriculture
Corn, soybeans, dairy products, hogs, cattle, turkeys, wheat

Statehood
May 11, 1858; 32nd state

GEO WHIZ

Nett Lake on the Bois Forte Chippewa reservation, in northern Minnesota, is the largest contiguous wild rice lake in the world. Native people have been gathering what the Indians call *manoomin* for thousands of years.

The Mayo Clinic, a world-famous medical research center founded in 1889 by Dr. William W. Mayo, is in Rochester.

The Boundary Waters Canoe Area Wilderness, along the Minnesota-Ontario border, was the first wilderness area in the U.S. to be set aside for canoeing.

COMMON LOON
SHOWY LADY'S SLIPPER

French fur traders began arriving in present-day Minnesota in the mid-17th century. Statehood was established in 1858, and most remaining Indians were forced from the state after a decisive battle in 1862. During the late 1800s large numbers of Germans, Scandinavians, and other immigrants settled a land rich in wildlife, timber, minerals, and fertile soils. Today, farming is concentrated in the south and west. In the northeast, the Mesabi Range's open-pit mines make the state the country's source of iron ore. Most of the ore is shipped from Duluth. It, along with Superior, in nearby Wisconsin (see p. 113), is the leading Great Lakes port. Ships from the port reach the Atlantic Ocean via the St. Lawrence Seaway. Scattered across the state's landscape are thousands of lakes—ancient footprints of retreating glaciers—that draw anglers and canoeists. One of those lakes, Lake Itasca, is the source of the mighty Mississippi River, which flows through the Twin Cities of Minneapolis and St. Paul.

⇧ SUMMER FUN. Young girls play on a rope swing near Leech Lake in northern Minnesota. The state's many lakes are remnants of the last ice age, when glaciers gouged depressions that filled with water as the ice sheets retreated.

SHOPPER'S PARADISE

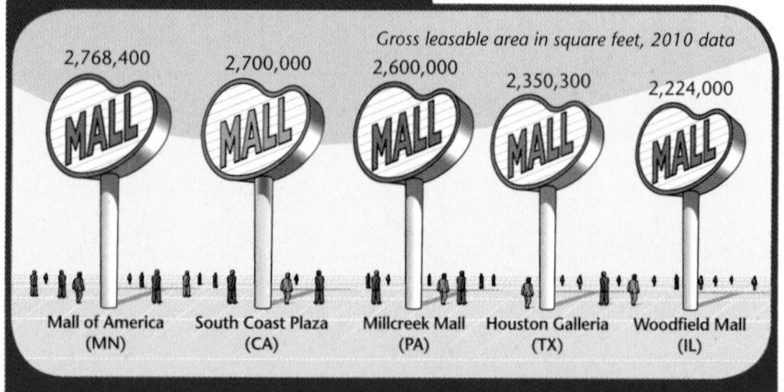
Gross leasable area in square feet, 2010 data
2,768,400
2,700,000
2,600,000
2,350,300
2,224,000
MALL
Mall of America (MN)
South Coast Plaza (CA)
Millcreek Mall (PA)
Houston Galleria (TX)
Woodfield Mall (IL)

Americans love to shop, and Bloomington's Mall of America includes more space for lease than any other mall in the country.

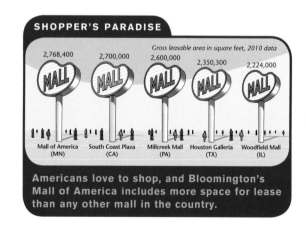

⇦ INLAND PORT. Duluth, on the northern shore of Lake Superior, is the westernmost deep-water port on the St. Lawrence Seaway. Barges and container ships move products such as iron ore and grain along the Great Lakes to the Atlantic Ocean and to markets around the world.

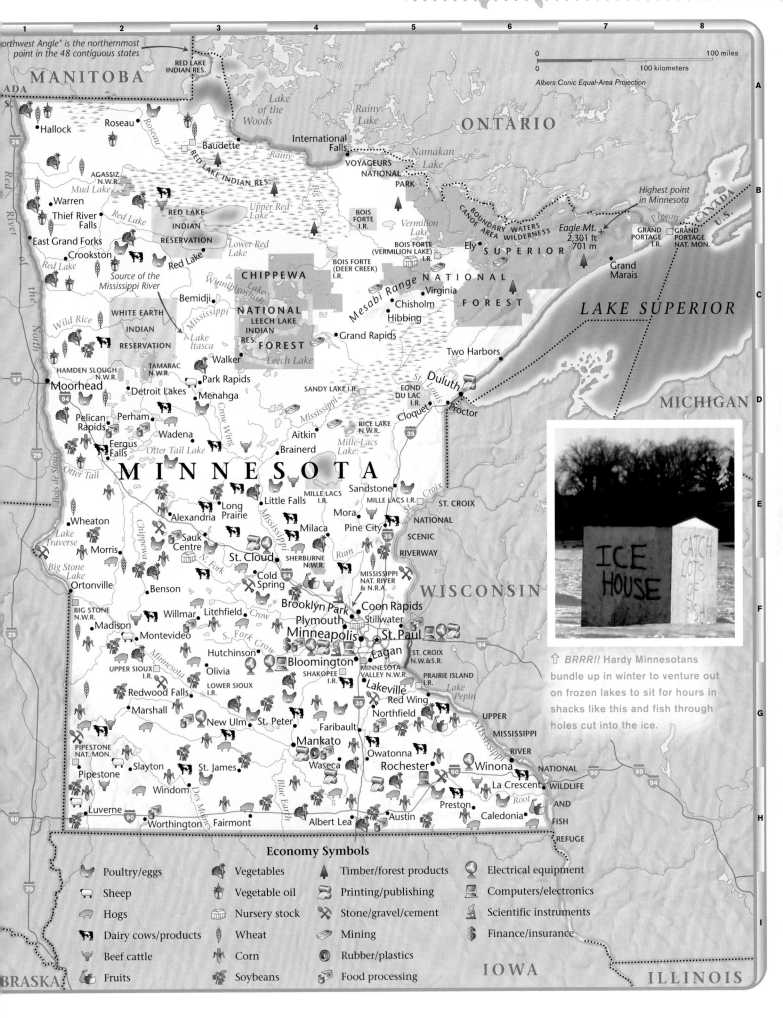

⇧ *BRRR!!* Hardy Minnesotans bundle up in winter to venture out on frozen lakes to sit for hours in shacks like this and fish through holes cut into the ice.

Economy Symbols

Poultry/eggs	Vegetables	Timber/forest products
Sheep	Vegetable oil	Printing/publishing
Hogs	Nursery stock	Stone/gravel/cement
Dairy cows/products	Wheat	Mining
Beef cattle	Corn	Rubber/plastics
Fruits	Soybeans	Food processing

Electrical equipment	
Computers/electronics	
Scientific instruments	
Finance/insurance	

THE SHOW-ME STATE:
MISSOURI

THE BASICS

STATS

Area
69,704 sq mi (180,534 sq mi)

Population
5,988,927

Capital
Jefferson City
Population 43,079

Largest city
Kansas City
Population 459,787

Ethnic/racial groups
82.8% white; 11.6% African American;
1.6% Asian; .5% Native American.
Hispanic (any race) 3.5%.

Industry
Transportation equipment, food
processing, chemicals, electrical
equipment, metal products

Agriculture
Cattle, soybeans, hogs, corn, poultry
and eggs, dairy products

Statehood
August 10, 1821; 24th state

GEO WHIZ

Camp Wood, near St. Louis,
was the starting point for Lew
is and Clark's Corps of Discovery,
commissioned by President
Thomas Jefferson to seek a water
route to the Pacific. Along the way
their encounters included hundreds
of new species of plants and animals,
nearly 50 Indian tribes, and the
Rocky Mountains.

In Ash Grove, near Springfield,
Father Moses Berry has turned his
family history into a museum for
slavery education. His family was
one of the few who didn't flee the
area after three falsely accused
black men were lynched in 1906.
The museum is the only one of
its kind in the Ozark region.

EASTERN BLUEBIRD
HAWTHORN

MISSOURI

The Osage people were among the
largest tribes in present-day Missouri
when the French began establishing
permanent settlements in the 1700s.
The U.S. obtained the territory in the 1803
Louisiana Purchase, and Lewis and Clark
began exploring the vast wilderness by
paddling up the Missouri River from the St.
Louis area. Missouri entered the Union as a
slave state in 1821. Though it remained in the Union during the Civil War,
sympathies were split between the North and South. For much
of the 1800s the state was the staging ground for pioneers
traveling to western frontiers on the Santa Fe and
Oregon Trails. Today, Missouri leads the country in
lead mining. Farmers raise cattle, hogs, poultry,
corn, and soybeans. Cotton and rice are grown
in the southeastern Bootheel region. Cross-
state river-port rivals St. Louis and Kansas
City are centers of transportation,
manufacturing, and finance. Lakes,
caves, scenic views, and Branson's
country music shows bring many
tourists to the Ozarks.

⇧ TALL HATS. Since its founding
in 1865 in St. Joseph, the Stetson
Company has been associated
with western hats worn by men
and women around the world.

HISTORICAL MARKERS

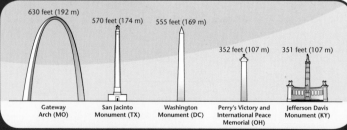

630 feet (192 m) — Gateway Arch (MO)
570 feet (174 m) — San Jacinto Monument (TX)
555 feet (169 m) — Washington Monument (DC)
352 feet (107 m) — Perry's Victory and International Peace Memorial (OH)
351 feet (107 m) — Jefferson Davis Monument (KY)

The tallest of all monuments in the U.S. is Gateway Arch
in St. Louis, which marks the departure point for westward-
bound pioneers during the 19th century.

⇨ HEADING WEST. The 630-foot (192-m) Gateway Arch honors
the role St. Louis played in U.S. westward expansion. Trams carry
one million tourists to the top of the arch each year.

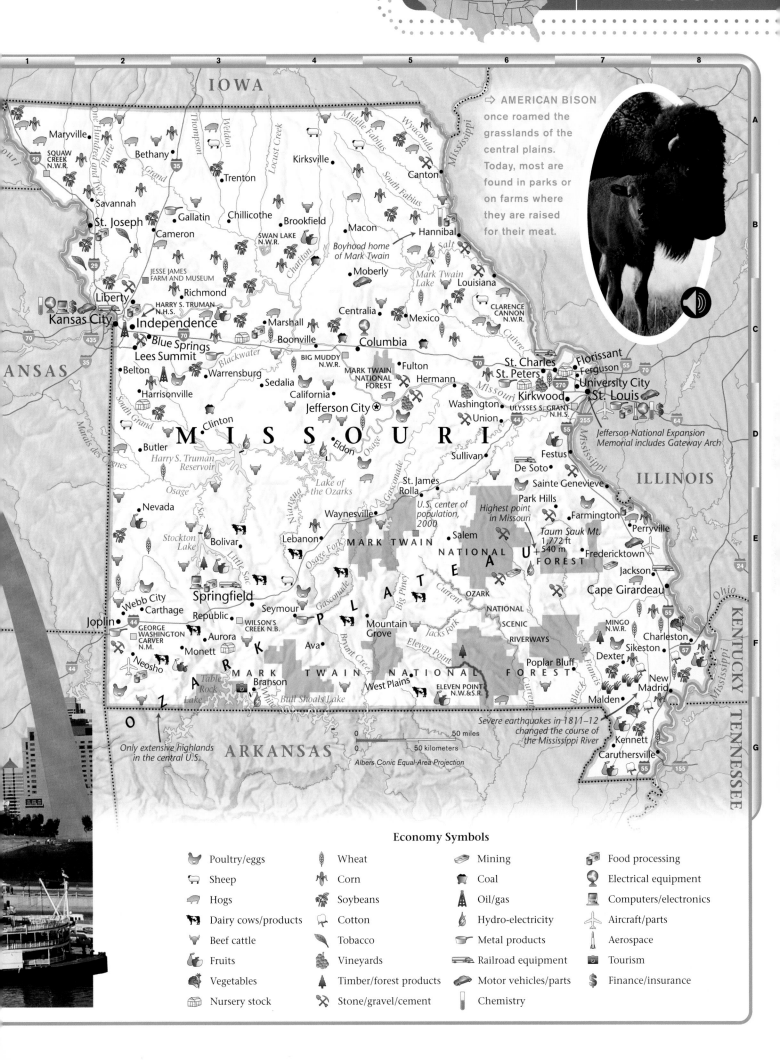

IOWA

1 2 3 4 5 6 7 8

→ AMERICAN BISON once roamed the grasslands of the central plains. Today, most are found in parks or on farms where they are raised for their meat.

Maryville
SQUAW CREEK N.W.R.
Bethany
Kirksville
Canton
Trenton
Savannah
Gallatin
Chillicothe
Brookfield
Macon
Hannibal
St. Joseph
Cameron
SWAN LAKE N.W.R.
Boyhood home of Mark Twain
Salt
Richmond
Moberly
Louisiana
JESSE JAMES FARM AND MUSEUM
Mark Twain Lake
CLARENCE CANNON N.W.R.
Liberty
HARRY S. TRUMAN N.H.S.
Centralia
Mexico
Kansas City
Independence
Marshall
Columbia
Blue Springs
Boonville
Lees Summit
BIG MUDDY N.W.R.
Fulton
St. Charles
Florissant
Ferguson
Belton
Warrensburg
MARK TWAIN NATIONAL FOREST
Hermann
St. Peters
University City
Harrisonville
Sedalia
Washington
Kirkwood
St. Louis
California
ULYSSES S. GRANT N.H.S.
Jefferson City ✪
Union
Clinton
Jefferson National Expansion Memorial includes Gateway Arch
Butler
Eldon
Sullivan
Festus
Harry S. Truman Reservoir
De Soto
Sainte Genevieve
ILLINOIS
Osage
Lake of the Ozarks
St. James
Rolla
Park Hills
Nevada
U.S. center of population, 2000
Highest point in Missouri
Farmington
Stockton Lake
Waynesville
Salem
Taum Sauk Mt. 1,772 ft +540 m
Perryville
Bolivar
Lebanon
MARK TWAIN
NATIONAL
PLATEAU
FOREST
Fredericktown
Webb City
Springfield
OZARK
Jackson
Joplin
Carthage
Seymour
NATIONAL
Cape Girardeau
GEORGE WASHINGTON CARVER N.M.
Republic
WILSON'S CREEK N.B.
Mountain Grove
SCENIC
MINGO N.W.R.
Aurora
Ava
RIVERWAYS
Charleston
Monett
Sikeston
Neosho
Dexter
Table Rock Lake
MARK TWAIN NATIONAL FOREST
Poplar Bluff
New Madrid
Branson
West Plains
ELEVEN POINT N.W.&S.R.
Malden
Bull Shoals Lake
Severe earthquakes in 1811–12 changed the course of the Mississippi River
Kennett
OZARK
Only extensive highlands in the central U.S.
Caruthersville

KANSAS

ARKANSAS

KENTUCKY

TENNESSEE

0 50 miles
0 50 kilometers
Albers Conic Equal-Area Projection

MISSOURI

Economy Symbols

Poultry/eggs	Wheat	Mining	Food processing
Sheep	Corn	Coal	Electrical equipment
Hogs	Soybeans	Oil/gas	Computers/electronics
Dairy cows/products	Cotton	Hydro-electricity	Aircraft/parts
Beef cattle	Tobacco	Metal products	Aerospace
Fruits	Vineyards	Railroad equipment	Tourism
Vegetables	Timber/forest products	Motor vehicles/parts	Finance/insurance
Nursery stock	Stone/gravel/cement	Chemistry	

THE CORNHUSKER STATE:
NEBRASKA

THE BASICS

STATS

Area
77,354 sq mi (200,346 sq km)

Population
1,826,341

Capital
Lincoln
Population 258,379

Largest city
Omaha
Population 408,958

Ethnic/racial groups
86.1% white; 4.5% African American; 1.8% Asian; 1.0% Native American. Hispanic (any race) 9.2%.

Industry
Food processing, machinery, electrical equipment, printing and publishing

Agriculture
Cattle, corn, hogs, soybeans, wheat, sorghum

Statehood
March 1, 1867; 37th state

GEO WHIZ

Many of Nebraska's early settlers were called sodbusters because they cut chunks of the grassy prairie (sod) to build their houses. These building blocks became known as "Nebraska marble."

Nebraska's state fossil is the mammoth. Fossils of these prehistoric elephants have been found in all 93 counties. The state estimates that as many as ten mammoths are buried beneath an average square mile of territory.

Boys Town, founded in 1917 as a home for troubled boys, has provided a haven for girls since 1979. They now make up about half the population of 500 kids in this village-style community near Omaha.

WESTERN MEADOWLARK
GOLDENROD

NEBRASKA

For thousands of westbound pioneers on the Oregon and California Trails, Scotts Bluff and Chimney Rock were unforgettable landmarks, towering above the North Platte River. Once reserved for Indians by the government, Nebraska was opened for white settlement in 1854. Following statehood in 1867, ranchers clashed with farmers in an unsuccessful bid to preserve open rangelands. Before white settlers arrived, Indians hunted bison and grew corn, pumpkins, beans, and squash. Today, farms and ranches cover nearly all of the state. Ranchers graze beef cattle on the grass-covered Sand Hills, while farmers grow corn, soybeans, and wheat elsewhere. The vast underground Ogallala Aquifer feeds center-pivot irrigation systems needed to water crops in areas that do not receive enough rain. Processing the state's farm products, especially meatpacking, is a big part of the economy. Omaha, which sits along the Missouri River, is a center of finance, insurance, and agribusiness. Lincoln, the state capital, has the only unicameral, or one-house, legislature in the United States.

⇧ TAKING FLIGHT. Migratory Sandhill cranes pass through Nebraska in late winter, stopping in the Platte River Valley to feed and rest.

⇩ RIDER DOWN. The Big Rodeo is an annual event in tiny Burwell (population 1,130) in Nebraska's Sand Hills. The town, sometimes called "the place where the Wild West meets the 21st century," has hosted the rodeo for more than 80 years.

Map:

1 2

OGLALA NATIONAL GRASSLAND
White
Chadron
Crawford
Pine Ridge
Rush
NEBRASK
NATIONAL FOREST

WYOMING

AGATE FOSSIL BEDS NAT. MON.

Fossils of extinct mammals tha here about 20 million years ag

NORTH PLATTE N.W.R.
Allian

Scottsbluff

SCOTTS BLUFF N.M.
Gering
CHIMNEY ROCK N.H.S.

Bridgeport

Pumpkin
Creek
North

Highest point in Nebraska

Kimball
Lodgepole Cr.
Sidney

Panorama Point
+5,423 ft, 1,653 m

COLORAD

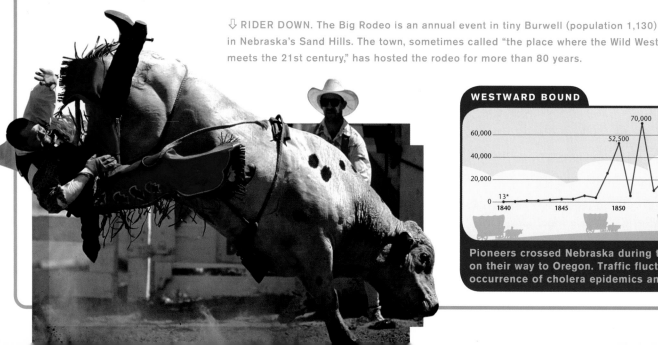

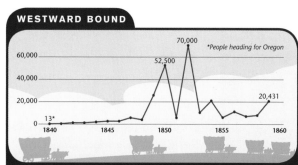

WESTWARD BOUND

70,000
*People heading for Oregon
60,000
52,500
40,000
20,431
20,000
13*
0
1840   1845   1850   1855   1860

Pioneers crossed Nebraska during the 19th century on their way to Oregon. Traffic fluctuated with the occurrence of cholera epidemics and Indian wars.

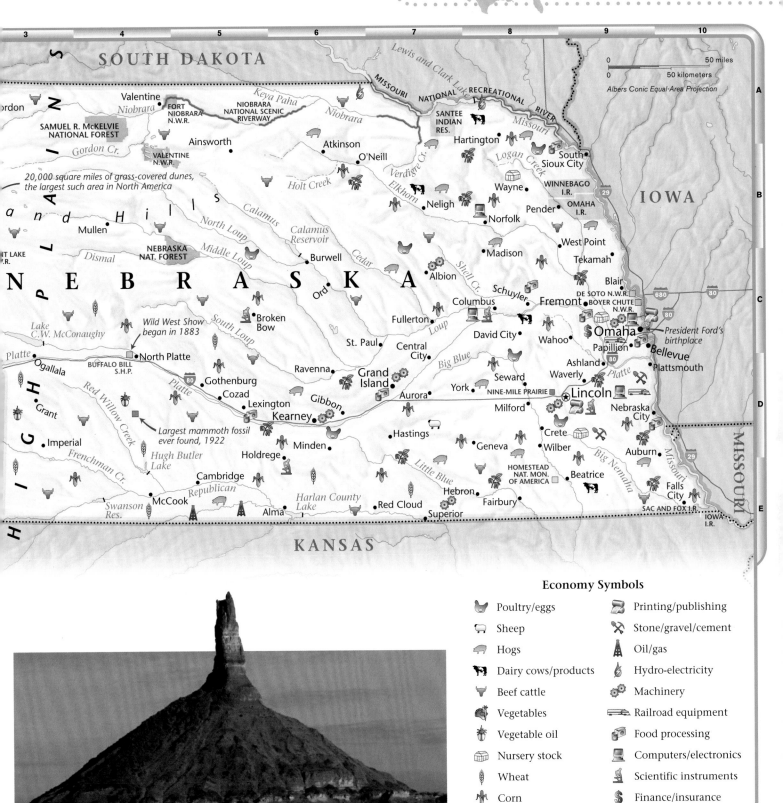

SOUTH DAKOTA

Gordon

Valentine

Niobrara

FORT NIOBRARA N.W.R.

Keya Paha

NIOBRARA NATIONAL SCENIC RIVERWAY

Niobrara

MISSOURI NATIONAL RECREATIONAL RIVER

Lewis and Clark Lake

SANTEE INDIAN RES.

Hartington

SAMUEL R. McKELVIE NATIONAL FOREST

Gordon Cr.

Ainsworth

Atkinson

O'Neill

Verdigre Cr.

Logan Creek

South Sioux City

Missouri

IOWA

20,000 square miles of grass-covered dunes, the largest such area in North America

Holt Creek

Calamus

Calamus Reservoir

Elkhorn

Wayne

WINNEBAGO I.R.

29

Mullen

Neligh

Pender

OMAHA I.R.

S
a
n
d
H
i
l
l
s

North Loup

Middle Loup

Norfolk

West Point

Cedar

Burwell

Madison

Tekamah

N E B R A S K A

NEBRASKA NAT. FOREST

Dismal

Ord

Albion

Shell Cr.

Schuyler

Blair

DE SOTO N.W.R.

BOYER CHUTE N.W.R.

680

80

Lake C.W. McConaughy

Wild West Show began in 1883

Broken Bow

Columbus

Fremont

80

South Loup

Fullerton

Loup

David City

Wahoo

Omaha

President Ford's birthplace

Platte

Ogallala

BUFFALO BILL S.H.P.

North Platte

St. Paul

Ravenna

Central City

Big Blue

Seward

Ashland

Waverly

Papillion

Bellevue

Plattsmouth

Red Willow Creek

Gothenburg

Cozad

Grand Island

Gibbon

Aurora

York

NINE-MILE PRAIRIE

Lincoln

Platte

Grant

Lexington

Kearney

Largest mammoth fossil ever found, 1922

Milford

Nebraska City

Imperial

Frenchman Cr.

Hugh Butler Lake

Minden

Hastings

Geneva

Crete

Wilber

Auburn

Missouri

H I G H   P L A I N S

Holdrege

Republican

Cambridge

McCook

Swanson Res.

Alma

Harlan County Lake

Red Cloud

Hebron

Fairbury

HOMESTEAD NAT. MON. OF AMERICA

Beatrice

Big Nemaha

Falls City

SAC AND FOX I.R.

Little Blue

Superior

IOWA I.R.

MISSOURI

KANSAS

0 — 50 miles
0 — 50 kilometers
Albers Conic Equal-Area Projection

Economy Symbols

- Poultry/eggs
- Sheep
- Hogs
- Dairy cows/products
- Beef cattle
- Vegetables
- Vegetable oil
- Nursery stock
- Wheat
- Corn
- Soybeans

- Printing/publishing
- Stone/gravel/cement
- Oil/gas
- Hydro-electricity
- Machinery
- Railroad equipment
- Food processing
- Computers/electronics
- Scientific instruments
- Finance/insurance

⬅ **THE WAY WEST.** Longhorn cattle and a bison stand knee-deep in grass below Chimney Rock, which rises more than 300 feet (91 m) above western Nebraska's rolling landscape. An important landmark on the Oregon Trail for 19th-century westbound pioneers and now a national historic site, the formation is being worn away by forces of erosion.

NORTH DAKOTA

During the winter of 1804–05, Lewis and Clark camped at a Mandan village where they met Sacagawea, the Shoshone woman who helped guide them through the Rockies and onto the Pacific Ocean. White settlement of the vast grassy plains coincided with the growth of railroads, and statehood was gained in 1889. The geographic center of North America is southwest of Rugby. The state's interior location helps give it a huge annual temperature range. A record low temperature of -60°F (-51°C) and record high of 121°F (49°C) were recorded in 1936. Fargo, located on the northward flowing Red River of the North, is the state's largest city. Garrison Dam, on the Missouri River, generates electricity and provides water for irrigation. The state leads the country in the production of flax-seed, canola, sunflowers, and barley, but it is wheat, cattle, and soybeans that provide the greatest income. Oil and lignite coal are impor-tant in the western part of the state.

THE BASICS

STATS

Area
70,700 sq mi (183,113 sq km)

Population
672,591

Capital
Bismarck
Population 61,272

Largest city
Fargo
Population 105,549

Ethnic/racial groups
90.0% white; 5.4% Native American; 1.2% African American; 1.0% Asian. Hispanic (any race) 2.0%.

Industry
Services, government, finance, construction, transportation, oil and gas

Agriculture
Wheat, cattle, sunflowers, barley, soybeans

Statehood
November 2, 1889; 39th state

GEO WHIZ

Teenage Indian guide Sacagawea (also known as Sakakawea) joined the Lewis and Clark expedition in the spring of 1805 after the explorers spent the winter in the Mandan-Hidatsa villages near present-day Washburn. Today, the state's largest reservoir is named in her honor.

Devils Lake has earned the title Perch Capital of the World for the large number of walleye—a kind of perch—that anglers catch there.

North Dakota's landscape boasts some of the world's largest outdoor animal sculptures, including Salem Sue, the world's largest Holstein cow; a 60-ton buffalo; a 40-by-60-foot (12-by-18-m) grasshopper; a giant snowmobiling turtle; and Wally the Giant Walleye.

WESTERN MEADOWLARK

WILD PRAIRIE ROSE

⇧ VIGILANT LOOKOUT. A black-tailed prairie dog watches for signs of danger. This member of the squirrel family lives in burrows in the Great Plains.

SASKATC

Crosby

WRITING ROCK S.H.S

LAKE ZAHL N.W.R.

Williston

Tio

Lake Sakakawea

FORT UNION TRADING POST N.H.S.

LITT

Watford City

THEODORE ROOSEVELT N.P. (NORTH UNIT)

MISSOURI

THEODORE ROOSEVELT N.P. (ELKHORN RANCH SITE)

NATIONAL

Beach

Medora

THEODORE ROO N.P. (SOUTH U

Dick

GRASSLAND

White But 3,506 ft 1,069 m

Bowman

Highest po in North D

Little Missouri

MONTANA

Yellowstone

Little Missouri

Missouri

Little Muddy

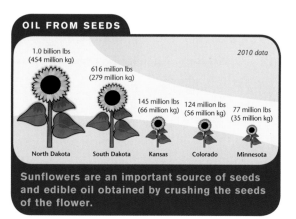

OIL FROM SEEDS

2010 data

1.0 billion lbs (454 million kg)
North Dakota

616 million lbs (279 million kg)
South Dakota

145 million lbs (66 million kg)
Kansas

124 million lbs (56 million kg)
Colorado

77 million lbs (35 million kg)
Minnesota

Sunflowers are an important source of seeds and edible oil obtained by crushing the seeds of the flower.

⇨ RUNNING FREE. A wild horse runs through a landscape dramatically eroded by the Little Missouri River in Theodore Roosevelt National Park in North Dakota's Badlands region.

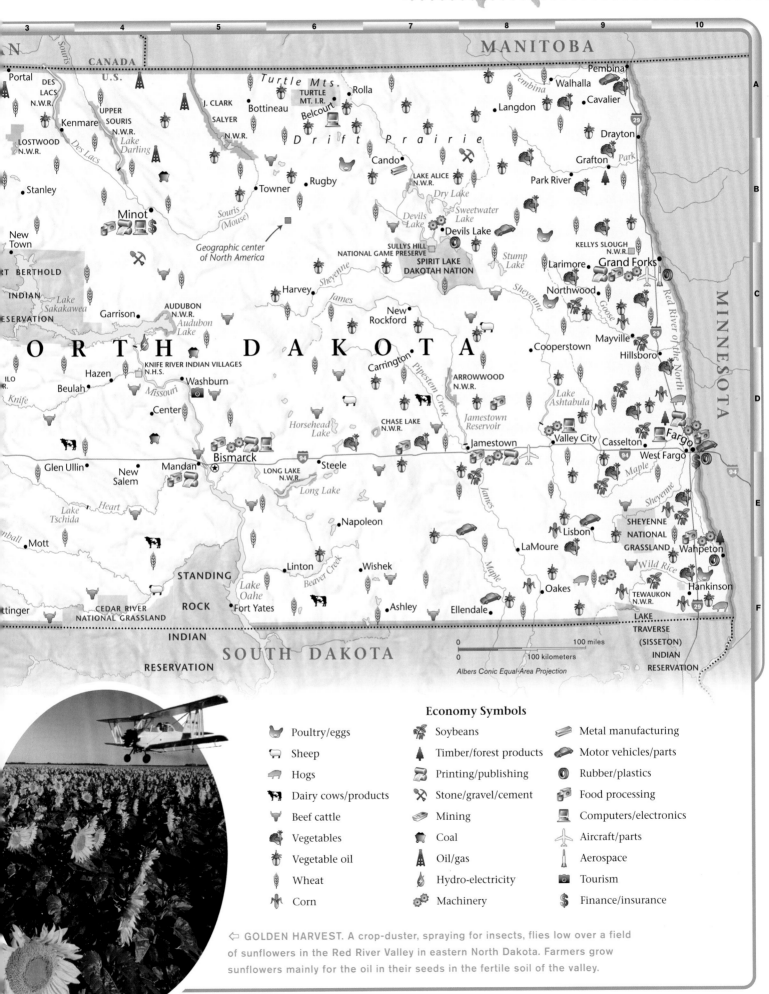

MANITOBA

CANADA
U.S.

Portal

DES
LACS
N.W.R.

UPPER
SOURIS
N.W.R.

Kenmare

LOSTWOOD
N.W.R.

*Lake
Darling*

Des Lacs

Stanley

New
Town

Minot

RT BERTHOLD

INDIAN

RESERVATION

*Lake
Sakakawea*

Garrison

ILO
R.

Hazen

Beulah

Knife

Center

Glen Ullin

New
Salem

Mandan

Bismarck

*Lake
Tschida*

Heart

Mott

mball

ttinger

CEDAR RIVER
NATIONAL GRASSLAND

STANDING

ROCK

INDIAN

RESERVATION

SOUTH DAKOTA

Turtle Mts.

TURTLE
MT. I.R.

Belcourt

Bottineau

J. CLARK
SALYER
N.W.R.

Rolla

D r i f t   P r a i r i e

Towner

Rugby

Cando

Geographic center
of North America

*Souris
(Mouse)*

Sheyenne

Harvey

James

New
Rockford

AUDUBON
N.W.R.

*Audubon
Lake*

KNIFE RIVER INDIAN VILLAGES
N.H.S.

Washburn

Missouri

*Horsehead
Lake*

Carrington

CHASE LAKE
N.W.R.

LAKE ALICE
N.W.R.

Dry Lake

*Devils
Lake*

Devils Lake

SULLYS HILL
NATIONAL GAME PRESERVE

SPIRIT LAKE
DAKOTAH NATION

*Sweetwater
Lake*

*Stump
Lake*

Sheyenne

ARROWWOOD
N.W.R.

*Jamestown
Reservoir*

Jamestown

Pipestem Creek

Steele

LONG LAKE
N.W.R.

Long Lake

Napoleon

Linton

Beaver Creek

Wishek

Ashley

Fort Yates

*Lake
Oahe*

Pembina

Walhalla

Cavalier

Langdon

Drayton

Grafton

Park

Park River

Larimore

Northwood

Grand Forks

KELLYS SLOUGH
N.W.R.

Cooperstown

Mayville

Hillsboro

*Lake
Ashtabula*

Valley City

Casselton

Fargo

West Fargo

Maple

Sheyenne

Lisbon

LaMoure

SHEYENNE
NATIONAL
GRASSLAND

Wild Rice

Wahpeton

Oakes

TEWAUKON
N.W.R.

Ellendale

Hankinson

LAKE
TRAVERSE
(SISSETON)

INDIAN
RESERVATION

Pembina

Red River of the North

Goose

MINNESOTA

0   100 miles
0   100 kilometers
Albers Conic Equal-Area Projection

Economy Symbols

Poultry/eggs	Soybeans	Metal manufacturing
Sheep	Timber/forest products	Motor vehicles/parts
Hogs	Printing/publishing	Rubber/plastics
Dairy cows/products	Stone/gravel/cement	Food processing
Beef cattle	Mining	Computers/electronics
Vegetables	Coal	Aircraft/parts
Vegetable oil	Oil/gas	Aerospace
Wheat	Hydro-electricity	Tourism
Corn	Machinery	Finance/insurance

⇦ GOLDEN HARVEST. A crop-duster, spraying for insects, flies low over a field of sunflowers in the Red River Valley in eastern North Dakota. Farmers grow sunflowers mainly for the oil in their seeds in the fertile soil of the valley.

THE BUCKEYE STATE:
OHIO

STATS

Area
44,825 sq mi (116,097 sq km)

Population
11,536,504

Capital
Columbus
Population 787,033

Largest city
Columbus
Population 787,033

Ethnic/racial groups
82.7% white; 12.2% African American; 1.7% Asian; .2% Native American. Hispanic (any race) 3.1%.

Industry
Transportation equipment, metal products, machinery, food processing, electrical equipment

Agriculture
Soybeans, dairy products, corn, hogs, cattle, poultry and eggs

Statehood
March 1, 1803; 17th state

GEO WHIZ

Cedar Point Amusement Park, in Sandusky, is known as the Roller Coaster Capital of the World. Top Thrill Dragster, the tallest and fastest roller coaster on Earth when it was built in 2003, is 420 feet (128 m) high with a top speed of 120 miles per hour (193 kmph)!

Ohio's state tree is the buckeye, so-called because the nut it produces resembles the eye of a buck. A buck is a male deer.

Ohio's state insect is the ladybird beetle, more commonly known as the ladybug. Use of these beetles to control plant-eating pests greatly reduces the need for chemical pesticides.

CARDINAL
SCARLET CARNATION

OHIO

Ohio and the rest of the Northwest Territory became part of the United States after the Revolutionary War. The movement of white settlers into the region led to conflicts with the native inhab-

⇧ INLAND URBAN CENTER. Cincinnati's skyline sparkles in the red glow of twilight. Founded in 1788, the modern city boasts education and medical centers as well as headquarters for companies such as Procter & Gamble.

itants until 1794 when Indian resistance was defeated at Fallen Timbers. Ohio entered the Union nine years later. Lake Erie in the north and the Ohio River in the south, along with canals and railroads, provided transportation links that spurred early immigration and commerce. The state became an industrial giant, producing steel, machinery, rubber, and glass. From 1869 to 1923, 7 of 12 U.S. presidents were Ohioans. With 18 electoral votes, seventh highest in the country, Ohio is still a big player in presidential elections. Education, government, and finance employ many people in Columbus, the capital and largest city. Manufacturing in Cleveland, Toledo, Cincinnati, and other cities remains a vital segment of the state's economy. Farmers on Ohio's western, glaciated plains grow soybeans and corn, the two largest cash crops.

⇩ TRADITIONAL TRAVEL. Horse and buggy are a familiar sight in central Ohio, location of the world's largest Amish population.

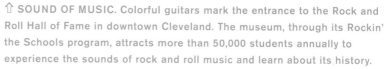

⇧ SOUND OF MUSIC. Colorful guitars mark the entrance to the Rock and Roll Hall of Fame in downtown Cleveland. The museum, through its Rockin' the Schools program, attracts more than 50,000 students annually to experience the sounds of rock and roll music and learn about its history.

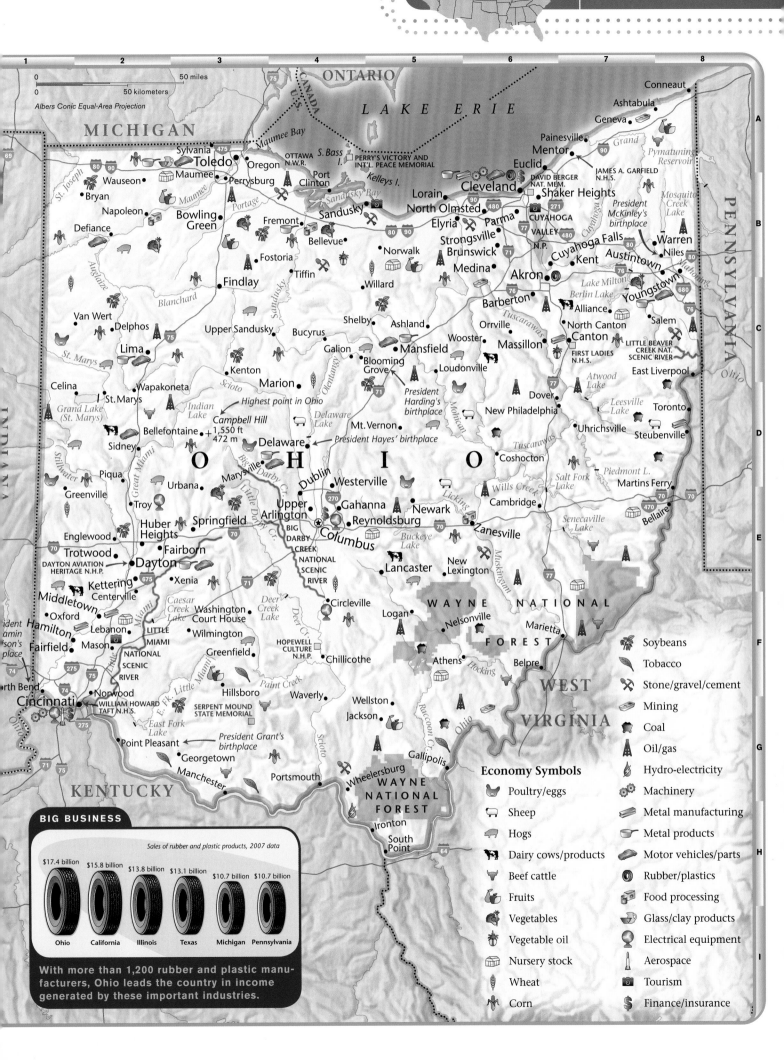

ONTARIO

CANADA
U.S.

LAKE ERIE

MICHIGAN

Conneaut
Ashtabula
Geneva
Painesville
Mentor
Euclid
DAVID BERGER NAT. MEM.
JAMES A. GARFIELD N.H.S.
Grand
Pymatuning Reservoir
Mosquito Creek Lake

Sylvania
Toledo
Maumee
Oregon
Perrysburg
Port Clinton
Sandusky
S. Bass I.
Kelleys I.
PERRY'S VICTORY AND INT'L. PEACE MEMORIAL
Cleveland
Shaker Heights
CUYAHOGA VALLEY N.P.
President McKinley's birthplace

Wauseon
Maumee Bay
Maumee
Portage
Lorain
North Olmsted
Elyria
Parma
Strongsville
Brunswick
Medina
Cuyahoga Falls
Kent
Austintown
Warren
Niles

Bryan
Napoleon
Defiance
St. Joseph
Bowling Green
Fremont
Bellevue
Norwalk
Akron
Barberton
Orrville
Wooster
Massillon
Canton
North Canton
Alliance
Lake Milton
Berlin Lake
Youngstown
Salem

Auglaize
Fostoria
Tiffin
Findlay
Blanchard
Sandusky
Willard
Shelby
Ashland
Bucyrus
Galion
Mansfield
Blooming Grove
Loudonville
Tuscarawas
First Ladies N.H.S.
Little Beaver Creek Nat. Scenic River

Van Wert
Delphos
Lima
Celina
St. Marys
Wapakoneta
Kenton
Marion
Upper Sandusky
Scioto
Indian Lake
Delaware Lake
Mt. Vernon
President Harding's birthplace
President Hayes' birthplace
Dover
New Philadelphia
Uhrichsville
Atwood Lake
Leesville Lake
East Liverpool
Toronto
Steubenville

Grand Lake (St. Marys)
Bellefontaine
Campbell Hill +1,550 ft 472 m
Highest point in Ohio
Delaware
Coshocton
Salt Fork Lake
Piedmont L.
Martins Ferry

OHIO

Sidney
Piqua
Urbana
Marysville
Dublin
Westerville
Gahanna
Newark
Cambridge
Senecaville Lake
Bellaire

Greenville
Troy
Springfield
Upper Arlington
Reynoldsburg
Columbus
Zanesville
Wills Creek
Licking
Muskingum

Englewood
Trotwood
Dayton
Fairborn
DAYTON AVIATION HERITAGE N.H.P.
BIG DARBY CREEK NATIONAL SCENIC RIVER
Buckeye Lake
Lancaster
New Lexington

Kettering
Centerville
Middletown
Xenia
Caesar Creek Lake
Washington Court House
Deer Creek Lake
Circleville
Logan
Nelsonville
Marietta
WAYNE NATIONAL FOREST

Oxford
Hamilton
Lebanon
Mason
LITTLE MIAMI NATIONAL SCENIC RIVER
Wilmington
Greenfield
HOPEWELL CULTURE N.H.P.
Chillicothe
Athens
Belpre

Fairfield
North Bend
President Benjamin Harrison's place
Cincinnati
Norwood
WILLIAM HOWARD TAFT N.H.S.
East Fork Lake
Hillsboro
Waverly
Paint Creek
Wellston
Jackson
WEST VIRGINIA

SERPENT MOUND STATE MEMORIAL
President Grant's birthplace
Point Pleasant
Georgetown
Manchester
Portsmouth
Wheelersburg
Gallipolis
Ohio
Raccoon Cr.
Scioto
Hocking
WAYNE NATIONAL FOREST
Ironton
South Point

KENTUCKY

PENNSYLVANIA
INDIANA

Economy Symbols

Poultry/eggs
Sheep
Hogs
Dairy cows/products
Beef cattle
Fruits
Vegetables
Vegetable oil
Nursery stock
Wheat
Corn

Soybeans
Tobacco
Stone/gravel/cement
Mining
Coal
Oil/gas
Hydro-electricity
Machinery
Metal manufacturing
Metal products
Motor vehicles/parts
Rubber/plastics
Food processing
Glass/clay products
Electrical equipment
Aerospace
Tourism
Finance/insurance

Albers Conic Equal-Area Projection
0 50 miles
0 50 kilometers

BIG BUSINESS

Sales of rubber and plastic products, 2007 data

Ohio	California	Illinois	Texas	Michigan	Pennsylvania
$17.4 billion	$15.8 billion	$13.8 billion	$13.1 billion	$10.7 billion	$10.7 billion

With more than 1,200 rubber and plastic manufacturers, Ohio leads the country in income generated by these important industries.

THE MOUNT RUSHMORE STATE:
SOUTH DAKOTA

SOUTH DAKOTA

After the discovery of Black Hills gold in 1874, prospectors poured in and established lawless mining towns such as Deadwood. Indians fought this invasion but were defeated, and statehood came in 1889. Today, South Dakota has several reservations, and nearly 9 percent of the state's people are Native Americans. The Missouri River flows through the center of the state, creating two distinct regions. To the east, farmers grow corn and soybeans on the fertile, rolling prairie. To the west, where it is too dry for most crops, farmers grow wheat and graze cattle and sheep on the vast plains. In the southwest, the Black Hills, named for the dark coniferous trees blanketing their slopes, are still a rich source of gold. Millions of tourists visit the area to see Mount Rushmore and a giant sculpture of Crazy Horse that has been in the works since 1948. Nearby, the fossil-rich Badlands, a region of eroded buttes and pinnacles, dominate the landscape.

THE BASICS

STATS

Area
77,117 sq mi (199,732 sq km)

Population
814,180

Capital
Pierre
Population 13,646

Largest city
Sioux Falls
Population 153,888

Ethnic/racial groups
85.9% white; 8.8% Native American; 1.3% African American; .9% Asian. Hispanic (any race) 2.7%.

Industry
Finance, services, manufacturing, government, retail trade, transportation and utilities, wholesale trade, construction, mining

Agriculture
Cattle, corn, soybeans, wheat, hogs, hay, dairy products

Statehood
November 2, 1889; 40th state

GEO WHIZ

Thirty years ago, black-footed ferrets were on the brink of extinction. Now, thanks to captive breeding programs, the world's largest wild black-footed ferret population is thriving in a black-tailed prairie dog colony in south-central South Dakota.

Called Shrine of Democracy by its creator Gutzon Borglum, Mount Rushmore National Monument features the faces of George Washington, Thomas Jefferson, Abraham Lincoln, and Theodore Roosevelt. Each is 60 feet (18 m) tall.

The Black Hills Institute of Geological Research in Hill City has been involved in digging up eight *Tyrannosaurus rex* skeletons, including Sue, Stan, Bucky, and WREX. In addition to research work, the institute prepares museum-quality reproductions.

RING-NECKED PHEASANT

PASQUEFLOWER

⇨ **HONORING AGRICULTURE.** The face of the Corn Palace in Mitchell is renewed each year using thousands of bushels of grain to create pictures depicting the role of agriculture in the state's history.

ALTERNATIVE BEEF

Bison sold 2007 data

South Dakota	Nebraska	North Dakota	Colorado	Montana	Wyoming
10,862	7,266	6,042	5,456	5,270	4,668

Bison meat is popular among health-conscious consumers because it is lower in calories, fat, and cholesterol than other meats.

MITCHELL CORN PALACE

LIFE ON THE FARM 2005

Map labels:
MONTANA
WYOMING
CUSTER NATIONAL FOREST
Little Missouri
S. Fork C
Buffalo
Geographic cer of the 50 states
Belle Fourche
90
Spearfish
Deadwood
Sturgis
Lead
BLACK
Belle Four
Highest mount east of the Rock
Black Hawk
Rapid C
HILLS
Black Hills
MOUNT RUSHMORE N.M.
CRAZY HORSE MEMORIAL
Harney Peak 7,242 ft 2,207 m
Custer
CUSTER S.P.
JEWEL CAVE N.M.
NAT.
BUFFAL
WIND CAVE N.P.
Hot Springs
GAP
Cheyenne
FOREST
Edgemont
NAT.
IN D
GRASSLAND
White
0   50 m
0   50 kilometers
Albers Equal-Area Conic Projection

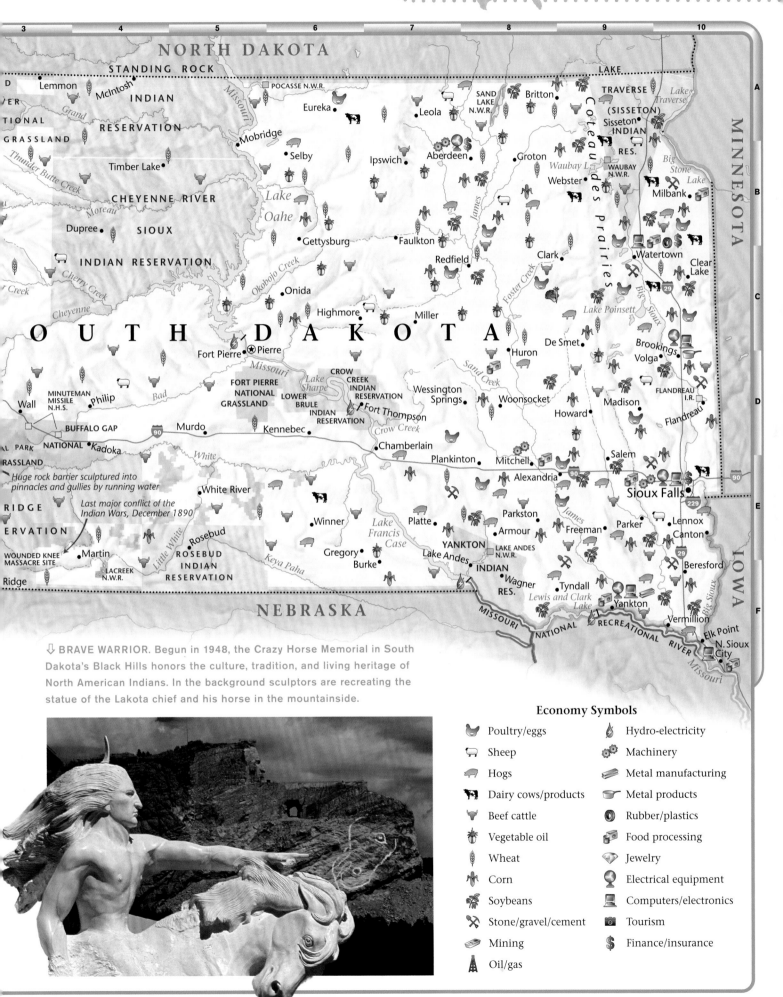

NORTH DAKOTA

STANDING ROCK
INDIAN
RESERVATION

Lemmon
McIntosh

Grand

NATIONAL
GRASSLAND

Thunder Butte Creek

Timber Lake

CHEYENNE RIVER

Dupree
Moreau

SIOUX

INDIAN RESERVATION

Cherry Creek

Cheyenne

Mobridge

Selby

Lake
Oahe

Eureka
Leola

Ipswich
Aberdeen

SAND
LAKE
N.W.R.

Britton

Groton

Webster

POCASSE N.W.R.

Coteau des

TRAVERSE
(SISSETON)
Sisseton

SISSETON
INDIAN
RES.

Waubay L.
WAUBAY
N.W.R.

Big
Stone
Lake

Milbank

Lake
Traverse

Prairies

MINNESOTA

Gettysburg
Faulkton

Redfield
Clark

Watertown

Clear
Lake

S O U T H   D A K O T A

Okobojo Creek

Onida

Highmore
Miller

Foster Creek

Lake Poinsett

De Smet
Huron

Big Sioux

Brookings
Volga

FLANDREAU
I.R.

Fort Pierre
Pierre

Missouri

Lake
Sharpe

CROW
CREEK
INDIAN
RESERVATION

Sand Creek

Madison

Howard

Flandreau

Wall

MINUTEMAN
MISSILE
N.H.S.

Philip

Bad

FORT PIERRE
NATIONAL
GRASSLAND

LOWER
BRULE
INDIAN
RESERVATION

Fort Thompson

Crow Creek

Wessington
Springs

Woonsocket

NATIONAL
Kadoka

Murdo

Kennebec

Chamberlain

Salem

AL PARK

RASSLAND

*Huge rock barrier sculptured into
pinnacles and gullies by running water*

BUFFALO GAP

White

Plankinton
Mitchell

Alexandria

Sioux Falls

RIDGE

*Last major conflict of the
Indian Wars, December 1890*

White River

Winner

Lake
Francis
Case

Platte

Parkston

James

Parker

Lennox
Canton

ERVATION

WOUNDED KNEE
MASSACRE SITE

Martin

Rosebud

ROSEBUD
INDIAN
RESERVATION

Gregory
Burke

Armour

Freeman

Beresford

Ridge

LACREEK
N.W.R.

Little White

Keya Paha

YANKTON
Lake Andes

LAKE ANDES
N.W.R.

INDIAN
RES.

Wagner

Tyndall

Lewis and Clark
Lake

Yankton

IOWA

Vermillion

Elk Point

N. Sioux
City

NEBRASKA

MISSOURI
NATIONAL
RECREATIONAL
RIVER

⇩ **BRAVE WARRIOR.** Begun in 1948, the Crazy Horse Memorial in South
Dakota's Black Hills honors the culture, tradition, and living heritage of
North American Indians. In the background sculptors are recreating the
statue of the Lakota chief and his horse in the mountainside.

Economy Symbols

Poultry/eggs	Hydro-electricity
Sheep	Machinery
Hogs	Metal manufacturing
Dairy cows/products	Metal products
Beef cattle	Rubber/plastics
Vegetable oil	Food processing
Wheat	Jewelry
Corn	Electrical equipment
Soybeans	Computers/electronics
Stone/gravel/cement	Tourism
Mining	Finance/insurance
Oil/gas	

THE BADGER STATE: WISCONSIN

WISCONSIN

1848

THE BASICS

STATS

Area
65,498 sq mi (169,639 sq km)

Population
5,686,986

Capital
Madison
Population 233,209

Largest city
Milwaukee
Population 594,833

Ethnic/racial groups
86.2% white; 6.3% African American; 2.3% Asian; 1.0% Native American. Hispanic (any race) 5.9%.

Industry
Industrial machinery, paper products, food processing, metal products, electronic equipment, transportation

Agriculture
Dairy products, cattle, corn, poultry and eggs, soybeans

Statehood
May 29, 1848; 30th state

GEO WHIZ

The Indian Community School in Milwaukee offers courses in native languages, history, and rituals. In all of its programs—from math to tribal creation stories—seven core values are stressed: bravery, love, truth, wisdom, humility, loyalty, and respect.

Bogs left by retreating ice-age glaciers provide excellent conditions for raising cranberries. Wisconsin leads the nation in cranberry farming, producing more than half of the estimated 575 million pounds (261 million kg) consumed by Americans annually.

Wisconsin is nicknamed the Badger State, not for the animal but for the men who mined lead in the state during the 1820s. They dug living spaces by burrowing like badgers into the hillside.

ROBIN
WOOD VIOLET

WISCONSIN

Frenchman Jean Nicolet was the first European to reach present-day Wisconsin when he stepped ashore from Green Bay in 1634. After decades of getting along, relations with the region's Indians soured as the number of settlers increased. The Black Hawk War in 1832 ended the last major Indian resistance, and statehood came in 1848. Many Milwaukee residents are descendants of German immigrants who labored in the city's breweries and meatpacking plants. Even as the economic importance of health care and other services has increased, food processing and the manufacture of machinery and metal products remains significant for the state. More than one million dairy cows graze in America's Dairyland, as the state is often called. It leads the country in cheese production, and is the second-largest producer of milk and butter. Other farmers grow crops ranging from corn and soybeans to potatoes and cranberries. Northern Wisconsin is sparsely populated but heavily forested, and is the source of paper and paper products produced by the state.

⇧ TASTY GRAZING. The largest concentration of Brown Swiss cows in the U.S. is in Wisconsin, where the milk of this breed is prized by cheese manufacturers.

⇧ CITY BY THE LAKE. Milwaukee, on the shore of Lake Michigan, derives its name from the Algonquian word for "beautiful land." The city, known for brewing and manufacturing, also has a growing service sector.

⇐ RURAL ECONOMY. The dairy industry is an important part of Wisconsin's rural economy, and dairy farmers control most of the state's farmland.

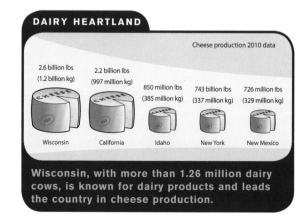

DAIRY HEARTLAND

Cheese production 2010 data

Wisconsin	California	Idaho	New York	New Mexico
2.6 billion lbs (1.2 billion kg)	2.2 billion lbs (997 million kg)	850 million lbs (385 million kg)	743 billion lbs (337 million kg)	726 million lbs (329 million kg)

Wisconsin, with more than 1.26 million dairy cows, is known for dairy products and leads the country in cheese production.

LAKE SUPERIOR

MICHIGAN

Apostle Islands

APOSTLE ISLANDS NATIONAL LAKESHORE
RED CLIFF I.R.
Madeline Island
BAD RIVER INDIAN RES.

Superior
CHEQUAMEGON-
Washburn
Ashland
Hurley

NICOLET

Land O'Lakes

Hayward

Turtle-Flambeau Flowage

LAC DU FLAMBEAU INDIAN RES.
CHEQUAMEGON-
Eagle River
Niagara

ST. CROIX
Lake Chippewa
Park Falls
NICOLET

NATIONAL
Spooner
LAC COURTE OREILLES I.R.
Rhinelander
SOKAOGON CHIPPEWA I.R.

SCENIC
NATIONAL
FOREST COUNTY POTAWATOMI I.R.

RIVERWAY
ST. CROIX INDIAN RES.
Rice Lake
Ladysmith
Highest point in Wisconsin
Timms Hill 1,951ft 595 m
Tomahawk
FOREST

St. Croix Falls
Medford
Merrill
Antigo
Marinette

New Richmond
MENOMINEE INDIAN RES.
Oconto
Sturgeon Bay

Hudson
Chippewa Falls
Wausau
WOLF N.W.&S.R.
Shawano

River Falls
Eau Claire
Altoona
STOCKBRIDGE I.R.
Ashwaubenon
Green Bay
De Pere

ST. CROIX N.W.&S.R.
Menomonie
Marshfield
Big Eau Pleine Reservoir
Lake Du Bay
ONEIDA INDIAN RES.

WISCONSIN
Lake Wissota
Stevens Point
Plover
New London
Appleton
Kaukauna

Pepin
Black River Falls
WISCONSIN WINNEBAGO I.R.
Wisconsin Rapids
Waupaca
Menasha
Neenah
Two Rivers

Lake Pepin
Petenwell Lake
Lake Poygan
Oshkosh
Manitowoc

TREMPEALEAU N.W.R.
NECEDAH N.W.R.
Castle Rock Lake
Ripon
Fond du Lac
Sheboygan

Sparta
Tomah
Wisconsin Dells
Waupun
HORICON N.W.R.

Onalaska
Viroqua
Reedsburg
Portage
Beaver Dam
West Bend
Port Washington

La Crosse
Richland Center
Baraboo
Lake Wisconsin
Sun Prairie
Menomonee Falls
Mequon

Prairie du Chien
TALIESIN
Middleton
Watertown
Brookfield
Wauwatosa

MICHIGAN

Dodgeville
Monona
Madison
Fort Atkinson
Waukesha
Milwaukee
West Allis
S. Milwaukee

Lancaster
Stoughton
Whitewater
Racine

Platteville
Janesville
Burlington
Lake Geneva
Pleasant Prairie
Kenosha

IOWA
Monroe
Beloit

ILLINOIS

INDIANA

Economy Symbols

- Fishing
- Poultry/eggs
- Sheep
- Hogs
- Dairy cows/products
- Beef cattle
- Fruits
- Vegetables
- Nursery stock
- Corn
- Soybeans
- Tobacco
- Timber/forest products
- Printing/publishing
- Stone/gravel/cement
- Mining
- Hydro-electricity
- Machinery
- Metal products
- Shipbuilding
- Railroad equipment
- Motor vehicles/parts
- Chemistry
- Food processing
- Electrical equipment
- Computers/electronics
- Scientific instruments
- Aircraft/parts
- Tourism

50 miles
50 kilometers
Albers Conic Equal-Area Projection

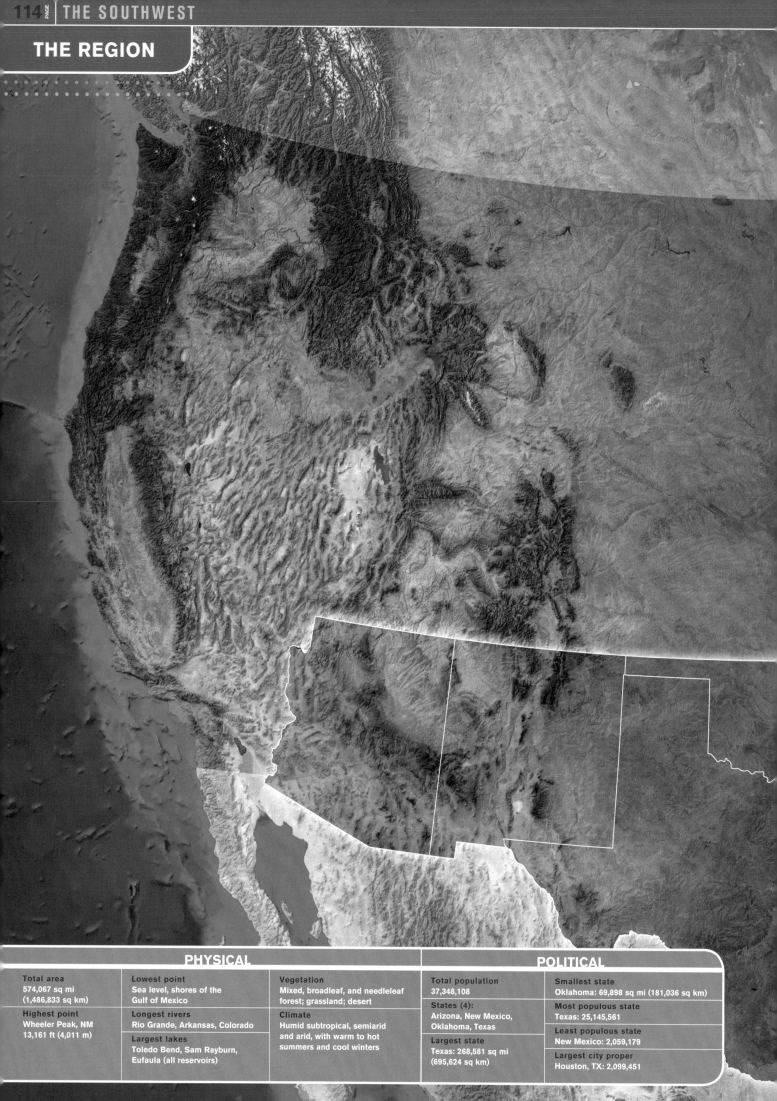

THE REGION

PHYSICAL

Total area 574,067 sq mi (1,486,833 sq km)	**Lowest point** Sea level, shores of the Gulf of Mexico	**Vegetation** Mixed, broadleaf, and needleleaf forest; grassland; desert
Highest point Wheeler Peak, NM 13,161 ft (4,011 m)	**Longest rivers** Rio Grande, Arkansas, Colorado	**Climate** Humid subtropical, semiarid and arid, with warm to hot summers and cool winters
	Largest lakes Toledo Bend, Sam Rayburn, Eufaula (all reservoirs)	

POLITICAL

Total population 37,348,108	**Smallest state** Oklahoma: 69,898 sq mi (181,036 sq km)
States (4): Arizona, New Mexico, Oklahoma, Texas	**Most populous state** Texas: 25,145,561
Largest state Texas: 268,581 sq mi (695,624 sq km)	**Least populous state** New Mexico: 2,059,179
	Largest city proper Houston, TX: 2,099,451

The Southwest

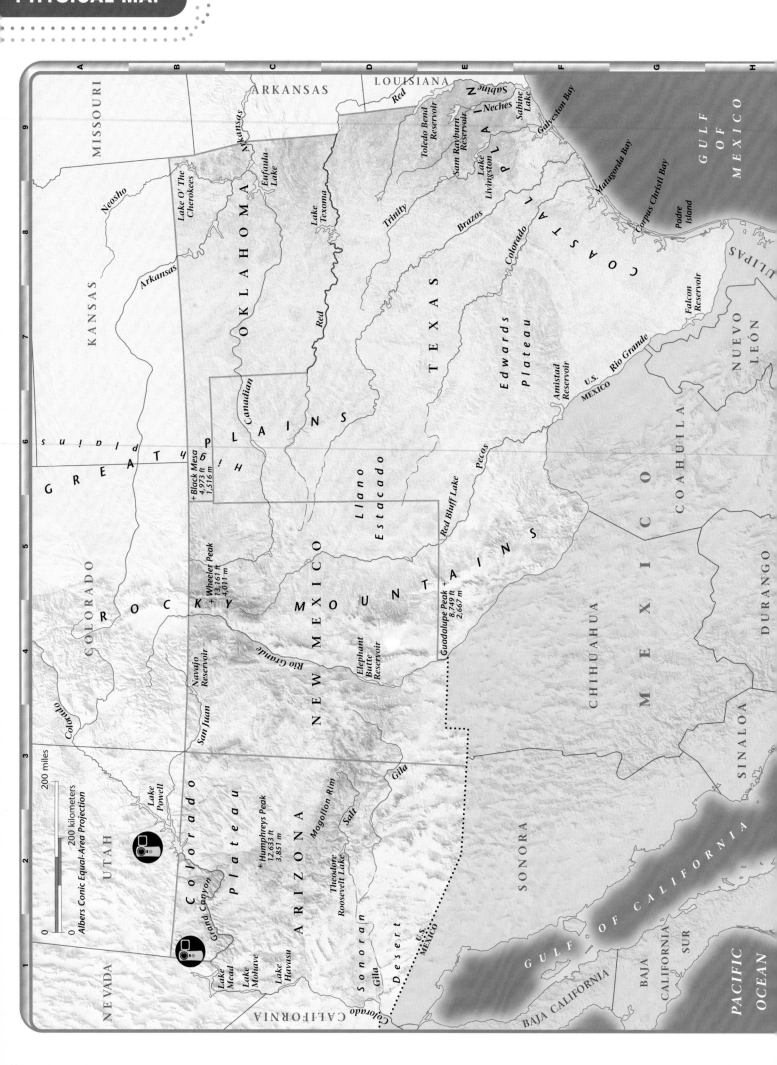

A B C D E F G H

MISSOURI

ARKANSAS

LOUISIANA

Red

Sabine

Neches

Toledo Bend Reservoir

Sam Rayburn Reservoir

Galveston Bay

Lake Livingston

Matagorda Bay

GULF OF MEXICO

Neosho

Lake O' The Cherokees

Eufaula Lake

Lake Texoma

Trinity

Brazos

Colorado

Corpus Christi Bay

Padre Island

TAMAULIPAS

Arkansas

Arkansas

OKLAHOMA

Red

TEXAS

COASTAL

Falcon Reservoir

KANSAS

Canadian

High

PLAINS

Edwards Plateau

Amistad Reservoir

U.S. Rio Grande

MEXICO

NUEVO LEÓN

GREAT PLAINS

+ Black Mesa
4,973 ft
1,516 m

Llano Estacado

Pecos

Red Bluff Lake

COAHUILA

Plains

ROCKY

Wheeler Peak
+ 13,161 ft
4,011 m

NEW MEXICO

MOUNTAINS

Guadalupe Peak +
8,749 ft
2,667 m

MEXICO

CHIHUAHUA

DURANGO

COLORADO

Colorado

San Juan

Navajo Reservoir

Rio Grande

Elephant Butte Reservoir

U.S. MEXICO

Gila

Lake Powell

Colorado Plateau

+ Humphreys Peak
12,633 ft
3,851 m

Mogollon Rim

Salt

Theodore Roosevelt Lake

ARIZONA

SONORA

SINALOA

UTAH

Grand Canyon

Sonoran Desert

Gila

U.S. MEXICO

GULF OF CALIFORNIA

Lake Mead

Lake Mohave

Lake Havasu

Colorado

BAJA CALIFORNIA

BAJA CALIFORNIA SUR

PACIFIC OCEAN

NEVADA

CALIFORNIA

200 miles

200 kilometers

Albers Conic Equal-Area Projection

9 8 7 6 5 4 3 2 1

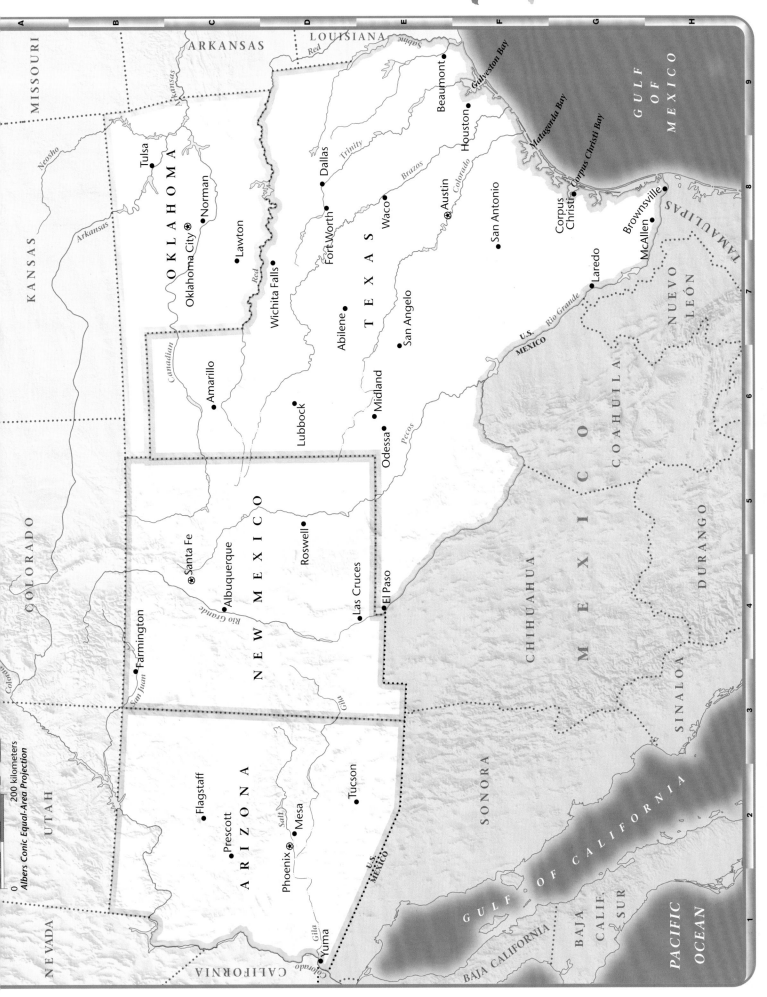

A B C D E F G H

MISSOURI

ARKANSAS

LOUISIANA

Red

Sabine

Neosho

Arkansas

KANSAS

Arkansas

Tulsa

OKLAHOMA

Norman

Oklahoma City ✪

Lawton

Canadian

Red

Wichita Falls

Amarillo

Lubbock

Trinity

Dallas

Fort Worth

Brazos

Abilene

TEXAS

Waco

San Angelo

Midland

Pecos

Odessa

Colorado

Austin ✪

San Antonio

Beaumont

Galveston Bay

Houston

Matagorda Bay

GULF OF MEXICO

Corpus Christi Bay

Corpus Christi

Brownsville

McAllen

Laredo

U.S. Rio Grande
MEXICO

TAMAULIPAS

NUEVO LEÓN

COLORADO

NEW MEXICO

Santa Fe ✪

Albuquerque

Roswell

Las Cruces

El Paso

Rio Grande

Farmington

San Juan

Gila

M E X I C O

CHIHUAHUA

COAHUILA

DURANGO

UTAH

NEVADA

ARIZONA

Flagstaff

Prescott

Mesa

Phoenix ✪

Salt

Tucson

Gila

Yuma

Colorado

CALIFORNIA

U.S.
MEXICO

SONORA

SINALOA

BAJA CALIFORNIA

BAJA CALIF. SUR

GULF OF CALIFORNIA

PACIFIC OCEAN

9 8 7 6 5 4 3 2 1

0   200 kilometers
Albers Conic Equal-Area Projection

⇨ SKY STONE. According to Indian legend, turquoise stole its color from the sky. This Zuni woman is wearing turquoise jewelry for a festival in Phoenix. Zuni Indians, whose reservation is in western New Mexico, have made jewelry for more than one thousand years.

The Southwest
FROM CANYONS TO GRASSLANDS

Legendary cities of gold lured Spanish conquistadors to the Southwest in the 1500s. Today, the promise of economic opportunities brings people from other states as well as immigrants, both legal and illegal, from countries south of the border. This part of the Sunbelt region boasts future-oriented cities while preserving Wild West tales and Native American traditions. Stretching from the humid Gulf Coast to Arizona's deserts, the landscape is as diverse as its climate, ranging from sprawling plains in the east to plateaus cut by dramatic canyons in the west. Water is a major concern in the Southwest, one of the country's fastest-growing regions.

⇩ HIGH SOCIETY. Dressed in an elegant ball gown, a young woman participates in the Society of Martha Washington Pageant in Laredo, Texas. This event presents daughters of wealthy and long-established Hispanic families to the local community.

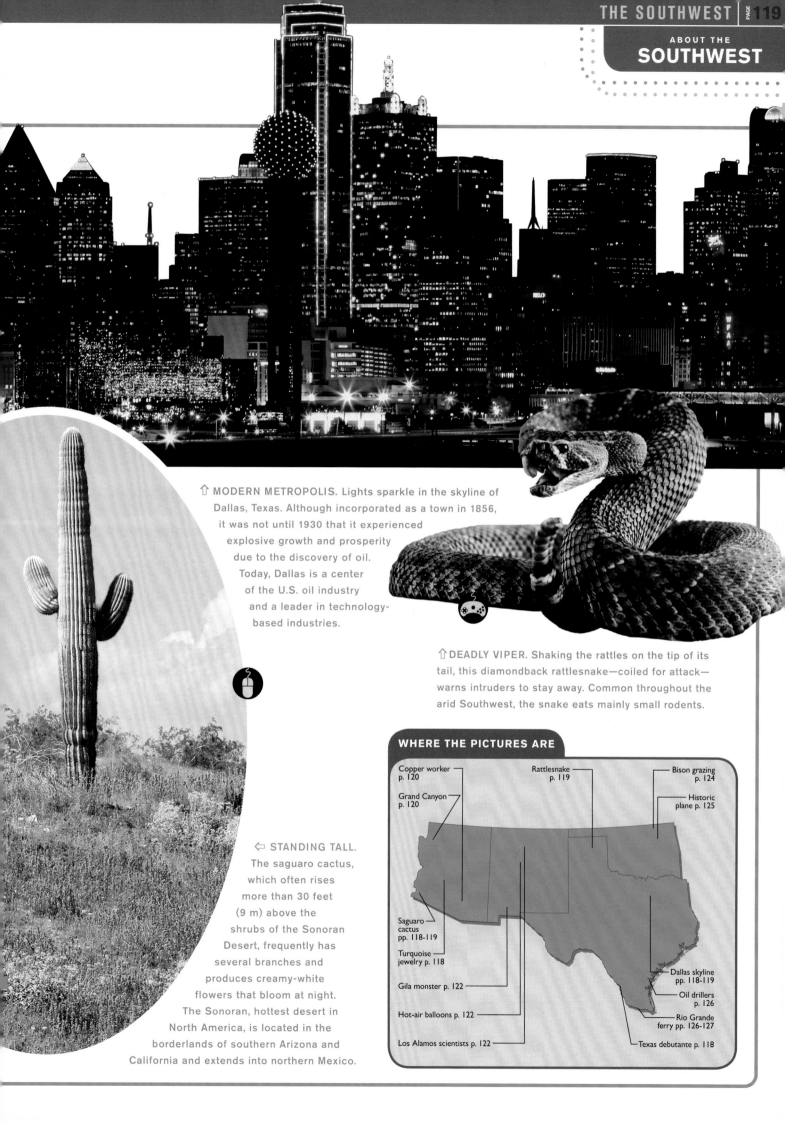

⇧ MODERN METROPOLIS. Lights sparkle in the skyline of Dallas, Texas. Although incorporated as a town in 1856, it was not until 1930 that it experienced explosive growth and prosperity due to the discovery of oil. Today, Dallas is a center of the U.S. oil industry and a leader in technology-based industries.

⇧ DEADLY VIPER. Shaking the rattles on the tip of its tail, this diamondback rattlesnake—coiled for attack—warns intruders to stay away. Common throughout the arid Southwest, the snake eats mainly small rodents.

⇦ STANDING TALL. The saguaro cactus, which often rises more than 30 feet (9 m) above the shrubs of the Sonoran Desert, frequently has several branches and produces creamy-white flowers that bloom at night. The Sonoran, hottest desert in North America, is located in the borderlands of southern Arizona and California and extends into northern Mexico.

WHERE THE PICTURES ARE

Copper worker p. 120

Grand Canyon p. 120

Rattlesnake p. 119

Bison grazing p. 124

Historic plane p. 125

Saguaro cactus pp. 118-119

Turquoise jewelry p. 118

Gila monster p. 122

Hot-air balloons p. 122

Los Alamos scientists p. 122

Dallas skyline pp. 118-119

Oil drillers p. 126

Rio Grande ferry pp. 126-127

Texas debutante p. 118

THE GRAND CANYON STATE:
ARIZONA

THE BASICS

STATS

Area
113,998 sq mi (295,256 sq km)

Population
6,392,017

Capital
Phoenix
Population 1,445,632

Largest city
Phoenix
Population 1,445,632

Ethnic/racial groups
73.0% white; 4.6% Native American;
4.1% African American; 2.8% Asian.
Hispanic (any race) 29.6%.

Industry
Real estate, manufactured goods,
retail, state and local government,
transportation and public utilities,
wholesale trade, health services,
tourism, electronics

Agriculture
Vegetables, cattle, dairy products,
cotton, fruit, nursery stock, nuts

Statehood
February 14, 1912; 48th state

GEO WHIZ

The California condor, once common
throughout the Southwest, nearly
became extinct in 1987. Through
captive breeding and other conservation measures, the species has
been reintroduced to the wild in areas
such as the Grand Canyon.

People have been carving pictures called
petroglyphs into rock cliffs in Verde
Valley near Flagstaff for thousands
of years. The meanings of most are
a mystery, but others reveal the
plants and animals of bygone eras.

Introduced as wild game for sports-
men, bullfrogs have made Arizona
their new home on the range. With
no natural predators and plenty to
eat, bullfrogs are taking over.

CACTUS WREN
SAGUARO

ARIZONA

The Europeans to first visit what is now Arizona were the Spanish in the 1500s. The territory passed from Spain to Mexico and then to the United States over the next three centuries. In the 1800s settlers clashed with the Apache warriors Cochise and Geronimo—and with one another in lawless towns like Tombstone. Youngest of the 48 contiguous states, statehood arrived in 1912. Arizona's economy was long based on the Five C's—copper, cattle, cotton, citrus, and climate—but manufacturing and service industries have gained prominence. A fast-growing population, sprawling cities, and agricultural irrigation strain limited water supplies in this dry state, which depends on water from the Colorado River and underground aquifers. Tourists flock to the Colorado Plateau in the north to see stunning vistas of the Grand Canyon, Painted Desert, and Monument Valley. To the south, the Sonoran Desert's unique ecosystem includes the giant saguaro cactus. Indian reservations scattered around the state offer outsiders the chance to learn about tribal history and culture.

⇧ HOT WORK. A man in protective clothing works near a furnace that melts and refines copper ore at Magma Copper Company near Tucson. Arizona is one of the largest copper-producing regions in the world.

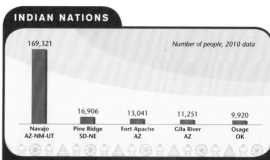

INDIAN NATIONS

Number of people, 2010 data

169,321	16,906	13,041	11,251	9,920
Navajo AZ-NM-UT	Pine Ridge SD-NE	Fort Apache AZ	Gila River AZ	Osage OK

More than 200,000 Indians live on reservations in the Southwest. The most populous is the Navajo Reservation in Arizona and adjoining states.

⇩ NATURAL WONDER. Carved by the rushing waters of the Colorado River, the Grand Canyon's geologic features and fossil record reveal almost two billion years of Earth's history. Archaeological evidence indicates human habitation dating back 12,000 years.

Economy Symbols

- Poultry/eggs
- Sheep
- Hogs
- Dairy cows/products
- Beef cattle
- Fruits
- Vegetables
- Nursery stock
- Wheat
- Cotton
- Timber/forest products
- Mining
- Coal
- Oil/gas
- Hydro-electricity
- Metal products
- Chemistry
- Food processing
- Electrical equipment
- Computers/electronics
- Aircraft/parts
- Aerospace

Only spot in the U.S. where the borders of four states come together

Highest point in Arizona
Humphreys Peak
12,633 ft
3,851 m

Hopi pueblo, oldest continuously inhabited town in U.S., dating from prehistoric times

Earth's largest known meteor crater, one mile wide

0   100 miles
0   100 kilometers

Albers Conic Equal-Area Projection

THE BASICS

STATS

Area
121,590 sq mi (314,917 sq km)

Population
2,059,179

Capital
Santa Fe
Population 67,947

Largest city
Albuquerque
Population 545,852

Ethnic/racial groups
68.4% white; 9.4% Native American; 2.1% African American; 1.4% Asian. Hispanic (any race) 46.3%.

Industry
Electronic equipment, state and local government, real estate, business services, federal government, oil and gas extraction, health services

Agriculture
Cattle, dairy products, hay, chili peppers, onions

Statehood
January 6, 1912; 47th state

GEO WHIZ

Carlsbad Caverns National Park has more than a hundred caves, including the deepest limestone cavern in the U.S. From May through October, visitors can watch hundreds of thousands of Mexican free-tailed bats emerge from the cavern on their nightly search for food.

Taos Pueblo, in north-central New Mexico, has been continuously inhabited by Pueblo people for more than 1,000 years. When Spanish explorers reached it in 1540, they thought they had found one of the fabled golden cities of Cibola.

In 2007 voters in a county in south-central New Mexico approved a tax to help fund construction of a spaceport where rockets will launch tourists into space.

ROADRUNNER
YUCCA

NEW MEXICO

New Mexico is among the youngest states—statehood was established in 1912—but its capital city is the country's oldest. The Spanish founded Santa Fe in 1610, a decade before the *Mayflower* reached America. Beginning in the 1820s, the Santa Fe Trail brought trade and settlers, and the United States acquired all the territory from Mexico by 1853. Most large cities are in the center of the state, along the Rio Grande. The Rocky Mountains divide the plains in the east from eroded mesas and canyons in the west. Cattle and sheep ranching on the plains is the chief agricultural activity, but hay, onions, and chili peppers are also important. Copper, potash, and natural gas produce mineral wealth. Cultural richness created by the historic interaction of Indian, Hispanic, and Anglo peoples abounds. Visitors experience this unique culture in the state's spicy cuisine, the famous art galleries of Taos, and the crafts made by Indians on the state's many reservations.

⬆ PAINFUL BITE. The strikingly patterned gila monster, the most poisonous lizard native to the United States, lives in desert areas of the Southwest.

⬆ FLYING HIGH. Brightly colored balloons rise into a brilliant blue October sky during Albuquerque's annual International Balloon Fiesta, the largest such event in the world. During the 9-day festival more than 700 hot-air balloons drift on variable air currents created by surrounding mountains.

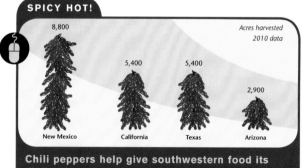

SPICY HOT!

Acres harvested 2010 data

8,800	5,400	5,400	2,900
New Mexico	California	Texas	Arizona

Chili peppers help give southwestern food its distinctive taste. New Mexico leads the country in acres planted of this fiery flavor enhancer.

⬅ NUCLEAR MYSTERIES. Scientists at Los Alamos National Laboratory, a leading scientific and engineering research institution responsible for national security, use 3-D simulations to study nuclear explosions.

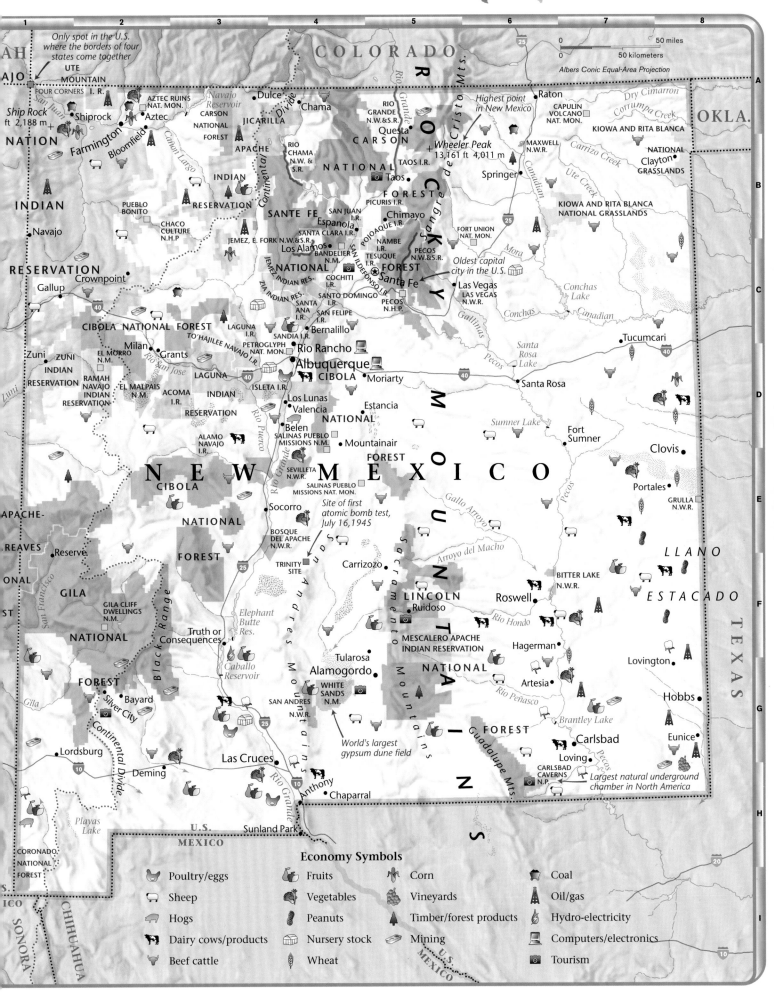

COLORADO

OKLA.

Only spot in the U.S. where the borders of four states come together

FOUR CORNERS I.R.

Ship Rock ft 2,188 m

UTE MOUNTAIN

Shiprock

Farmington

Bloomfield

Aztec

AZTEC RUINS NAT. MON.

Navajo Reservoir

Dulce

Chama

RIO GRANDE N.W.& S.R.

Raton

CAPULIN VOLCANO NAT. MON.

Highest point in New Mexico

Wheeler Peak 13,161 ft 4,011 m

KIOWA AND RITA BLANCA NATIONAL

Dry Cimarron

Corrumpa Creek

CARSON NATIONAL FOREST

JICARILLA

APACHE

INDIAN

RESERVATION

Questa

CARSON

Carrizo Creek

Clayton

NATIONAL GRASSLANDS

MAXWELL N.W.R.

Springer

Canadian

NATION

INDIAN

RESERVATION

Navajo

Gallup

Crownpoint

PUEBLO BONITO

CHACO CULTURE N.H.P.

RIO CHAMA N.W. & S.R.

SANTE FE

Espanola

JEMEZ, E. FORK N.W.& S.R.

Los Alamos

BANDELIER N.M.

NATIONAL

SAN JUAN I.R.

Chimayo

SANTA CLARA I.R.

POJOAQUE I.R.

SAN ILDEFONSO I.R.

NAMBE I.R.

TESUQUE I.R.

PICURIS I.R.

Taos

TAOS I.R.

PECOS N.W.& S.R.

FORT UNION NAT. MON.

Oldest capital city in the U.S.

Santa Fe

Las Vegas

LAS VEGAS N.W.R.

Mora

FORT UNION NAT. MON.

KIOWA AND RITA BLANCA NATIONAL GRASSLANDS

Conchas Lake

CIBOLA NATIONAL FOREST

LAGUNA I.R.

TO'HAJIILEE NAVAJO I.R.

PETROGLYPH NAT. MON.

Rio Rancho

Albuquerque

SANDIA I.R.

Bernalillo

COCHITI I.R.

SANTO DOMINGO I.R.

SAN FELIPE I.R.

SANTA ANA I.R.

ZIA INDIAN RES.

JEMEZ INDIAN RES.

Zuni

ZUNI INDIAN RESERVATION

EL MORRO N.M.

Milan

Grants

RAMAH NAVAJO INDIAN RESERVATION

EL MALPAIS N.M.

ACOMA I.R.

LAGUNA

INDIAN

RESERVATION

ISLETA I.R.

CIBOLA

Moriarty

Santa Rosa

Santa Rosa Lake

Pecos

Tucumcari

Los Lunas

Valencia

Belen

SALINAS PUEBLO MISSIONS N.M.

Mountainair

Estancia

NATIONAL

Sumner Lake

Fort Sumner

Clovis

ALAMO NAVAJO I.R.

N E W   M E X I C O

CIBOLA

SEVILLETA N.W.R.

SALINAS PUEBLO MISSIONS NAT. MON.

FOREST

Gallo Arroyo

Portales

GRULLA N.W.R.

NATIONAL

Socorro

Site of first atomic bomb test, July 16, 1945

BOSQUE DEL APACHE N.W.R.

TRINITY SITE

FOREST

Carrizozo

Arroyo del Macho

BITTER LAKE N.W.R.

Roswell

L L A N O

E S T A C A D O

APACHE-

REAVES

Reserve

ONAL

GILA

ST

San Francisco

GILA CLIFF DWELLINGS N.M.

NATIONAL

FOREST

Black Range

Elephant Butte Res.

Truth or Consequences

Caballo Reservoir

LINCOLN

Ruidoso

MESCALERO APACHE INDIAN RESERVATION

Rio Hondo

Hagerman

Artesia

Lovington

Hobbs

Gila

FOREST

Bayard

Silver City

Continental Divide

Tularosa

Alamogordo

WHITE SANDS N.M.

SAN ANDRES N.W.R.

World's largest gypsum dune field

NATIONAL

Rio Peñasco

FOREST

Brantley Lake

Carlsbad

Eunice

Lordsburg

Deming

Las Cruces

Anthony

Chaparral

Rio Grande

Loving

CARLSBAD CAVERNS N.P.

Largest natural underground chamber in North America

Guadalupe Mts.

Pecos

T E X A S

CORONADO NATIONAL FOREST

Playas Lake

Sunland Park

U.S.

MEXICO

20

S.

ICO

SONORA

CHIHUAHUA

MEXICO

U.S.

10

Economy Symbols

Poultry/eggs	Corn	Coal
Sheep	Vineyards	Oil/gas
Hogs	Peanuts	Hydro-electricity
Dairy cows/products	Nursery stock	Computers/electronics
Beef cattle	Wheat	Tourism
Fruits	Timber/forest products	
Vegetables	Mining	

0   50 miles

0   50 kilometers

Albers Conic Equal-Area Projection

OKLAHOMA

THE BASICS

STATS

Area
69,898 sq mi (181,036 sq km)

Population
3,751,351

Capital
Oklahoma City
Population 579,999

Largest city
Oklahoma City
Population 579,999

Ethnic/racial groups
72.2% white; 8.6% Native American;
7.4% African American; 1.7% Asian.
Hispanic (any race) 8.9%.

Industry
Manufacturing, services, government,
finance, insurance, real estate

Agriculture
Cattle, wheat, hogs, poultry, nursery
stock

Statehood
November 16, 1907; 46th state

GEO WHIZ

An area of Oklahoma City has earned
the nickname Little Saigon. In the
1960s the city opened its doors
to tens of thousands of refugees
from Vietnam. Today, the area is a
thriving business district that includes
people of other Asian nationalities.

"Hillbilly Speed Bump" is one of several
nicknames for the armadillo.
Native to South America, large
populations of this armor-plated
mammal are found as far north
as Oklahoma.

Before it became a state in 1907,
Oklahoma was known as Indian
Territory. Today 39 tribes, including
Cherokees, Osages, Creeks,
and Choctaws, have their
headquarters in the state.

SCISSOR-TAILED
FLYCATCHER
MISTLETOE

OKLAHOMA

The U.S. government declared most of present-day Oklahoma Indian Territory in 1834. To reach this new homeland, southeastern Indians were forced to travel the Trail of Tears, named for its brutal conditions. By 1889 areas were opened for white homesteaders who staked claims in frenzied land runs. White and Indian lands were combined to form the state of Oklahoma in 1907. During the 1930s, many Okies fled drought and dust storms that smothered everything in sight. Some traveled as far as California in search of work. Better farming methods and the return of rain helped agriculture recover, and today cattle and wheat are the chief products. Oil and natural gas wells are found throughout the state. The Red River, colored by the region's iron-rich soils, marks the state's southern boundary. Along the eastern border, the Ozark Plateau and Ouachita Mountains form rugged bluffs and valleys. To the west, rolling plains rise toward the High Plains in the state's panhandle.

WEATHER ALERT

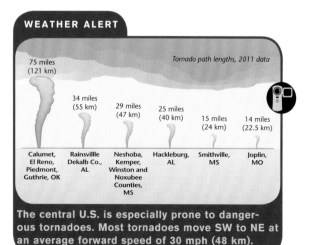

Tornado path lengths, 2011 data

75 miles
(121 km)

34 miles
(55 km)

29 miles
(47 km)

25 miles
(40 km)

15 miles
(24 km)

14 miles
(22.5 km)

Calumet,
El Reno,
Piedmont,
Guthrie, OK

Rainsville
Dekalb Co.,
AL

Neshoba,
Kemper,
Winston and
Noxubee
Counties,
MS

Hackleburg,
AL

Smithville,
MS

Joplin,
MO

The central U.S. is especially prone to dangerous tornadoes. Most tornadoes move SW to NE at
an average forward speed of 30 mph (48 km).

⇧ NATURAL LANDSCAPE. A bison herd grazes in the Tallgrass Prairie Preserve, near Pawhuska. In years when rain is abundant, the grasses can grow as tall as 8 feet (2.5 m). Tallgrass prairie once covered 140 million acres (57 million ha), extending from Minnesota to Texas, but today less than 10 percent remains because of urban sprawl and cropland expansion.

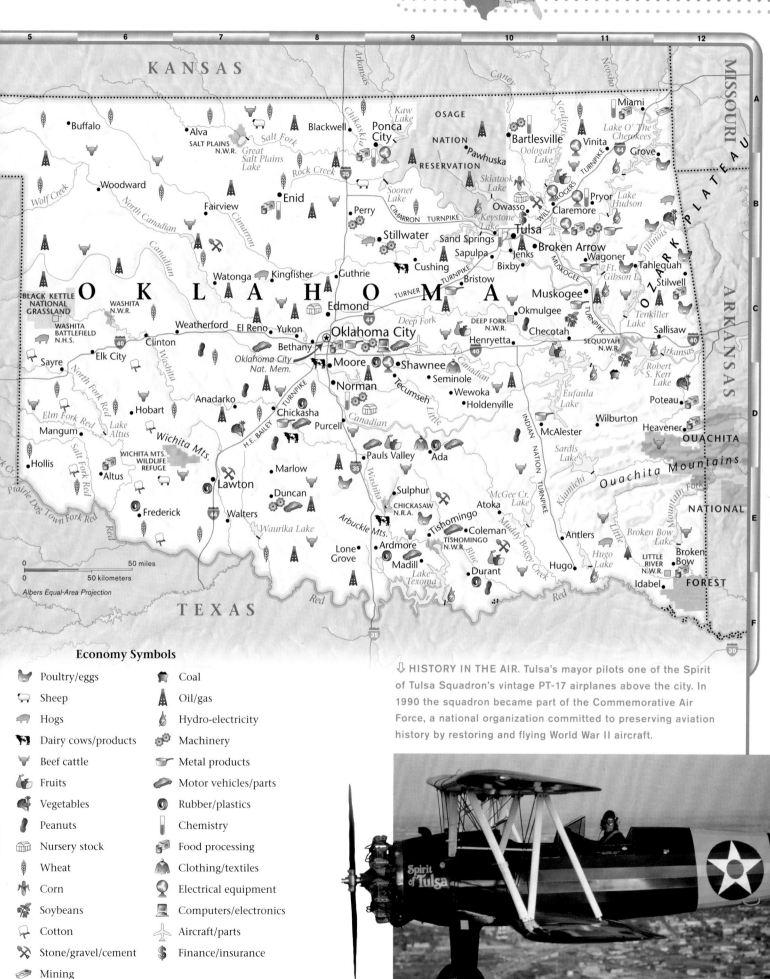

KANSAS

MISSOURI

TEXAS

ARKANSAS

OZARK PLATEAU

OUACHITA Mountains

OUACHITA NATIONAL FOREST

Buffalo · Alva · Blackwell · Ponca City · Bartlesville · Miami · Vinita · Grove
Woodward · Fairview · Enid · Perry · Pawhuska · Skiatook · Claremore · Pryor · Owasso
OSAGE NATION RESERVATION
Watonga · Kingfisher · Stillwater · Cushing · Tulsa · Broken Arrow · Wagoner · Tahlequah · Stilwell
Weatherford · El Reno · Yukon · Guthrie · Edmond · Sapulpa · Bixby · Muskogee · Okmulgee · Checotah · Sallisaw
Clinton · Oklahoma City · Bethany · Moore · Shawnee · Henryetta
Sayre · Elk City · Anadarko · Norman · Tecumseh · Seminole · Wewoka · Holdenville · Poteau
Mangum · Hobart · Chickasha · Purcell · McAlester · Wilburton · Heavener
Hollis · Altus · Lawton · Marlow · Pauls Valley · Ada · Atoka · Antlers
Frederick · Walters · Duncan · Sulphur · Coleman · Tishomingo · Hugo · Broken Bow
Lone Grove · Ardmore · Madill · Durant · Idabel

BLACK KETTLE NATIONAL GRASSLAND
WASHITA BATTLEFIELD N.H.S.
WASHITA N.W.R.
SALT PLAINS N.W.R.
WICHITA MTS. WILDLIFE REFUGE
DEEP FORK N.W.R.
SEQUOYAH N.W.R.
CHICKASAW N.R.A.
TISHOMINGO N.W.R.
LITTLE RIVER N.W.R.

Great Salt Plains Lake · Kaw Lake · Sooner Lake · Oologah Lake · Lake O' The Cherokees · Skiatook Lake · Keystone Lake · Lake Hudson · Ft. Gibson L. · Tenkiller Lake · Deep Fork · Robert S. Kerr Lake · Eufaula Lake · Sardis Lake · McGee Cr. Lake · Waurika Lake · Lake Altus · Lake Texoma · Hugo Lake · Broken Bow Lake

Wolf Creek · North Canadian · Cimarron · Canadian · Washita · North Fork Red · Elm Fork Red · Salt Fork Red · Prairie Dog Town Fork Red · Red · Arkansas · Salt Fork · Rock Creek · Chikaskia · Arkansas · Caney · Verdigris · Neosho · Illinois · Muskogee · Little · Deep Fork · Indian Nation · Kiamichi · Muddy Boggy Creek · Blue · Mountain Fork · Little

CIMARRON TURNPIKE · TURNER TURNPIKE · WILL ROGERS TURNPIKE · MUSKOGEE TURNPIKE · INDIAN NATION TURNPIKE · H.E. BAILEY TURNPIKE

Wichita Mts. · Arbuckle Mts.

50 miles
50 kilometers
Albers Equal-Area Projection

Economy Symbols

- Poultry/eggs
- Sheep
- Hogs
- Dairy cows/products
- Beef cattle
- Fruits
- Vegetables
- Peanuts
- Nursery stock
- Wheat
- Corn
- Soybeans
- Cotton
- Stone/gravel/cement
- Mining

- Coal
- Oil/gas
- Hydro-electricity
- Machinery
- Metal products
- Motor vehicles/parts
- Rubber/plastics
- Chemistry
- Food processing
- Clothing/textiles
- Electrical equipment
- Computers/electronics
- Aircraft/parts
- Finance/insurance

⇩ HISTORY IN THE AIR. Tulsa's mayor pilots one of the Spirit of Tulsa Squadron's vintage PT-17 airplanes above the city. In 1990 the squadron became part of the Commemorative Air Force, a national organization committed to preserving aviation history by restoring and flying World War II aircraft.

Spirit of Tulsa

TEXAS

Huge size, geographic diversity, and rich natural resources make Texas seem like its own country. In fact, it was an independent republic after throwing off Mexican rule in 1836. A famous battle in the fight for independence produced the Texan battle cry "Remember the Alamo!" In 1845 Texas was annexed by the United States. Texas is the second largest state (behind Alaska) and the second most populous (behind California). It is a top producer of many agricultural products, including cattle, sheep, cotton, citrus fruits, vegetables, rice, and pecans. It also has huge oil and natural gas fields and is a manufacturing powerhouse. Pine forests cover East Texas, the wettest region. The Gulf Coast has swamps and extensive barrier islands. Grassy plains stretch across the northern panhandle, while the rolling Hill Country is famous for beautiful wildflowers. Mountains, valleys, and sandy plains sprawl across dry West Texas. The Rio Grande, sometimes barely a trickle, separates Texas and Mexico.

THE BASICS

STATS

Area
268,581 sq mi (695,624 sq km)

Population
25,145,561

Capital
Austin
Population 790,390

Largest city
Houston
Population 2,099,451

Ethnic/racial groups
70.4% white; 11.8% African American; 3.8% Asian; .7% Native American. Hispanic (any race) 37.6%.

Industry
Chemicals, machinery, electronics and computers, food products, petroleum and natural gas, transportation equipment

Agriculture
Cattle, sheep, poultry, cotton, sorghum, wheat, rice, hay, peanuts, pecans

Statehood
December 29, 1845; 28th state

GEO WHIZ

The Fossil Rim Wildlife Research Center in the Texas Hill Country is breeding black rhinos and other endangered African animals. The goal is to reintroduce offspring into the wild in their native environment. Meanwhile, visitors get a chance to see a bit of Africa in Texas.

Six national flags have flown over Texas during the course of its history—the Spanish, French, Mexican, Texan, Confederate, and American.

Texas has a long history of Bigfoot sightings. The ape-man creature was part of local Indian lore, and white settlers told stories about a wild woman along the Navidad River. The Texas Bigfoot Research Center has collected hundreds of eyewitness reports, footprint casts, and hair samples of what locals call Wooly Booger.

MOCKINGBIRD
BLUEBONNET

⇧ BLACK GOLD. Workers plug an oil well. Discovery of oil early in the 20th century transformed life in Texas. Today, the state leads the U.S. in oil and natural gas production.

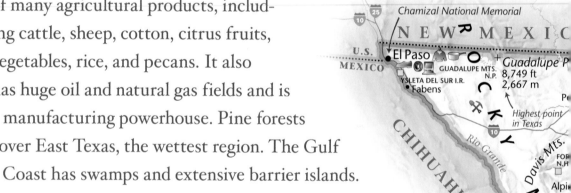

Chamizal National Memorial
NEW MEXICO
U.S.
MEXICO
El Paso
GUADALUPE MTS. N.P.
YSLETA DEL SUR I.R.
Fabens
Guadalupe P
8,749 ft
2,667 m
Highest point in Texas
CHIHUAHUA
Rio Grande
Davis Mts.
FOR
N.H
Alpi
Mar
Presidio

ROUNDUP

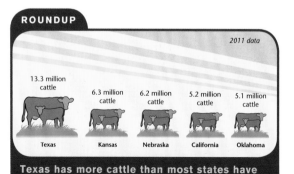

2011 data

13.3 million cattle — Texas
6.3 million cattle — Kansas
6.2 million cattle — Nebraska
5.2 million cattle — California
5.1 million cattle — Oklahoma

Texas has more cattle than most states have people. Only California, Texas, New York, and Florida have larger human populations.

⇨ BORDERLAND RELIC. Los Ebanos Ferry, which takes its name from a grove of ebony trees growing nearby, is the last remaining government-licensed, hand-pulled ferry on any U.S. border. The privately owned ferry, near Mission, Texas, can carry three cars at a time across the Rio Grande.

Economy Symbols

- Fishing
- Shellfish
- Poultry/eggs
- Sheep
- Hogs
- Dairy cows/products
- Beef cattle
- Fruits
- Vegetables
- Peanuts
- Nursery stock
- Wheat
- Corn
- Rice
- Soybeans
- Cotton
- Timber/forest products
- Stone/gravel/cement
- Mining
- Oil/gas
- Hydro-electricity
- Machinery
- Metal manufacturing
- Metal products
- Motor vehicles/parts
- Rubber/plastics
- Chemistry
- Food processing
- Clothing/textiles
- Leather products
- Computers/electronic
- Aircraft/parts
- Tourism

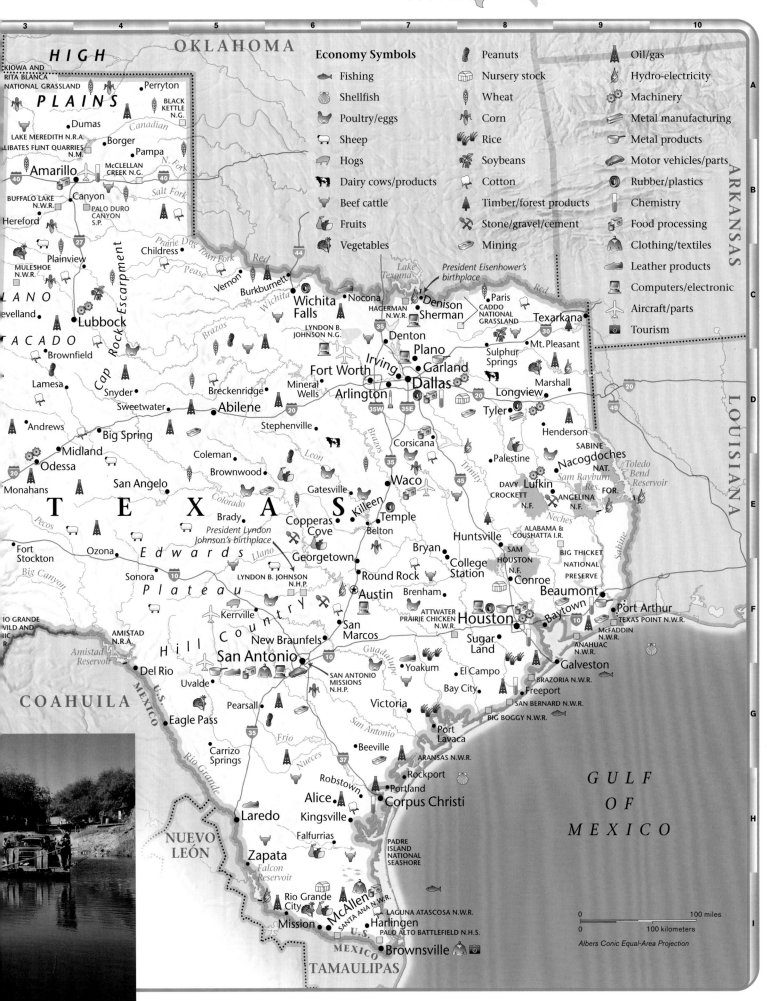

OKLAHOMA

HIGH PLAINS

KIOWA AND RITA BLANCA NATIONAL GRASSLAND

Perryton
BLACK KETTLE N.G.
Dumas
LAKE MEREDITH N.R.A.
ALIBATES FLINT QUARRIES N.M.
Borger
Pampa
Amarillo
McCLELLAN CREEK N.G.
Canyon
BUFFALO LAKE N.W.R.
PALO DURO CANYON S.P.
Hereford
MULESHOE N.W.R.
Plainview
Childress

Canadian
N. Fork
Salt Fork
Prairie Dog Town Fork
Pease
Red
Wichita

LLANO ESTACADO
Cleveland
Lubbock
Brownfield
Lamesa
Snyder
Sweetwater
Andrews
Big Spring
Midland
Odessa
Monahans

Cap Rock Escarpment

Vernon
Burkburnett
Wichita Falls
Nocona
HAGERMAN N.W.R.
Denison
Sherman
LYNDON B. JOHNSON N.G.
Denton
Plano
Irving
Fort Worth
Garland
Arlington
Dallas
Longview
Mineral Wells
Breckenridge
Abilene
Stephenville
Tyler
Henderson
Coleman
Corsicana
Brownwood
Palestine
Gatesville
Waco
Killeen
Temple
Belton
Brady
Copperas Cove
Georgetown
Round Rock
Bryan
College Station
Conroe
Austin
Brenham
Huntsville
Kerrville
San Marcos
New Braunfels
San Antonio
Houston
Sugar Land
Baytown
Port Arthur
Beaumont
Galveston
Freeport

President Eisenhower's birthplace
Paris
CADDO NATIONAL GRASSLAND
Texarkana
Mt. Pleasant
Sulphur Springs
Marshall
SABINE NAT. FOR.
Nacogdoches
Lufkin
Toledo Bend Reservoir
DAVY CROCKETT N.F.
ANGELINA N.F.
ALABAMA & COUSHATTA I.R.
BIG THICKET NATIONAL PRESERVE
SAM HOUSTON N.F.

ARKANSAS
LOUISIANA

President Lyndon Johnson's birthplace
LYNDON B. JOHNSON N.H.P.

T E X A S

Edwards Plateau
Hill Country
Fort Stockton
Ozona
Sonora
Del Rio
Uvalde
Eagle Pass
Pearsall
Carrizo Springs
Laredo
Zapata
Rio Grande City
Mission
McAllen
Harlingen
Brownsville
Alice
Kingsville
Falfurrias
Robstown
Portland
Corpus Christi
Port Lavaca
Beeville
Victoria
Bay City
El Campo
Yoakum
Rockport

Big Canyon
AMISTAD N.R.A.
RIO GRANDE WILD AND SCENIC
Amistad Reservoir
Pecos
Colorado
Leon
Brazos
Trinity
Neches
Sabine
Llano
Guadalupe
San Antonio
Nueces
Frio
Rio Grande
Falcon Reservoir
Sam Rayburn Res.

San Marcos
ATTWATER PRAIRIE CHICKEN N.W.R.
BRAZORIA N.W.R.
SAN BERNARD N.W.R.
BIG BOGGY N.W.R.
ARANSAS N.W.R.
McFADDIN N.W.R.
ANAHUAC N.W.R.
TEXAS POINT N.W.R.
SANTA ANA N.W.R.
LAGUNA ATASCOSA N.W.R.
PALO ALTO BATTLEFIELD N.H.S.
PADRE ISLAND NATIONAL SEASHORE

SAN ANTONIO MISSIONS N.H.P.

COAHUILA
MEXICO
NUEVO LEÓN
TAMAULIPAS

MEXICO
U.S.

GULF OF MEXICO

0   100 miles
0   100 kilometers
Albers Conic Equal-Area Projection

THE REGION

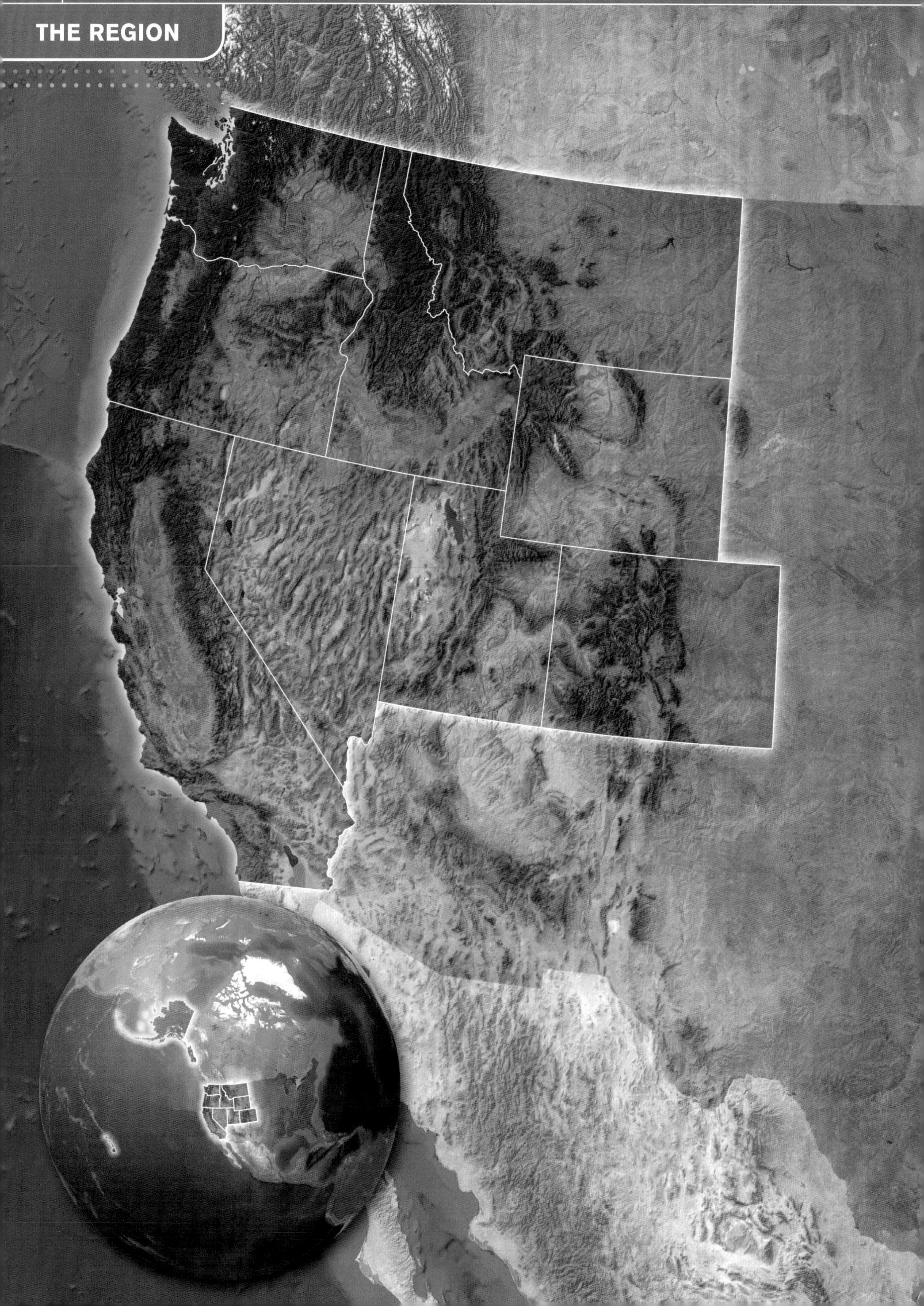

The West

PHYSICAL

Total area
1,635,555 sq mi
(4,236,083 sq km)

Highest point
Mount McKinley (Denali),
AK: 20,320 ft (6,194 m)

Lowest point
Death Valley, CA:
-282 ft (-86 m)

Longest rivers
Missouri, Yukon,
Rio Grande, Colorado

Largest lakes
Great Salt, Iliamna,
Becharof

Vegetation
Needleleaf, broadleaf, and mixed
forest; grassland; desert; tundra
(Alaska); tropical (Hawai'i)

Climate
Mild along the coast, with warm
summers and mild winters; semiarid
to arid inland; polar in parts of
Alaska; tropical in Hawai'i

POLITICAL

Total population
63,494,357

States (11):
Alaska, California, Colorado, Hawai'i,
Idaho, Montana, Nevada, Oregon,
Utah, Washington, Wyoming

Largest state
Alaska: 663,267 sq mi
(1,717,862 sq km)

Smallest state
Hawai'i: 10,931 sq mi (28,311 sq km)

Most populous state
California: 37,253,956

Least populous state
Wyoming: 563,626

Largest city proper
Los Angeles, CA: 3,792,621

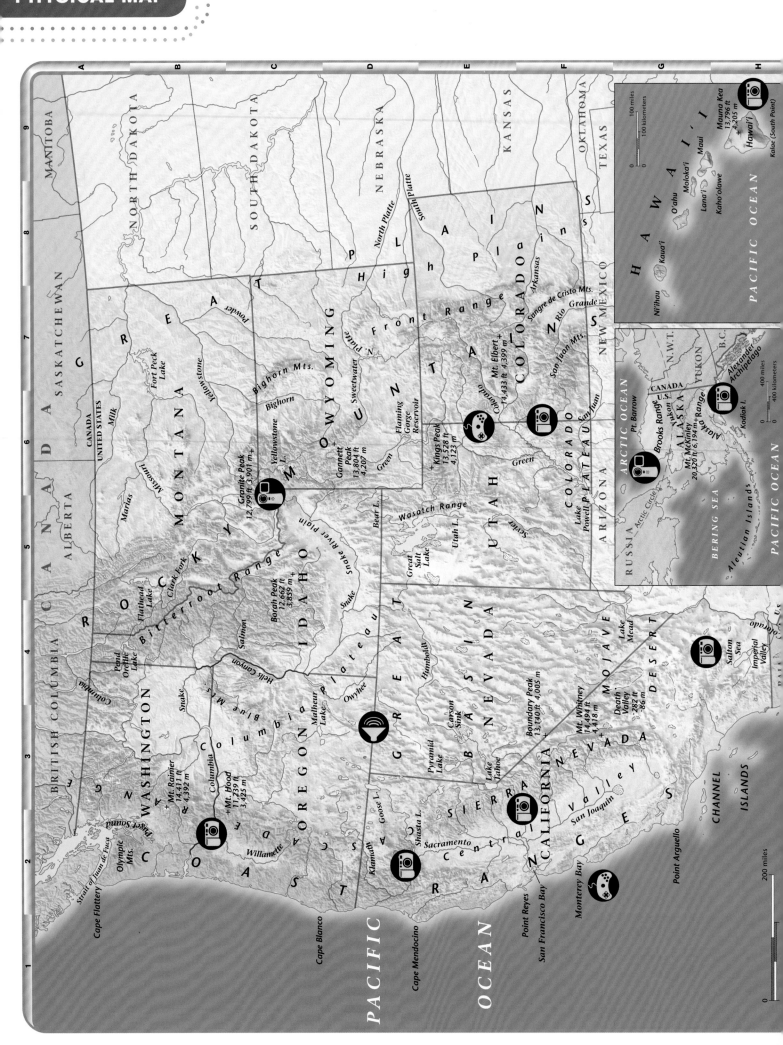

A B C D E F G H

9 8 7 6 5 4 3 2 1

CANADA

ALBERTA

NORTH DAKOTA

SOUTH DAKOTA

NEBRASKA

KANSAS

OKLAHOMA

TEXAS

NEW MEXICO

ARIZONA

MONTANA

WYOMING

COLORADO

UTAH

IDAHO

NEVADA

WASHINGTON

OREGON

CALIFORNIA

CANADA
UNITED STATES

Milk

Missouri

Marias

Yellowstone

Powder

Bighorn

Sweetwater

North Platte

South Platte

Arkansas

Rio Grande

Colorado

San Juan

Green

Green

Snake

Salmon

Owyhee

Columbia

Snake

Humboldt

Sevier

Great Salt Lake

Klamath

Sacramento

San Joaquin

Colorado

U.S.
MEXICO

SONORA

MEXICO

BAJA
CALIF.

Great Falls

Missoula

Helena ⊛

Butte

Billings

Bozeman

Cody

Gillette

Casper

Cheyenne ⊛

Laramie

Fort Collins

Boulder

Denver ⊛

Colorado Springs

Pueblo

Grand
Junction

Rock
Springs

Logan

Ogden

Salt Lake City ⊛

Provo

St. George

Idaho Falls

Pocatello

Boise ⊛

Twin Falls

Elko

Las
Vegas

Henderson

San Bernardino

Riverside

Oceanside

San Diego

Los Angeles

Long Beach

Bakersfield

Fresno

Salinas

Reno

Carson City ⊛

Sacramento ⊛

Stockton

Oakland

San Jose

San Francisco

Santa Rosa

Redding

Eureka

Medford

Klamath Falls

Bend

Eugene

Salem ⊛

Portland

Vancouver

Pendleton

Walla
Walla

Yakima

Spokane

Coeur
d'Alene

Lewiston

Olympia ⊛

Tacoma

Seattle

Bellingham

PACIFIC

OCEAN

200 miles
200 kilometers
0
Albers Conic Equal-Area Projection

HAWAI‘I

Ni‘ihau

Kaua‘i

O‘ahu

Honolulu

Moloka‘i

Lāna‘i

Kaho‘olawe

Maui

Hawai‘i

Hilo

PACIFIC OCEAN

100 miles
100 kilometers
0
0

RUSSIA

ARCTIC OCEAN

Arctic Circle

CANADA
U.S.

N.W.T.

YUKON

B.C.

Juneau ⊛

Fairbanks

Anchorage

ALASKA

Yukon

Kodiak I.

Aleutian Islands

BERING SEA

PACIFIC OCEAN

400 miles
400 kilometers
0
0

⇨ OLD AND NEW. A cable car carries passengers on a steep hill in San Francisco. In the background modern buildings, including the Transamerica Pyramid, rise above older neighborhoods in this earthquake-prone city.

The West

THE HIGH FRONTIER

The western states, which make up almost half of the country's land area, have diverse landscapes and climates, ranging from the frozen heights of Denali, in Alaska, to the desolation of Death Valley, in California, and the lush, tropical islands of Hawai'i. More than half the region's population lives in California, and the Los Angeles metropolitan area is second only to New York City. Yet many parts of the region are sparsely populated, and much of the land is set aside as parkland and military bases. The region also faces many natural hazards—earthquakes, landslides, wildfires, and even volcanic eruptions.

⇨ NORTHERN GIANT. Mount McKinley, called Denali—the "High One"—by native Athabascans, is North America's highest peak, rising more than 20,000 feet (6,100 m) in the Alaska Range. The same tectonic forces that trigger earthquakes in Alaska are slowly pushing this huge block of granite ever higher.

WHERE THE PICTURES ARE

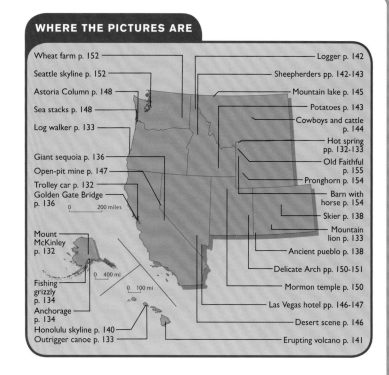

Wheat farm p. 152
Seattle skyline p. 152
Astoria Column p. 148
Sea stacks p. 148
Log walker p. 133
Giant sequoia p. 136
Open-pit mine p. 147
Trolley car p. 132
Golden Gate Bridge p. 136
0   200 miles
Mount McKinley p. 132
0   400 mi
Fishing grizzly p. 134
Anchorage p. 134
0   100 mi
Honolulu skyline p. 140
Outrigger canoe p. 133

Logger p. 142
Sheepherders pp. 142-143
Mountain lake p. 145
Potatoes p. 143
Cowboys and cattle p. 144
Hot spring pp. 132-133
Old Faithful p. 155
Pronghorn p. 154
Barn with horse p. 154
Skier p. 138
Mountain lion p. 133
Ancient pueblo p. 138
Delicate Arch pp. 150-151
Mormon temple p. 150
Las Vegas hotel pp. 146-147
Desert scene p. 146
Erupting volcano p. 141

⇧ ELUSIVE PREDATOR. Known by many names, including cougar and mountain lion, these big cats are found mainly in remote mountainous areas of the West, where they hunt deer and smaller animals.

⇦ STEAMY BATH. Colorful, mineral-rich hot springs are just one geothermal feature of Yellowstone National Park. Runoff from rain and snowmelt seeps into cracks in the ground, sinking to a depth of 10,000 feet (3,050 m), where it is heated by molten rock before rising back to the surface.

⇩ BALANCING ACT. For many years, rivers have been used to move logs from forest to market, taking advantage of the buoyancy of logs and the power of moving water. A logger stands on a floating log raft in Coos Bay, Oregon.

⇧ TRADITIONAL SAILING CRAFT. A Hawaiian outrigger canoe on Waikiki Beach promises fun in the surf for visitors to the 50th state. An important part of Polynesian culture, the canoes were once used to travel from island to island.

THE LAST FRONTIER STATE:
ALASKA

ALASKA

| 1 | 2 | 3 |

Alaska—from *Alyeska*, an Aleut word meaning "great land"—was purchased by the U.S. from Russia in 1867 for just two cents an acre. Many people thought it was a bad investment, but it soon paid off when gold was discovered, and again when major petroleum deposits were discovered in 1968. Today, an 800-mile-long pipeline (1,287 km) links North Slope oil fields to the ice-free port at Valdez, but opponents worry about long-term environmental impact. Everything is big in Alaska. It is the largest state, with one-sixth of the country's land area; it has the highest peak in the U.S., Mt. McKinley (Denali); and the largest earthquake ever recorded in the U.S.—a 9.2 magnitude—occurred there in 1964. It is first in forestland, a leading source of seafood, and a major oil producer. Alaska's population includes a higher percentage of native people than that of any other state.

⇧TIME FOR LUNCH. A grizzly bear wades into the rushing waters of Brooks Falls, in Katmai National Park, to catch a leaping salmon.

THE BASICS

STATS

Area
663,267 sq mi (1,717,862 sq km)

Population
710,231

Capital
Juneau
Population 31,275

Largest city
Anchorage
Population 291,826

Ethnic/racial groups
66.7% white; 14.8% Native American; 5.4% Asian; 3.3% African American. Hispanic (any race) 5.5%.

Industry
Petroleum products, government, services, trade

Agriculture
Shellfish, seafood, nursery stock, vegetables, dairy products, feed crops

Statehood
January 3, 1959; 49th state

GEO WHIZ

During the summer humpback whales migrate to Alaskan waters, where they work together to catch fish. While swimming in circles, the whales blow bubbles that form a net around schools of herring. Each whale can eat hundreds of fish in one gulp.

Global warming and population growth are changing the route of the Iditarod, the world's most famous sled-dog race. Since 2002 lack of snow in Wasilla has forced the starting point for the competition to move 30 miles (48 km) farther north to Willow.

The Tongass National Forest, where conservationists are battling to stop the harvesting of 1,000-year-old trees, is the largest national forest in the United States.

WILLOW PTARMIGAN
FORGET-ME-NOT

CHUKC
SEA

RUSSIA

RUSSIA
U.S.

Bering Strait
Little Diomede

Cape Prince of Wales
only 2.5 miles from Russia

St. Lawrence I.

Nor

Yu
Delta

Emmor

Mou
Vi

St. Matthew I.
ALASKA MARITIME N.W.R.

Hooper Bay

YUKO

Nelson I.

Nunivak I.

B E R I N G

S E A

St. Paul
Pribilof
Islands

ALASKA MARITIME N.W.R.

A L E U T I A N   I S L A N D S
IZEMBEK N.W.R.
Unimak I.
A

Unalaska I.   ALEUTIAN WORLD WAR II N.H.A.
Dutch Harbor
Umnak I.   Unalaska   Sana

Yunaska I.   Islands of Four Mountains

ALASKA MARITIME NATIONAL WIL

⇐ NORTHERN METROPOLIS. Anchorage, established in 1915 as a construction port for the Alaska Railroad, sits in the shadow of the snow-covered Chugach Mountains.

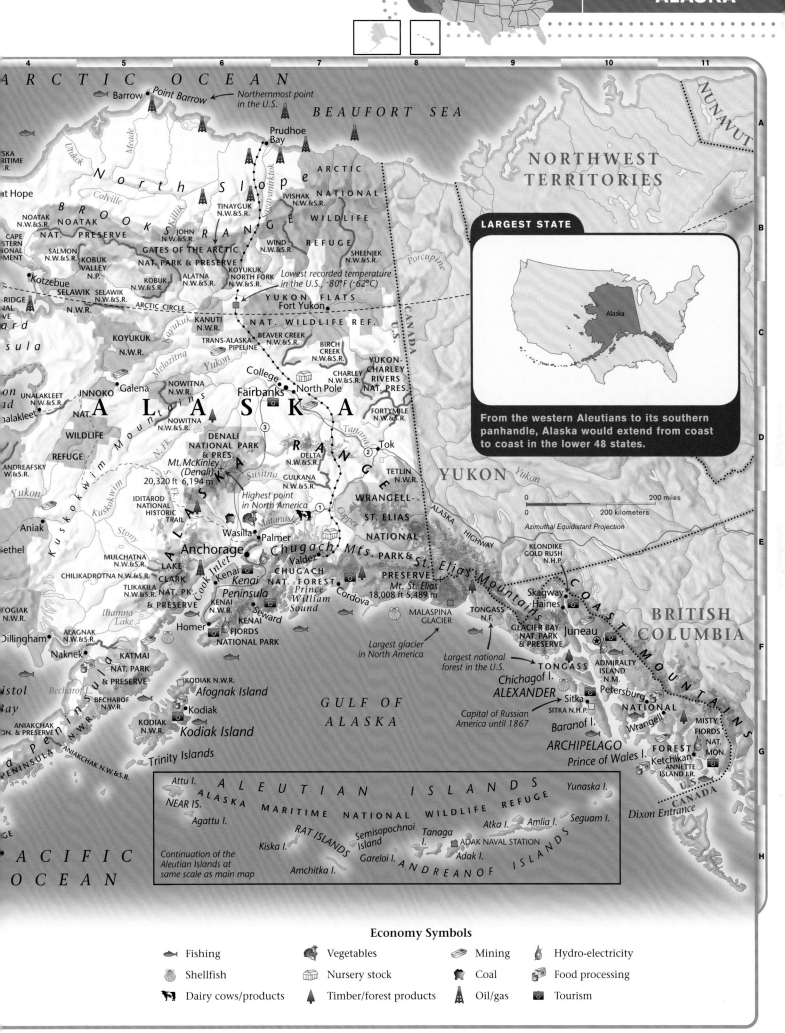

4 **5** **6** **7** **8** **9** **10** **11**

A R C T I C O C E A N

Barrow • Point Barrow ← Northernmost point in the U.S.

B E A U F O R T   S E A

Prudhoe Bay

ARCTIC

NUNAVUT

North Slope

Meade
Ukok
Colville

t Hope

SKA
ARITIME

BROOKS RANGE

NOATAK NAT. PRESERVE
NOATAK N.W.&S.R.
CAPE
STERN
ONAL
MENT

Kotzebue

SALMON N.W.&S.R.
KOBUK VALLEY N.P.

GATES OF THE ARCTIC
NAT. PARK & PRESERVE

TINAYGUK N.W.&S.R.
JOHN N.W.&S.R.

KOYUKUK, NORTH FORK N.W.&S.R.

IVISHAK N.W.&S.R.

WIND N.W.&S.R.

ARCTIC
NATIONAL
WILDLIFE
REFUGE

SHEENJEK N.W.&S.R.

NORTHWEST
TERRITORIES

Porcupine

Lowest recorded temperature in the U.S., -80°F (-62°C)

RIDGE
NAL
VE
ard
sula

SELAWIK N.W.R.
SELAWIK N.W.&S.R.

KOBUK N.W.&S.R.
ALATNA N.W.&S.R.

ARCTIC CIRCLE

KANUTI N.W.R.

YUKON FLATS
Fort Yukon
NAT. WILDLIFE REF.

BEAVER CREEK N.W.&S.R.

CANADA U.S.

LARGEST STATE

on
nd
nalakleet

KOYUKUK N.W.R.

TRANS-ALASKA PIPELINE

BIRCH CREEK N.W.&S.R.

CHARLEY N.W.&S.R.

YUKON-CHARLEY RIVERS NAT. PRES.

Alaska

UNALAKLEET N.W.&S.R.
INNOKO N.W.R.
Galena

NOWITNA N.W.R.
College
Fairbanks • North Pole

A L A S K A

NAT.
WILDLIFE
REFUGE

NOWITNA N.W.&S.R.

Melozitna
Yukon
Koyukuk

DENALI NATIONAL PARK & PRES.

FORTYMILE N.W.&S.R.

From the western Aleutians to its southern panhandle, Alaska would extend from coast to coast in the lower 48 states.

ANDREAFSKY W.&S.R.

Mt. McKinley (Denali) 20,320 ft 6,194 m

Kuskokwim Mountains
N. Fk.

ALASKA RANGE

Tanana

DELTA N.W.&S.R.

Tok

TETLIN N.W.R.

YUKON

Yukon

Yukon

Highest point in North America

GULKANA N.W.&S.R.

WRANGELL-ST. ELIAS NATIONAL

Aniak

IDITAROD NATIONAL HISTORIC TRAIL

Susitna

Wasilla
Palmer

Copper

PARK &
PRESERVE

ALASKA HIGHWAY

200 miles
200 kilometers
Azimuthal Equidistant Projection

ethel

Kuskokwim
Stony

Matanuska

Anchorage

Chugach Mts.

Mt. St. Elias 18,008 ft 5,489 m

St. Elias Mountains

KLONDIKE GOLD RUSH N.H.P.

MULCHATNA N.W.&S.R.
LAKE CLARK
CHILIKADROTNA N.W.&S.R.

Iliamna Lake

Cook Inlet

Kenai
CHUGACH NAT. FOREST

Valdez

Prince William Sound

Cordova

MALASPINA GLACIER

TONGASS N.F.

Skagway
Haines

COAST

TLIKAKILA N.W.&S.R.
LAKE CLARK NAT. PK. & PRESERVE

KENAI N.W.R.

Kenai Peninsula

Seward

Largest glacier in North America

GLACIER BAY NAT. PARK & PRESERVE

Juneau

MOUNTAINS

BRITISH
COLUMBIA

OGIAK N.W.R.

Homer

KENAI FJORDS NATIONAL PARK

Largest national forest in the U.S.

TONGASS

ADMIRALTY ISLAND N.M.

Dillingham •

ALAGNAK N.W.&S.R.

Naknek •

KATMAI NAT. PARK & PRESERVE

Becharof L.

KODIAK N.W.R.
Afognak Island

Chichagof I.
ALEXANDER

Capital of Russian America until 1867

Sitka
SITKA N.H.P.

NATIONAL

Petersburg

istol
ay

BECHAROF N.W.R.

Kodiak

GULF OF
ALASKA

Baranof I.

Wrangell

MISTY FIORDS NAT. MON.

ANIAKCHAK NON. & PRESERVE

KODIAK N.W.R.

Kodiak Island

ARCHIPELAGO

FOREST

a
PENINSULA

ANIAKCHAK N.W.&S.R.

Trinity Islands

Prince of Wales I.

Ketchikan
ANNETTE ISLAND I.R.

U.S.
CANADA

GE

P A C I F I C
O C E A N

Attu I.
NEAR IS.
A L E U T I A N   I S L A N D S
ALASKA MARITIME NATIONAL WILDLIFE REFUGE
Yunaska I.

Agattu I.

RAT ISLANDS

Kiska I.

Semisopochnoi Island

Tanaga I.

ADAK NAVAL STATION

Atka I.   Amlia I.   Seguam I.

Dixon Entrance

Continuation of the Aleutian Islands at same scale as main map

Amchitka I.

Gareloi I.

A N D R E A N O F   I S L A N D S

Adak I.

CANADA

Economy Symbols

🐟 Fishing	🦫 Vegetables	▭ Mining	💧 Hydro-electricity
🐚 Shellfish	🏠 Nursery stock	⛏ Coal	📷 Food processing
🐄 Dairy cows/products	🌲 Timber/forest products	🛢 Oil/gas	📷 Tourism

THE GOLDEN STATE:
CALIFORNIA

CALIFORNIA REPUBLIC

THE BASICS

STATS

Area
163,696 sq mi (423,972 sq km)

Population
37,253,956

Capital
Sacramento
Population 466,488

Largest city
Los Angeles
Population 3,792,621

Ethnic/racial groups
57.6% white; 13.0% Asian; 6.2% African American; 1.0% Native American. Hispanic (any race) 37.6%.

Industry
Electronic components and equipment, computers and computer software, tourism, food processing, entertainment, clothing

Agriculture
Fruits and vegetables, dairy products, cattle, forest products, commercial fishing

Statehood
September 9, 1850; 31st state

GEO WHIZ

Every December one of the largest gatherings of northern elephant seals in the world converges on the beaches of Año Nuevo State Reserve, south of San Francisco, to rest, mate, and give birth.

The Monterey Bay Aquarium has been working to save endangered sea otters for 20 years. Rescued animals that cannot be rehabilitated for re-release into the wild find a permanent home at the aquarium.

Castroville, known as the Artichoke Capital of the World, crowned future movie legend Marilyn Monroe its first-ever artichoke queen in 1947.

CALIFORNIA QUAIL
GOLDEN POPPY

CALIFORNIA

The coast of what is now California was visited by Spanish and English explorers in the mid-1500s, but colonization did not begin until 1769 when the first of 21 Spanish missions was established at San Diego. The missions, built to bring Christianity to the many native people living in the area, eventually extended up the coast as far as Sonoma along a road known as El Camino Real. The U.S. gained control of California in 1847, following a war with Mexico. The next year gold was discovered near Sutter's Mill, triggering a gold rush and migration from the eastern U.S. and around the world. Today, California is the most populous state, and its economy ranks above that of most of the world's countries. It is a major source of fruits, nuts, and vegetables, accounting for more than half of the U.S. output. The state is an industrial leader, producing jet aircraft, ships, and high-tech equipment. It is also a center for the enter-tainment industry.

⇧ ENGINEERING WONDER. Stretching more than a mile (1.6 km) across the entrance to San Francisco Bay, the Golden Gate Bridge opened to traffic in 1937. The bridge is painted vermilion orange, a color chosen in part because it is visible in fog.

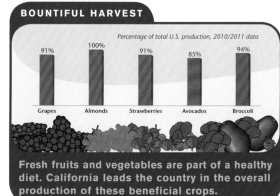

BOUNTIFUL HARVEST

Percentage of total U.S. production, 2010/2011 data

Grapes	Almonds	Strawberries	Avocados	Broccoli
91%	100%	91%	85%	94%

Fresh fruits and vegetables are part of a healthy diet. California leads the country in the overall production of these beneficial crops.

⇦ FOREST GIANT. Sequoias in Yosemite National Park's Mariposa Grove exceed 200 feet (61 m), making them the world's tallest trees. The trees, some of which are 3,000 years old, grow in isolated groves on the western slopes of the Sierra Nevada.

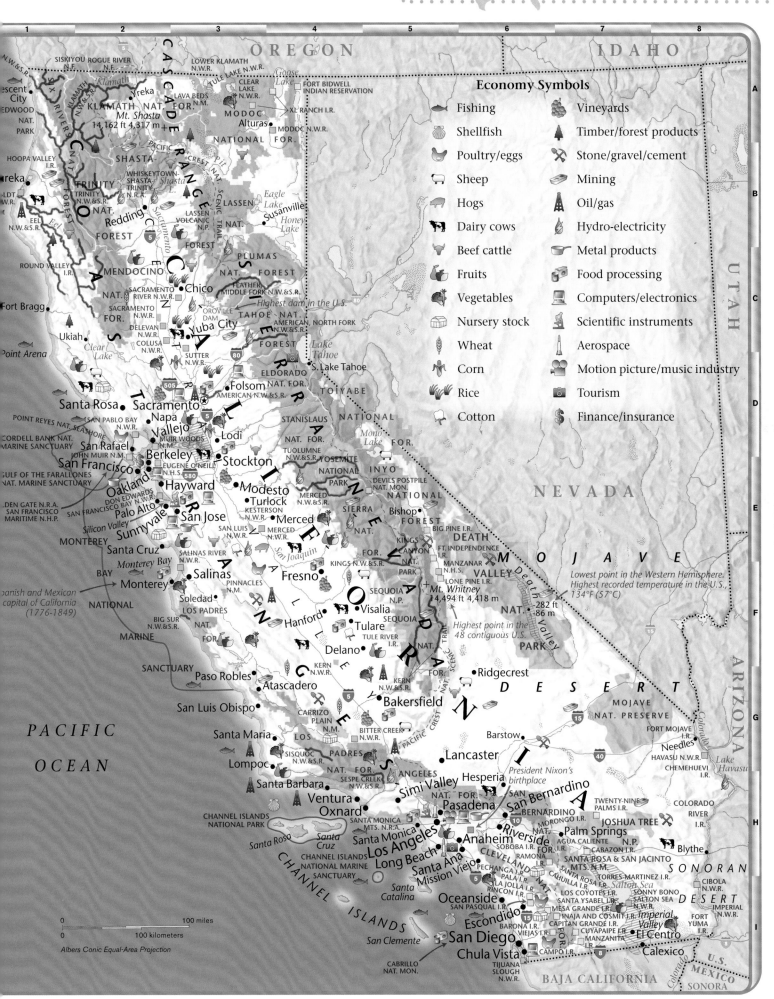

Economy Symbols

- Fishing
- Shellfish
- Poultry/eggs
- Sheep
- Hogs
- Dairy cows
- Beef cattle
- Fruits
- Vegetables
- Nursery stock
- Wheat
- Corn
- Rice
- Cotton

- Vineyards
- Timber/forest products
- Stone/gravel/cement
- Mining
- Oil/gas
- Hydro-electricity
- Metal products
- Food processing
- Computers/electronics
- Scientific instruments
- Aerospace
- Motion picture/music industry
- Tourism
- Finance/insurance

OREGON

IDAHO

NEVADA

UTAH

ARIZONA

PACIFIC OCEAN

*Mt. Shasta
14,162 ft 4,317 m*

Mt. Whitney
14,494 ft 4,418 m
*Highest point in the
48 contiguous U.S.*

-282 ft
-86 m
*Lowest point in the Western Hemisphere.
Highest recorded temperature in the U.S.,
134°F (57°C)*

DEATH VALLEY

MOJAVE DESERT

SONORAN DESERT

Los Angeles
San Diego
Sacramento
San Francisco
Fresno
Bakersfield

100 miles
100 kilometers
Albers Conic Equal-Area Projection

BAJA CALIFORNIA

MEXICO
SONORA

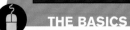

THE BASICS

STATS

Area
104,094 sq mi (269,602 sq km)

Population
5,029,196

Capital
Denver
Population 600,158

Largest city
Denver
Population 600,158

Ethnic/racial groups
81.3% white; 4.0% African American;
2.8% Asian; 1.1% Native American.
Hispanic (any race) 20.7%.

Industry
Real estate, government, durable
goods, communications, health and
other services, nondurable goods,
transportation

Agriculture
Cattle, corn, wheat, dairy products, hay

Statehood
August 1, 1876; 38th state

GEO WHIZ

The Black Canyon of the Gunnison is
one of the newest national parks
in the Rockies. As it flows through
the canyon, the Gunnison River
drops an average of 95 feet (29 m)
per mile—one of the steepest descents
in North America. The craggy rock walls
are a mecca for rock climbers.

Colorado's lynx population is making
a comeback, thanks to a program
that releases wild
cats captured in
Canada into
Colorado's
southern Rockies.
Since the program began in
1999, more than 200 cats have
been released and at least
141 lynx kittens have
been born.

LARK BUNTING
COLUMBINE

COLORADO

Indians were the earliest inhabitants of present-day Colorado. Some were cliff dwellers; others were plains dwellers. Spanish explorers arrived in Colorado in 1541. In 1803 eastern Colorado became U.S. territory as part of the Louisiana Purchase. Gold was discovered in 1858, and thousands were attracted by the prospect of quick wealth. The sudden jump in population led to conflict with native Cheyennes and Arapahos over control of the land, but the settlers prevailed. Completion of the transcontinental railroad in 1869 helped link Colorado to the eastern states and opened its doors for growth. Cattle ranching and farming developed on the High Plains of eastern Colorado, while the mountainous western part of the state focused on mining. Today, mining is still important in Colorado, but the focus has shifted to energy resources—oil, natural gas, and coal. Agriculture is also an important source of income, with cattle accounting for almost half of farm income. And Colorado's majestic mountains attract thousands of tourists each year.

⇧ THRILLING SPORT.
Colorado's snow-covered
mountains attract winter
sports enthusiasts from
near and far. In the past
skis were used by gold
prospectors. Today, skiing
and snowboarding are
big moneymakers in the
state's recreation and
tourism industry.

⇦ ANCIENT CULTURE. Ancestral Puebloans lived from about
A.D. 600 to A.D. 1300 in the canyons that today are a part of Mesa
Verde National Park. More than 600 stone structures were built
on protected cliffs of the canyon walls; others were located on
mesas. These dwellings hold many clues to a past way of life.

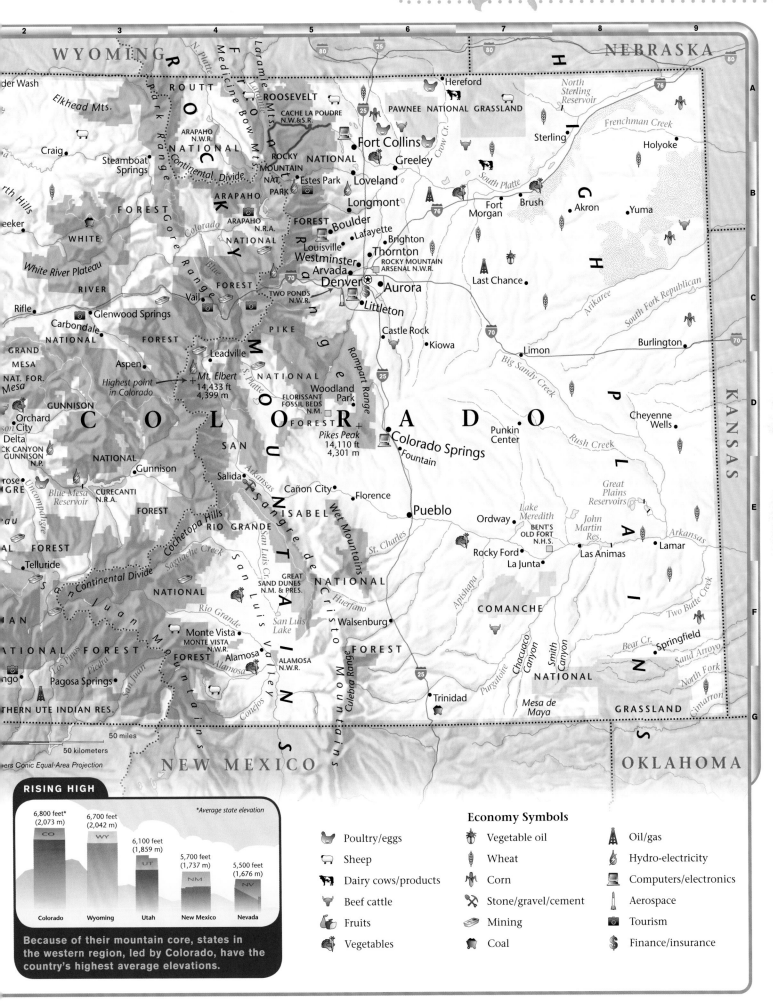

WYOMING

NEBRASKA

der Wash

Elkhead Mts.

ROUTT

N. Platte R.

Medicine Bow Mts.

Laramie Mts.

ROOSEVELT

CACHE LA POUDRE N.W.&S.R.

Hereford

PAWNEE NATIONAL GRASSLAND

North Sterling Reservoir

Frenchman Creek

Craig

Steamboat Springs

PARK RANGE

ARAPAHO N.W.R.

NATIONAL

Fort Collins

Greeley

Crow Cr.

Sterling

Holyoke

rth Hills

Continental Divide

FOREST

ROCKY MOUNTAIN NAT. PARK

NATIONAL

Estes Park

Loveland

South Platte

Fort Morgan

Brush

Akron

Yuma

eeker

WHITE

ARAPAHO

Colorado R.

ARAPAHO N.R.A.

Longmont

Boulder

Lafayette

Brighton

I-76

White River Plateau

RIVER

NATIONAL

Gore Range

Blue R.

FOREST

FOREST

Louisville

Westminster

Thornton

ROCKY MOUNTAIN ARSENAL N.W.R.

Last Chance

Arikaree R.

South Fork Republican

Rifle

Glenwood Springs

Vail

Front Range

I-70

Arvada

Denver

Aurora

TWO PONDS N.W.R.

Carbondale

Littleton

NATIONAL

PIKE

Castle Rock

Kiowa

Big Sandy Creek

Limon

Burlington

I-70

GRAND MESA

Leadville

Mt. Elbert 14,433 ft 4,399 m

Highest point in Colorado

S. Platte R.

NATIONAL

Rampart Range

Woodland Park

Cheyenne Wells

Mesa

NAT. FOR.

Aspen

MOUNTAIN

FLORISSANT FOSSIL BEDS N.M.

FOREST

Pikes Peak 14,110 ft 4,301 m

Colorado Springs

Fountain

Punkin Center

Rush Creek

Orchard City

Delta

GUNNISON

SAN

COLORADO

Great Plains Reservoirs

CK CANYON GUNNISON N.P.

NATIONAL

Gunnison

Arkansas R.

Salida

Cañon City

Florence

Pueblo

Ordway

Lake Meredith

John Martin Res.

Arkansas R.

Lamar

rose GRE

Blue Mesa Reservoir

CURECANTI N.R.A.

Uncompahgre R.

FOREST

ISABEL

Wet Mountains

St. Charles R.

Rocky Ford

La Junta

BENT'S OLD FORT N.H.S.

Las Animas

au

AL FOREST

Telluride

Cochetopa Hills

RIO GRANDE

Sangre de Cristo

Saguache Creek

San Luis Cr.

GREAT SAND DUNES N.M. & PRES.

NATIONAL

Huerfano R.

Apishapa R.

COMANCHE

Two Butte Creek

M N

Continental Divide

San Juan

NATIONAL

Rio Grande

San Luis Lake

San Luis Valley

MOUNTAINS

FOREST

Walsenburg

Chacuaco Canyon

Smith Canyon

Springfield

Bear Cr.

Sand Arroyo

ATIONAL FOREST

Monte Vista

MONTE VISTA N.W.R.

Alamosa

ALAMOSA N.W.R.

Sangre de Cristo Mountains

Culebra Range

FOREST

I-25

Purgatoire R.

NATIONAL

North Fork

ngo

Pagosa Springs

San Juan Mountains

Piedra R.

Conejos R.

Los Pinos R.

Alamosa R.

Trinidad

Mesa de Maya

GRASSLAND

Cimarron R.

THERN UTE INDIAN RES.

NEW MEXICO

OKLAHOMA

KANSAS

HIGH

PLAINS

50 miles

50 kilometers

ers Conic Equal-Area Projection

Economy Symbols

Poultry/eggs	Vegetable oil	Oil/gas
Sheep	Wheat	Hydro-electricity
Dairy cows/products	Corn	Computers/electronics
Beef cattle	Stone/gravel/cement	Aerospace
Fruits	Mining	Tourism
Vegetables	Coal	Finance/insurance

HAWAI'I

Some 1,500 years ago, Polynesians traveling in large canoes arrived from the south to settle the volcanic islands that make up Hawai'i. In 1778 Captain James Cook claimed the islands for Britain, and soon Hawai'i became a center of the whaling industry and a major producer of sugarcane. The spread of sugarcane plantations led to the importation of workers from Asia. Hawai'i became a U.S. territory in 1900. Naval installations, established as fueling depots and to protect U.S. interests in the Pacific, were attacked by the Japanese in 1941, an act that officially brought the U.S. into World War II. In 1959 Hawai'i became the 50th state. Tourism, agriculture, and the military, with bases centered on O'ahu's Pearl Harbor, are the cornerstone of Hawai'i's economy today. Jet airline service makes the distant islands accessible to tourists from both the mainland U.S. and Asia as well as from Australia and New Zealand. Hawai'i is still a major producer of sugarcane, along with nursery products and pineapples.

THE BASICS

STATS

Area
10,931 sq mi (28,311 sq km)

Population
1,360,301

Capital
Honolulu
Population 337,256

Largest city
Honolulu
Population 337,256

Ethnic/racial groups
38.6% Asian; 24.7% white; 10.0% Hawaiian/Pacific Islander; 1.6% African American. Hispanic (any race) 10.5%.

Industry
Tourism, trade, finance, food processing, petroleum refining, stone, clay, glass products

Agriculture
Sugarcane, pineapples, nursery stock, tropical fruit, livestock, macadamia nuts

Statehood
August 21, 1959; 50th state

GEO WHIZ

The shallow waters off the coast of Hawai'i are home to some of the world's most interesting sea creatures: marine worms. They were among the first sea animals more than 500 million years ago.

Hawai'i is the most isolated population center on Earth. It is more than 2,300 miles (3,700 km) from California, 3,850 miles (6,196 km) from Japan, and 4,900 miles (7,886 km) from China.

Everywhere else in the world caterpillars feed on plants. In Hawai'i there are 20 species that eat meat. Scientists have recorded the world's only known carnivorous caterpillars munching on ants.

You can ski two different ways on the same day in Hawai'i: on water at the beach and on snow on the slopes of Mauna Kea, a 13,796-foot-high volcano (4,205 m) on the Big Island.

HAWAIIAN GOOSE (NENE)
HIBISCUS

↑ ISLAND PARADISE. High-rise hotels light up Waikiki, the center of Honolulu's tourist industry. Thousands of visitors flock to the islands each year to enjoy the warm climate, sandy beaches, and rich, multicultural heritage of Hawai'i.

One of the world's rainiest spots

KAUA'I
Princeville
KILAUEA P.
N.W.R.
HANALEI N.W.R.
Wai'ale'ale
5,148 ft
1,569 m
Kapa'
Lehua I.
Hanan
Pu'uwai
Kekaha
Lihu'e
Kaulakahi Channel
NI'IHAU
Kalaheo
Kalaheo

Kure Atoll
Midway Islands
Pearl and Hermes At

NORTHWESTERN HI

Lisianski I.
Lc
I.

0   400 mi
0   400 kilometers
Oblique Mercator Projection

DANGER FROM BELOW

Continuous eruptions since 1983	Intermittent eruptions since 1980	Last eruption 1894	Last eruption 1790s	Last eruption 1786

Mt. Rainier, WA
Mount Hood, OR
Mount Shasta, CA
Mount St. Helens, WA
Kilauea, HI

Volcanoes release molten rock and gases from beneath Earth's crust, often with explosive force that can put people and property at great risk.

THE ALOHA STATE:
HAWAI'I

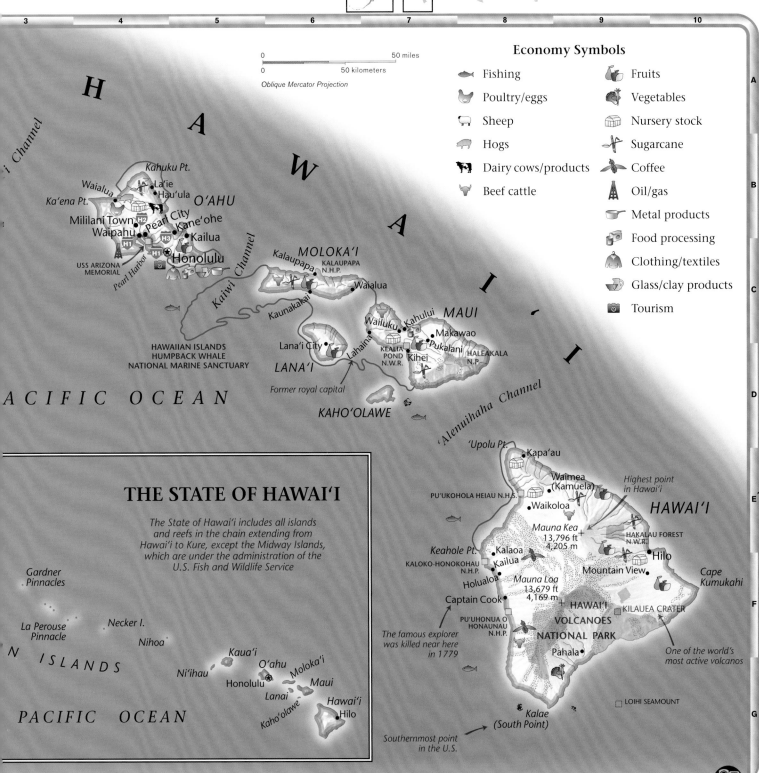

0 ————— 50 miles
0 ————— 50 kilometers
Oblique Mercator Projection

Economy Symbols

- Fishing
- Poultry/eggs
- Sheep
- Hogs
- Dairy cows/products
- Beef cattle
- Fruits
- Vegetables
- Nursery stock
- Sugarcane
- Coffee
- Oil/gas
- Metal products
- Food processing
- Clothing/textiles
- Glass/clay products
- Tourism

H A W A I ' I

O'AHU
Kahuku Pt.
Waialua
La'ie
Hau'ula
Ka'ena Pt.
Mililani Town
Pearl City
Kane'ohe
Waipahu
Kailua
Honolulu
USS ARIZONA MEMORIAL
Pearl Harbor
Kaiwi Channel

MOLOKA'I
Kalaupapa
KALAUPAPA N.H.P.
Waialua
Kaunakakai

HAWAIIAN ISLANDS
HUMPBACK WHALE
NATIONAL MARINE
SANCTUARY

LANA'I
Lana'i City
Lahaina
Former royal capital

MAUI
Wailuku
Kahului
Makawao
Pukalani
KEALIA POND N.W.R.
Kihei
HALEAKALA N.P.

KAHO'OLAWE

'Alenuihaha Channel

PACIFIC OCEAN

'Upolu Pt.
Kapa'au
Waimea (Kamuela)
Highest point in Hawai'i
PU'UKOHOLA HEIAU N.H.S.
Waikoloa
HAWAI'I
Keahole Pt.
Mauna Kea
13,796 ft
4,205 m
HAKALAU FOREST N.W.R.
KALOKO-HONOKOHAU N.H.P.
Kalaoa
Kailua
Hilo
Holualoa
Mountain View
Mauna Loa
13,679 ft
4,169 m
Cape Kumukahi
Captain Cook
The famous explorer was killed near here in 1779
PU'UHONUA O HONAUNAU N.H.P.
HAWAI'I VOLCANOES NATIONAL PARK
KILAUEA CRATER
Pahala
One of the world's most active volcanos
Kalae (South Point)
Southernmost point in the U.S.
LOIHI SEAMOUNT

THE STATE OF HAWAI'I

*The State of Hawai'i includes all islands
and reefs in the chain extending from
Hawai'i to Kure, except the Midway Islands,
which are under the administration of the
U.S. Fish and Wildlife Service*

Gardner
Pinnacles

La Perouse
Pinnacle

Necker I.

Nihoa

N ISLANDS

Kaua'i
Ni'ihau
O'ahu
Moloka'i
Maui
Honolulu
Lanai
Kaho'olawe
Hawai'i
Hilo

PACIFIC OCEAN

➪ **FIERY CREATION.** Hawai'i is the fastest-
growing state in the U.S.—not in people,
but in land. Active volcanoes are constantly
creating new land as lava continues to flow.
The Pu'u 'O'o vent on Kīlauea has added
more than 568 acres (230 ha) of new land
since it began erupting in 1983.

THE GEM STATE:
IDAHO

IDAHO

THE BASICS

STATS

Area
83,570 sq mi (216,447 sq km)

Population
1,567,582

Capital
Boise
Population 205,671

Largest city
Boise
Population 205,671

Ethnic/racial groups
89.1% white; 1.4% Native American; 1.2% Asian; .6% African American. Hispanic (any race) 11.2%.

Industry
Electronics and computer equipment, tourism, food processing, forest products, mining, chemicals

Agriculture
Potatoes, dairy products, cattle, wheat, alfalfa hay, sugar beets, barley, trout

Statehood
July 3, 1890; 43rd state

GEO WHIZ

Before the last ice age, mammoths, woolly rhinos, giant ground sloths, and other huge mammal species roamed what is now Idaho. Fossils of these prehistoric creatures are on display at the Museum of Idaho, in Idaho Falls.

Wood duck chicks born in Idaho and other Rocky Mountain states undergo an amazing rite of passage the day after they are born. If they want to eat, they have to jump as much as 60 feet (18 m) from their tree-hole nest to the water below, where their mother waits for them.

In preparation for their mission to the Moon, Apollo astronauts visited Craters of the Moon National Monument to study its volcanic geology and experience firsthand its harsh environment.

MOUNTAIN BLUEBIRD
SYRINGA (MOCK ORANGE)

Some of the earliest Native American sites in what is now Idaho date back 10,000 to 12,000 years. In the 18th and early 19th centuries, contact between native people and Europeans brought not only trade and cultural change but also diseases that

⇧ WOOLLY RUSH HOUR. Sheep fill a roadway in Idaho's Salmon River Valley. The herds move twice a year. In the spring they migrate north to mountain pastures. In the fall they return to the Snake River plains in the south.

wiped out many native groups. Present-day Idaho was part of the 1803 Louisiana Purchase, and in 1805 it was explored during the famous Lewis and Clark expedition. In 1843 wagons crossed into Idaho on the Oregon Trail. The arrival of white settlers brought conflict with the Indians, which continued until 1890 when Idaho became a state. Today, farming plays an important role in Idaho's economy. More than one-fifth of the land is planted with crops, especially wheat, sugar beets, barley, and potatoes. The state supports the use of alternative sources of energy, including geothermal, ethanol, wind, and biomass. The economy has diversified to include manufacturing and high-tech industries. The state's rugged natural beauty also attracts tourists year-round.

ANCIENT STAPLE FOOD

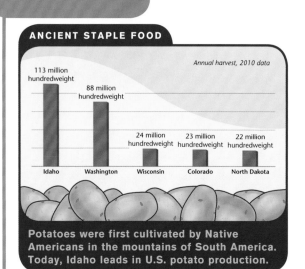

Annual harvest, 2010 data

Idaho	Washington	Wisconsin	Colorado	North Dakota
113 million hundredweight	88 million hundredweight	24 million hundredweight	23 million hundredweight	22 million hundredweight

Potatoes were first cultivated by Native Americans in the mountains of South America. Today, Idaho leads in U.S. potato production.

⇧ TIMBER! More than 40 percent of Idaho's land area is tree-covered, much of it in national forests. Lumber and paper products, most of which are sold to other states, are important to the state economy.

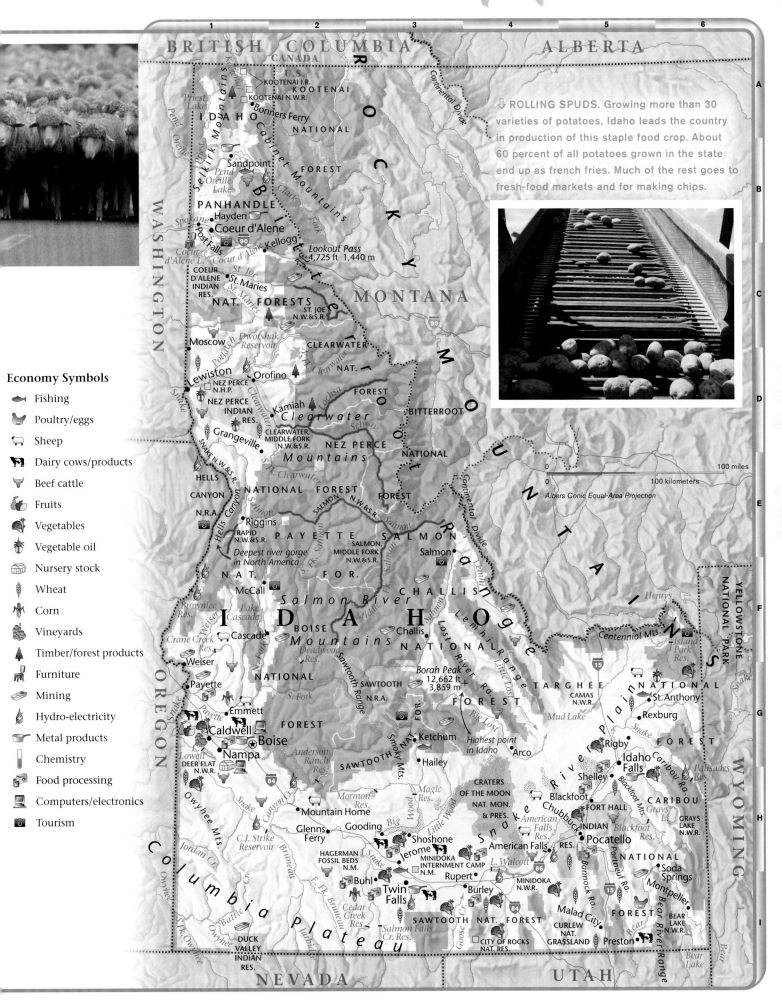

⇩ ROLLING SPUDS. Growing more than 30 varieties of potatoes, Idaho leads the country in production of this staple food crop. About 60 percent of all potatoes grown in the state end up as french fries. Much of the rest goes to fresh-food markets and for making chips.

Economy Symbols

- 🐟 Fishing
- 🐔 Poultry/eggs
- 🐑 Sheep
- 🐄 Dairy cows/products
- 🐂 Beef cattle
- 🍓 Fruits
- 🥬 Vegetables
- 🌱 Vegetable oil
- 🏠 Nursery stock
- 🌾 Wheat
- 🌽 Corn
- 🍇 Vineyards
- 🌲 Timber/forest products
- 🪑 Furniture
- ⛏ Mining
- 💧 Hydro-electricity
- 🍳 Metal products
- 🧪 Chemistry
- 📷 Food processing
- 💻 Computers/electronics
- 📷 Tourism

BRITISH COLUMBIA — **ALBERTA**
CANADA / U.S.

Priest Lake, Kootenai I.R., KOOTENAI N.W.R., KOOTENAI NATIONAL FOREST
Bonners Ferry
Sandpoint
Pend Oreille Lake
PANHANDLE
Hayden
Spokane, Coeur d'Alene
Post Falls, Kellogg
Lookout Pass 4,725 ft 1,440 m
Coeur d'Alene L.
COEUR D'ALENE INDIAN RES.
St. Joe, St. Maries
NAT. FORESTS
ST. JOE N.W.&S.R.
MONTANA
Moscow
Dworshak Reservoir
CLEARWATER NAT. FOREST
Lewiston
NEZ PERCE N.H.P.
Orofino
NEZ PERCE INDIAN RES.
Kamiah
Clearwater
BITTERROOT
CLEARWATER, MIDDLE FORK N.W.&S.R.
Grangeville
NEZ PERCE NATIONAL FOREST
Mountains
HELLS CANYON N.R.A.
NATIONAL FOREST
Riggins
RAPID N.W.&S.R.
PAYETTE SALMON-
SALMON, MIDDLE FORK N.W.&S.R.
Salmon
Deepest river gorge in North America
McCall
CHALLIS
Salmon River
IDAHO
BOISE
Challis
Borah Peak 12,662 ft 3,859 m
Highest point in Idaho
Cascade
Mountains
Deadwood Res.
NATIONAL
Brownlee Res.
Lake Cascade
Crane Creek
Weiser
SAWTOOTH N.R.A.
TARGHEE NATIONAL FOREST
CAMAS N.W.R.
St. Anthony
Payette
S. Fork
FOREST
Rexburg
Emmett
SAWTOOTH
Ketchum
Arco
Rigby
Caldwell
Idaho Falls
Boise
Nampa
Anderson Ranch Res.
Hailey
Shelley
DEER FLAT N.W.R.
Magic Res.
CRATERS OF THE MOON NAT. MON. & PRES.
Blackfoot
L. Lowell
Mormon Res.
Chubbuck
FORT HALL
Mountain Home
INDIAN RES.
Glenns Ferry
Gooding
Shoshone
American Falls
Pocatello
C.J. Strike Reservoir
Jerome
MINIDOKA INTERNMENT CAMP N.M.
American Falls Res.
Soda Springs
HAGERMAN FOSSIL BEDS N.M.
L. Walcott
Rupert
Buhl
Burley
Montpelier
Twin Falls
MINIDOKA N.W.R.
Malad City
BEAR LAKE N.W.R.
Cedar Creek Res.
SAWTOOTH NAT. FOREST
CURLEW NAT. GRASSLAND
Preston
DUCK VALLEY INDIAN RES.
Salmon Falls Cr. Res.
CITY OF ROCKS NAT. RES.
Bear Lake
NEVADA — **UTAH**

ROCKY MOUNTAINS
Bitterroot Range
Continental Divide
Snake River Plain
Columbia Plateau

0   100 miles
0   100 kilometers
Albers Conic Equal-Area Projection

WYOMING
YELLOWSTONE NATIONAL PARK
CARIBOU NATIONAL FOREST
GRAYS LAKE N.W.R.

MONTANA

THE BASICS

STATS

Area
147,042 sq mi (380,840 sq km)

Population
989,415

Capital
Helena
Population 28,190

Largest city
Billings
Population 104,170

Ethnic/racial groups
89.4% white; 6.3% Native American
.6% Asian; .4% African American.
Hispanic (any race) 2.9%.

Industry
Forest products, food processing,
mining, construction, tourism

Agriculture
Wheat, cattle, barley, hay, sugar beets,
dairy products

Statehood
November 8, 1889; 41st state

GEO WHIZ

The fossil of a dinosaur about the size of a large turkey is being called the missing link between Asian and North American horned dinosaurs. Paleontologist Jack Horner, who served as the model for the character of Alan Grant in the *Jurassic Park* movies, discovered the fossil while sitting on it during a lunch break at a dig near Choteau.

Montana is the only state with river systems that empty into the Gulf of Mexico, Hudson Bay, and the Pacific Ocean.

Grasshopper Glacier is littered with the bodies of thousands of grasshoppers that became trapped in the ice sometime before the species became extinct 200 years ago.

WESTERN MEADOWLARK
BITTERROOT

MONTANA

Long before the arrival of Europeans, numerous native groups lived and hunted in the plains and mountains of present-day Montana. While contact between European explorers and Native Americans was often peaceful, Montana was the site of the historic 1876 Battle of the Little Bighorn, in which Lakota (Sioux) and Cheyenne warriors defeated George Armstrong Custer's troops. In the mid-19th century the discovery of gold and silver attracted many prospectors, and later cattle ranching became big business, adding to tensions with the Indians. Montana became the 41st state in 1889. Today, Indians still make up more than 6 percent of the state's population—only four other states have a larger percent. Agriculture is an important part of the economy, producing wheat, hay, and barley as well as beef cattle. Mining and timber industries have seen a decline, but service industries and tourism are growing. Montana's natural environment, including Glacier and Yellowstone National Parks, remains one of its greatest resources.

⬆ STEP BACK IN TIME. Just like in the past, Montana ranchers move their cattle herds from low winter pastures to higher elevations for summer grazing. Some ranches allow adventurous tourists to participate in the drives.

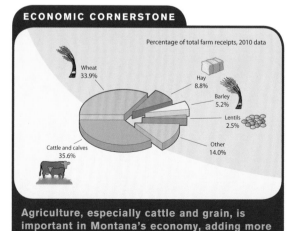

ECONOMIC CORNERSTONE

Percentage of total farm receipts, 2010 data

Wheat 33.9%
Hay 8.8%
Barley 5.2%
Lentils 2.5%
Other 14.0%
Cattle and calves 35.6%

Agriculture, especially cattle and grain, is important in Montana's economy, adding more than $3 billion to the state income each year.

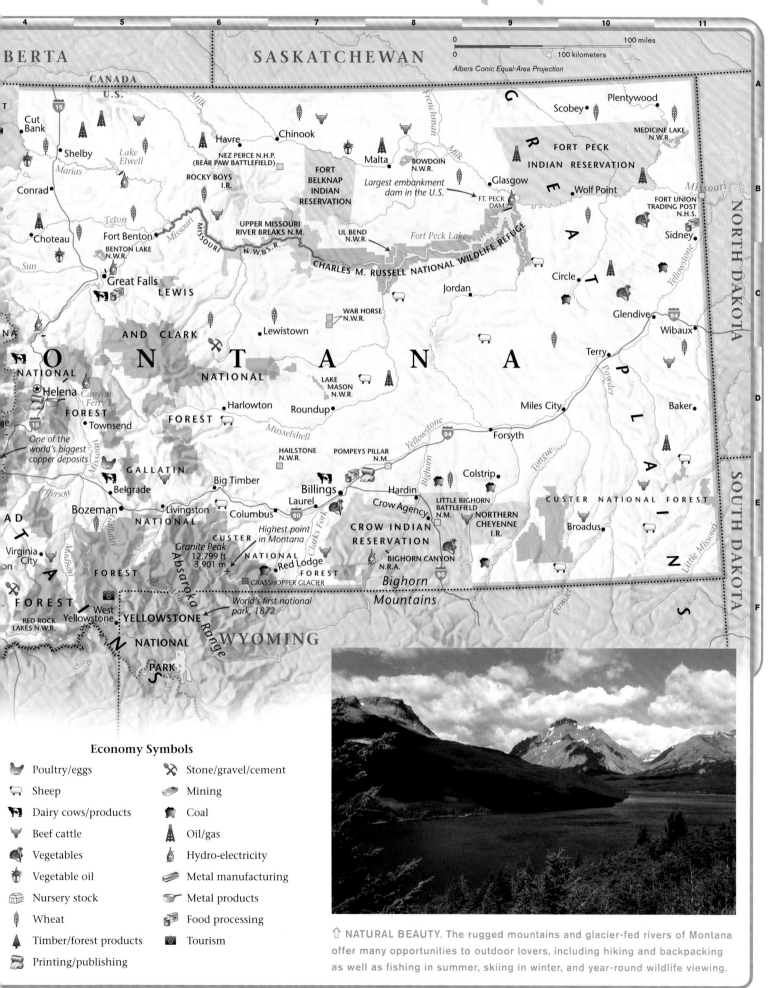

ALBERTA

SASKATCHEWAN

0   100 miles
0   100 kilometers
Albers Conic Equal-Area Projection

CANADA
U.S.

Cut Bank

Shelby

Lake Elwell

Conrad

Marias

Choteau

Teton

Fort Benton

Sun

BENTON LAKE N.W.R.

Great Falls

LEWIS

AND CLARK

NATIONAL

Helena

Canyon Ferry L.

FOREST

Townsend

One of the world's biggest copper deposits

NATIONAL

FOREST

GALLATIN

Belgrade

Bozeman

Virginia City

FOREST

Red Rock Lakes N.W.R.

West Yellowstone

YELLOWSTONE

NATIONAL

PARK

World's first national park, 1872

Havre

Chinook

NEZ PERCE N.H.P.
(BEAR PAW BATTLEFIELD)

ROCKY BOYS I.R.

FORT BELKNAP INDIAN RESERVATION

UPPER MISSOURI RIVER BREAKS N.M.

Missouri

N.W.&S.R.

Lewistown

WAR HORSE N.W.R.

LAKE MASON N.W.R.

Harlowton

Roundup

Musselshell

HAILSTONE N.W.R.

Big Timber

POMPEYS PILLAR N.M.

Billings

Laurel

Columbus

Livingston

Highest point in Montana

Granite Peak
12,799 ft
3,901 m

CUSTER

NATIONAL

FOREST

Red Lodge

GRASSHOPPER GLACIER

Absaroka Range

Malta

BOWDOIN N.W.R.

Largest embankment dam in the U.S.

FT. PECK DAM

UL BEND N.W.R.

CHARLES M. RUSSELL NATIONAL WILDLIFE REFUGE

Fort Peck Lake

Jordan

Frenchman

Milk

GREAT

Scobey

Plentywood

FORT PECK INDIAN RESERVATION

Glasgow

Wolf Point

MEDICINE LAKE N.W.R.

Missouri

FORT UNION TRADING POST N.H.S.

Sidney

Circle

Glendive

Wibaux

Terry

Yellowstone

PLAINS

Miles City

Forsyth

Baker

Yellowstone

Hardin

Crow Agency

Colstrip

LITTLE BIGHORN BATTLEFIELD N.M.

NORTHERN CHEYENNE I.R.

CROW INDIAN RESERVATION

BIGHORN CANYON N.R.A.

Bighorn Mountains

Bighorn

Tongue

Powder

CUSTER NATIONAL FOREST

Broadus

Little Missouri

NORTH DAKOTA

SOUTH DAKOTA

WYOMING

Economy Symbols

- Poultry/eggs
- Sheep
- Dairy cows/products
- Beef cattle
- Vegetables
- Vegetable oil
- Nursery stock
- Wheat
- Timber/forest products
- Printing/publishing

- Stone/gravel/cement
- Mining
- Coal
- Oil/gas
- Hydro-electricity
- Metal manufacturing
- Metal products
- Food processing
- Tourism

⇧ NATURAL BEAUTY. The rugged mountains and glacier-fed rivers of Montana offer many opportunities to outdoor lovers, including hiking and backpacking as well as fishing in summer, skiing in winter, and year-round wildlife viewing.

THE BASICS

STATS

Area
110,561 sq mi (286,352 sq km)

Population
2,700,551

Capital
Carson City
Population 55,274

Largest city
Las Vegas
Population 583,756

Ethnic/racial groups
66.2% white; 8.1% African American;
7.2% Asian; 1.2% Native American.
Hispanic (any race) 26.5%.

Industry
Tourism and gaming, mining, printing
and publishing, food processing,
electrical equipment

Agriculture
Cattle, hay, dairy products

Statehood
October 31, 1864; 36th state

GEO WHIZ

Lehman Caves, in Great Basin
National Park, contains the best
collection of shield, or angel wing,
formations in the country.

The Applegate Trail, named for two
brothers who first traveled it in 1846,
offered a shorter alternative to
the Oregon Trail. The trail
headed south from Idaho,
across Nevada's Black Rock
Desert into northern California
and then north into Oregon.

So many people claim to have seen
extraterrestrials along a 98-mile
(158-km) stretch of Nevada Highway
375 that the state transportation
board named it Extraterrestrial
Highway in 1996.

MOUNTAIN BLUEBIRD
SAGEBRUSH

NEVADA

Nevada's earliest settlers were native people about whom little is known. Around two thousand years ago, they began establishing permanent dwellings of clay and stone perched atop rocky ledges in what is today the state of Nevada. This was what Spanish explorers saw when they arrived in 1776. In years following, many expeditions passing through the area faced challenges of a difficult environment and native groups protecting their land. In the mid-1800s, gold and silver were discovered. In 1861, the Nevada Territory was created, and three years later statehood was granted. Today, the Nevada landscape is dotted with ghost towns—places once prosperous, but now abandoned except for curious tourists. Mining is now overshadowed by other economic activities. Casinos, modern hotels, and lavish entertainment attract thousands of visitors each year. Hoover Dam, on the Colorado River, supplies water and power to much of Nevada as well as two adjoining states. But water promises to be a challenge to Nevada's future growth.

⇧ TURNING BACK TIME. The Luxor, recreating a scene from ancient Egypt, is one of the many hotel-casinos that attract thousands of tourists to the four-mile (7-km) section of Las Vegas known as the Strip.

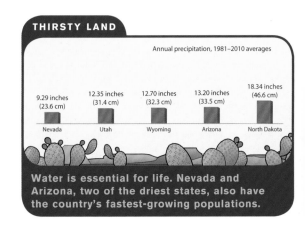

THIRSTY LAND

Annual precipitation, 1981–2010 averages

Nevada	Utah	Wyoming	Arizona	North Dakota
9.29 inches (23.6 cm)	12.35 inches (31.4 cm)	12.70 inches (32.3 cm)	13.20 inches (33.5 cm)	18.34 inches (46.6 cm)

Water is essential for life. Nevada and Arizona, two of the driest states, also have the country's fastest-growing populations.

⇦ PRICKLY GARDEN. Nevada's desert environment includes many varieties of cactuses. Saguaro and aloe plants as well as other xerophytes—plants that tolerate very dry conditions—thrive in this rocky garden.

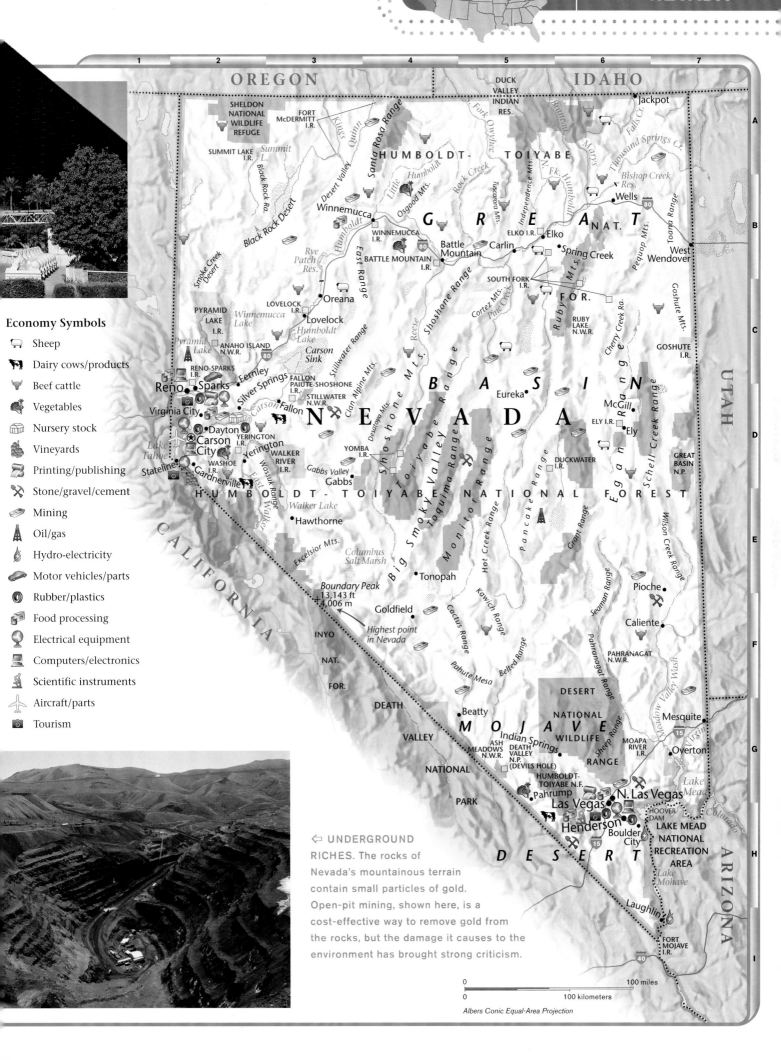

Economy Symbols

- 🐑 Sheep
- 🐄 Dairy cows/products
- 🐂 Beef cattle
- 🥬 Vegetables
- Nursery stock
- Vineyards
- Printing/publishing
- ⚒ Stone/gravel/cement
- Mining
- Oil/gas
- Hydro-electricity
- Motor vehicles/parts
- Rubber/plastics
- 📷 Food processing
- Electrical equipment
- 💻 Computers/electronics
- 🔬 Scientific instruments
- ✈ Aircraft/parts
- 📷 Tourism

OREGON   IDAHO

DUCK VALLEY INDIAN RES.

SHELDON NATIONAL WILDLIFE REFUGE

FORT McDERMITT I.R.

Jackpot

SUMMIT LAKE I.R.

Summit L.

Santa Rosa Range

Kings

Quinn

N. Fk. Owyhee

Marys

Falls Cr.

Brunea

Thousand Springs Cr.

Desert Valley

Black Rock Ra.

HUMBOLDT- TOIYABE

Humboldt

Bishop Creek Res.

Black Rock Desert

Osgood Mts.

Little Humboldt

Rock Creek

N. Fk. Humboldt

Toana Range

Winnemucca

Smoke Creek Desert

Humboldt

Rye Patch Res.

WINNEMUCCA I.R.

East Range

BATTLE MOUNTAIN I.R.

Battle Mountain

Tuscarora Mts.

Independence Mts.

ELKO I.R.

Carlin

Elko

Spring Creek

Wells

West Wendover

Pequop Mts.

GREAT

NAT.

Oreana

LOVELOCK I.R.

Lovelock

Humboldt Lake

Stillwater Range

Reese River

Shoshone Range

SOUTH FORK I.R.

Cortez Mts.

Pine Creek

Ruby Mts.

FOR.

RUBY LAKE N.W.R.

Cherry Creek Ra.

Goshute Mts.

GOSHUTE I.R.

PYRAMID LAKE I.R.

Winnemucca Lake

ANAHO ISLAND N.W.R.

Pyramid Lake

RENO-SPARKS I.R.

Fernley

Silver Springs

FALLON PAIUTE-SHOSHONE I.R.

Carson Sink

Clan Alpine Mts.

BASIN

Eureka

Egan Range

Schell Creek Range

McGill

GOSHUTE I.R.

Reno   Sparks

Virginia City

STILLWATER N.W.R.

Fallon

Desatoya Mts.

NEVADA

ELY I.R.

Ely

Dayton

YERINGTON I.R.

WASHOE

YOMBA I.R.

Toiyabe Range

Toquima Range

Monitor Range

DUCKWATER I.R.

GREAT BASIN N.P.

Carson City

Lake Tahoe

Stateline

Gardnerville

Yerington

WALKER RIVER I.R.

Wassuk Range

Gabbs Valley

Gabbs

Shoshone Mts.

Toiyabe Valley

Pancake Range

Grant Range

Wilson Creek Range

HUMBOLDT- TOIYABE

East Walker

Walker Lake

NATIONAL   FOREST

Hawthorne

Big Smoky Valley

Hot Creek Range

Seaman Range

Pioche

Excelsior Mts.

Columbus Salt Marsh

Tonopah

Monitor Range

Kawich Range

Caliente

Boundary Peak 13,143 ft 4,006 m

Goldfield

Cactus Range

Pahranagat Range

PAHRANAGAT N.W.R.

INYO

NAT.

Highest point in Nevada

Belted Range

Pahute Mesa

Meadow Valley Wash

FOR.

DEATH

Beatty

DESERT

NATIONAL

Mesquite

VALLEY

MOJAVE

Indian Springs

WILDLIFE

Sheep Range

MOAPA RIVER I.R.

Overton

NATIONAL

ASH MEADOWS N.W.R.

DEATH VALLEY N.P. (DEVILS HOLE)

RANGE

HUMBOLDT-TOIYABE N.F.

15

Lake Mead

PARK

Pahrump

Las Vegas

N. Las Vegas

HOOVER DAM

Colorado

Lake Mohave

Henderson

Boulder City

LAKE MEAD NATIONAL RECREATION AREA

MOJAVE   DESERT

ARIZONA

Laughlin

FORT MOJAVE I.R.

⇐ UNDERGROUND RICHES. The rocks of Nevada's mountainous terrain contain small particles of gold. Open-pit mining, shown here, is a cost-effective way to remove gold from the rocks, but the damage it causes to the environment has brought strong criticism.

UTAH

CALIFORNIA

0   100 miles
0   100 kilometers

Albers Conic Equal-Area Projection

THE BEAVER STATE:
OREGON

STATE OF OREGON

1859

THE BASICS

STATS

Area
98,381 sq mi (254,806 sq km)

Population
3,831,074

Capital
Salem
Population 154,637

Largest city
Portland
Population 583,776

Ethnic/racial groups
83.6% white; 3.7% Asian; 1.8% African American; 1.4% Native American. Hispanic (any race) 11.7%.

Industry
Real estate, retail and wholesale trade, electronic equipment, health services, construction, forest products, business services

Agriculture
Nursery stock, hay, cattle, grass seed, wheat, dairy products, potatoes

Statehood
February 14, 1859; 33rd state

GEO WHIZ

To recover wetlands and save two endangered fish species, 100 tons of explosives were used to blast through levees so that water from the Williamson River could again flow into Upper Klamath Lake.

Crater Lake, at 1,943 feet (592 m), is the deepest in the United States. It fills a depression created when an eruption caused the top of a mountain to collapse. Wizard Island, at the center of the 6-mile-wide lake (10 km), is the top of a volcano.

Snow-covered Mount Hood dominates the Portland skyline. The peak is one of the most active volcanoes in the Cascade Range. Its last eruption occurred just a few years before Lewis and Clark reached the region.

WESTERN MEADOWLARK
OREGON GRAPE

OREGON

Long before the Oregon Trail brought settlers from the eastern U.S., Indians fished and hunted in Oregon's coastal waters and forested valleys. Spanish explorers sailed along Oregon's coast in 1543, and in the 18th century fur traders from Europe set up forts in the region. In the mid-1800s settlers began farming the rich soil of the Willamette Valley. Oregon achieved statehood in 1859, and by 1883 Oregon was linked to the East by railroad, and Portland had become an important shipping center. Today, forestry, fishing, and agriculture make up an important part of the state's economy, but Oregon is making an effort to diversify into manufacturing and high-tech industries, as well. Dams on the Columbia River generate inexpensive electricity to support energy-hungry industries, such as aluminum production. Computers, electronics, and research-based industries are expanding. The state's natural beauty—snow-capped volcanoes, old-growth forests, and rocky coastline—makes tourism an important growth industry.

⇧ TOWER OF HISTORY. The 125-foot (38-m) Astoria Column, built in 1926 near the mouth of the Columbia River, is decorated with historic scenes of exploration and settlement along the Pacific Northwest coast.

⇦ CHANGING LANDSCAPE. Oregon's Pacific coast is a lesson on erosion and deposition. Rocky outcrops called sea stacks are leftovers of a former coastline that has been eroded by waves. The sandy beach is a result of eroded material being deposited along the shore.

Map labels:

PACIFIC OCEAN

FT. CLATSOP NAT. MEM.
Seaside
CAPE MEARES N.W.R.
Tillamook
Lincoln City
Newport
Florence
OREGON DUNES
N.R.A.
Reed
COOS, LOWER, UMPQUA, AND SUISLAW I.R.
Coos Bay
Coos Bay
North Be
COQUILLE I.R.
Coquille
BANDON MARSH N.W.R.
Cape Blanco
ELK N.W.&S.R.
SISKIYOU
Gold Beach
CHETCO N.W.&S.R.
Brookings
SMITH, N. FORK N.W.&S.R.
ILLIN N.W
NATION

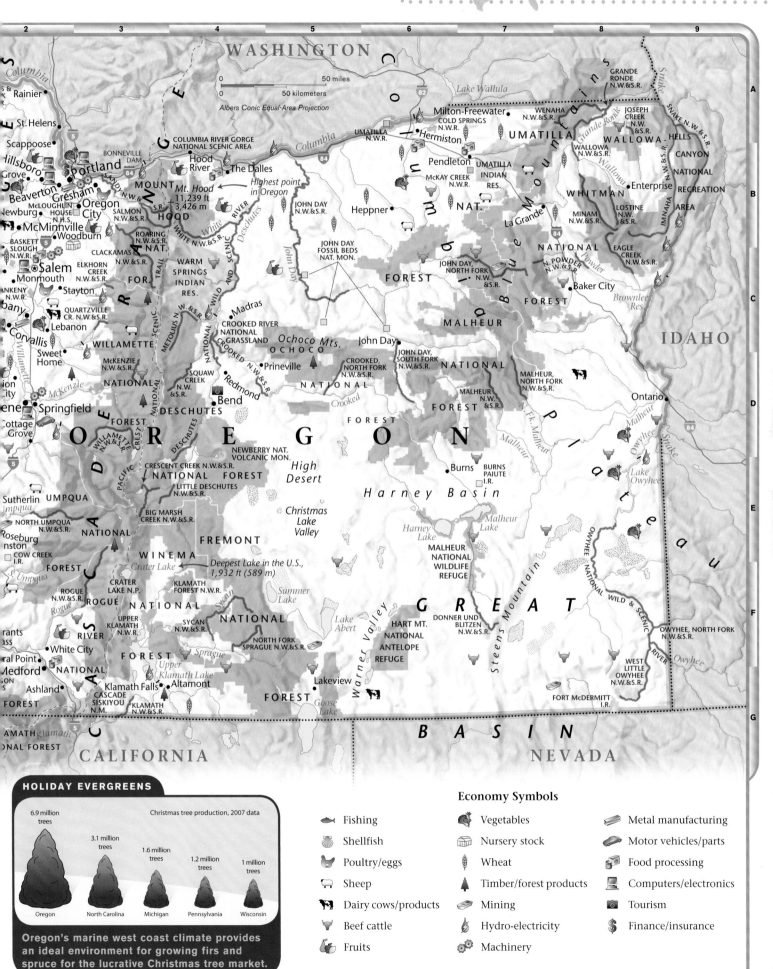

WASHINGTON

50 miles
50 kilometers
Albers Conic Equal-Area Projection

Columbia

Rainier
St. Helens
Scappoose
Hillsboro
Grove
Portland
Beaverton
Gresham
Newburg
McLOUGHLIN HOUSE N.H.S.
Oregon City
McMinnville
Woodburn
BASKETT SLOUGH
Salem
Monmouth
Stayton
ANKENY N.W.R.
Albany
Corvallis
Sweet Home
Lebanon
Sutherlin
Roseburg
Johnston
COW CREEK I.R.
grants pass
White City
ral Point
Medford
Ashland

BONNEVILLE DAM
Hood River
The Dalles
COLUMBIA RIVER GORGE NATIONAL SCENIC AREA
Mt. Hood
Highest point in Oregon 11,239 ft 3,426 m
MOUNT HOOD
SALMON N.W.&S.R.
ROARING R. N.W.&S.R.
CLACKAMAS N.W.&S.R.
WARM SPRINGS INDIAN RES.
ELKHORN CREEK N.W.&S.R.
QUARTZVILLE CR. N.W.&S.R.
WILLAMETTE
McKENZIE N.W.&S.R.
SQUAW CREEK N.W.&S.R.
METOLIUS N.W.&S.R.
CROOKED RIVER NATIONAL GRASSLAND
Madras
Prineville
Redmond
Bend
NATIONAL
FOR.
DESCHUTES
NEWBERRY NAT. VOLCANIC MON.
CRESCENT CREEK N.W.&S.R.
NATIONAL FOREST
LITTLE DESCHUTES N.W.&S.R.
BIG MARSH CREEK N.W.&S.R.
FREMONT
WINEMA
Crater Lake
Deepest Lake in the U.S., 1,932 ft (589 m)
CRATER LAKE N.P.
KLAMATH FOREST N.W.R.
NATIONAL
UPPER KLAMATH N.W.R.
ROGUE N.W.&S.R.
ROGUE RIVER
SYCAN N.W.&S.R.
NORTH FORK SPRAGUE N.W.&S.R.
NATIONAL
FOREST
Upper Klamath Lake
Klamath Falls
Altamont
CASCADE SISKIYOU N.M.
KLAMATH N.W.&S.R.

Columbia
Lake Wallula
Milton-Freewater
COLD SPRINGS N.W.R.
Hermiston
UMATILLA N.W.R.
WENAHA N.W.&S.R.
GRANDE RONDE N.W.&S.R.
Pendleton
UMATILLA INDIAN RES.
McKAY CREEK N.W.R.
Heppner
JOHN DAY N.W.&S.R.
JOHN DAY, NORTH FORK N.W. &S.R.
John Day
FOREST
MALHEUR
Ochoco Mts.
OCHOCO
CROOKED, NORTH FORK N.W.&S.R.
NATIONAL
FOREST
Crooked
JOHN DAY FOSSIL BEDS NAT. MON.
JOHN DAY, SOUTH FORK N.W.&S.R.
MALHEUR, NORTH FORK N.W.&S.R.
MALHEUR N.W. &S.R.
NATIONAL
FOREST
Burns
BURNS PAIUTE I.R.
High Desert
Christmas Lake Valley
Harney Basin
Harney Lake
Malheur Lake
MALHEUR NATIONAL WILDLIFE REFUGE
Summer Lake
Lake Abert
Sycan
Sprague
HART MT. NATIONAL ANTELOPE REFUGE
DONNER UND BLITZEN N.W.&S.R.
Warner Valley
Steens Mountain
GREAT
Lakeview
FORT McDERMITT I.R.
Goose Lake

UMATILLA
Grande Ronde
NAT.
La Grande
WHITMAN
MINAM N.W. &S.R.
N. POWDER N.W.&S.R.
Powder
Baker City
MALHEUR
Ontario
N. Fk. Malheur
Malheur
GRANDE RONDE N.W.&S.R.
JOSEPH CREEK N.W. &S.R.
WALLOWA
WALLOWA N.W.&S.R.
Wallowa
Enterprise
LOSTINE N.W. &S.R.
EAGLE CREEK N.W.&S.R.
HELLS CANYON NATIONAL RECREATION AREA
SNAKE N.W.&S.R.
IMNAHA
Brownlee Res.
IDAHO
Lake Owyhee
Malheur
OWYHEE NATIONAL WILD & SCENIC RIVER
Owyhee
OWYHEE, NORTH FORK N.W.&S.R.
WEST LITTLE OWYHEE N.W.&S.R.
Owyhee
Snake
Plateau

CALIFORNIA   NEVADA
BASIN
KLAMATH NAT. FOREST

Economy Symbols

- Fishing
- Shellfish
- Poultry/eggs
- Sheep
- Dairy cows/products
- Beef cattle
- Fruits
- Vegetables
- Nursery stock
- Wheat
- Timber/forest products
- Mining
- Hydro-electricity
- Machinery
- Metal manufacturing
- Motor vehicles/parts
- Food processing
- Computers/electronics
- Tourism
- Finance/insurance

THE BASICS

STATS

Area
84,899 sq mi (219,888 sq km)

Population
2,763,885

Capital
Salt Lake City
Population 186,440

Largest city
Salt Lake City
Population 186,440

Ethnic/racial groups
86.1% white; 2.0% Asian; 1.2% Native American; 1.1% African American. Hispanic (any race) 13.0%.

Industry
Government, manufacturing, real estate, construction, health services, business services, banking

Agriculture
Cattle, dairy products, hay, poultry and eggs, wheat

Statehood
January 4, 1896; 45th state

GEO WHIZ

A giant, duck-billed dinosaur is among the many kinds of dinosaur fossils that have been found in the Grand Staircase–Escalante National Monument. Scientists think the plant eater was at least 30 feet (9 m) long and had a mouthful of 300 teeth.

Drought has caused the level of Lake Powell to drop by more than 100 feet (30 meters), revealing much of the spectacular scenery of Glen Canyon that was drowned in 1963 when a dam created the lake.

Great Salt Lake is the largest natural lake west of the Mississippi River. The lake, which has a high level of evaporation, is about eight times saltier than the ocean.

CALIFORNIA GULL
SEGO LILY

UTAH

For thousands of years, present-day Utah was populated by Native Americans living in small hunter-gatherer groups, including the Utes for whom the state is named. Spanish explorers passed through Utah in 1776, and in the early 19th century trappers came from the East searching for beavers. In 1847, the arrival of Mormons seeking freedom to practice their religion marked the beginning of widespread settlement of the territory. They established farms and introduced irrigation. Discovery of precious metals in the 1860s brought miners to the territory. Today, almost 70 percent of Utah's land is set aside by the federal government for use by the military and defense industries and as national parks, which attract large numbers of tourists annually. As a result, government is a leading employer in the state. Another important force in Utah is the Church of Latter-day Saints (Mormons), which has influenced culture and politics in the state for more than a century. More than half the state's population is Mormon.

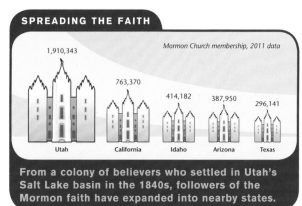

⇑ NATURE'S HANDIWORK. Arches National Park includes more than 2,000 arches carved by forces of water and ice, extreme temperatures, and the shifting of underground salt beds over a period of 100 million years. Delicate Arch stands on the edge of a canyon, with the La Sal Mountains in the distance.

SPREADING THE FAITH

Mormon Church membership, 2011 data

Utah	California	Idaho	Arizona	Texas
1,910,343	763,370	414,182	387,950	296,141

From a colony of believers who settled in Utah's Salt Lake basin in the 1840s, followers of the Mormon faith have expanded into nearby states.

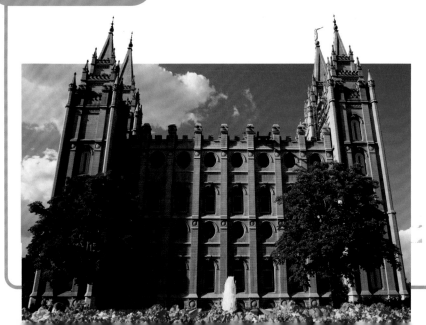

⇐ MONUMENT TO FAITH. Completed in 1893, the Salt Lake Temple is where Mormons gather to worship and participate in religious ceremonies. Church members regard temples as the most sacred places on Earth.

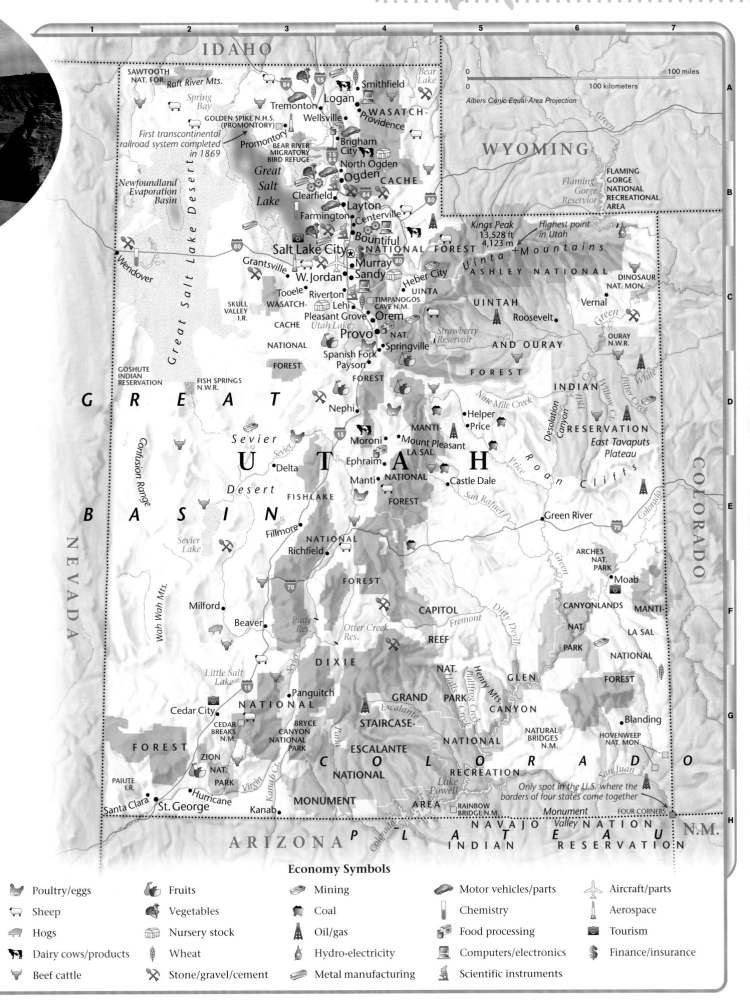

IDAHO

WYOMING

NEVADA

COLORADO

ARIZONA

N.M.

SAWTOOTH NAT. FOR.
Raft River Mts.
Spring Bay
GOLDEN SPIKE N.H.S. (PROMONTORY)
First transcontinental railroad system completed in 1869
Promontory
Newfoundland Evaporation Basin

Smithfield
Logan
WASATCH-
Providence
Tremonton
Wellsville
Brigham City
BEAR RIVER MIGRATORY BIRD REFUGE
North Ogden
Ogden
CACHE
Clearfield
Layton
Farmington
Centerville
Bountiful
Salt Lake City
NATIONAL FOREST
Murray
Grantsville
W. Jordan
Sandy
Heber City
Tooele
Riverton
WASATCH-
Lehi
CACHE
Pleasant Grove
Orem
NATIONAL
Provo
FOREST
Spanish Fork
Payson
Springville

Bear Lake
Flaming Gorge Reservoir
FLAMING GORGE NATIONAL RECREATIONAL AREA
Kings Peak 13,528 ft 4,123 m
Highest point in Utah
Uinta Mountains
ASHLEY NATIONAL
UINTA
UINTAH
Roosevelt
Strawberry Reservoir
AND OURAY
FOREST
DINOSAUR NAT. MON.
Vernal
OURAY N.W.R.
INDIAN
RESERVATION
East Tavaputs Plateau

Great Salt Lake
Great Salt Lake Desert

Wendover

GOSHUTE INDIAN RESERVATION
SKULL VALLEY I.R.
FISH SPRINGS N.W.R.
Confusion Range
Sevier
Sevier
Delta
Fillmore
Sevier Lake
FISHLAKE
Richfield

GREAT
BASIN
Desert
UTAH
Nephi
Moroni
Mount Pleasant
Ephraim
Manti
Castle Dale
Helper
Price
MANTI-
LA SAL
NATIONAL
FOREST
Nine Mile Creek
Desolation Canyon
Roan
Price
San Rafael
Cliffs
Green River
Bitter Creek
Willow Cr.
White

Wah Wah Mts.
Milford
Beaver
Piute Res.
Otter Creek Res.
NATIONAL
FOREST
CAPITOL REEF
Fremont
Dirty Devil
Green
ARCHES NAT. PARK
Moab
CANYONLANDS
NAT.
PARK
MANTI-
LA SAL
NATIONAL
FOREST

Little Salt Lake
Panguitch
Cedar City
CEDAR BREAKS N.M.
FOREST
ZION NAT. PARK
PAIUTE I.R.
Santa Clara
St. George
Hurricane
Kanab
NATIONAL
Sevier
DIXIE
BRYCE CANYON NATIONAL PARK
GRAND STAIRCASE-
ESCALANTE
NATIONAL
MONUMENT
Virgin
Kanab Cr.
Paria
Escalante
Henry Mts.
Bullfrog Creek
Halls Creek
GLEN
CANYON
NATURAL BRIDGES N.M.
Lake Powell
RAINBOW BRIDGE N.M.
NATIONAL
RECREATION
AREA
HOVENWEEP NAT. MON.
Blanding
San Juan
Only spot in the U.S. where the borders of four states come together
FOUR CORNERS
NAVAJO NATION Valley
Monument Valley
INDIAN RESERVATION
Colorado
ARIZONA PLATEAU

Economy Symbols

Poultry/eggs	Fruits	Mining	Motor vehicles/parts	Aircraft/parts
Sheep	Vegetables	Coal	Chemistry	Aerospace
Hogs	Nursery stock	Oil/gas	Food processing	Tourism
Dairy cows/products	Wheat	Hydro-electricity	Computers/electronics	Finance/insurance
Beef cattle	Stone/gravel/cement	Metal manufacturing	Scientific instruments	

THE EVERGREEN STATE:
WASHINGTON

THE BASICS

STATS

Area
71,300 sq mi (184,666 sq km)

Population
6,724,540

Capital
Olympia
Population 46,478

Largest city
Seattle
Population 608,660

Ethnic/racial groups
77.3% white; 7.2% Asian; 3.6% African American; 1.5% Native American. Hispanic (any race) 11.2%.

Industry
Aerospace, tourism, food processing, forest products, paper products, industrial machinery, printing and publishing, metals, computer software

Agriculture
Seafood, apples, dairy products, wheat, cattle, potatoes, hay

Statehood
November 11, 1889; 42nd state

GEO WHIZ

The forests of the Olympic Peninsula are among the world's rainiest places. The Hoh Rain Forest is one of the planet's few temperate rain forests.

Mount St. Helens, the most active volcano in the lower 48 states, is close to both Seattle and Portland, Oregon. The eruption in May 1980 reduced its elevation by 1,314 feet (401 m), triggering the largest landslide in recorded history.

Orcas, also known as killer whales, are the world's largest dolphins. The 90 or so that call the waters of Puget Sound home have been placed on the government's Endangered Species List.

AMERICAN GOLDFINCH

COAST RHODODENDRON

WASHINGTON

Long before Europeans explored the coast of the Pacific Northwest, Native Americans inhabited the area, living mainly off abundant seafood found in coastal waters and rivers. In the late 18th century, first Spanish sailors and then British explorers, including Captain James Cook, visited the region. Under treaties with Spain (1819) and Britain (1846), the U.S. gained control of the land, and in 1853 the Washington Territory was formally separated from the Oregon Territory. Settlers soon based their livelihood on fishing, farming, and lumbering. Washington became the 42nd state in 1889. The 20th century was a time of growth and development in Washington. Seattle became a major Pacific seaport. The Grand Coulee Dam, completed in 1941, provided the region with inexpensive electricity. Today, manufacturing, led by Boeing and Microsoft, is a mainstay of the economy. Washington leads the country in production of apples and sweet cherries, and the state is home to the headquarters of the popular Starbucks chain of coffee shops.

⇩ HARVEST TIME. Once a semiarid grassland, the Palouse region north of the Snake River in eastern Washington is now a major wheat-producing area.

⇧ PACIFIC GATEWAY. The city of Seattle, easily recognizable by its distinctive Space Needle tower, is a major West Coast port and home to the North Pacific fishing fleet.

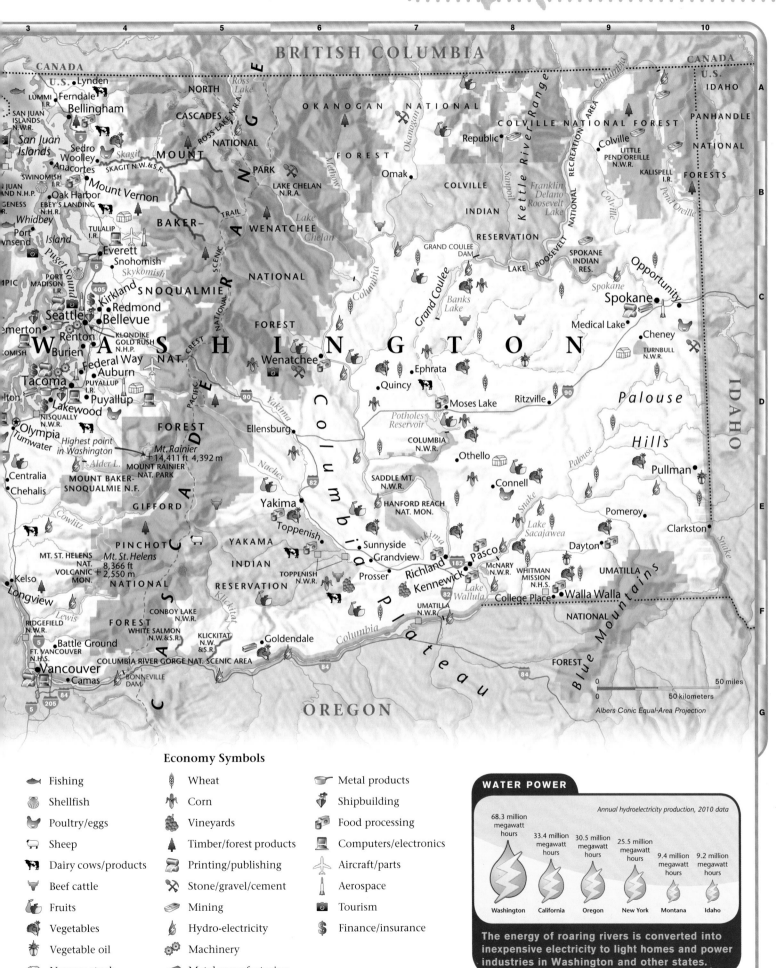

BRITISH COLUMBIA

CANADA
U.S.

CANADA
U.S.
IDAHO

PANHANDLE

NATIONAL

FORESTS

IDAHO

OREGON

Mt. Rainier
+14,411 ft 4,392 m
Highest point in Washington

Mt. St. Helens
8,366 ft
2,550 m

50 miles

50 kilometers

Albers Conic Equal-Area Projection

Economy Symbols

- Fishing
- Shellfish
- Poultry/eggs
- Sheep
- Dairy cows/products
- Beef cattle
- Fruits
- Vegetables
- Vegetable oil
- Nursery stock

- Wheat
- Corn
- Vineyards
- Timber/forest products
- Printing/publishing
- Stone/gravel/cement
- Mining
- Hydro-electricity
- Machinery
- Metal manufacturing

- Metal products
- Shipbuilding
- Food processing
- Computers/electronics
- Aircraft/parts
- Aerospace
- Tourism
- Finance/insurance

WATER POWER

Annual hydroelectricity production, 2010 data

Washington	California	Oregon	New York	Montana	Idaho
68.3 million megawatt hours	33.4 million megawatt hours	30.5 million megawatt hours	25.5 million megawatt hours	9.4 million megawatt hours	9.2 million megawatt hours

The energy of roaring rivers is converted into inexpensive electricity to light homes and power industries in Washington and other states.

THE BASICS

STATS

Area
97,814 sq mi (253,337 sq km)

Population
563,626

Capital
Cheyenne
Population 59,466

Largest city
Cheyenne
Population 59,466

Ethnic/racial groups
90.7% white; 2.4% Native American; .8% African American; .8% Asian. Hispanic (any race) 8.9%.

Industry
Oil and natural gas, mining, generation of electricity, chemicals, tourism

Agriculture
Cattle, sugar beets, sheep, hay, wheat

Statehood
July 10, 1890; 44th state

GEO WHIZ

The successful reintroduction of wolves into Yellowstone National Park, a program that began in the mid-1990s, has become a model for saving endangered carnivores around the world. In 2010 there were almost 350 wolves in 45 packs living in the Northern Rockies of Wyoming.

The National Elk Refuge, in Jackson Hole, provides a winter home for some 5,000 elk. The herd's migration from the refuge to their summer home in Yellowstone National Park is the longest elk herd migration in the lower 48 states.

Devils Tower, a huge formation of igneous rock near Sundance, was the country's first national monument. It was featured in the science-fiction classic *Close Encounters of the Third Kind.*

WESTERN MEADOWLARK
INDIAN PAINTBRUSH

WYOMING

When Europeans arrived in the 18th century in what would become Wyoming, various native groups were already there, living as nomads following herds of deer and bison across the plains. In the early 19th century fur traders moved into Wyoming, and settlers followed later along the Oregon Trail. Laramie and many of the state's other towns developed around old army forts built to protect wagon trains traveling through Wyoming. Today, fewer than 600,000 people live in all of Wyoming. The state's economy is based on agriculture—mainly grain and livestock production—and mining, especially energy resources. The state has some of the world's largest surface coal mines. In addition, it produces petroleum, natural gas, industrial metals, and precious gems. The natural environment is also a major resource. People come to Wyoming for fishing and hunting, for rodeos, and for the state's majestic mountains and parks. Yellowstone, established in 1872, was the world's first national park.

⇧ WANT TO RACE? Unique to the High Plains of the West, the pronghorn can sprint up to 60 miles per hour (97 kmph).

⇩ DRAMATIC LANDSCAPE. Rising more than 13,000 feet (3,900 m), the jagged peaks of the Tetons, one of the youngest mountain ranges of the West, tower over a barn on the valley floor.

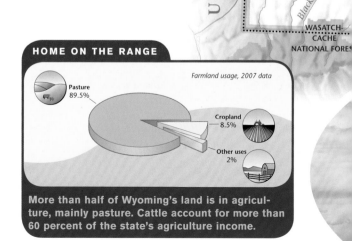

HOME ON THE RANGE

Farmland usage, 2007 data

Pasture 89.5%

Cropland 8.5%

Other uses 2%

More than half of Wyoming's land is in agriculture, mainly pasture. Cattle account for more than 60 percent of the state's agriculture income.

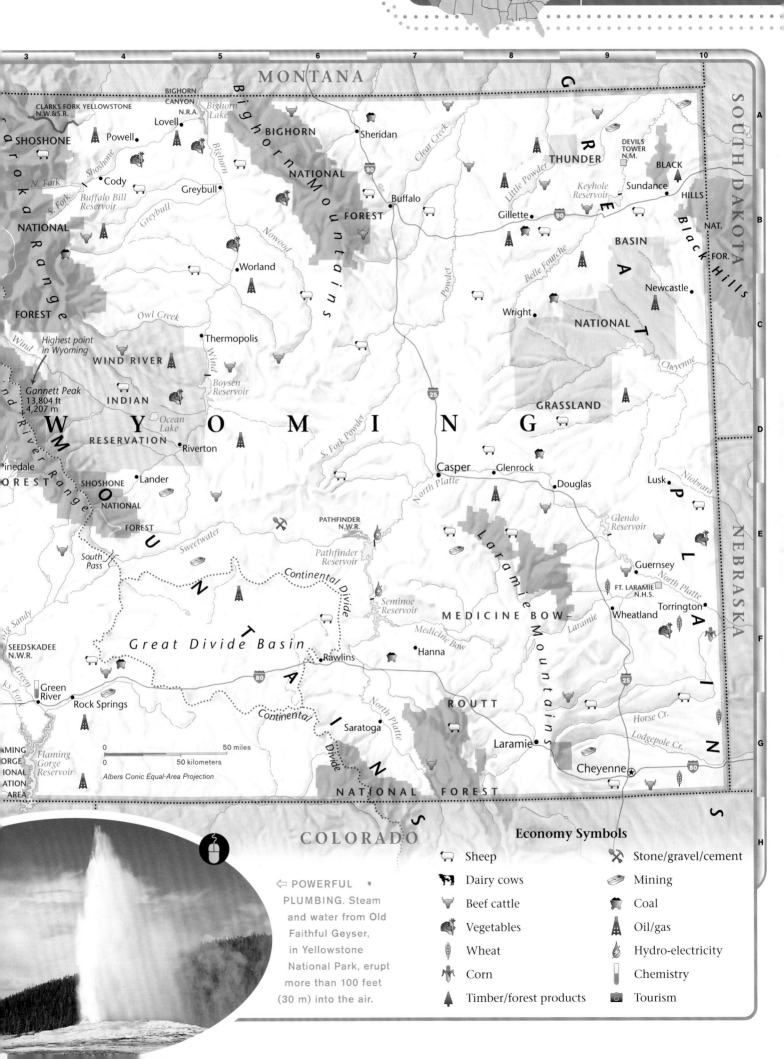

MONTANA

SOUTH DAKOTA

CLARKS FORK YELLOWSTONE
N.W.&S.R.

BIGHORN
CANYON
N.R.A.

Bighorn
Lake

BIGHORN

DEVILS
TOWER
N.M.

BLACK

NAT.
FOR.

SHOSHONE

Powell

Lovell

Sheridan

THUNDER

Sundance

HILLS

Cody

N. Fork

Shoshone

Greybull

NATIONAL

Clear Creek

Little Powder

Keyhole
Reservoir

Gillette

Buffalo

Black Hills

NATIONAL

Buffalo Bill
Reservoir

Greybull

Nowood

FOREST

90

BASIN

RANGE

Worland

Owl Creek

Belle Fourche

Wright

Newcastle

NATIONAL

FOREST

Thermopolis

Wind

Powder

Cheyenne

GREAT

Highest point
in Wyoming

WIND RIVER

Boysen
Reservoir

Gannett Peak
13,804 ft
4,207 m

INDIAN

Ocean
Lake

W   Y   O   M   I   N   G

GRASSLAND

inedale

RESERVATION

Riverton

S. Fork Powder

Wind River Range

SHOSHONE

Lander

Casper

Glenrock

Lusk

Niobrara

OREST

NATIONAL

Douglas

Glendo
Reservoir

M   O   U   N   T   A   I   N   S

FOREST

PATHFINDER
N.W.R.

P

SEEDSKADEE
N.W.R.

Sweetwater

Pathfinder
Reservoir

Laramie Mountains

Guernsey

South
Pass

Continental Divide

Seminoe
Reservoir

FT. LARAMIE
N.H.S.

North Platte

Torrington

L

Big Sandy

Great Divide Basin

MEDICINE BOW-

Wheatland

A

Green River

Rawlins

80

Medicine Bow

Laramie

Green

Hanna

I

Flaming
Gorge
Reservoir

Rock Springs

North Platte

ROUTT

Horse Cr.

MING
ORGE
IONAL
ATION
AREA

0   50 miles

0   50 kilometers

Albers Conic Equal-Area Projection

Saratoga

Continental

Divide

Laramie

Lodgepole Cr.

N

Cheyenne

80

NATIONAL   FOREST

S

COLORADO

NEBRASKA

Economy Symbols

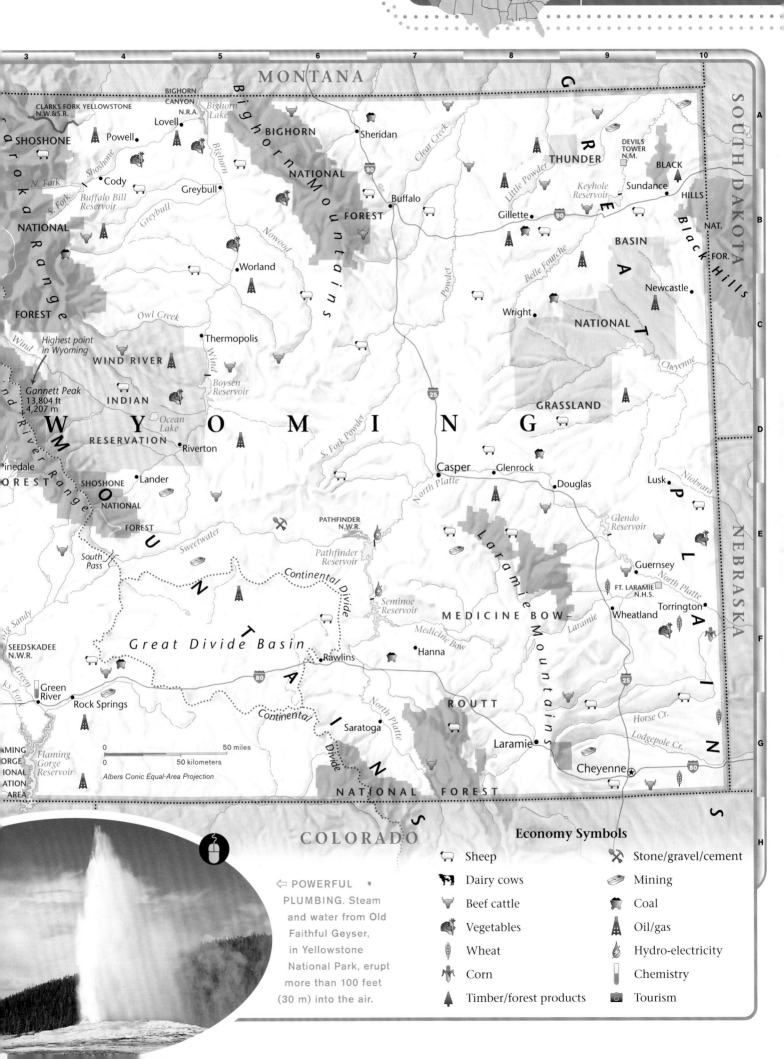

POWERFUL
PLUMBING. Steam
and water from Old
Faithful Geyser,
in Yellowstone
National Park, erupt
more than 100 feet
(30 m) into the air.

Symbol	Name	Symbol	Name
	Sheep		Stone/gravel/cement
	Dairy cows		Mining
	Beef cattle		Coal
	Vegetables		Oil/gas
	Wheat		Hydro-electricity
	Corn		Chemistry
	Timber/forest products		Tourism

The Territories

ACROSS TWO SEAS

Listed below are the 5 largest of the 14 U.S. territories, along with their flags and key information. Two of these are in the Caribbean Sea, and the other three are in the Pacific Ocean. Can you find the other 9 U.S. territories on the map?

U.S. CARIBBEAN TERRITORIES

PUERTO RICO

Area: 3,508 sq mi (9,086 sq km)

Population: 3,989,133

Capital: San Juan
Population 2,730,000

Languages: Spanish, English

U.S. VIRGIN ISLANDS

Area: 149 sq mi (386 sq km)

Population: 109,666

Capital: Charlotte Amalie
Population 54,000

Languages: English, Spanish or Spanish Creole, French or French Creole

U.S. PACIFIC TERRITORIES

AMERICAN SAMOA

Area: 77 sq mi (199 sq km)

Population: 67,242

Capital: Pago Pago
Population 60,000

Language: Samoan

GUAM

Area: 217 sq mi (561 sq km)

Population: 183,286

Capital: Hagåtña (Agana)
Population 153,000

Languages: English, Chamorro, Philippine languages

NORTHERN MARIANA ISLANDS

Area: 184 sq mi (477 sq km)

Population: 46,050

Capital: Saipan (Capitol Hill)
Population 1,500

Languages: Philippine languages, Chinese, Chamorro, English

OTHER U.S. TERRITORIES

Baker Island, Howland Island, Jarvis Island, Johnston Atoll, Kingman Reef, Midway Islands, Navassa Island, Palmyra Atoll, Wake Island

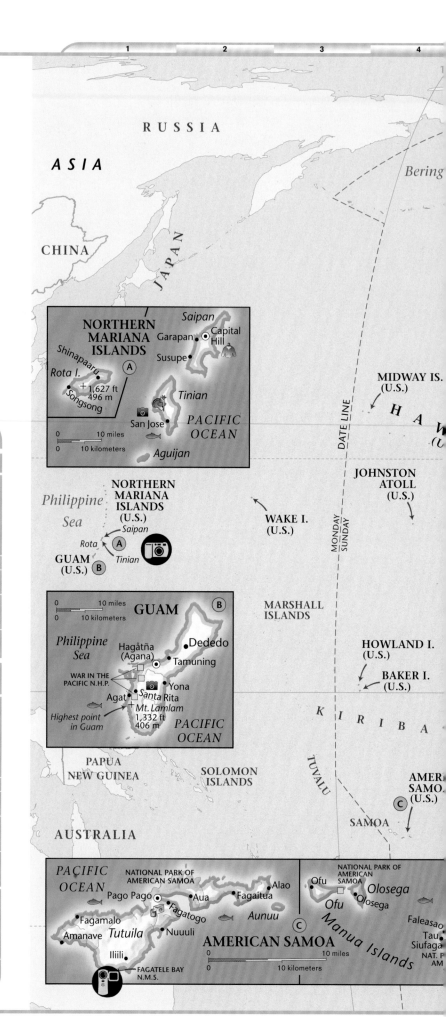

RUSSIA

ASIA

Bering

CHINA

JAPAN

NORTHERN MARIANA ISLANDS
Saipan
Garapan • ⊙ Capital Hill
Susupe •
Shinapaaru
Rota I. Ⓐ
+1,627 ft 496 m
Songsong
Tinian
San Jose •
PACIFIC OCEAN
Aguijan

0 — 10 miles
0 — 10 kilometers

Philippine Sea

NORTHERN MARIANA ISLANDS (U.S.)
Saipan
Rota Ⓐ
GUAM (U.S.) Ⓑ Tinian

MIDWAY IS. (U.S.)
H A W

DATE LINE

JOHNSTON ATOLL (U.S.)

WAKE I. (U.S.)

MONDAY SUNDAY

0 — 10 miles
0 — 10 kilometers
GUAM Ⓑ
Philippine Sea
Hagåtña (Agana) ⊙ • Dededo
• Tamuning
WAR IN THE PACIFIC N.H.P.
• Yona
Agat • Santa Rita
Highest point in Guam
+Mt. Lamlam 1,332 ft 406 m
PACIFIC OCEAN

MARSHALL ISLANDS

HOWLAND I. (U.S.)

BAKER I. (U.S.)

K I R I B A

PAPUA NEW GUINEA

SOLOMON ISLANDS

TUVALU

AMER SAMO (U.S.) Ⓒ

SAMOA

AUSTRALIA

PACIFIC OCEAN
NATIONAL PARK OF AMERICAN SAMOA
Pago Pago ⊙
Fagatogo
Fagamalo
Amanave Tutuila
Iliili
FAGATELE BAY N.M.S.
• Aua • Fagaitua • Alao
Aunuu
• Nuuuli
AMERICAN SAMOA

NATIONAL PARK OF AMERICAN SAMOA
Ofu • Olosega
Ofu • Olosega
Manua Islands
Faleasao
Tau
Siufaga
NAT. P
AM

0 — 10 miles
0 — 10 kilometers

Economy Symbols

- Fishing
- Shellfish
- Fruits
- Vegetables
- Sugarcane
- Tobacco
- Coffee
- Chemistry
- Food processing
- Clothing/textiles
- Jewelry
- Electrical equipment
- Tourism

0 — 2,000 miles
0 — 2,000 kilometers

Eckert 4 Equal-Area Projection

GREENLAND
(DENMARK)

ALASKA
(U.S.)

CANADA

NORTH

AMERICA

UNITED STATES

ATLANTIC

OCEAN

TROPIC OF CANCER

MEXICO

Gulf of
Mexico

BAHAMAS

DOMINICAN
REPUBLIC

CUBA

PUERTO RICO (U.S.)

JAMAICA   HAITI

U.S. VIRGIN IS.
(U.S.)

BELIZE

NAVASSA I.
(U.S.)

HONDURAS

Caribbean Sea

GUATEMALA

NICARAGUA

EL SALVADOR

COSTA RICA

GUYANA

VENEZUELA

SURINAME

PANAMA

COLOMBIA

KINGMAN REEF
(U.S.)

PACIFIC OCEAN

PALMYRA ATOLL
(U.S.)

EQUATOR

FRENCH
GUIANA
(FRANCE)

JARVIS I.
(U.S.)

ECUADOR

SOUTH

AMERICA

BRAZIL

PERU

BOLIVIA

FRENCH
POLYNESIA
(FRANCE)

U.S. VIRGIN ISLANDS

ATLANTIC OCEAN

Crown
Mt.
1,556 ft
474 m

St. Thomas

Charlotte Amalie

Cruz Bay

St. John

BUCK ISLAND
N.W.R.

VIRGIN
ISLANDS
N.P.

0 — 20 miles
0 — 20 kilometers

Caribbean Sea

GREEN CAY
N.W.R.

BUCK
ISLAND
REEF N.M.

SALT RIVER BAY N.H.P.
& ECOLOGICAL PRES.

CHRISTIANSTED
N.H.S.

Frederiksted

Christiansted

St. Croix

PACIFIC
OCEAN

Maia

Leusoalii

ta Mountain
170 ft
6 m

TROPIC OF CAPRICORN

PUERTO RICO

Arecibo

Vega Baja

San Juan

SAN JUAN
N.H.S.

ATLANTIC
OCEAN

Aguadilla

Cataño

Carolina

Trujillo Alto

CULEBRA
N.W.R.

Fajardo

CARIBBEAN N.F.
(EL YUNQUE)

Culebra I.

Mayagüez

Cordillera Central

Caguas

Humacao

LAGUNA
CARTAGENA
N.W.R.

Cerro de Punta
4,390 ft 1,338 m
Highest point
in Puerto Rico

Cayey

Guayama

Vieques I.

CABO ROJO
N.W.R.

Ponce

0 — 20 miles
0 — 20 kilometers

Caribbean Sea

⇨ PRESERVING TRADITION. Young dancers from American Samoa, dressed in costumes of feathers and pandanus leaves, prepare to perform in the Pacific Arts Festival, which is held once every four years to promote Pacific cultures.

The Territories
ISLANDS IN THE FAMILY

Fourteen territories and commonwealths scattered across the Pacific and Caribbean came under U.S. influence after wars or various international agreements. Because they are neither states nor independent countries, the U.S. government provides economic and military aid. Puerto Rico's nearly four million residents give it a population greater than that of 24 U.S. states. Many tourists seeking sunny beaches visit the Virgin Islands, purchased from Denmark for $25 million in 1917. American Samoa, Guam, and the Northern Mariana Islands in the Pacific have sizable popula-

⇧ RELIC OF THE PAST. Sugar mill ruins on St. John, in the U.S. Virgin Islands, recall a way of life that dominated the Caribbean in the 18th and 19th centuries. Plantations used slave labor to grow cane and make it into sugar and molasses.

tions, but several tiny atolls have no civilian residents and are administered by the U.S. military or government departments. In most cases, citizens of these territories are also eligible for American citizenship.

WHERE THE PICTURES ARE

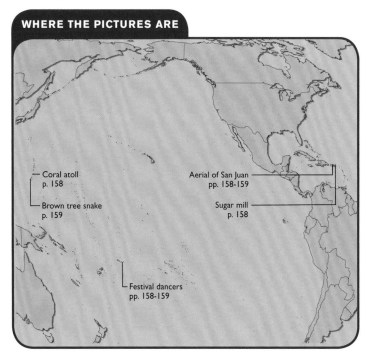

Coral atoll
p. 158

Brown tree snake
p. 159

Festival dancers
pp. 158-159

Aerial of San Juan
pp. 158-159

Sugar mill
p. 158

⇐ PACIFIC JEWEL. Managaha Island sits in the blue-green waters of a lagoon formed by a long reef along Saipan's western coast. Marine biologists fear that portions of the reef are dying due to pollution. The lagoon holds wrecks from battles fought in Northern Mariana waters during World War II.

⇐ ATLANTIC PLAYGROUND. Modern hotels, catering to more than 3 million tourists annually, rise above sandy beaches in San Juan, Puerto Rico. Founded in 1521, the city has one of the best natural harbors in the Caribbean.

⇓ UNWELCOME STOWAWAY. The brown tree snake probably arrived in Guam on cargo ships in the 1950s. The snake has greatly reduced the island's bird and small mammal populations and causes power outages when it climbs electric poles.

U.S. FACTS & FIGURES

THE COUNTRY

STATS

Founding
1776

Area
3,794,083 sq mi (9,826,675 sq km)

Population (December 2011)
312,782,167

Capital
Washington, D.C.

Population
601,723

Largest city
New York

Population
8,782,166

Ethnic/racial groups
72.4% white; 12.6% African American;
4.8% Asian; .9% Native American.
Hispanic (any race) 16.3%.

Languages
(most widely spoken)
English, Spanish

Economy
Services: 76.7% of GDP
Industry: 22.2% of GDP
Agriculture: 1.2% of GDP

BALD EAGLE,
NATIONAL SYMBOL

Top States

Listed below are major farm products, fish, and minerals and the states that currently lead in their production. Following each list is a ranking of the top states in each category.

Farm Products

Cattle and calves: Texas, Kansas, Nebraska, Iowa
Dairy products: California, Wisconsin, New York, Pennsylvania
Soybeans: Iowa, Illinois, Minnesota, Nebraska
Corn for grain: Iowa, Illinois, Nebraska, Minnesota
Hogs and pigs: Iowa, North Carolina, Minnesota, Illinois
Broiler chickens: Georgia, Arkansas, Alabama, North Carolina
Wheat: North Dakota, Kansas, Montana, Washington
Cotton: Texas, Georgia, North Carolina, Arkansas
Eggs: Iowa, Ohio, Pennsylvania, Indiana
Hay: Texas, California, Missouri, South Dakota
Tobacco: North Carolina, Kentucky, Tennessee, Virginia
Turkeys: Minnesota, North Carolina, Missouri, Indiana
Oranges: Florida, California, Texas, Arizona
Potatoes: Idaho, Washington, Wisconsin, Colorado
Grapes: California, Washington, New York
Tomatoes (processed): Florida, Georgia, California

Rice: Arkansas, California, Louisiana, Mississippi

Top Ten in Farm Products
(by net farm income)

1. California
2. Iowa
3. Illinois
4. Nebraska
5. Minnesota
6. North Carolina
7. Indiana
8. South Dakota
9. Kansas
10. Georgia

Fish

Shrimp: Louisiana, Texas, Florida, Alabama
Crabs: Alaska, Louisiana, Oregon, Maryland, California
Lobsters: Maine, Massachusetts, Florida, Rhode Island
Salmon: Alaska, Washington, Oregon, California
Pollock: Alaska, Massachusetts, Maine, New Hampshire

Top Five in Fisheries
(by value of catch)

1. Alaska
2. Massachusetts
3. Maine
4. Louisiana
5. Washington

Minerals

Crude oil: Texas, Alaska, California, North Dakota, New Mexico
Natural gas: Texas, Wyoming, Oklahoma, Louisiana, Colorado
Coal: Wyoming, West Virginia, Kentucky, Pennsylvania, Montana
Crushed stone: Texas, Pennsylvania, Missouri, Illinois, Florida
Copper: Arizona, Utah, Nevada, New Mexico, Montana
Cement: Texas, California, Missouri, Pennsylvania, Alabama
Construction sand and gravel: Texas, California, Arizona, Colorado, Wisconsin
Gold: Nevada, Alaska, Utah, Colorado, California
Iron ore: Michigan, Minnesota
Clay: Georgia, Wyoming, Alabama, Texas, North Carolina
Phosphate rock: Florida, North Carolina, Idaho, Utah
Lime: Alabama, Kentucky, Missouri, Nevada, Ohio
Salt: Louisiana, Texas, New York, Kansas, Utah
Sulfur: Louisiana, Texas

Top Ten in Minerals

1. Nevada
2. Arizona
3. Florida
4. Utah
5. California
6. Texas
7. Alaska
8. Minnesota
9. Missouri
10. Wyoming

Extremes

World's Strongest Surface Wind
231 mph (372 kmph), Mount Washington, New Hampshire, April 12, 1934

World's Tallest Living Tree
"Hyperion," a coast redwood in Redwood National Park, California, 379.1 ft (115.55 m) high

World's Oldest Living Tree
Methuselah bristlecone pine, California; 4,789 years old

World's Largest Gorge
Grand Canyon, Arizona; 290 mi (466 km) long, 600 ft to 18 mi (183 m to 29 km) wide, 1 mile (1.6 km) deep

Highest Temperature in U.S.
134°F (56.6°C), Death Valley, California, July 10, 1913

Lowest Temperature in U.S.
Minus 80°F (-62.2°C) at Prospect Creek, Alaska, January 23, 1971

Highest Point in U.S.
Mount McKinley (Denali), Alaska; 20,320 ft (6,194 m)

Lowest Point in U.S.
Death Valley, California; 282 feet (86 m) below sea level

Longest River System in U.S.
Mississippi-Missouri; 3,710 mi (5,971 km) long

Rainiest Spot in U.S.
Wai'ale'ale (mountain), Hawai'i: average annual rainfall 460 in (1,168 cm)

Metropolitan Areas With More Than Five Million People
A metropolitan area is a city and its surrounding suburban areas. (2010 data)

1. New York, pop. 18,897,109
2. Los Angeles, pop. 12,828,837
3. Chicago, pop. 9,461,105
4. Dallas–Fort Worth, pop. 6,371,773
5. Philadelphia, pop. 5,965,343
6. Houston, pop. 5,946,800
7. Washington, D.C., pop. 5,582,170
8. Miami, pop. 5,564,635
9. Atlanta, pop. 5,268,860

GLOSSARY

aquaculture raising fish or shellfish in controlled ponds or waterways for commercial use

atoll a circular coral reef enclosing a tropical lagoon

arid climate type of dry climate in which annual precipitation is often less than 10 inches (25 cm)

biomass total weight of all organisms found in a given area

bituminous coal a soft form of coal used in industries and power plants

bog a poorly drained area with wet, spongy ground

broadleaf forest trees with wide leaves that are shed during the winter season

butte a high, steep-sided rock formation created by the erosion of a mesa

canal an artificial waterway that is used by ships or to carry water for irrigation

center-pivot irrigation an irrigation system that rotates around a piped water source at its middle, often resulting in circular field patterns

continental climate temperature extremes with long cold winters and heavy snowfall

continental divide an elevated area that separates rivers flowing toward opposite sides of a continent; in the U.S. this divide follows the crest of the Rocky Mountains

copra dried coconut meat from which oil is extracted to make a variety of products, including soap, candles, and cosmetics

Creole a simplified or modified form of a language, such as French or Spanish, used for communication between two groups; spoken in some Caribbean islands

delta lowland formed by silt, sand, and gravel deposited by a river at its mouth

desert vegetation plants such as cactus and dry shrubs that have adapted to conditions of low, often irregular precipitation

fork in a river, the place where two streams join

Fortune 500 company ranking of the top 500 U.S. companies based on total revenue

fossil remains of or an impression left by the remains of plants or animals preserved in rock

geothermal energy a clean, renewable form of energy derived from heat that flows continuously from Earth's interior

grassland areas with medium to short grasses; found where precipitation is not sufficient to support tree growth

gross domestic product (GDP) the total value of goods and services produced in a country in a year

highland climate found in association with high mountains where elevation affects temperature and precipitation

hundredweight in the U.S., a commercial unit of measure equal to 100 pounds

ice age a very long period of cold climate when glaciers often cover large areas of land

intermittent river/lake a stream or lake that contains water only part of the time, usually after heavy rain or snowmelt

lava molten rock from Earth's interior that flows out on the surface during volcanic activity

levee an embankment, usually earth or concrete, built to prevent a river from overflowing

lignite low-grade coal used mainly to produce heat in thermal-electric generators

marine west coast climate type of mild climate found on the mid-latitude West Coast of the U.S.

Mediterranean climate type of mild climate found on the West Coast of the U.S., south of the marine west coast climate

mesa an eroded plateau, broader than it is high, that is found in arid or semiarid regions

metropolitan area a city and its surrounding suburbs or communities

mild climate moderate temperatures with distinct seasons and ample precipitation

nursery stock young plants, including fruits, vegetables, shrubs, and trees, raised in a greenhouse or nursery

pinnacle a tall pillar of rock standing alone or on a summit

plain a large area of relatively flat land that is often covered with grasses

plateau a relatively flat area, larger than a mesa, that rises above the surrounding landscape

population density the average number of people living on each square mile or square kilometer of a specific land area

precipitate process of depositing dissolved minerals as water evaporates, as in limestone caves

rangeland areas of grass prairie that are used for grazing livestock

reactor a device that uses controlled nuclear fission to divide an atomic nucleus to generate power

Richter scale ranking of the power of an earthquake; the higher the number, the stronger the quake

Rust Belt a region made up of northeastern and midwestern states that have experienced a decline in heavy industry and an out-migration of population

scale on a map, a means of explaining the relationship between distances on the map and actual distances on Earth's surface

stalactite column of limestone hanging from the ceiling of a cave that forms as underground water drips down and evaporates, leaving dissolved minerals behind

stalagmite column of limestone that forms on the floor of a cave when underground water drips down and evaporates, leaving dissolved minerals behind

staple main item in an economy; also, main food for domestic consumption

Sunbelt a region made up of southern and western states that are experiencing major in-migration of population and rapid economic growth

territory land that is under the jurisdiction of a country but that is not a state or a province

tropical zone the area bounded by the Tropic of Cancer and the Tropic of Capricorn, where it is usually warm year-round

tundra vegetation plants, often stunted in size, that have adapted to periods of extreme cold and a short growing season; found in polar regions and high elevations

urban areas in which natural vegetation has been replaced by towns or cities, where the main economic activity is nonagricultural

volcanic pipe a vertical opening beneath a volcano through which molten rock has passed

wetland land that is either covered with or saturated by water; includes swamps, marshes, and bogs

OUTSIDE WEB SITES

The following Web sites will provide you with additional valuable information about various topics discussed in this atlas. You can find direct links to each by going to the atlas URL (www.nationalgeographic.com/kids-usa-atlas) and clicking on "Resources."

General information:
States: www.state.al.us (This is for Alabama; for each state insert the two-letter state abbreviation where "al" is now.)

D.C. and the Territories:
Washington, D.C.: kids.dc.gov/kids_main_content.html
American Samoa: www.samoanet.com
Guam: ns.gov.gu
Northern Marianas: www.saipan.com/gov
Puerto Rico: www.prstar.net
U.S. Virgin Islands: www.gov.vi

Natural Environment:
Biomes: www.blueplanetbiomes.org
Climate: www.eoearth.org
Global Warming: www.nrdc.org/globalWarming

Climate:
www.noaa.gov/climate.html
www.worldclimate.com (for cities)
www.cpc.noaa.gov

Natural Hazards:
General: www.usgs.gov/hazards
Droughts: www.drought.unl.edu/DM/monitor.html
Earthquakes: earthquake.usgs.gov
Hurricanes: hurricanes.noaa.gov
Tornadoes: www.tornadoproject.com
Tsunamis: www.noaa.gov/tsunamis.html
Volcanoes: www.geo.mtu.edu/volcanoes
Wildfires: www.nifc.gov/ and www.fs.fed.us/fire

Population:
States: quickfacts.census.gov/qfd
Cities: www.city-data.com
Population migration: www.census.gov/prod/2001pubs/p23-204.pdf
Hispanic population: www.census.gov/prod/2003pubs/p20-545.pdf

Getting Green:
www.epa.gov/
www.earthday.org
www.footprintnetwork.org/index.php

Bird sounds:
www.animalbehaviorarchive.org/loginPublic.do

Mapping site:
earth.google.com

PLACE-NAME INDEX

Map references are in boldface (**50**) type. Letters and numbers following in lightface (D12) locate the place-names using the map grid. (Refer to page 7 for more details.)

A

Abbeville, AL **61** G6
Abbeville, LA **71** G4
Abbeville, SC **76** C2
Aberdeen, MD **39** A8
Aberdeen, MS **73** C5
Aberdeen, SD **111** B8
Aberdeen, WA **152** D2
Abert, Lake, OR **149** F5
Abilene, KS **97** C7
Abilene, TX **127** D5
Abingdon, VA **80** E3
Abraham Lincoln Birthplace National Historic Site, KY **69** D6
Absaroka Range, MT, WY **155** A3
Absecon, NJ **45** H3
Acadia N.P., ME **37** G6
Ada, OK **125** D9
Adak Island, AK **135** H8
Adams, MA **40** A1
Adamsville, RI **51** E7
Adel, GA **67** H4
Adirondack Mountains, NY **47** B7
Adirondack Park, NY **47** C7
Admiralty Island Nat. Mon., AK **135** F10
Adrian, MI **99** I7
Afognak Island, AK **135** F6
Afton, WY **154** E1
Agana *see* Hagåtña, GU **156** F1
Agat, GU **156** G1
Agate Fossil Beds Nat. Mon., NE **104** B1
Agattu Island, AK **135** H6
Agawam, MA **41** D3
Agua Fria (river), AZ **121** E4
Agua Fria Nat. Mon., AZ **121** E4
Aguadilla, PR **157** H9
Aguijan (island), MP **156** D1
Ahoskie, NC **75** B9
Aiken, SC **77** E4
Ainsworth, NE **105** B5
Aitkin, MN **101** D4
Ajo, AZ **121** G3
Akron, CO **139** B8
Akron, OH **109** B6
Alabama (river), AL **61** F3
Alabaster, AL **61** D3
Alagnak N.W.&S.R., AK **135** F5
Alamogordo, NM **123** G5
Alamosa, CO **139** F4
Alamosa (river), CO **139** F4
Alao, AS **156** H2
Alapaha (river), GA **67** H4
Alaska Highway, AK **135** E8
Alaska Peninsula, AK **134** G3
Alaska Range, AK **135** E6
Alaska, Gulf of, AK **135** G7
Alatna N.W.&S.R., AK **135** B6
Albany, GA **67** G3
Albany, KY **69** E7
Albany, NY **47** E8
Albany, OR **149** C2
Albemarle, NC **75** C5
Albemarle Sound, NC **75** B10
Albert Lea, MN **101** H4
Albertville, AL **61** B4
Albion, MI **99** H6
Albion, NE **105** C7
Albuquerque, NM **123** D4
Alburg, VT **53** A1
Alcoa, TN **79** C8
Alder Lake, WA **153** E4
'Alenuihaha Channel, HI **141** D7
Aleutian Islands, AK **135** G6
Aleutian World War II National Historic Area, AK **134** H2
Alexander Archipelago, AK **135** F9
Alexander City, AL **61** D5
Alexandria, IN **93** D4
Alexandria, LA **71** D4
Alexandria, MN **101** E2
Alexandria, SD **111** E9
Alexandria, VA **81** B10
Algoma, WI **113** E7
Algona, IA **95** B4
Alibates Flint Quarries Nat. Mon., TX **127** B4
Alice, TX **127** H6
Aliceville, AL **61** D1
Aliquippa, PA **48** D1
Allagash (river), ME **37** B4
Allagash, ME **37** A4
Allagash Lake, ME **37** C4
Allagash Wilderness Waterway, ME **37** C4
Allatoona Lake, GA **67** C2
Allegheny (river), PA **48** D2
Allegheny Mountains, **28** G2
Allegheny N.W.&S.R., PA **49** B3
Allegheny Portage Railroad National Historic Site, PA **49** D4
Allegheny Reservoir, PA **49** A3
Allendale, SC **77** F4
Allenton, RI **51** E4
Allentown, PA **49** D9
Alliance, NE **104** B2
Alliance, OH **109** C7
Alligator (river), NC **75** B10
Alma, MI **99** G6
Alma, NE **105** E6
Alpena, MI **99** E7
Alpine, TX **126** F2
Altamaha (river), GA **67** G6
Altamont, OR **149** G3
Altavista, VA **81** E7
Alton, IL **91** F3
Alton Bay, NH **43** G4
Altoona, PA **49** D4
Altoona, WI **113** D3
Alturas, CA **137** A4
Altus, OK **125** E6
Altus, Lake, OK **125** D6
Alva, OK **125** A7
Amana Colonies (site), IA **95** D8
Amanave, AS **156** I1
Amarillo, TX **127** B3
Amchitka Island, AK **135** H7
American Falls, ID **143** H4
American Falls Reservoir, ID **143** H4
American N.W.&S.R., CA **137** D3
American Samoa (territory), US **156** G4
American, North Fork N.W.&S.R., CA **137** C4
Americus, GA **67** F3
Ames, IA **95** D5
Amesbury, MA **41** A7
Amherst, MA **41** C3
Amherst, NY **46** D2
Amistad N.R.A., TX **127** F4
Amistad Reservoir, TX **127** F4
Amite, LA **71** F7
Amlia Island, AK **135** H9
Ammonoosuc (river), NH **43** D3
Amory, MS **73** C5
Amsterdam, NY **47** D8
Anaconda, MT **144** D3
Anacortes, WA **153** B3
Anadarko, OK **125** D7
Anamosa, IA **95** C9
Anchorage, AK **135** E6
Andalusia, AL **61** G4
Anderson, IN **93** D4
Anderson, SC **76** C2
Anderson Ranch Reservoir, ID **143** G2
Andersonville National Historic Site, GA **67** F3
Andreafsky N.W.&S.R., AK **135** D4
Andreanof Islands, AK **135** H8
Andrew Johnson National Historic Site, TN **79** B10
Andrews, TX **127** D3
Androscoggin (river), ME, NH **43** C4
Angola, IN **93** A5
Aniak, AK **135** E4
Aniakchak N.W.&S.R., AK **135** G4
Aniakchak Nat. Mon. and Preserve, AK **135** G4
Ankeny, IA **95** D5
Ann Arbor, MI **99** H7
Ann, Cape, MA **41** A8
Anna, IL **91** I4
Anna, Lake, VA **81** C9
Annapolis, MD **39** C8
Anniston, AL **61** C5
Ansonia, CT **33** D3
Anthony, KS **97** E6
Anthony, NM **123** H4
Anthony, RI **51** D4
Antietam N.B., MD **39** B5
Antigo, WI **113** D5
Antlers, OK **125** E11
Antrim, NH **43** H2
Apache-Sitgreaves National Forests, AZ, NM **121** E7
Apalachicola (river), FL **65** B3
Apishapa (river), CO **139** F7
Apostle Islands, WI **113** A4
Apostle Islands National Lakeshore, WI **113** A3
Appalachian Mountains, **56** C5
Appalachian National Scenic Trail, **47** G7
Appalachian Plateau, **28** F2
Apple (river), WI **113** D2
Appleton, WI **113** E6
Appomattox, VA **81** D7
Appomattox (river), VA **81** D8
Appomattox Court House N.H.P., VA **81** D7
Arapaho N.R.A., CO **139** B5
Arbuckle Mountains, OK **125** E8
Arcadia, FL **65** F7
Archbald, PA **49** B9
Arches N.P., UT **151** E6
Arco, ID **143** G4
Ardmore, OK **125** E9
Arecibo, PR **157** H10
Arena, Point, CA **137** D1
Arikaree (river), CO **139** C8
Arkabutla Lake, MS **73** A3
Arkadelphia, AR **63** E3
Arkansas (river), **56** C1
Arkansas City, KS **97** F7
Arkansas Post National Memorial, AR **63** E6
Arlington, TX **127** D7
Arlington, VA **81** B10
Arlington, VT **53** H2
Arlington Heights, IL **91** B5
Armour, SD **111** E8
Aroostook (river), ME **37** C5
Arroyo del Macho (river), NM **123** F5
Artesia, NM **123** G6
Arvada, CO **139** C5
Arvon, Mount, MI **99** C3
Asbury Park, NJ **45** E5
Ash Lawn-Highland (site), VA **81** C8
Ashaway, RI **51** F2
Ashdown, AR **63** F1
Asheboro, NC **75** B6
Asheville, NC **74** C2
Ashland, KY **69** B10
Ashland, ME **37** B5
Ashland, NE **105** D9
Ashland, NH **43** F3
Ashland, OH **109** C5
Ashland, OR **149** G2
Ashland, VA **81** D9
Ashland, WI **113** A3
Ashley, ND **107** F7
Ashtabula, OH **109** A7
Ashtabula, Lake, ND **107** D9
Ashton, RI **51** A4
Ashuelot (river), NH **43** I1
Ashwaubenon, WI **113** E7
Aspen, CO **139** D3
Assateague Island, MD **39** F11
Assateague Island National Seashore, MD, VA **39** F11
Assawoman Canal, DE **35** I7
Assawompset Pond, MA **41** D8
Astoria, OR **148** A1
Atascadero, CA **137** G3
Atchafalaya (river), LA **71** F5
Atchafalaya Bay, LA **71** H5
Atchison, KS **97** B9
Athens, AL **61** A3
Athens, GA **67** C4
Athens, OH **109** F5
Athens, TN **79** C8
Athol, MA **41** B4
Atka Island, AK **135** H9
Atkinson, NE **105** B6
Atkinson, NH **43** I4
Atlanta, GA **67** C2
Atlantic, IA **95** E3
Atlantic City, NJ **45** H4
Atlantic City Expressway, NJ **45** G2
Atmore, AL **61** H2
Atoka, OK **125** E10
Attleboro, MA **41** D6
Attu Island, AK **135** G6
Atwood Lake, OH **109** C7
Au Sable (river), MI **99** E6
Au Sable N.W.&S.R., MI **99** E7
Aua, AS **156** I2
Aubrey Cliffs, AZ **121** B3
Auburn, AL **61** E5
Auburn, IN **93** B5
Auburn, MA **41** C5
Auburn, ME **37** G3
Auburn, NE **105** D9
Auburn, NY **47** D5
Auburn, WA **153** D4
Audubon Lake, ND **107** C5
Auglaize (river), OH **109** B2
Augusta, GA **67** D6
Augusta, KS **97** E7
Augusta, ME **37** G3
Aunuu (island), AS **156** I2
Aurora, CO **139** C6
Aurora, IL **91** B5
Aurora, MO **103** F3
Aurora, NE **105** D7
Austin, MN **101** H5
Austin, RI **51** E3
Austin, TX **127** F6
Austintown, OH **109** B8
Ava, MO **103** F4
Avery Island, LA **71** G4
Aziscohos Lake, ME **37** E2
Aztec, NM **123** A2
Aztec Ruins Nat. Mon., NM **123** A2

B

B. Everett Jordan Lake, NC **75** B6
Backbone Mountain, MD **38** B1
Bad (river), SD **111** D4
Bad Axe, MI **99** F8
Badlands (region), ND **106** E2
Badlands N.P., SD **110** E2
Bainbridge, GA **67** H2
Baker, MT **145** D11
Baker (river), NH **43** F2
Baker City, OR **149** C8
Baker Island (territory), US **156** F4
Bakersfield, CA **137** G5
Bald Knob, AR **63** C5
Baldwyn, MS **73** B5
Baltic, CT **33** C7
Baltimore, MD **39** B7
Bamberg, SC **77** E5
Bandelier Nat. Mon., NM **123** C4
Bangor, ME **37** F5
Bangor, PA **49** E9
Banks Lake, WA **153** C7
Bannock Range, ID **143** H5
Bantam Lake, CT **33** B3
Bar Harbor, ME **37** G6
Baraboo, WI **113** F5
Baranof Island, AK **135** G10
Barataria Bay, LA **71** H8
Barberton, OH **109** C6
Bardstown, KY **69** C6
Barkhamsted Reservoir, CT **33** A4
Barkley, Lake, KY, TN **68** E3
Barnegat Bay, NJ **45** F5
Barnstable, MA **41** E9
Barnwell, SC **77** E4
Barre, VT **53** D3
Barren (river), KY **69** D5
Barren River Lake, KY **69** E5
Barrington, RI **51** C5
Barrow, AK **135** A5
Barrow, Point, AK **135** A5
Barstow, CA **137** G6
Bartholomew, Bayou (river), LA **71** B4
Bartlesville, OK **125** A10
Bartlett, TN **78** C1
Barton, VT **53** B4
Bastrop, LA **71** A5
Batavia, NY **46** D3
Batesburg-Leesville, SC **77** D4
Batesville, AR **63** B5
Batesville, MS **73** B3
Bath, ME **37** H3
Bath, NY **47** E4
Baton Rouge, LA **71** F6
Batten Kill (river), VT **53** H1
Battle Creek, ID **143** I1
Battle Creek, MI **99** H5
Battle Ground, WA **153** F3
Battle Mountain, NV **147** B4
Baudette, MN **101** A3
Baxter Springs, KS **97** E10
Bay City, MI **99** G7
Bay City, TX **127** G8
Bay Minette, AL **61** H2
Bay St. Louis, MS **73** I4
Bayard, NM **123** G2
Bayonet Point, FL **65** D6
Bayonne, NJ **45** C5
Bayou Bartholomew (river), AR **63** E5
Bayou La Batre, AL **61** I1
Baytown, TX **127** F8
Beach, ND **106** D1
Beach Haven, NJ **45** G4
Beacon, NY **47** G8
Bear, DE **35** B4
Bear (river), ID, WY **143** I5
Bear Creek, AL **61** B2
Bear Creek, CO, KS **139** F8
Bear Creek N.W.&S.R., MI **99** F5
Bear Lake, ID, UT **151** A5
Bear River Migratory Bird Refuge, UT **151** B3
Bear River Range, ID **143** I6
Bearcamp (river), NH **43** F4
Beardstown, IL **91** E2
Beatrice, NE **105** E9
Beatty, NV **147** G5
Beaufort, SC **77** G6
Beaufort Sea, AK **135** A7
Beaumont, TX **127** F9
Beaver, OK **124** A4
Beaver, UT **151** F3
Beaver (river), OK **124** A4
Beaver (river), PA **48** C1
Beaver Creek, KS **96** B1
Beaver Creek, ND **107** F6
Beaver Creek N.W.&S.R., AK **135** C7
Beaver Dam, WI **113** G6
Beaver Falls, PA **48** D1
Beaver Island, MI **99** D5
Beaver Lake (lake), AR **63** A2
Beaverton, OR **149** B2
Becharof Lake, AK **135** F5
Beckley, WV **83** G4
Bedford, IA **95** F4
Bedford, IN **93** G3
Bedford, PA **49** E4
Bedford, VA **81** D6
Beebe, AR **63** C5
Beech Grove, IN **93** E4
Beeville, TX **127** G6
Bel Air, MD **39** A8
Belcourt, ND **107** A6
Belding, MI **99** G5
Belen, NM **123** D4
Belfast, ME **37** G4
Belgrade, MT **145** E5
Bella Vista, AR **63** A1
Bellaire, OH **109** E8
Belle Fourche, SD **110** C1
Belle Fourche (river), SD, WY **110** C2
Belle Glade, FL **65** F9
Bellefontaine, OH **109** D3
Bellefonte, DE **35** A5
Belleville, IL **91** G3
Belleville, KS **97** A6
Bellevue, NE **105** C9
Bellevue, OH **109** B4
Bellevue, WA **153** C4
Bellingham, MA **41** D6
Bellingham, WA **153** A3
Bellows Falls, VT **53** H4
Belmar, NJ **45** E5
Beloit, KS **97** B6
Beloit, WI **113** H6
Belpre, OH **109** F6
Belted Range, NV **147** F5
Belton, MO **103** C2
Belton, SC **76** C2
Belton, TX **127** E7
Belvidere, IL **91** A4
Bemidji, MN **101** C3
Bend, OR **149** D4
Bennettsville, SC **77** B8
Bennington, VT **53** I1
Benson, AZ **121** H6
Benson, MN **101** F2
Benton, AR **63** D4
Benton, IL **91** H4
Benton Harbor, MI **99** H4
Bentonville, AR **63** A1
Bent's Old Fort National Historic Site, CO **139** E7
Berea, KY **69** D8
Beresford, SD **111** F10
Bering Sea, AK **134** F2
Bering Strait, AK **134** C2
Berkeley, CA **137** E2
Berkeley (site), VA **81** D10
Berkeley Heights, NJ **45** C4
Berlin, MD **39** E11
Berlin, NH **43** C4
Berlin Lake, OH **109** C7
Bernalillo, NM **123** C4
Bernardsville, NJ **45** C3
Berryville, AR **63** A2
Bessemer, AL **61** D3
Bethany, MO **103** A3
Bethany, OK **125** C8
Bethany Beach, DE **35** I7
Bethel, AK **135** E4
Bethel, CT **33** D2
Bethel, ME **37** G2
Bethesda, MD **39** C6
Bethlehem, CT **33** C3
Bethlehem, PA **49** D9
Bettendorf, IA **95** D10

Beulah — Cascade

Beulah, ND **107** D4
Beverly, MA **41** B8
Biddeford, ME **37** H2
Big Bend N.P., TX **127** F3
Big Black (river), MS **73** E2
Big Blue (river), KS, NE **97** A7
Big Blue (river), IN **93** E4
Big Canyon (river), TX **127** F3
Big Coal (river), WV **83** G3
Big Cypress National Preserve, FL **65** G8
Big Cypress Swamp, FL **65** G8
Big Darby Creek, OH **109** D3
Big Darby Creek National Scenic River, OH **109** E4
Big Eau Pleine Reservoir, WI **113** D4
Big Fork (river), MN **101** B4
Big Hole N.B., MT **144** E3
Big Lake, ME **37** E6
Big Lost (river), ID **143** G4
Big Marsh Creek N.W.&S.R., OR **149** E3
Big Muddy (river), IL **91** H4
Big Nemaha (river), NE **105** E9
Big Piney (river), MO **103** F5
Big Piney Creek, AR **63** C3
Big Piney Creek N.W.&S.R., AR **63** B3
Big Raccoon Creek, IN **93** E2
Big Rapids, MI **99** G5
Big Sandy (river), AZ **121** D3
Big Sandy (river), KY, WV **82** F1
Big Sandy (river), WY **155** F3
Big Sandy Creek, CO **139** D7
Big Sioux (river), IA, SD **94** B1
Big Smoky Valley, NV **147** E4
Big South Fork National River and Recreation Area, KY, TN **79** A7
Big Spring, TX **127** D4
Big Stone Gap, VA **80** E2
Big Stone Lake, MN, SD **101** F1
Big Sunflower (river), MS **73** C2
Big Sur N.W.&S.R., CA **137** F3
Big Thicket National Preserve, TX **127** E9
Big Timber, MT **145** E6
Big Wood (river), ID **143** H3
Bighorn (river), MT, WY **130** C6
Bighorn Canyon N.R.A., MT, WY **145** F8
Bighorn Lake, WY **155** A5
Bighorn Mountains, MT, WY **155** A5
Bill Williams (river), AZ **121** E2
Billings, MT **145** E7
Biloxi, MS **73** I5
Biltmore House (site), NC **74** C2
Bingham, ME **37** E3
Binghamton, NY **47** F6
Birch Creek N.W.&S.R., AK **135** C7
Birmingham, AL **61** C3
Bisbee, AZ **121** H7
Biscayne Bay, FL **65** H9
Biscayne N.P., FL **65** H9
Bishop, CA **137** E5
Bishop Creek Reservoir, NV **147** B6
Bismarck, ND **107** E5
Bison, SD **111** B3
Bistineau, Lake, LA **70** B2
Bitter Creek, UT **151** D7
Bitterroot Range, ID, MT **143** B1
Bixby, OK **125** C10
Black (river), VT **53** G3
Black (river), AR, MO **63** B6
Black (river), AZ **121** F7
Black (river), MI **99** G8
Black (river), NY **47** C6
Black (river), SC **77** E8
Black (river), WI **113** E3
Black Belt (region), AL **61** E2
Black Canyon of the Gunnison N.P., CO **139** D2
Black Creek, MS **73** H5
Black Creek N.W.&S.R., MS **73** H4
Black Hawk, SD **110** D2
Black Hills, SD **110** D1
Black Hills, WY **155** B10
Black Mesa (peak), OK **124** A1
Black Mesa, AZ **121** B6
Black Mountain, KY **69** E10
Black Mountain, NC **74** C3
Black Mountains, AZ **121** C2
Black N.W.&S.R., MI **99** C1
Black Range, NM **123** G2
Black River Falls, WI **113** E3
Black Rock Desert, NV **147** B2
Black Rock Range, NV **147** A2
Black Warrior (river), AL **61** E2
Blackfoot, ID **143** H5
Blackfoot Mountains, ID **143** H5
Blackfoot Reservoir, ID **143** H5
Blacks Fork (river), WY **154** G2
Blacksburg, VA **81** E5
Blackstone, VA **81** E9
Blackstone (river), MA, RI **51** A4
Blackwater (river), MO **103** C3
Blackwell, OK **125** A8
Blades, DE **35** H5
Blair, NE **105** C9
Blakely, GA **67** G1
Blanchard, IA **95** F3
Blanchard (river), OH **109** C2
Blanco, Cape, OR **148** F1
Blanding, UT **151** G6
Block Island, RI **51** I3
Block Island, RI **51** H3
Block Island Sound, NY **47** G11
Bloodsworth Island, MD **39** F9
Bloomfield, CT **33** B5
Bloomfield, IA **95** F7
Bloomfield, NM **123** A2
Blooming Grove, OH **109** C4
Bloomington, IL **91** D4
Bloomington, IN **93** F3
Bloomington, MN **101** F4
Bloomsburg, PA **49** C7
Blue (river), CO **139** C4
Blue (river), IN **93** H3
Blue (river), OK **125** E10
Blue Earth (river), MN **101** H4
Blue Grass Parkway, KY **69** C6
Blue Hill Bay, ME **37** G5
Blue Mesa Reservoir, CO **139** E3
Blue Mountain, NH **43** B3
Blue Mountain, PA **49** D7
Blue Mountains, OR **149** C7
Blue Ridge, GA, NC, VA **56** C5
Blue Ridge Parkway, VA **81** F5
Blue Springs, MO **103** C2
Bluefield, VA **80** E4
Bluefield, WV **83** H3
Bluegrass Region, KY **69** B7
Bluestone (river), WV **83** H3
Bluestone Lake, WV **83** H4
Bluestone National Scenic River, WV **83** H4
Blythe, CA **137** H8
Blytheville, AR **63** B8
Boaz, AL **61** B4
Boca Raton, FL **65** G9
Bogalusa, LA **71** E8
Bogue Chitto (river), LA, MS **71** E8
Bois Blanc Island, MI **99** D6
Bois Brule (river), WI **113** B3
Bois de Sioux (river), MN **101** E1
Boise, ID **143** G1
Boise City, OK **124** A2
Bolivar, MO **103** E3
Bolivar, TN **78** C2
Bombay Hook Island, DE **35** D5
Bomoseen, Lake, VT **53** F1
Bonne Springs, KS **97** B10
Bonners Ferry, ID **143** A1
Bonneville Dam, OR, WA **149** B3
Booker T. Washington Nat. Mon., VA **81** E6
Boone, IA **95** C5
Boone, NC **74** B3
Boone (river), IA **95** B5
Booneville, AR **63** C2
Booneville, MS **73** A5
Boonsboro, MD **39** A5
Boonville, IN **93** I2
Boonville, MO **103** C4
Boothbay Harbor, ME **37** H4
Borah Peak, ID **143** G3
Borger, TX **127** B4
Borgne, Lake, LA **71** G8
Bossier City, LA **70** B1
Boston, MA **41** C7
Boston Harbor Islands N.R.A., MA **41** C7
Boston Mountains, AR **63** B2
Boston N.H.P., MA **41** B7
Bottineau, ND **107** A5
Boulder, CO **139** B5
Boulder City, NV **147** H6
Boundary Peak, NV **147** E3
Boundary Waters Canoe Area Wilderness, MN **101** B5
Bountiful, UT **151** B4
Bow Lake (lake), NH **43** H4
Bowers Beach, DE **35** F6
Bowie, MD **39** C7
Bowling Green, KY **69** E5
Bowling Green, OH **109** B3
Bowman, ND **106** F2
Boyer (river), IA **95** D3
Boyne City, MI **99** E6
Boysen Reservoir, WY **155** D5
Bozeman, MT **145** E5
Bradenton, FL **65** E6
Bradford, PA **49** A4
Bradford, RI **51** F2
Bradford, VT **53** E4
Brady, TX **127** E5
Brainerd, MN **101** D4
Brandenburg, KY **69** C5
Brandon, MS **73** F3
Brandon, VT **53** E2
Brandywine, DE **35** A5
Brandywine Creek, DE **35** A5
Branford, CT **33** E4
Branson, MO **103** F3
Brantley Lake, NM **123** G7
Brasstown Bald (peak), GA **67** A3
Brattleboro, VT **53** I3
Brazil, IN **93** F2
Brazos (river), TX **127** C5
Breaks Interstate Park, KY **69** D11
Breaux Bridge, LA **71** F4
Breckenridge, TX **127** D5
Bremerton, WA **153** C3
Brenham, TX **127** F7
Brentwood, NY **47** H9
Brentwood, TN **79** B5
Breton Islands, LA **71** H10
Breton Sound, LA **71** H9
Brevard, NC **74** C2
Brewer, ME **37** F5
Brewton, AL **61** H3
Brices Cross Roads National Battlefield Site, MS **73** B5
Bridgeport, CT **33** E3
Bridgeport, NE **104** C2
Bridgeport, WV **83** D5
Bridgeton, NJ **45** H1
Bridgeville, DE **35** H5
Bridgewater, MA **41** D7
Bridgewater, VA **81** C7
Bridgton, ME **37** G2
Brigantine, NJ **45** H4
Brigham City, UT **151** A4
Brighton, CO **139** B6
Brinkley, AR **63** D6
Bristol, NH **43** F3
Bristol, RI **51** D6
Bristol, TN **79** A11
Bristol, VA **80** F3
Bristol, VT **53** D2
Bristol Bay, AK **135** F4
Bristow, OK **125** C10
Britton, SD **111** A8
Britton Hill (peak), FL **64** A2
Broad (river), GA **67** C5
Broad (river), NC, SC **77** A4
Broad Brook, CT **33** A5
Broadkill Beach, DE **35** G7
Broadus, MT **145** E10
Brockton, MA **41** D7
Broken Arrow, OK **125** B10
Broken Bow, NE **105** C5
Broken Bow, OK **125** E12
Broken Bow Lake, OK **125** E12
Bromley Mountain, VT **53** G2
Brookfield, MO **103** B4
Brookfield, WI **113** G7
Brookhaven, MS **73** G2
Brookings, OR **148** G1
Brookings, SD **111** D10
Brookline, MA **41** C7
Brooklyn, CT **33** B8
Brooklyn Park, MN **101** F4
Brooks Range, AK **135** B4
Brookside, DE **35** B4
Brookville Lake, IN **93** F5
Brown v. Board of Education N.H.S., KS **97** C8
Brownfield, TX **127** D3
Browning, MT **144** B3
Brownlee Reservoir, ID, OR **143** F1
Browns Mills, NJ **45** F3
Brownsville, TN **78** C2
Brownsville, TX **127** I7
Brownville Junction, ME **37** E4
Brownwood, TX **127** E5
Brule (river), MI, WI **113** B6
Bruneau (river), ID, NV **143** H2
Bruneau, East Fork (river), ID **143** I2
Brunswick, GA **67** H7
Brunswick, MD **39** B5
Brunswick, ME **37** H3
Brunswick, OH **109** B6
Brush, CO **139** B7
Bryan, OH **109** B2
Bryan, TX **127** E7
Bryant, AR **63** D4
Bryant Creek, MO **103** F4
Bryce Canyon N.P., UT **151** G3
Buck Creek, OK **125** D5
Buck Island Reef Nat. Mon., VI **157** I8
Buckeye Lake, OH **109** E5
Buckhannon, WV **83** D5
Buckner Creek, KS **97** D3
Bucksport, ME **37** F5
Bucktown, MD **39** E9
Bucyrus, OH **109** C4
Budd Lake, NJ **45** B3
Buena Vista, VA **81** D7
Buffalo, NY **46** D2
Buffalo, OK **125** A5
Buffalo, SD **110** A2
Buffalo (river), TN **79** C4
Buffalo, WY **155** B7
Buffalo (river), AR **63** B2
Buffalo Bill Reservoir, WY **155** B4
Buffalo N.W.&S.R., AR **63** B2
Buffalo National River, AR **63** B3
Buhl, ID **143** I3
Bull Shoals Lake, AR, MO **63** A3
Bullfrog Creek, UT **151** G5
Bullhead City, AZ **121** D2
Bunkie, LA **71** E4
Burien, WA **153** C4
Burkburnett, TX **127** C6
Burke, SD **111** F7
Burley, ID **143** I5
Burlington, CO **139** C9
Burlington, IA **95** F9
Burlington, KS **97** D9
Burlington, NC **75** B6
Burlington, NJ **45** E2
Burlington, VT **53** C1
Burlington, WI **113** H6
Burns, OR **149** E6
Burt Lake, MI **99** D6
Burton, MI **99** G7
Burton, SC **77** G6
Burwell, NE **105** C6
Butler, MO **103** D2
Butler, PA **48** C2
Butte, MT **145** E4
Buzzards Bay, MA **41** E8

C

C.J. Strike Reservoir, ID **143** H1
C.W. McConaughy, Lake, NE **105** C3
Caballo Reservoir, NM **123** G3
Cabinet Mountains, ID, MT **144** A1
Cabot, AR **63** D5
Cabot, Mount, NH **43** C4
Cabrillo Nat. Mon., CA **137** I5
Cacapon (river), WV **83** D8
Cache (river), AR **63** C6
Cache La Poudre N.W.&S.R., CO **139** A5
Cactus Range, NV **147** F4
Caddo Lake, LA **70** A1
Cadillac, MI **99** F5
Cadillac Mountain, ME **37** G6
Caesar Creek Lake, OH **109** F2
Cagles Mill Lake, IN **93** F2
Caguas, PR **157** I11
Cahaba (river), AL **61** E3
Cairo, GA **67** H3
Cairo, IL **91** I4
Calais, ME **37** E7
Calamus (river), NE **105** B5
Calamus Reservoir, NE **105** B6
Calcasieu (river), LA **71** F3
Calcasieu Lake, LA **70** G2
Caldwell, ID **143** G1
Caldwell, NJ **45** C4
Caledonia, MN **101** H6
Calexico, CA **137** I7
Calhoun, GA **67** B2
Caliente, NV **147** F7
California, MO **103** D4
California, Gulf of, **116** F1
Caloosahatchee (river), FL **65** F8
Calvert City, KY **68** E2
Camas, WA **153** G3
Cambridge, MA **41** B7
Cambridge, MD **39** D9
Cambridge, NE **105** E5
Cambridge, OH **109** E6
Camden, AR **63** F3
Camden, DE **35** E5
Camden, ME **37** G4
Camden, NJ **45** F2
Camden, SC **77** C6
Camels Hump (peak), VT **53** C2
Cameron, MO **103** B2
Camilla, GA **67** H3
Campbell Hill (peak), OH **109** D3
Campbellsville, KY **69** D6
Campe Verde, AZ **121** D5
Canaan, CT **33** A2
Canaan, NH **43** F2
Canaan, VT **53** A6
Canadian (river), NM, OK, TX **116** C6
Canadian, North (river), OK **125** B6
Canandaigua, NY **47** D4
Canaveral National Seashore, FL **65** C8
Canaveral, Cape, FL **65** D9
Candlewood, Lake, CT **33** D2
Cando, ND **107** B7
Cane River Creole N.H.P. and Heritage Area, LA **70** D2
Caney (river), KS, OK **125** A10
Caney Fork (river), TN **79** C6
Cannonball (river), ND **107** E3
Cañon City, CO **139** E5
Cañon Largo (river), NM **123** B3
Canoochee (river), GA **67** F6
Canterbury, NH **43** G3
Canton, IL **91** D3
Canton, MO **103** A5
Canton, MS **73** E3
Canton, OH **109** C7
Canton, SD **111** E10
Canyon, TX **127** B3
Canyon Creek, ID **143** H1
Canyon de Chelly Nat. Mon., AZ **121** B7
Canyon Ferry Lake, MT **145** D5
Canyonlands N.P., UT **151** F6
Canyons of the Ancients Nat. Mon., CO **138** F1
Cap Rock Escarpment, TX **127** D4
Cape Charles, VA **81** D11
Cape Cod Bay, MA **41** D9
Cape Cod Canal, MA **41** D8
Cape Cod National Seashore, MA **41** D10
Cape Coral, FL **65** G7
Cape Elizabeth, ME **37** H3
Cape Fear (river), NC **75** D7
Cape Girardeau, MO **103** E8
Cape Hatteras National Seashore, NC **75** C11
Cape Island, SC **77** F8
Cape Krusenstern Nat. Mon., AK **135** B4
Cape Lookout National Seashore, NC **75** D10
Cape May, NJ **45** I2
Cape May Canal, NJ **45** I2
Cape May Court House, NJ **45** I3
Capitol Hill, MP **156** C2
Capitol Reef N.P., UT **151** F5
Captain Cook, HI **141** F8
Capulin Volcano Nat. Mon., NM **123** A7
Carbondale, CO **139** C3
Carbondale, IL **91** H4
Carbondale, PA **49** B9
Caribou, ME **37** B6
Caribou Range, ID **143** G6
Carl Sandburg Home National Historic Site, NC **74** C3
Carlin, NV **147** B5
Carlinville, IL **91** F3
Carlisle, PA **49** E6
Carlsbad, NM **123** G7
Carlsbad Caverns N.P., NM **123** H6
Carlyle Lake, IL **91** G4
Carmel, IN **93** E4
Carmi, IL **91** H5
Caro, MI **99** G7
Carolina, PR **157** H11
Carolina, RI **51** F3
Carp N.W.&S.R., MI **99** D5
Carrington, ND **107** D7
Carrizo Creek, NM **123** B7
Carrizo Plain Nat. Mon., CA **137** G4
Carrizo Springs, TX **127** G5
Carrizozo, NM **123** F5
Carroll, IA **95** C3
Carrollton, GA **67** D1
Carson (river), NV **147** D2
Carson City, NV **147** D2
Carson Sink (river), NV **147** C3
Carthage, IL **91** D2
Carthage, MO **103** F2
Carthage, MS **73** E4
Caruthersville, MO **103** G8
Cary, NC **75** B7
Casa Grande, AZ **121** F5
Casa Grande Ruins Nat. Mon., AZ **121** F5
Cascade, ID **143** F1

Cascade Range — Crossville

Cascade Range, **130** C2
Cascade Siskiyou Nat. Mon., OR **149** G3
Cascade, Lake, ID **143** F1
Casco Bay, ME **37** H3
Casper, WY **155** D7
Cass (river), MI **99** G7
Casselman (river), PA **49** F3
Casselton, ND **107** D9
Castillo de San Marcos Nat. Mon., FL **65** B8
Castine, ME **37** G5
Castle Dale, UT **151** E5
Castle Rock, CO **139** C6
Castle Rock Lake, WI **113** F5
Castleton, VT **53** F2
Catahoula Lake, LA **71** D4
Catalina, AZ **121** G6
Cataño, PR **157** H11
Catawba (river), NC, SC **77** B5
Cathedral Bluffs, CO **138** B1
Catoctin Mountain Park, MD **39** A5
Catonsville, MD **39** B7
Catskill, NY **47** E8
Catskill Mountains, NY **47** F8
Catskill Park, NY **47** F7
Cattaraugus Creek, NY **46** E2
Cavalier, ND **107** A9
Cave City, KY **69** D6
Cave Run Lake, KY **69** C9
Cayce, SC **77** D5
Cayey, PR **157** I11
Cayuga Lake, NY **47** E5
Cecil M. Harden Lake, IN **93** E2
Cedar (river), NE **105** C6
Cedar (river), IA **95** A6
Cedar (river), MI **99** D3
Cedar Bluff Reservoir, KS **97** C3
Cedar Breaks Nat. Mon., UT **151** G2
Cedar City, UT **151** G2
Cedar Creek, ND **106** E2
Cedar Creek, IN **93** B5
Cedar Creek Reservoir, ID **143** I2
Cedar Falls, IA **95** C7
Cedar Rapids, IA **95** D8
Celina, OH **109** D2
Centennial Mountains, ID **143** F5
Center, ND **107** D4
Center Hill Lake, TN **79** B6
Center Ossipee, NH **43** F4
Center Point, AL **61** C3
Center Sandwich, NH **43** F4
Centereach, NY **47** H9
Centerville, IA **95** F6
Centerville, OH **109** E2
Centerville, UT **151** B4
Central City, IA **95** C8
Central City, NE **105** C7
Central Falls, RI **51** B5
Central Lowland (plain), **86** E5
Central Point, OR **149** F2
Central Valley, CA **137** B2
Centralia, IL **91** G4
Centralia, MO **103** C5
Centralia, WA **153** E3
Centreville, MS **73** H1
Cerro de Punta (mountains), PR **157** I10
Chaco Culture N.H.P., NM **123** B2
Chacuaco Canyon, CO **139** F7
Chadron, NE **104** A2
Challis, ID **143** F3
Chalmette, LA **71** G8
Chama, NM **123** A4
Chamberlain, SD **111** D7
Chamberlain Lake, ME **37** C4
Chambersburg, PA **49** E5
Champaign, IL **91** E5
Champlain, Lake, NY, VT **47** B9
Chandeleur Islands, LA **71** G10
Chandeleur Sound, LA **71** G10
Chandler, AZ **121** F5
Channel Islands, CA **137** H3
Channel Islands N.P., CA **137** H3
Channel Islands National Marine Sanctuary, CA **137** H4
Chanute, KS **97** E9
Chaparral, NM **123** H4
Chapel Hill, NC **75** B6
Chappaquiddick Island, MA **41** F9
Chariton, IA **95** E6
Chariton (river), IA, MO **103** B4
Charles (river), MA **41** C6
Charles City, IA **95** B7
Charles Mound, IL **91** A3
Charles Pinckney National Historic Site, SC **77** F8
Charles Town, WV **83** D10
Charleston, IL **91** F5
Charleston, MO **103** F8
Charleston, SC **77** G7
Charleston, WV **83** F3
Charlestown, IN **93** H4
Charlestown, NH **43** G1
Charlestown, RI **51** G3
Charley N.W.&S.R., AK **135** C7
Charlotte, MI **99** H6
Charlotte, NC **75** C4
Charlotte Amalie, VI **157** G7
Charlotte Harbor, FL **65** F7
Charlottesville, VA **81** C8
Chatham, MA **41** E10
Chattahoochee (river), AL, GA **56** D5
Chattahoochee River N.R.A., GA **67** C2
Chattanooga, TN **79** D6
Chattooga (river), SC **76** B1
Chattooga N.W.&S.R., GA, NC, SC **67** A4
Chautauqua Lake, NY **46** E1
Cheaha Mountain, AL **61** C5
Cheat (river), WV **83** C6
Cheat Mountain, WV **83** F6
Cheboygan, MI **99** D6
Checotah, OK **125** C11
Cheektowaga, NY **46** D2
Cheesequake, NJ **45** D4
Chehalis, WA **153** E3
Chehalis (river), WA **152** D2
Chelan, Lake, WA **153** B6
Chelmsford, MA **41** B6
Chemung (river), NY **47** E4
Cheney, WA **153** C9
Cheney Reservoir, KS **97** D6
Chepachet, RI **51** B3
Cheraw, SC **77** B7
Cherokee, IA **94** B2
Cherokee Lake, TN **79** A9
Cherokee Village, AR **63** A5
Cherokees, Lake O' The, OK **125** A11
Cherry Creek, SD **111** C3
Cherry Creek Range, NV **147** C6
Cherry Hill, NJ **45** F2
Chesapeake, VA **81** E11
Chesapeake and Delaware Canal, DE, MD **35** C4
Chesapeake and Ohio Canal, MD **38** A2
Chesapeake and Ohio Canal N.H.P., MD **39** B5
Chesapeake Bay, MD, VA **28** H4
Chesapeake Bay Bridge *see* William Preston Lane Jr. Memorial Bridge, MD **39** C8
Chesapeake Bay Bridge-Tunnel, VA **81** E11
Chesapeake Beach, MD **39** D8
Cheshire, CT **33** D4
Cheshire Reservoir, MA **40** B1
Chester, IL **91** H3
Chester, PA **49** F9
Chester, SC **77** B5
Chester, VA **81** D9
Chester, VT **53** G3
Chester, WV **83** A5
Chester (bay), MD **39** C8
Chesterfield, CT **33** D7
Chestertown, MD **39** B9
Chesuncook Lake, ME **37** D4
Cheswold, DE **35** E5
Chetco (river), OR **148** G1
Chetco N.W.&S.R., OR **148** G1
Chevelon Creek, AZ **121** D6
Cheyenne, WY **155** G9
Cheyenne (river), SD, WY **111** C3
Cheyenne Bottoms (lake), KS **97** C5
Cheyenne Wells, CO **139** D9
Chicago, IL **91** B6
Chichagof Island, AK **135** F9
Chickamauga and Chattanooga N.M.P., GA, TN **67** A1
Chickamauga Lake, TN **79** C7
Chickasaw N.R.A., OK **125** E9
Chickasawhay (river), MS **73** G5
Chickasha, OK **125** D8
Chico, CA **137** C3
Chicopee (river), MA **41** C3
Chicopee, MA **41** C3
Chikaskia (river), OK **125** A8
Childress, TX **127** C5
Chilikadrotna N.W.&S.R., AK **135** E5
Chillicothe, IL **91** C3
Chillicothe, MO **103** B3
Chillicothe, OH **109** F4
Chimayo, NM **123** B5
Chimney Rock National Historic Site, NE **104** C1
Chincoteague, VA **81** C12
Chincoteague Bay, MD **39** F11
Chinle, AZ **121** B7
Chinle Wash (river), AZ **121** A7
Chino Valley, AZ **121** D4
Chinook, MT **145** B7
Chippewa (river), MN **101** E2
Chippewa (river), WI **113** C3
Chippewa Falls, WI **113** D3
Chippewa, Lake, WI **113** B3
Chiputneticook Lakes, ME **37** D6
Chiricahua Nat. Mon., AZ **121** H7
Chisholm, MN **101** C5
Chittenden Reservoir, VT **53** E2
Choctawhatchee (river), AL, FL **64** B2
Choptank (bay), MD **39** D8
Choptank (river), MD **39** D9
Choteau, MT **145** B4
Chowan (river), NC **75** A9
Christiansburg, VA **81** E5
Christiansted, VI **157** I8
Christiansted National Historic Site, VI **157** I7
Christina (river), DE **35** B4
Christmas Lake Valley, OR **149** E5
Chubbuck, ID **143** H5
Chugach Mountains, AK **135** E7
Chukchi Sea, AK **134** A3
Chula Vista, CA **137** I6
Church Hill, TN **79** A10
Churchill Lake, ME **37** C4
Cicero, IL **91** B5
Cimarron (river), CO, KS, OK **125** B7
Cimarron Turnpike, OK **125** B9
Cimarron, North Fork (river), CO, KS **96** E1
Cincinnati, OH **109** G1
Cinnaminson, NJ **45** F2
Circle, MT **145** C10
Circleville, OH **109** F4
Citronelle, AL **61** H1
City of Rocks National Reserve, ID **143** I4
Clackamas N.W.&S.R., OR **149** C3
Clan Alpine Mountains, NV **147** D3
Clanton, AL **61** E3
Clara Barton National Historic Site, MD **39** C6
Claremont, NH **43** G1
Claremore, OK **125** B10
Clarinda, IA **95** F3
Clarion, PA **49** C3
Clarion (river), PA **49** C3
Clarion N.W.&S.R., PA **49** C3
Clark, SD **111** C9
Clark Fork (river), MT **144** B1
Clarks Fork (river), MT **145** E7
Clarks Fork Yellowstone N.W.&S.R., WY **155** A3
Clarksburg, WV **83** D5
Clarksdale, MS **73** B2
Clarkston, WA **153** E10
Clarksville, AR **63** C2
Clarksville, TN **79** A4
Clay Center, KS **97** B7
Claymont, DE **35** A6
Clayton, DE **35** D4
Clayton, NM **123** B8
Clear Creek, AZ **121** D5
Clear Creek, WY **155** A7
Clear Lake, CA **137** C2
Clear Lake, IA **95** A5
Clear Lake, SD **111** C10
Clearfield, PA **49** C4
Clearfield, UT **151** B3
Clearwater, FL **65** E6
Clearwater, SC **77** E3
Clearwater (river), ID **143** D1
Clearwater Mountains, ID **143** D2
Clearwater, Middle Fork N.W.&S.R., ID **143** D2
Clearwater, North Fork (river), ID **143** D2
Clearwater, South Fork (river), ID **143** E2
Clemson, SC **76** B2
Cleveland, MS **73** C2
Cleveland, OH **109** B6
Cleveland, TN **79** D7
Clifton, AZ **121** F7
Clifton, NJ **45** B4
Clifton Forge, VA **81** D6
Clinch (river), TN, VA **79** A9
Clinch Mountain, VA **80** E3
Clingmans Dome (peak), TN **79** C9
Clinton, AR **63** B4
Clinton, CT **33** E5
Clinton, IA **95** D10
Clinton, IL **91** E4
Clinton, IN **93** E2
Clinton, MO **103** D3
Clinton, MS **73** E2
Clinton, NC **75** C7
Clinton, OK **125** C6
Clinton, SC **77** C3
Clinton, TN **79** B8
Cloquet, MN **101** D5
Clovis, NM **123** E8
Clyde (river), VT **53** A5
Coast Mountains, AK **135** E10
Coast Ranges, CA **137** B2
Coast Ranges, **130** B2
Coastal Plain, **56** E2
Coatesville, PA **49** E8
Cobble Mountain Reservoir, MA **40** C2
Cobleskill, NY **47** E7
Cocheco (river), NH **43** G5
Cochetopa Hills, CO **139** E4
Cockeysville, MD **39** A7
Coconino Plateau, AZ **121** C4
Cod, Cape, MA **41** E9
Cody, WY **155** B4
Coeur d'Alene, ID **143** B1
Coeur d'Alene (river), ID **143** C1
Coeur d'Alene Lake, ID **143** C1
Coffeyville, KS **97** F9
Cohansey (river), NJ **45** H1
Colby, KS **96** B2
Colchester, CT **33** C6
Cold Spring, MN **101** F3
Coldwater, MI **99** I6
Coldwater (river), MS **73** B2
Colebrook, NH **43** B3
Coleman, OK **125** E10
Coleman, TX **127** E5
College, AK **135** C7
College Place, WA **153** F8
College Station, TX **127** E7
Collierville, TN **78** D1
Collins, MS **73** G4
Collinsville, CT **33** B4
Collinsville, VA **81** E6
Colonial Beach, VA **81** C10
Colonial N.H.P., VA **81** D10
Colorado (river), **130** H4
Colorado City, AZ **121** A3
Colorado Nat. Mon., CO **138** D1
Colorado Plateau, AZ **116** B2
Colorado Springs, CO **139** D6
Colstrip, MT **145** E9
Columbia, MD **39** B7
Columbia, MO **103** C4
Columbia, MS **73** G3
Columbia, PA **49** E7
Columbia, SC **77** D5
Columbia, TN **79** C4
Columbia (river), OR, WA **149** A2
Columbia City, IN **93** B5
Columbia Falls, MT **144** B2
Columbia Plateau, OR **130** B3
Columbia River Gorge National Scenic Area, OR, WA **153** F4
Columbus, GA **67** F1
Columbus, IN **93** F4
Columbus, KS **97** E10
Columbus, MS **73** C5
Columbus, MT **145** E7
Columbus, NE **105** C8
Columbus, OH **109** E4
Columbus Salt Marsh (river), NV **147** E3
Colville, WA **153** B9
Colville (river), AK **135** B5
Colville (river), WA **153** B9
Combahee (river), SC **77** G6
Combs Mountain Parkway, KY **69** C9
Compensating Reservoir, CT **33** B4
Conanicut Island, RI **51** E5
Conchas (river), NM **123** C6
Conchas Lake, NM **123** C7
Concord, MA **41** B6
Concord, NC **75** C5
Concord, NH **43** H3
Concord (river), MA **41** B6
Concordia, KS **97** B6
Conecuh (river), AL **61** G4
Conejos (river), CO **139** G4
Conemaugh (river), PA **49** D3
Confusion Range, UT **151** D1
Congamond Lakes, CT **33** A4
Congaree (river), SC **77** D5
Congaree N.P., SC **77** D5
Conneaut, OH **109** A8
Connecticut (river), CT, MA, NH, VT **28** D6
Connell, WA **153** E8
Connellsville, PA **48** E2
Connersville, IN **93** E5
Conrad, MT **145** B4
Conroe, TX **127** F8
Continental Divide, CO, ID, MT, NM, WY **143** E4
Contoocook, NH **43** H3
Contoocook (river), NH **43** H3
Conway, AR **63** C4
Conway, NH **43** E4
Conway, SC **77** D9
Conway Lake, NH **43** E4
Cook Inlet, AK **135** E6
Cookeville, TN **79** B6
Coolidge, AZ **121** F5
Coon Rapids, MN **101** F4
Cooper (river), SC **77** F7
Cooperstown, ND **107** D8
Cooperstown, NY **47** E7
Coos (river), OR **148** E1
Coos Bay, OR **148** E1
Coosa (river), AL, GA **61** D4
Coosawattee (river), GA **67** B2
Coosawhatchie (river), SC **77** F5
Copper (river), AK **135** E7
Copperas Cove, TX **127** E6
Coquille, OR **148** E1
Coral Springs, FL **65** G9
Coralville, IA **95** D8
Coram, NY **47** H9
Corbin, KY **69** E8
Cordele, GA **67** F3
Cordell Bank National Marine Sanctuary, CA **137** D1
Cordillera Central (mountains), PR **157** I9
Cordova, AK **135** E7
Core Sound, NC **75** D10
Corinth, MS **73** A5
Corning, AR **63** A7
Corning, NY **47** F4
Coronado Nat. Mon., AZ **121** H6
Corpus Christi, TX **127** H7
Corpus Christi Bay, TX **116** G8
Corrumpa Creek, NM **123** A7
Corry, PA **48** A2
Corsicana, TX **127** D7
Cortez, CO **138** F1
Cortez Mountains, NV **147** C5
Cortland, NY **47** E5
Corvallis, OR **149** C2
Corydon, IN **93** H4
Coshocton, OH **109** D6
Cossatot (river), AR **63** E1
Cossatot N.W.&S.R., AR **63** E1
Coteau des Prairies, SD **111** A9
Cottage Grove, OR **149** D2
Cottonwood, AZ **121** D4
Coudersport, PA **49** B5
Council Bluffs, IA **94** E2
Council Grove, KS **97** C8
Coventry, CT **33** B6
Coventry Center, RI **51** D3
Covington, GA **67** D3
Covington, KY **69** A8
Covington, LA **71** F8
Covington, VA **81** D6
Cowlitz (river), WA **153** E3
Cowpasture (river), VA **81** C6
Cowpens N.B., SC **77** A4
Cozad, NE **105** D5
Craig, CO **139** B2
Crane Creek Reservoir, ID **143** F1
Cranston, RI **51** C4
Crater Lake, OR **149** F3
Crater Lake N.P., OR **149** F3
Craters of the Moon Nat. Mon. and Preserve, ID **143** H4
Crawford, NE **104** A1
Crawfordsville, IN **93** D2
Crazy Horse Memorial, SD **110** D1
Crescent City, CA **137** A1
Crescent Creek N.W.&S.R., OR **149** E3
Cresco, IA **95** A7
Creston, IA **95** E4
Crestview, FL **64** A2
Crestwood Village, NJ **45** F4
Crete, NE **105** D8
Crisfield, MD **39** F9
Crooked (river), OR **149** D5
Crooked N.W.&S.R., OR **149** C4
Crooked, North Fork N.W.&S.R., OR **149** D5
Crookston, MN **101** C1
Crosby, ND **106** A2
Crossett, AR **63** G5
Crossville, TN **79** B7

Crow Agency, MT **145** E8
Crow Creek, CO **139** B6
Crow Creek, SD **111** D7
Crow Wing (river), MN **101** D3
Crow, North Fork (river), MN **101** E3
Crow, South Fork (river), MN **101** F3
Crowley, LA **71** G4
Crowleys Ridge, AR **63** C7
Crown Mountain, VI **157** G7
Crown Point, IN **93** B2
Crownpoint, NM **123** C2
Cruz Bay, VI **157** G8
Crystal Lake, NH **43** G4
Crystal Springs, MS **73** F2
Cuivre (river), MO **103** C6
Culebra Island, PR **157** I12
Culebra Range, CO **139** G5
Cullman, AL **61** B3
Culpeper, VA **81** B8
Cumberland, KY **69** E10
Cumberland, MD **38** A2
Cumberland (river), KY, TN **56** C4
Cumberland Gap, KY, VA **69** E9
Cumberland Gap N.H.P., KY, TN, VA **69** E9
Cumberland Hill, RI **51** A4
Cumberland Island, GA **67** H7
Cumberland Island National Seashore, GA **67** H7
Cumberland Mountains, KY **69** E9
Cumberland Plateau, **56** C5
Cumberland, Lake, KY **69** E7
Curecanti N.R.A., CO **139** E3
Current (river), MO **103** E5
Currituck Sound, NC **75** A10
Cushing, OK **125** C9
Custer, SD **110** D1
Cut Bank, MT **145** A4
Cuyahoga (river), OH **109** B7
Cuyahoga Falls, OH **109** B6
Cuyahoga Valley N.P., OH **109** B6
Cynthiana, KY **69** B8
Cypress Swamp, DE **35** I6

D

Dagsboro, DE **35** I6
Dahlonega, GA **67** B3
Dale City, VA **81** B9
Dale Hollow Lake, KY,TN **79** A7
Daleville, AL **61** G5
Dallas, OR **149** C2
Dallas, TX **127** D7
Dalton, GA **67** B2
Dalton, MA **40** B1
Dan (river), NC, VA **75** A6
Danbury, CT **33** D2
Danforth, ME **37** D6
Danielson, CT **33** B8
Dannemora, NY **47** A8
Dansville, NY **46** E3
Danvers, MA **41** B7
Danville, IL **91** E6
Danville, KY **69** D7
Danville, VA **81** F7
Daphne, AL **61** I1
D'Arbonne, Bayou (river), LA **71** B3
Dardanelle, AR **63** C3
Dardanelle, Lake, AR **63** C2
Darien, CT **33** F2
Darling, Lake, ND **107** B4
Darlington, SC **77** C7
Daufuskie Island, SC **77** H5
Dauphin Island, AL **61** I1
Davenport, IA **95** D9
David Berger National Memorial, OH **109** B6
David City, NE **105** C8
Davis Mountains, TX **126** F2
Davis, Mount, PA **49** F3
Dawson, GA **67** G2
Dayton, NV **147** D2
Dayton, OH **109** E2
Dayton, TN **79** C7
Dayton, WA **153** E9
Dayton Aviation Heritage N.H.P., OH **109** E2
Daytona Beach, FL **65** C8
Dayville, CT **33** B8
De Gray Lake, AR **63** E3
De Land, FL **65** C8
De Pere, WI **113** E7
De Queen, AR **63** E1
De Quincy, LA **70** F2
De Ridder, LA **70** E2
De Smet, SD **111** C9
De Soto, MO **103** D6
De Soto National Memorial, FL **65** E6
De Witt, AR **63** E6
De Witt, IA **95** D9
Dead (river), ME **37** E3
Deadwood, SD **110** C1
Deadwood Reservoir, ID **143** F2
Deale, MD **39** D8
Dearborn, MI **99** H7
Death Valley, CA **137** F6
Death Valley N.P., CA, NV **137** E6
Decatur, AL **61** B3
Decatur, IL **91** E4
Decatur, IN **93** C6
Decorah, IA **95** A8
Dededo, GU **156** F2
Deep (river), NC **75** C6
Deep Creek Lake, MD **38** A1
Deep Fork (river), OK **125** C9
Deep River, CT **33** D6
Deepwater Point, DE **35** E6
Deer Creek, OH **109** F4
Deer Creek, MS **73** E2
Deer Creek Lake, OH **109** F4
Deer Isle, ME **37** G5
Deer Lodge, MT **145** D4
Deerfield, MA **41** B3
Deerfield (river), MA **40** B2
Defiance, OH **109** B2
DeKalb, IL **91** B4
Del Rio, TX **127** G4
Delano, CA **137** F4
Delaware, OH **109** D4
Delaware (river), DE, NJ, PA **28** F4
Delaware and Raritan Canal, NJ **45** E3
Delaware Bay, DE, NJ **28** G4
Delaware City, DE **35** B5
Delaware Lake, OH **109** D4
Delaware Memorial Bridge, DE **35** B5
Delaware Water Gap N.R.A., NJ, PA **45** B2
Delaware, East Branch (river), NY **47** F7
Delaware, West Branch (river), NY **47** F7
Delmar, DE **35** I5
Delmarva Peninsula, DE, MD, VA **28** H4
Delphos, OH **109** C2
Delray Beach, FL **65** G9
Delta, CO **139** D2
Delta, UT **151** E3
Delta N.W.&S.R., AK **135** D7
Deltona, FL **65** D8
Deming, NM **123** H2
Demopolis, AL **61** E2
Denali (peak) *see* McKinley, Mount, AK **135** D6
Denali N.P. and Preserve, AK **135** D6
Denham Springs, LA **71** F6
Denison, IA **95** C3
Denison, TX **127** C7
Dennis, MA **41** E10
Denton, MD **39** C9
Denton, TX **127** C7
Denver, CO **139** C6
Derby, KS **97** E7
Derby Center, VT **53** A4
Derby Line, VT **53** A4
Dermott, AR **63** F6
Derry, NH **43** I4
Des Lacs (river), ND **107** B4
Des Moines, IA **95** D5
Des Moines (river), IA, MN **95** B4
Des Plaines (river), IL **91** B5
Desatoya Mountains, NV **147** D4
Deschutes (river), OR **149** B4
Deschutes N.W.&S.R., OR **149** D4
Desert National Wildlife Range, NV **147** F6
Desert Valley, NV **147** B3
Desolation Canyon, UT **151** D6
Detroit, MI **99** H8
Detroit (river), MI **99** H8
Detroit Lakes, MN **101** D2
Devils Lake (lake), ND **107** B7
Devils Lake, ND **107** B7
Devils Postpile Nat. Mon., CA **137** E5
Devils Tower Nat. Mon., WY **155** A9
Dewey Beach, DE **35** H7
Dexter, ME **37** E4
Dexter, MO **103** F7
Dickinson, ND **106** D2
Dickson, TN **79** B4
Dillingham, AK **135** F4
Dillon, MT **145** F4
Dillon, SC **77** C8
Dinosaur Nat. Mon., CO, UT **138** A1
Dirty Devil (river), UT **151** F5
Disappointment, Cape, WA **152** E1
Dismal (river), NE **105** C4
Dixon, IL **91** B3
Dixon Entrance (strait), AK **135** H10
Dodge City, KS **97** D3
Dodgeville, WI **113** G4
Dolan Springs, AZ **121** C2
Dolores, CO **138** E1
Donaldsonville, LA **71** G6
Donner Und Blitzen N.W.&S.R., OR **149** F7
Door Peninsula, WI **113** E7
Dothan, AL **61** G5
Double Trouble, NJ **45** F4
Douglas, AZ **121** H7
Douglas, GA **67** G5
Douglas, WY **155** E8
Douglas Lake, TN **79** B9
Dover, DE **35** E5
Dover, NH **43** H5
Dover, NJ **45** B3
Dover, OH **109** D6
Dover-Foxcroft, ME **37** E4
Dowagiac, MI **99** I5
Doylestown, PA **49** E10
Dracut, MA **41** A6
Drayton, ND **107** A9
Drift Prairie, ND **107** B7
Driskill Mountain, LA **71** B3
Drummond Island, MI **99** D7
Dry Cimarron (river), NM **123** A7
Dry Lake, ND **107** B7
Dry Tortugas N.P., FL **65** I6
Du Bay, Lake, WI **113** D5
Du Bois, PA **49** C4
Du Quoin, IL **91** H4
Dublin, GA **67** E5
Dublin, OH **109** E4
Dubuque, IA **95** C9
Duck (river), TN **79** C4
Dulce, NM **123** A3
Duluth, MN **101** D5
Dumas, AR **63** F6
Dumas, TX **127** A3
Dunbar, WV **83** F3
Duncan, OK **125** E8
Dundalk, MD **39** B8
Dunkirk, NY **46** E1
Dunmore, PA **49** B9
Dunmore, Lake, VT **53** E2
Dunn, NC **75** C7
Dupree, SD **111** B4
Durango, CO **139** G2
Durant, OK **125** F10
Durham, CT **33** D5
Durham, NC **75** B7
Durham, NH **43** H5
Dutch Harbor, AK **134** H2
Dworshak Reservoir, ID **143** C2
Dyersburg, TN **78** B1
Dyersville, IA **95** C9

E

Eagan, MN **101** F5
Eagar, AZ **121** E7
Eagle Creek, KY **69** B7
Eagle Creek N.W.&S.R., OR **149** C8
Eagle Lake, CA **137** B4
Eagle Lake, ME **37** B5
Eagle Lake, ME **37** C4
Eagle Lake, ME **37** A5
Eagle Mountain, MN **101** B7
Eagle Pass, TX **127** G4
Eagle River, WI **113** C5
Earle, AR **63** C7
Easley, SC **76** B2
East Brunswick, NJ **45** D4
East Chicago, IN **93** A2
East Derry, NH **43** I4
East Falmouth, MA **41** E9
East Fork Lake, OH **109** G2
East Grand Forks, MN **101** B1
East Greenwich, RI **51** D4
East Hampton, CT **33** C6
East Hartford, CT **33** B5
East Hartland, CT **33** A4
East Haven, CT **33** E4
East Lansing, MI **99** H6
East Liverpool, OH **109** C8
East Millinocket, ME **37** D5
East Mountain, VT **53** B5
East Okoboji Lake, IA **95** A3
East Point, GA **67** C2
East Providence, RI **51** B5
East Range, NV **147** B3
East Ridge, TN **79** D7
East River, CT **33** E5
East St. Louis, IL **91** G3
East Tavaputs Plateau, UT **151** D6
Eastern Bay, MD **39** C8
Easthampton, MA **40** C2
Eastman, GA **67** F4
Easton, MD **39** D9
Easton, PA **49** D9
Eastport, ME **37** F7
Eatonton, GA **67** D4
Eatontown, NJ **45** D5
Eau Claire, WI **113** D3
Ebey's Landing National Historical Reserve, WA **153** B3
Eden, NC **75** A6
Edenton, NC **75** B9
Edgartown, MA **41** F9
Edgefield, SC **77** D3
Edgemont, SD **110** E1
Edgewood, MD **39** B8
Edison, NJ **45** D4
Edison National Historic Site, NJ **45** C4
Edisto (river), SC **77** F6
Edisto Island, SC **77** G6
Edisto, North Fork (river), SC **77** E5
Edisto, South Fork (river), SC **77** E4
Edmond, OK **125** C8
Edward T. Breathitt Parkway, KY **68** D3
Edwards Plateau, TX **127** E5
Edwardsville, IL **91** G3
Eel (river), CA **137** B1
Eel (river), IN **93** B4
Eel (river), IN **93** F2
Eel N.W.&S.R., CA **137** B1
Effigy Mounds Nat. Mon., IA **95** A8
Effingham, IL **91** F5
Egan Range, NV **147** E6
Egg Harbor City, NJ **45** G3
Eisenhower National Historic Site, PA **49** F6
El Campo, TX **127** G7
El Centro, CA **137** I7
El Dorado, AR **63** G4
El Dorado, KS **97** D7
El Dorado Lake, KS **97** D7
El Malpais Nat. Mon., NM **123** D2
El Morro Nat. Mon., NM **123** D2
El Paso, TX **126** D1
El Reno, OK **125** C7
Elbert, Mount, CO **139** D4
Elberton, GA **67** C5
Eldon, MO **103** D4
Eldora, IA **95** C6
Eleanor Roosevelt National Historic Site, NY **47** F8
Elephant Butte Reservoir, NM **123** F3
Eleven Point (river), MO **103** F5
Eleven Point N.W.&S.R., MO **103** F6
Elgin, IL **91** B5
Elizabeth, NJ **45** C4
Elizabeth City, NC **75** A10
Elizabeth Islands, MA **41** F7
Elizabethton, TN **79** B11
Elizabethtown, KY **69** C6
Elizabethtown, PA **49** E7
Elk (river), KS **97** E8
Elk (river), WV **83** F5
Elk City, OK **125** C6
Elk City Lake, KS **97** E9
Elk N.W.&S.R., OR **148** F1
Elk Point, SD **111** F10
Elkhart, IN **93** A4
Elkhart, KS **96** F1
Elkhead Mountains, CO **139** A2
Elkhorn (river), NE **105** B7
Elkhorn Creek N.W.&S.R., OR **149** C3
Elkins, WV **83** E6
Elko, NV **147** B5
Elkton, MD **39** A9
Ellendale, DE **35** G6
Ellendale, ND **107** F8
Ellensburg, WA **153** D6
Ellicott City, MD **39** B7
Ellington, CT **33** A6
Ellis (river), NH **43** D4
Ellis Island, NY, NJ **47** H8
Ellisville, MS **73** G4
Ellsworth, KS **97** C5
Ellsworth, ME **37** F5
Elmira, NY **47** F4
Eloy, AZ **121** G5
Elsmere, DE **35** A5
Elwell, Lake, MT **145** B5
Elwood, IN **93** D4
Ely, MN **101** C6
Ely, NV **147** D6
Elyria, OH **109** B5
Embarras (river), IL **91** F5
Emmetsburg, IA **95** A4
Emmett, ID **143** G1
Emmonak, AK **134** D3
Emporia, KS **97** C8
Emporia, VA **81** E9
Emporium, PA **49** B5
Endicott, NY **47** F5
Endwell, NY **47** F6
Enfield, CT **33** A5
Enfield, NH **43** F2
England, AR **63** D5
Englewood, OH **109** E2
Enid, OK **125** B8
Enid Lake, MS **73** B3
Enosburg Falls, VT **53** A3
Enterprise, AL **61** G5
Enterprise, OR **149** B8
Ephraim, UT **151** E4
Ephrata, PA **49** E8
Ephrata, WA **153** D7
Equinox, Mount, VT **53** H2
Erie, PA **48** A2
Erie Canal, NY **46** D2
Erie, Lake, **86** E9
Erling, Lake, AR **63** G2
Erwin, TN **79** B10
Escalante (river), UT **151** G4
Escanaba, MI **99** D4
Escondido, CA **137** I6
Esmond, RI **51** B4
Espanola, NM **123** B4
Essex, CT **33** D6
Essex, MD **39** B8
Essex Junction, VT **53** C2
Estancia, NM **123** D4
Estes Park, CO **139** B5
Estherville, IA **95** A3
Etowah (river), GA **67** B1
Euclid, OH **109** A6
Eudora, AR **63** G6
Eufaula, AL **61** F6
Eufaula Lake, OK **125** D11
Eugene, OR **149** D2
Eugene O'Neill National Historic Site, CA **137** E2
Eunice, LA **71** F4
Eunice, NM **123** G8
Eureka, CA **137** B1
Eureka, KS **97** D8
Eureka, MT **144** A2
Eureka, NV **147** D5
Eureka, SD **111** A6
Eureka Springs, AR **63** A2
Evangeline, LA **71** F3
Evans, GA **67** D6
Evanston, IL **91** B6
Evanston, WY **154** G1
Evansville, IN **93** I1
Everett, WA **153** C4
Everglades N.P., FL **65** H9
Evergreen, AL **61** G3
Ewing, NJ **45** E3
Excelsior Mountains, NV **147** E3
Exeter, NH **43** H5
Exeter, RI **51** E4

F

Fabens, TX **126** E1
Fabius, Middle (river), MO **103** A4
Fabius, South (river), MO **103** B5
Fagaitua, AS **156** H2
Fagamalo, AS **156** I1
Fagatele Bay National Marine Sanctuary, AS **156** I1
Fagatogo, AS **156** I1
Fair Haven, VT **53** F1
Fairbanks, AK **135** D7
Fairborn, OH **109** E2
Fairbury, NE **105** E8
Fairfield, CT **33** E2
Fairfield, IA **95** E8
Fairfield, IL **91** G5
Fairfield, OH **109** F1
Fairfield, VT **53** B3
Fairfield Bay, AR **63** B4
Fairhaven, MA **41** E8
Fairhope, AL **61** I1
Fairmont, MN **101** H3
Fairmont, WV **83** C5
Fairmount, NY **47** D5
Fairview, KY **69** E4
Fairview, OK **125** B7
Fajardo, PR **157** H12
Falcon Reservoir, TX **127** H5
Faleasao, AS **156** I4
Falfurrias, TX **127** H6
Fall (river), KS **97** D8

Fall Line — Green River

Fall Line (escarpment), NJ, PA **28** G4
Fall River, MA **41** E7
Fallon, NV **147** D3
Falls City, NE **105** E10
Falls Creek, NV **147** A6
Falls Lake, NC **75** B7
Falmouth, MA **41** F8
Falmouth, ME **37** H3
Fargo, ND **107** D10
Faribault, MN **101** G4
Farmington, ME **37** F3
Farmington, MO **103** E7
Farmington, NH **43** G5
Farmington, NM **123** A2
Farmington, UT **151** B4
Farmington (river), CT **33** B4
Farmington N.W.&S.R., CT **33** A3
Farmington, East Branch (river), CT **33** A4
Farmington, West Branch (river), CT, MA **33** A3
Farmville, VA **81** D8
Farragut, TN **79** B8
Father Marquette National Memorial, MI **99** D6
Faulkton, SD **111** B7
Fayette, AL **61** C2
Fayetteville, AR **63** B1
Fayetteville, NC **75** C7
Fayetteville, TN **79** D5
Fayetteville, WV **83** G4
Fear, Cape, NC **75** E8
Feather, Middle Fork N.W.&S.R., CA **137** C3
Federal Way, WA **153** D4
Federalsburg, MD **39** D9
Felton, DE **35** F5
Fenwick Island, DE **35** I7
Fergus Falls, MN **101** D2
Ferguson, MO **103** C7
Fernandina Beach, FL **65** A8
Ferndale, WA **153** A3
Fernley, NV **147** C2
Ferriday, LA **71** D5
Festus, MO **103** D7
Fillmore, UT **151** E3
Findlay, OH **109** C3
Finger Lakes, NY **47** E4
Fire Island National Seashore, NY **47** H9
First Connecticut Lake, NH **43** A4
First Ladies National Historic Site, OH **109** C7
Fish (river), ME **37** B5
Fish Creek, WV **83** C4
Fishing Bay, MD **39** E9
Fitchburg, MA **41** B5
Fitzgerald, GA **67** G4
Flagstaff, AZ **121** C5
Flagstaff Lake, ME **37** E2
Flambeau (river), WI **113** C3
Flaming Gorge N.R.A., WY **155** G3
Flaming Gorge Reservoir, UT, WY **155** G3
Flandreau, SD **111** D10
Flat N.W.&S.R., MI **99** G5
Flat River Reservoir, RI **51** D3
Flathead (river), MT **144** C2
Flathead Lake, MT **144** B3
Flathead N.W.&S.R., MT **144** B3
Flathead, South Fork (river), MT **144** B3
Flatrock (river), IN **93** F4
Flattery, Cape, WA **152** B1
Flatwoods, KY **69** B10
Flemington, NJ **45** D2
Flint, MI **99** G7
Flint (river), GA **67** E2
Flint (river), MI **99** G7
Flint Hills, KS **97** E7
Flora, IL **91** G5
Florence, AL **61** A2
Florence, AZ **121** F5
Florence, CO **139** E5
Florence, KY **69** A7
Florence, OR **148** D1
Florence, SC **77** C8
Florida Bay, FL **65** H9
Florida Keys (islands), FL **65** I8
Florida Keys National Marine Sanctuary, FL **65** I7
Florida, Straits of, FL **65** I9
Florida's Turnpike, FL **65** E8
Florissant, MO **103** C7
Florissant Fossil Beds Nat. Mon., CO **139** D5
Floyd (river), IA **94** B2
Foley, AL **61** I2
Follansbee, WV **83** A5
Folsom, CA **137** D3
Fond du Lac, WI **113** F6
Fontana Lake, NC **74** C1
Fontenelle Reservoir, WY **154** F2
Ford (river), MI **99** C3
Fordyce, AR **63** F4
Forest, MS **73** E4
Forest Acres, SC **77** D5
Forest City, IA **95** A5
Forest City, NC **74** C3
Forest Grove, OR **149** B2
Forrest City, AR **63** D7
Forsyth, MT **145** D9
Fort Atkinson, WI **113** G6
Fort Benton, MT **145** B5
Fort Bowie National Historic Site, AZ **121** G7
Fort Bragg, CA **137** C1
Fort Caroline National Memorial, FL **65** B8
Fort Clatsop National Memorial, OR **148** A1
Fort Collins, CO **139** B5
Fort Davis National Historic Site, TX **126** E2
Fort Defiance, AZ **121** C7
Fort Dodge, IA **95** C4
Fort Donelson N.B., TN **78** A3
Fort Fairfield, ME **37** B6
Fort Foote Park, MD **39** D6
Fort Frederica Nat. Mon., GA **67** H7
Fort Gibson Lake, OK **125** C11
Fort Kent, ME **37** A5
Fort Knox (site), KY **69** C6
Fort Laramie National Historic Site, WY **155** F9
Fort Larned National Historic Site, KS **97** D4
Fort Lauderdale, FL **65** G9
Fort Lee, NJ **45** C5
Fort Loudoun Lake, TN **79** B8
Fort Madison, IA **95** F8
Fort Matanzas Nat. Mon., FL **65** B8
Fort McHenry Nat. Mon. and Historic Shrine, MD **39** B8
Fort Mill, SC **77** A5
Fort Morgan, CO **139** B7
Fort Myers, FL **65** F7
Fort Necessity N.B., PA **48** F2
Fort Payne, AL **61** B5
Fort Peck Dam, MT **145** B9
Fort Peck Lake, MT **145** B8
Fort Pickens, FL **64** B1
Fort Pierce, FL **65** E9
Fort Pierre, SD **111** D5
Fort Pulaski Nat. Mon., GA **67** F8
Fort Raleigh National Historic Site, NC **75** B10
Fort Scott, KS **97** D10
Fort Scott National Historic Site, KS **97** D10
Fort Smith, AR **63** C1
Fort Smith National Historic Site, AR **63** B1
Fort Stanwix Nat. Mon., NY **47** C6
Fort Stockton, TX **127** E3
Fort Sumner, NM **123** D7
Fort Sumter Nat. Mon., SC **77** G7
Fort Thompson, SD **111** D6
Fort Ticonderoga, NY **47** C9
Fort Union Nat. Mon., NM **123** B6
Fort Union Trading Post National Historic Site, MT, ND **145** B11
Fort Vancouver National Historic Site, WA **153** F3
Fort Walton Beach, FL **64** B2
Fort Washington Park, MD **39** D6
Fort Wayne, IN **93** B5
Fort Worth, TX **127** D7
Fort Yates, ND **107** F5
Fort Yukon, AK **135** C7
Fortymile N.W.&S.R., AK **135** D8
Fossil Butte Nat. Mon., WY **154** F2
Foster Center, RI **51** C2
Foster Creek, SD **111** C8
Fostoria, OH **109** B3
Fountain, CO **139** D6
Four Corners (site), AZ, CO, NM, UT **121** A7
Four Mountains, Islands of, AK **134** H1
Fox, IL, WI **91** B5
Framingham, MA **41** C6
Francis Case, Lake, SD **111** E7
Francis, Lake, NH **43** B4
Franconia, NH **43** D3
Frankford, DE **35** I7
Frankfort, IN **93** D3
Frankfort, KY **69** B7
Franklin, IN **93** F4
Franklin, KY **69** E5
Franklin, LA **71** G5
Franklin, MA **41** D6
Franklin, NC **74** C1
Franklin, NH **43** G3
Franklin, NJ **45** B3
Franklin, TN **79** B5
Franklin, VA **81** E10
Franklin Delano Roosevelt Lake, WA **153** B9
Frederica, DE **35** F5
Frederick, MD **39** B5
Frederick, OK **125** E6
Fredericksburg, VA **81** C9
Fredericksburg and Spotsylvania County Battlefields Memorial N.M.P., VA **81** C9
Fredericktown, MO **103** E7
Frederiksted, VI **157** I7
Fredonia, KS **97** E8
Fredonia, NY **46** E1
Freehold, NJ **45** E4
Freeman, SD **111** E9
Freeman, Lake, IN **93** C3
Freeport, IL **91** A3
Freeport, TX **127** G8
Freeport, NY **47** H9
Fremont, MI **99** G5
Fremont, NE **105** C9
Fremont, OH **109** B4
Fremont (river), UT **151** F5
French Broad (river), TN **79** B10
Frenchman (river), MT **145** A8
Frenchman Creek, CO, NE **105** E4
Frenchville, ME **37** A5
Fresno, CA **137** F4
Friendship Hill National Historic Site, PA **48** F2
Frio (river), TX **127** G6
Frissell, Mount, CT **33** A2
Front Range, CO,WY **130** D7
Front Royal, VA **81** B8
Frostburg, MD **38** A2
Fruitland, MD **39** E10
Fryeburg, ME **37** G2
Fullerton, NE **105** C7
Fulton, KY **68** E1
Fulton, MO **103** C5
Fulton, MS **73** B5
Fulton, NY **47** D5
Fundy, Bay of, **28** C9

G

Gabbs, NV **147** D3
Gabbs Valley, NV **147** D3
Gadsden, AL **61** C4
Gaffney, SC **77** A4
Gahanna, OH **109** E4
Gaillard, Lake, CT **33** D4
Gainesville, FL **65** C7
Gainesville, GA **67** B3
Gaithersburg, MD **39** C6
Galax, VA **81** F5
Galena, AK **135** C5
Galena, IL **91** A2
Galesburg, IL **91** C2
Galilee, RI **51** G4
Galion, OH **109** C4
Gallatin, MO **103** B3
Gallatin, TN **79** B5
Gallatin (river), MT **145** E5
Gallinas (river), NM **123** C6
Gallipolis, OH **109** G5
Gallo Arroyo (river), NM **123** E5
Gallup, NM **123** C1
Galveston, TX **127** F9
Galveston Bay, TX **116** F9
Gannett Peak, WY **155** D3
Gantt, SC **76** B2
Garapan, MP **156** C2
Garden City, KS **96** D2
Garden City, SC **77** E9
Garden Peninsula, MI **99** D4
Garden State Parkway, NJ **45** G4
Gardiner, ME **37** G3
Gardner, MA **41** B4
Gardner Lake, CT **33** C6
Gardner Pinnacles, HI **141** F3
Gardnerville, NV **147** D2
Gareloi Island, AK **135** H8
Garland, TX **127** D7
Garner, NC **75** B7
Garnett, KS **97** D9
Garrison, ND **107** C4
Gary, IN **93** A2
Gas City, IN **93** D4
Gasconade (river), MO **103** F4
Gaston, Lake, NC, VA **75** A8
Gastonia, NC **75** C4
Gates, NY **46** D3
Gates of the Arctic N.P. and Preserve, AK **135** B6
Gatesville, TX **127** E6
Gateway N.R.A., NJ, NY **45** D5
Gatlinburg, TN **79** C9
Gauley (river), WV **83** F4
Gauley River N.R.A., WV **83** F4
Gay Head (point), MA **41** F8
Gaylord, MI **99** E6
Genesee (river), NY **46** E3
Geneseo, IL **91** C3
Geneseo, NY **46** E3
Geneva, AL **61** H5
Geneva, NE **105** D8
Geneva, NY **47** D4
Geneva, OH **109** A7
George Rogers Clark N.H.P., IN **93** G1
George Washington Birthplace Nat. Mon., VA **81** C10
George Washington Carver Nat. Mon., MO **103** F2
George, Lake, FL **65** C7
George, Lake, NY **47** C8
Georgetown, DE **35** H6
Georgetown, KY **69** C8
Georgetown, OH **109** G3
Georgetown, SC **77** E9
Georgetown, TX **127** F6
Georgia, Strait of, WA **152** A2
Gering, NE **104** B1
Germantown, MD **39** C6
Germantown, TN **78** D1
Gettysburg, PA **49** F6
Gettysburg, SD **111** B6
Gettysburg N.M.P., PA **49** F6
Gibbon, NE **105** D6
Gila (river), AZ **121** F7
Gila Bend, AZ **121** F4
Gila Cliff Dwellings Nat. Mon., NM **123** F2
Gilford Park, NJ **45** F5
Gillette, WY **155** B8
Glacier Bay N.P. and Preserve, AK **135** F9
Glacier N.P., MT **144** A3
Gladstone, MI **99** D4
Glasgow, DE **35** B4
Glasgow, KY **69** E6
Glasgow, MT **145** B9
Glassboro, NJ **45** G2
Glastonbury, CT **33** B5
Glen Burnie, MD **39** C7
Glen Canyon Dam, AZ **121** A5
Glen Canyon N.R.A., AZ, UT **151** G5
Glen Ullin, ND **107** E4
Glendale, AZ **121** F4
Glendale, RI **51** A3
Glendive, MT **145** C10
Glendo Reservoir, WY **155** E9
Glenns Ferry, ID **143** H2
Glenrock, WY **155** D8
Glens Falls, NY **47** D8
Glenwood, IA **94** E2
Glenwood Springs, CO **139** C3
Globe, AZ **121** F6
Gloucester, MA **41** B8
Gloversville, NY **47** D8
Gold Beach, OR **148** F1
Golden Beach, MD **39** E7
Golden Gate N.R.A., CA **137** E1
Golden Spike National Historic Site, UT **151** A3
Goldendale, WA **153** F5
Goldfield, NV **147** F4
Goldsboro, NC **75** C8
Gonzales, LA **71** G6
Gooding, ID **143** H3
Goodland, KS **96** B1
Goodlettsville, TN **79** B5
Goose (river), ND **107** C9
Goose Creek, ID **143** I3
Goose Creek, SC **77** F7
Goose Lake, CA, OR **137** A4
Goose Point, DE **35** D6
Gordon, NE **105** A3
Gordon Creek, NE **105** B4
Gore Range, CO **139** B4
Gorham, NH **43** D4
Goshen, IN **93** A4
Goshute Mountains, NV **147** C7
Gothenburg, NE **105** D5
Gouverneur, NY **47** B6
Grafton, ND **107** B9
Grafton, WV **83** D6
Graham Lake, ME **37** F5
Grambling, LA **71** B3
Granby, CT **33** A4
Grand (river), MI **99** G6
Grand (river), MO **103** A2
Grand (river), OH **109** A7
Grand (river), SD **111** A3
Grand Canyon, AZ **121** B4
Grand Canyon (canyon), AZ **121** B3
Grand Canyon N.P., AZ **121** B3
Grand Canyon-Parashant Nat. Mon., AZ **121** B3
Grand Coulee (valley), WA **153** C7
Grand Coulee Dam, WA **153** C8
Grand Detour, IL **91** B4
Grand Forks, ND **107** C10
Grand Haven, MI **99** G4
Grand Island, NE **105** D7
Grand Island N.R.A., MI **99** C4
Grand Isle, LA **71** I8
Grand Isle, VT **53** B1
Grand Junction, CO **138** D1
Grand Lake, LA **71** G3
Grand Lake, ME **37** D6
Grand Lake (St. Marys Lake), OH **109** D2
Grand Manan Channel, ME **37** F7
Grand Marais, MN **101** C7
Grand Mesa, CO **139** D2
Grand Portage Nat. Mon., MN **101** B8
Grand Rapids, MI **99** G5
Grand Rapids, MN **101** C4
Grand Staircase-Escalante Nat. Mon., UT **151** G4
Grand Teton N.P., WY **154** C2
Grand Traverse Bay, MI **99** D5
Grand Valley, CO **138** D1
Grand Wash Cliffs, AZ **121** B2
Grand, South (river), MO **103** D2
Grand, South Fork (river), SD **110** A2
Grande Ronde (river), OR **149** A8
Grande Ronde N.W.&S.R., OR **149** A8
Grandfather Mountain, NC **74** B3
Grandview, WA **153** E7
Grangeville, ID **143** D1
Granite City, IL **91** G3
Granite Peak, MT **145** E6
Graniteville, VT **53** D4
Grant, NE **105** D3
Grant Range, NV **147** E6
Grant-Kohrs Ranch National Historic Site, MT **145** D4
Grants, NM **123** D2
Grants Pass, OR **149** F2
Grantsville, UT **151** C3
Grasonville, MD **39** C8
Grasshopper Glacier (site), MT **145** F6
Grays Harbor, WA **152** D1
Grays Lake, ID **143** H6
Gray's Reef National Marine Sanctuary, GA **67** G8
Great Barrington, MA **40** C1
Great Basin, NV **147** B5
Great Basin N.P., NV **147** D7
Great Bay, NH **43** H5
Great Bay, NJ **45** G4
Great Bend, KS **97** C5
Great Dismal Swamp, NC, VA **56** B8
Great Divide Basin, WY **155** F5
Great Egg Harbor (river), NJ **45** G3
Great Egg Harbor N.W.&S.R., NJ **45** G3
Great Falls, MT **145** C5
Great Miami (river), OH **109** D2
Great Pee Dee (river), NC, SC **56** C6
Great Plains, **86** A1
Great Plains Reservoirs, CO **139** E8
Great Pond, ME **37** F3
Great Quittacus Pond, MA **41** E8
Great Sacandaga Lake, NY **47** D8
Great Salt Lake, UT **151** B3
Great Salt Lake Desert, UT **151** D2
Great Salt Plains Lake, OK **125** B7
Great Sand Dunes Nat. Mon. and Preserve, CO **139** F5
Great Smoky Mountains, NC, TN **74** C1
Great Smoky Mountains N.P., NC, TN **74** B1
Great Swamp, RI **51** F3
Greece, NY **46** D3
Greeley, CO **139** B6
Green (river), CO, UT, WY **130** F6
Green Bay, WI **113** E7
Green Bay (bay), WI **113** D7
Green Mountains, VT **53** H2
Green River, UT **151** E6

Green River — Jamestown

Green River, WY **155** G3
Green River Lake, KY **69** D7
Green Swamp, NC **75** E7
Green Valley, AZ **121** H6
Greenbelt Park, MD **39** C7
Greenbrier, AR **63** C4
Greenbrier (river), WV **83** G5
Greencastle, IN **93** E2
Greeneville, TN **79** B10
Greenfield, IN **93** E4
Greenfield, MA **41** B3
Greenfield, OH **109** F3
Greensboro, NC **75** B6
Greensburg, IN **93** F5
Greensburg, KS **97** E4
Greensburg, PA **49** E3
Greenville, AL **61** F3
Greenville, DE **35** A5
Greenville, ME **37** E4
Greenville, MS **73** D1
Greenville, NC **75** C8
Greenville, NH **43** I3
Greenville, OH **109** D1
Greenville, PA **48** B1
Greenville, RI **51** B3
Greenville, SC **76** B2
Greenville, MI **99** G5
Greenway (site), VA **81** D10
Greenwich, CT **33** F1
Greenwood, AR **63** C1
Greenwood, DE **35** G5
Greenwood, IN **93** E4
Greenwood, MS **73** C3
Greenwood, SC **77** C3
Greer, SC **77** B3
Greers Ferry Lake, AR **63** C4
Greeson, Lake, AR **63** E2
Gregory, SD **111** E6
Grenada, MS **73** C3
Grenada Lake, MS **73** C3
Gresham, OR **149** B3
Greybull, WY **155** B5
Greybull (river), WY **155** B4
Greylock, Mount, MA **40** A1
Greys (river), WY **154** D2
Griffin, GA **67** D3
Grinnell, IA **95** D6
Gros Ventre (river), WY **154** C2
Groton, SD **111** B8
Groton, CT **33** D7
Grove, OK **125** B12
Grove City, PA **48** C2
Groveton, NH **43** C3
Guadalupe (river), TX **127** F7
Guadalupe Mountains, NM **123** G6
Guadalupe Mountains N.P., TX **126** E1
Guadalupe Peak, TX **126** E2
Guam (territory), US **156** E1
Guayama, PR **157** I11
Guernsey, WY **155** E9
Guilford, CT **33** E5
Guilford, ME **37** E4
Guilford Courthouse N.M.P., NC **75** B6
Gulf Islands National Seashore, FL, MS **64** B1
Gulf of the Farallones National Marine Sanctuary, CA **137** E2
Gulf Shores, AL **61** I2
Gulfport, MS **73** I4
Gulkana N.W.&S.R., AK **135** D7
Gunnison, CO **139** E3
Guntersville, AL **61** B4
Guntersville Lake, AL **61** B4
Gurdon, AR **63** F3
Guthrie, OK **125** C8
Guyandotte (river), WV **82** G2
Guymon, OK **124** A3

H

H.E. Bailey Turnpike, OK **125** D7
Hackensack, NJ **45** B5
Hackettstown, NJ **45** C3
Haddam, CT **33** D5
Haddonfield, NJ **45** F2
Hagåtña (Agana), GU **156** F1
Hagerman, NM **123** F6
Hagerman Fossil Beds Nat. Mon., ID **143** H2
Hagerstown, MD **39** A5
Hailey, ID **143** G3
Haines, AK **135** F9
Haines City, FL **65** E7
Hal Rogers Parkway, KY **69** D8
Haleakala N.P., HI **141** D8
Hallock, MN **101** A1
Halls Creek, UT **151** G5
Hamburg, AR **63** G5
Hamburg, NY **46** E2
Hamden, CT **33** D4
Hamilton, AL **61** B1
Hamilton, MT **144** D2
Hamilton, OH **109** F1
Hamilton, RI **51** E4
Hammonasset (river), CT **33** D5
Hammond, IN **93** A1
Hammond, LA **71** F7
Hammonton, NJ **45** G3
Hampton, IA **95** B6
Hampton, NH **43** H5
Hampton, SC **77** F5
Hampton, VA **81** E11
Hampton National Historic Site, MD **39** B7
Hams Fork (river), WY **154** F2
Hanahan, SC **77** F7
Hanamaʻulu, HI **140** A2
Hancock, MD **39** A4
Hanford, CA **137** F4
Hanford Reach Nat. Mon., WA **153** E7
Hankinson, ND **107** F10
Hanna, WY **155** F7
Hannibal, MO **103** B5
Hanover, NH **43** F2
Hanover, PA **49** F7
Harbeson, DE **35** H6
Harbor Beach, MI **99** F8
Hardin, MT **145** E8
Harding, Lake, GA **67** E1
Hardinsburg, KY **69** C5
Hardwick, VT **53** C4
Harlan, IA **95** D3
Harlan County Lake, NE **105** E6
Harlingen, TX **127** I7
Harlowton, MT **145** D6
Harmony, RI **51** B3
Harney Basin, OR **149** E6
Harney Lake, OR **149** E6
Harney Peak, SD **110** D2
Harpers Ferry N.H.P., WV **83** D10
Harriman, TN **79** B8
Harriman Reservoir, VT **53** I2
Harrington, DE **35** F5
Harris, RI **51** C4
Harrisburg, IL **91** H5
Harrisburg, PA **49** E7
Harrison, AR **63** A3
Harrison, TN **79** D7
Harrisonburg, VA **81** C7
Harrisonville, MO **103** D2
Harrisville, RI **51** A3
Harrodsburg, KY **69** C7
Harry S. Truman National Historic Site, MO **103** C2
Harry S. Truman Reservoir, MO **103** D3
Hart Mountain National Antelope Refuge, OR **149** F6
Hartford, CT **33** B5
Hartford City, IN **93** D5
Hartington, NE **105** A8
Hartland, ME **37** F4
Hartland, VT **53** F4
Hartselle, AL **61** B3
Hartsville, SC **77** C7
Hartwell, GA **67** B4
Hartwell Lake, GA, SC **76** C1
Harvard, IL **91** A4
Harvey, ND **107** C6
Harwinton, CT **33** B3
Hastings, MI **99** H5
Hastings, NE **105** D7
Hatchie (river), TN **78** C2
Hatteras Island, NC **75** B11
Hatteras, Cape, NC **75** C11
Hattiesburg, MS **73** G4
Hauʻula, HI **141** B4
Havasu, Lake, AZ, CA **121** D2
Havelock, NC **75** D9
Haverhill, MA **41** A7
Haverhill, NH **43** E2
Haverhill-Bath Bridge, NH **43** D2
Havre, MT **145** B6
Havre de Grace, MD **39** A9
Haw (river), NC **75** B6
Hawaiʻi (island), HI **141** E9
Hawaiʻi Volcanoes N.P., HI **141** F9
Hawaiian Islands Humpback Whale National Marine Sanctuary, HI **141** D5
Hawkeye Point (peak), IA **94** A2
Hawthorne, NV **147** E3
Hayden, ID **143** B1
Hays, KS **97** C4
Hayward, CA **137** E2
Hayward, WI **113** B3
Hazard, KY **69** D10
Hazardville, CT **33** A5
Hazen, ND **107** D4
Hazlehurst, GA **67** G5
Hazlehurst, MS **73** F2
Hazleton, PA **49** C8
Heart (river), ND **107** E4
Heavener, OK **125** D12
Heber City, UT **151** C4
Heber Springs, AR **63** C5
Hebron, NE **105** E8
Helena, AR **63** D7
Helena, MT **145** D4
Hells Canyon, ID **143** E1
Hells Canyon N.R.A., ID, OR **149** A9
Helper, UT **151** D5
Henderson, KY **68** C3
Henderson, NC **75** B7
Henderson, NV **147** H6
Henderson, TN **78** C2
Henderson, TX **127** D8
Hendersonville, NC **74** C2
Hendersonville, TN **79** B5
Henlopen, Cape, DE **35** G7
Hennepin Canal, IL **91** C3
Henniker, NH **43** H3
Henry Mountains, UT **151** G5
Henryetta, OK **125** C10
Henrys Lake, ID **143** F6
Heppner, OR **149** B6
Herbert Hoover National Historic Site, IA **95** D8
Hereford, CO **139** A6
Hereford, TX **127** B3
Hermann, MO **103** C5
Hermiston, OR **149** A6
Hershey, PA **49** E7
Hesperia, CA **137** H6
Hesston, KS **97** D6
Hettinger, ND **107** F3
Hialeah, FL **65** G9
Hiawatha, KS **97** A9
Hibbing, MN **101** C5
Hickory, NC **75** B4
High Bridge, NJ **45** C2
High Desert, OR **149** E5
High Plains, **130** D7
High Point, NC **75** B5
High Point (peak), NJ **45** A3
Highland Lake, NH **43** H2
Highland Lakes, NJ **45** A4
Highmore, SD **111** C6
Hightstown, NJ **45** E3
Hill Country (region), TX **127** H5
Hill Creek, UT **151** D6
Hillsboro, KS **97** D7
Hillsboro, ND **107** D10
Hillsboro, NH **43** H2
Hillsboro, OH **109** F3
Hillsboro, OR **149** B2
Hillsdale, MI **99** I6
Hillsdale Lake, KS **97** C10
Hilo, HI **141** F9
Hilton Head Island (island), SC **77** H6
Hilton Head Island, SC **77** H6
Hinesville, GA **67** G7
Hinsdale, NH **43** I1
Hinton, WV **83** G4
Hiwassee (river), TN **79** D8
Hiwassee Lake, NC **74** C1
Hobart, OK **125** D6
Hobbs, NM **123** G8
Hockanum (river), CT **33** B5
Hockessin, DE **35** A4
Hocking (river), OH **109** F6
Hoisington, KS **97** C5
Holbrook, AZ **121** D6
Holdenville, OK **125** D10
Holdrege, NE **105** D6
Holland, MI **99** H5
Hollandale, MS **73** D2
Hollidaysburg, PA **49** D4
Hollis, OK **125** E5
Holly Springs, MS **73** A4
Hollywood, FL **65** G9
Holston (river), TN, VA **79** A10
Holston, North Fork (river), VA **80** F3
Holston, South Fork (river), VA **80** F3
Holt Creek, NE **105** B6
Holton, KS **97** B9
Holualoa, HI **141** F8
Holyoke, CO **139** A9
Holyoke, MA **41** C3
Home of Franklin D. Roosevelt National Historic Site, NY **47** F8
Homer, AK **135** F6
Homer, LA **71** A3
Homestead, FL **65** H9
Homestead Nat. Mon. of America, NE **105** E8
Homewood, AL **61** D3
Homochitto (river), MS **73** G1
Homosassa Springs, FL **65** D6
Hondo, Rio (river), NM **123** F6
Honey Lake, CA **137** B4
Honolulu, HI **141** C4
Hood River, OR **149** B4
Hood, Mount, OR **149** B4
Hooper Bay, AK **134** E3
Hoopeston, IL **91** D6
Hoosic (river), MA **40** A1
Hoover, AL **61** D3
Hoover Dam, AZ, NV **121** B1
Hopatcong, NJ **45** B3
Hopatcong, Lake, NJ **45** B3
Hope, AR **63** F2
Hope, RI **51** C3
Hope Mills, NC **75** C7
Hope Valley, RI **51** E2
Hopewell, VA **81** D10
Hopewell Culture N.H.P., OH **109** F4
Hopewell Furnace National Historic Site, PA **49** E8
Hopkinsville, KY **68** E3
Hoquiam, WA **152** D2
Horn Lake, MS **73** A3
Hornell, NY **46** E3
Horse Creek, WY **155** G9
Horsehead Lake, ND **107** D6
Horseheads, NY **47** F4
Horsepasture N.W.&S.R., NC **74** C2
Horseshoe Bend, AR **63** A5
Horseshoe Bend N.M.P., AL **61** D5
Hot Creek Range, NV **147** E5
Hot Springs, AR **63** E3
Hot Springs, SD **110** E2
Hot Springs N.P., AR **63** D3
Houghton, MI **99** B2
Houghton Lake (lake), MI **99** F6
Houghton Lake, MI **99** F6
Houlton, ME **37** C6
Houma, LA **71** H7
Housatonic (river), CT, MA **33** D3
Houston, DE **35** F5
Houston, MS **73** C4
Houston, TX **127** F8
Hovenweep Nat. Mon., CO **138** F1
Howard, SD **111** D9
Howland, ME **37** E5
Howland Island (territory), US **156** F3
Hubbard Lake, MI **99** E7
Hubbell Trading Post National Historic Site, AZ **121** C7
Huber Heights, OH **109** E2
Hudson (river), NJ, NY **47** C8
Hudson, NY **47** E8
Hudson, WI **113** D1
Hudson, Lake, OK **125** B11
Huerfano (river), CO **139** F5
Hueytown, AL **61** D3
Hugh Butler Lake, NE **105** D4
Hugo, OK **125** E11
Hugo Lake, OK **125** E11
Hugoton, KS **96** E2
Humacao, PR **157** I11
Humboldt, IA **95** B4
Humboldt, TN **78** B2
Humboldt (river), NV **147** B3
Humboldt Lake, NV **147** C3
Humboldt, North Fork (river), NV **147** A5
Humphreys Peak, AZ **121** C5
Huntingburg, IN **93** H2
Huntingdon, PA **49** D5
Huntington, IN **93** C5
Huntington, WV **82** F1
Huntington, NY **47** H9
Huntington Lake, IN **93** C5
Huntsville, AL **61** A4
Huntsville, TX **127** E8
Hurley, WI **113** B4
Hurlock, MD **39** D9
Huron, SD **111** D8
Huron, Lake, **86** C8
Hurricane, UT **151** H2
Hurricane, WV **82** F2
Hurricane Creek N.W.&S.R., AR **63** B3
Hutchinson, KS **97** D6
Hutchinson, MN **101** F3
Hyannis, MA **41** E9
Hyattsville, MD **39** C7

I

Idabel, OK **125** F12
Idaho Falls, ID **143** G5
Iditarod National Historic Trail, AK **135** E5
Iliamna Lake, AK **135** F5
Iliili, AS **156** I1
Ilion, NY **47** D7
Illinois (river), IL **91** E2
Illinois (river), OK **125** B12
Illinois (river), OR **148** G1
Illinois N.W.&S.R., OR **148** F1
Immokalee, FL **65** G8
Imnaha N.W.&S.R., OR **149** B9
Imperial, NE **105** D3
Imperial Valley, CA **137** I7
Independence, IA **95** C8
Independence, KS **97** E9
Independence, MO **103** C2
Independence Mountains, NV **147** B5
Indian (river), FL **65** E9
Indian Head, MD **39** D6
Indian Lake, OH **109** D3
Indian N.W.&S.R., MI **99** C4
Indian Nation Turnpike, OK **125** D10
Indian River Bay, DE **35** I7
Indian River Inlet, DE **35** H8
Indian Springs, NV **147** G6
Indiana, PA **49** D3
Indiana Dunes National Lakeshore, IN **93** A2
Indianapolis, IN **93** E4
Indianola, IA **95** E5
Indianola, MS **73** D2
International Falls, MN **101** B4
Intracoastal Waterway, AL, FL, LA, NC, SC **61** I2
Iola, KS **97** D9
Ionia, MI **99** G6
Iowa (river), IA **95** B5
Iowa City, IA **95** D8
Iowa Falls, IA **95** C6
Ipswich, MA **41** A8
Ipswich, SD **111** B7
Irmo, SC **77** D5
Iron Mountain, MI **99** D3
Irondequoit, NY **46** D4
Ironton, OH **109** H5
Ironwood, MI **99** C1
Ironwood Forest Nat. Mon., AZ **121** G5
Iroquois (river), IL, IN **91** C5
Irving, TX **127** D7
Irvington, NJ **45** C4
Ishpeming, MI **99** C3
Island Falls, ME **37** C5
Island Park, RI **51** D6
Island Park Reservoir, ID **143** F6
Island Pond, VT **53** B5
Isle au Haut, ME **37** G5
Isle Royale, MI **99** A2
Isle Royale N.P., MI **99** A2
Isles of Shoals, ME, NH **37** I2
Itasca, Lake, MN **101** C3
Ithaca, NY **47** E5
Iuka, MS **73** A6
Ivishak N.W.&S.R., AK **135** B7

J

J. Percy Priest Lake, TN **79** B5
J. Strom Thurmond Reservoir, GA, SC **67** C5
Jack Lee, Lake, AR **63** G4
Jackman, ME **37** D3
Jackpot, NV **147** A6
Jacks Fork (river), MO **103** F5
Jackson, AL **61** G2
Jackson, KY **69** D9
Jackson, MI **99** H6
Jackson, MO **103** E7
Jackson, MS **73** F3
Jackson, OH **109** G5
Jackson, TN **78** C2
Jackson, WY **154** C2
Jackson Lake, WY **154** C2
Jacksonville, AL **61** C5
Jacksonville, AR **63** D5
Jacksonville, FL **65** B7
Jacksonville, IL **91** E3
Jacksonville, NC **75** D8
Jacksonville Beach, FL **65** B8
Jaffrey, NH **43** I2
James (river), ND, SD **86** C3
James (river), VA **81** D8
James A. Garfield National Historic Site, OH **109** A7
Jamestown, ND **107** D8

Jamestown — Little Deschutes N.W.&S.R.

Jamestown, NY **46** F2
Jamestown, RI **51** E5
Jamestown, VA **81** D10
Jamestown Reservoir, ND **107** D8
Janesville, WI **113** H6
Jarbidge (river), ID **143** I2
Jarvis Island (territory), US **157** G5
Jasper, AL **61** C2
Jasper, IN **93** H2
Jay Peak, VT **53** A3
Jeanerette, LA **71** G5
Jeannette, PA **48** E2
Jefferson, IA **95** D4
Jefferson (river), MT **145** E4
Jefferson City, MO **103** D5
Jefferson City, TN **79** B9
Jeffersontown, KY **69** B6
Jeffersonville, IN **93** H4
Jekyll Island, GA **67** H7
Jemez, E. Fork N.W.&S.R., NM **123** C4
Jenks, OK **125** B10
Jennings, LA **71** G3
Jericho, VT **53** C2
Jerimoth Hill (peak), RI **51** B2
Jerome, ID **143** H3
Jersey City, NJ **45** C5
Jersey Shore, PA **49** C6
Jerseyville, IL **91** F2
Jerusalem, RI **51** G4
Jesse James Farm and Museum, MO **103** B2
Jesup, GA **67** G6
Jewel Cave Nat. Mon., SD **110** E1
Jewett City, CT **33** C8
Jimmy Carter National Historic Site, GA **67** F2
John D. Rockefeller, Jr. Memorial Parkway, WY **154** B2
John Day, OR **149** C6
John Day (river), OR **149** C5
John Day Fossil Beds Nat. Mon., OR **149** C5
John Day N.W.&S.R., OR **149** B5
John Day, North Fork N.W.&S.R., OR **149** C7
John Day, South Fork N.W.&S.R., OR **149** D6
John F. Kennedy Space Center (site), FL **65** D9
John H. Kerr Reservoir, NC, VA **81** E8
John Martin Reservoir, CO **139** E8
John Muir Nat. Mon., CA **137** D2
John N.W.&S.R., AK **135** B6
John Redmond Reservoir, KS **97** D9
Johnson, VT **53** B3
Johnson City, TN **79** B10
Johnston, RI **51** B4
Johnston Atoll (territory), US **156** E4
Johnstown, PA **49** E3
Johnstown Flood National Memorial, PA **49** D4
Joliet, IL **91** C5
Jonesboro, AR **63** B7
Jonesboro, LA **71** C3
Jonesport, ME **37** F6
Joplin, MO **103** F2
Jordan, MT **145** C9
Jordan Creek, ID **143** H1
Joseph Creek N.W.&S.R., OR **149** A8
Joshua Tree N.P., CA **137** H7
Juan de Fuca, Strait of, WA **152** B1
Julia Butler Hansen Refuge, WA **152** E2
Julian M. Carroll Parkway, KY **68** E1
Jump (river), WI **113** C3
Junction City, KS **97** B7
Junction City, OR **149** D2
Juneau, AK **135** F10
Juniata (river), PA **49** D6
Jupiter, FL **65** F9

K

Ka'ena Point, HI **141** B4
Kadoka, SD **111** D4
Kaho'olawe (island), HI **141** D7
Kahuku Point, HI **141** B4
Kahului, HI **141** C7
Kaibab Plateau, AZ **121** B4
Kailua, HI **141** B5
Kailua, HI **141** F8
Kaiwi Channel, HI **141** C5
Kalae (South Point), HI **141** G8
Kalaheo, HI **140** A2
Kalamazoo, MI **99** H5
Kalamazoo (river), MI **99** H5
Kalaoa, HI **141** F8
Kalaupapa, HI **141** C6
Kalaupapa N.H.P., HI **141** C6
Kalispell, MT **144** B2
Kalkaska, MI **99** E5
Kaloko-Honokohau N.H.P., HI **141** F8
Kamiah, ID **143** D2
Kamuela *see* Waimea, HI **141** E8
Kanab, UT **151** H3
Kanab Creek, AZ, UT **121** B4
Kanawha (river), WV **83** F3
Kane'ohe, HI **141** B5
Kankakee, IL **91** C5
Kankakee (river), IL, IN **91** C5
Kannapolis, NC **75** C5
Kanopolis Lake, KS **97** C6
Kansas (river), KS **97** B9
Kansas City, KS **97** B10
Kansas City, MO **103** C2
Kapa'a, HI **140** A2
Kapa'au, HI **141** E8
Kaskaskia (river), IL **91** F4
Kaskaskia Island, IL **91** H3
Katahdin, Mount, ME **37** D5
Katmai N.P. and Preserve, AK **135** F5
Kaua'i (island), HI **140** A2
Kaukauna, WI **113** E6
Kaulakahi Channel, HI **140** A1
Kaunakakai, HI **141** C6
Kaw Lake, OK **125** A9
Kawich Range, NV **147** E5
Kayenta, AZ **121** B6
Keahole Point, HI **141** F8
Keansburg, NJ **45** D4
Kearney, NE **105** D6
Keene, NH **43** H2
Kekaha, HI **140** A1
Kelleys Island, OH **109** B5
Kellogg, ID **143** C1
Kelso, WA **153** F3
Kemmerer, WY **154** F2
Kenai, AK **135** E6
Kenai Fjords N.P., AK **135** F6
Kenai Peninsula, AK **135** E6
Kendall, FL **65** H9
Kendall Park, NJ **45** D3
Kendallville, IN **93** B5
Kenmare, ND **107** A3
Kennebec, SD **111** D6
Kennebec (river), ME **37** G3
Kennebunk, ME **37** I2
Kenner, LA **71** G7
Kennesaw Mountain National Battlefield Park, GA **67** C2
Kennett, MO **103** G7
Kennett Square, PA **49** F9
Kennewick, WA **153** F7
Kenosha, WI **113** H7
Kenova, WV **82** F1
Kent, CT **33** B2
Kent, OH **109** B7
Kent Island, MD **39** C8
Kenton, OH **109** C3
Kentucky (river), KY **69** B7
Kentucky Lake, KY **68** E2
Kentucky, Middle Fork (river), KY **69** D9
Kentucky, North Fork (river), KY **69** C9
Kentucky, South Fork (river), KY **69** D9
Kentwood, MI **99** G5
Keokuk, IA **95** F8
Keowee, Lake, SC **76** B2
Kern N.W.&S.R., CA **137** G5
Kernersville, NC **75** B5
Kerrville, TX **127** F5
Ketchikan, AK **135** G11
Ketchum, ID **143** G3
Kettering, OH **109** E2
Kettle River Range, WA **153** B8
Keuka Lake, NY **47** E4
Kewanee, IL **91** C3
Keweenaw N.H.P., MI **99** B2
Keweenaw Peninsula, MI **99** B3
Key Largo, FL **65** H9
Key West, FL **65** I7
Keya Paha (river), NE, SD **105** A5
Keyhole Reservoir, WY **155** B9
Keyser, WV **83** C8
Keystone Lake, OK **125** B10
Kiamichi (river), OK **125** E11
Kickapoo (river), WI **113** G3
Kihei, HI **141** D7
Kilauea Crater (site), HI **141** F9
Killeen, TX **127** E6
Killik (river), AK **135** B6
Killington Peak, VT **53** F3
Kimball, NE **104** C1
Kinderhook, NY **47** E8
Kingfield, ME **37** F3
Kingfisher, OK **125** C8
Kingman, AZ **121** D2
Kingman, KS **97** E6
Kingman Reef (territory), US **157** F5
Kings (river), NV **147** A3
Kings Canyon N.P., CA **137** E5
Kings Mountain, NC **75** C4
Kings Mountain N.M.P., SC **77** A4
Kings N.W.&S.R., CA **137** F5
Kings Peak, UT **151** B5
Kingsland, GA **67** H7
Kingsport, TN **79** A10
Kingston, NH **43** H5
Kingston, NY **47** F8
Kingston, PA **49** C8
Kingston, RI **51** F4
Kingstree, SC **77** E7
Kingsville, TX **127** H6
Kingwood, WV **83** C6
Kinsley, KS **97** D4
Kinston, NC **75** C8
Kiowa, CO **139** C6
Kirkland, WA **153** C4
Kirksville, MO **103** A4
Kirkwood, MO **103** D7
Kirwin Reservoir, KS **97** A4
Kiska Island, AK **135** H7
Kissimmee, FL **65** D8
Kissimmee (river), FL **65** E8
Kitt Peak National Observatory, AZ **121** H5
Kittanning, PA **49** D3
Kittatinny Mountains, NJ **45** B2
Kittery, ME **37** I2
Kitts Hummock, DE **35** E6
Kitty Hawk, NC **75** B10
Klamath (river), CA, OR **130** D2
Klamath Falls, OR **149** G3
Klamath N.W.&S.R., CA, OR **137** A1
Klickitat (river), WA **153** F5
Klickitat N.W.&S.R., WA **153** F5
Klondike Gold Rush N.H.P., AK **135** E9
Knife (river), ND **107** D3
Knife River Indian Villages National Historic Site, ND **107** D4
Knoxville, IA **95** E6
Knoxville, TN **79** B8
Kobuk N.W.&S.R., AK **135** C5
Kobuk Valley N.P., AK **135** B5
Kodiak, AK **135** G6
Kodiak Island, AK **135** G6
Kokomo, IN **93** D4
Koocanusa, Lake, MT **144** A2
Kootenai (river), ID, MT **143** A1
Kosciusko, MS **73** D4
Kotzebue, AK **135** B4
Koyukuk (river), AK **135** C5
Koyukuk, North Fork N.W.&S.R., AK **135** B6
Kumukahi, Cape, HI **141** F10
Kure Atoll, HI **140** E1
Kuskokwim (river), AK **135** C6
Kuskokwim Mountains, AK **135** E4
Kuskokwim, North Fork (river), AK **135** D5

L

L'Anse, MI **99** C2
La Crescent, MN **101** H6
La Crosse, WI **113** F3
La Follette, TN **79** B8
La Grande, OR **149** B7
La Grange, GA **67** E1
La Grange, KY **69** B6
La Junta, CO **139** F7
La Moine (river), IL **91** D2
La Perouse Pinnacle (island), HI **141** F3
La Plata, MD **39** E7
La Salle, IL **91** C4
La'ie, HI **141** B4
Laconia, NH **43** G4
Ladder Creek, KS **96** C2
Ladson, SC **77** F7
Ladysmith, WI **113** C3
LaFayette, GA **67** B1
Lafayette, IN **93** D2
Lafayette, LA **71** G4
Lafayette, CO **139** B5
Lafayette, Mount, NH **43** D3
Lafourche, Bayou (river), LA **71** H7
Lahaina, HI **141** C7
Lake Andes, SD **111** F8
Lake Charles, LA **70** G2
Lake City, FL **65** B6
Lake City, SC **77** D8
Lake Clark N.P. and Preserve, AK **135** E5
Lake Erie Beach, NY **46** E2
Lake Geneva, WI **113** H6
Lake Havasu City, AZ **121** D2
Lake Mead N.R.A., AZ, NV **121** C2
Lake Meredith N.R.A., TX **127** A4
Lake Placid, NY **47** B8
Lake Providence, LA **71** A6
Lake Roosevelt N.R.A., WA **153** C8
Lake Village, AR **63** G6
Lakehurst, NJ **45** F4
Lakeland, FL **65** E7
Lakeview, OR **149** G5
Lakeville, CT **33** A2
Lakeville, MN **101** G4
Lakewood, NJ **45** E4
Lakewood, WA **153** D3
Lakin, KS **96** D2
Lamar, CO **139** E9
Lambertville, MI **99** I7
Lambertville, NJ **45** D2
Lamesa, TX **127** D3
Lamlam, Mount, GU **156** G1
Lamoille (river), VT **53** B2
LaMoure, ND **107** E8
Lamprey (river), NH **43** H4
Lamprey N.W.&S.R., NH **43** H5
Lana'i (island), HI **141** D6
Lana'i City, HI **141** D6
Lancaster, CA **137** G5
Lancaster, NH **43** C3
Lancaster, OH **109** E5
Lancaster, PA **49** E8
Lancaster, SC **77** B6
Lancaster, WI **113** G4
Land Between the Lakes N.R.A., KY, TN **68** E3
Land O'Lakes, WI **113** B5
Lander, WY **155** D4
Lanett, AL **61** E6
Langdon, ND **107** A8
L'Anguille (river), AR **63** C6
Lansing, KS **97** B10
Lansing, MI **99** H6
LaPorte, IN **93** A3
Laramie, WY **155** G8
Laramie (river), CO, WY **155** F9
Laramie Mountains, CO, WY **155** E8
Laredo, TX **127** H5
Larimore, ND **107** C9
Larned, KS **97** D4
Larose, LA **71** H7
Las Animas, CO **139** E8
Las Cruces, NM **123** G4
Las Vegas, NM **123** C5
Las Vegas, NV **147** G6
Lassen Volcanic N.P., CA **137** B3
Last Chance, CO **139** C7
Lata Mountain, AS **157** I5
Laughlin, NV **147** I6
Laurel, DE **35** I5
Laurel, MS **73** G4
Laurel, MT **145** E7
Laurens, SC **77** C3
Laurinburg, NC **75** D6
Laurium, MI **99** B2
Lava Beds Nat. Mon., CA **137** A3
Lawrence, IN **93** E4
Lawrence, KS **97** B9
Lawrence, MA **41** A7
Lawrenceburg, IN **93** F6
Lawrenceburg, KY **69** C7
Lawrenceburg, TN **79** C4
Lawrenceville, IL **91** G6
Lawton, OK **125** E7
Laysan Island, HI **140** E2
Layton, UT **151** B4
Le Mars, IA **94** B2
Lead, SD **110** C1
Leadville, CO **139** D4
Leaf (river), MS **73** G5
Leavenworth, KS **97** B10
Lebanon, IN **93** D3
Lebanon, KS **97** A5
Lebanon, KY **69** D7
Lebanon, MO **103** E4
Lebanon, NH **43** F2
Lebanon, OH **109** F2
Lebanon, OR **149** C2
Lebanon, PA **49** E7
Lebanon, TN **79** B5
Lebanon, VA **80** E3
Lee, MA **40** C1
Leech Lake, MN **101** D3
Lees Summit, MO **103** C2
Leesburg, FL **65** D7
Leesburg, VA **81** A9
Leesville, LA **70** E2
Leesville Lake, OH **109** D7
Lehi, UT **151** C4
Lehigh (river), PA **49** C8
Lehua Island, HI **140** A1
Leitchfield, KY **69** D5
Leland, MS **73** D2
Lemhi (river), ID **143** F4
Lemhi Pass, MT **144** F3
Lemhi Range, ID **143** F3
Lemmon, SD **111** A3
Lemon, Lake, IN **93** F3
Lennox, SD **111** E10
Lenoir, NC **75** B4
Lenoir City, TN **79** B8
Lenox, MA **40** B1
Leola, SD **111** A7
Leominster, MA **41** B5
Leon (river), TX **127** E6
Leusoalii, AS **157** I5
Levelland, TX **127** C3
Levisa Fork (river), KY **69** C10
Levittown, NY **47** H9
Levittown, PA **49** E10
Lewes, DE **35** G7
Lewes and Rehoboth Canal, DE **35** G7
Lewis (river), WA **153** F3
Lewis and Clark Lake, NE, SD **111** F9
Lewis and Clark Memorial, MT **144** F3
Lewis Smith Lake, AL **61** B3
Lewisburg, PA **49** C7
Lewisburg, TN **79** C5
Lewisburg, WV **83** G5
Lewiston, ID **143** D1
Lewiston, ME **37** G3
Lewistown, MT **145** C6
Lewistown, PA **49** D6
Lexington, KY **69** C8
Lexington, MA **41** B7
Lexington, NC **75** B5
Lexington, NE **105** D5
Lexington, TN **78** C3
Lexington, VA **81** D7
Lexington Park, MD **39** E8
Libby, MT **144** B1
Liberal, KS **96** F2
Liberty, MO **103** C2
Licking (river), KY **69** A8
Licking (river), OH **109** E5
Licking, North Fork (river), KY **69** B8
Licking, South Fork (river), KY **69** B8
Lihu'e, HI **140** A2
Lillinonah, Lake, CT **33** D2
Lima, OH **109** C2
Limestone, ME **37** B6
Limon, CO **139** D7
Lincoln, DE **35** G6
Lincoln, IL **91** E4
Lincoln, ME **37** E5
Lincoln, NE **105** D9
Lincoln, NH **43** E3
Lincoln Boyhood National Memorial, IN **93** H2
Lincoln City, OR **148** C1
Lincoln Home National Historic Site, IL **91** E3
Lincolnton, NC **75** C4
Lindenwold, NJ **45** F2
Lindsborg, KS **97** C6
Linton, IN **93** G2
Linton, ND **107** F6
Lisbon, ND **107** E9
Lisbon, NH **43** D2
Lisbon Falls, ME **37** G3
Lisianski Island, HI **140** E2
Liston Point, DE **35** C5
Litchfield, CT **33** B3
Litchfield, IL **91** F3
Litchfield, MN **101** F3
Little (river), AR, OK **63** F1
Little (river), KY **68** E3
Little (river), LA **71** D4
Little (river), OK **125** D9
Little Beaver Creek National Scenic River, OH **109** C8
Little Bighorn Battlefield Nat. Mon., MT **145** E8
Little Blue (river), KS, NE **97** A7
Little Colorado (river), AZ **121** D7
Little Compton, RI **51** E6
Little Darby Creek, OH **109** E3
Little Deschutes N.W.&S.R., OR **149** E4

Little Diomede Island — Mio

Little Diomede Island, AK **134** C3
Little Egg Harbor, NJ **45** G4
Little Falls, MN **101** E3
Little Falls, NY **47** D7
Little Humboldt (river), NV **147** B4
Little Kanawha (river), WV **83** D3
Little Lost (river), ID **143** F4
Little Miami (river), OH **109** F2
Little Miami National Scenic River, OH **109** F2
Little Miami, East Fork (river), OH **109** G2
Little Missouri (river), AR, ND, SD **86** C1
Little Missouri, MT **145** F11
Little Missouri N.W.&S.R., AR **63** E2
Little Muddy (river), ND **106** B2
Little Pee Dee (river), NC, SC **77** D9
Little Powder (river), WY **155** B8
Little Red (river), AR **63** C5
Little River Canyon National Preserve, AL **61** B5
Little Rock, AR **63** D4
Little Rock Central High School National Historic Site, AR **63** D5
Little Sac (river), MO **103** E3
Little Salt Lake (dry lake), UT **151** G2
Little Sandy (river), KY **69** B10
Little Sioux (river), IA **94** C2
Little Snake (river), CO **139** A2
Little Tallahatchie (river), MS **73** B4
Little Wabash (river), IL **91** G5
Little White (river), SD **111** F4
Little Wood (river), ID **143** H3
Littleton, CO **139** C6
Littleton, ME **37** C6
Littleton, NH **43** D3
Live Oak, FL **65** B6
Livingston, AL **61** E1
Livingston, MT **145** E5
Livingston, Lake, TX **116** E9
Livonia, MI **99** H7
Llano (river), TX **127** E5
Llano Estacado (plain), NM, TX **116** D5
Lochsa (river), ID **143** D2
Lock Haven, PA **49** C6
Lockport, NY **46** D2
Locust Creek, MO **103** A4
Locust Fork (river), AL **61** C3
Lodgepole Creek, NE, WY **104** C1
Lodi, CA **137** D3
Logan, OH **109** F5
Logan, UT **151** A4
Logan, WV **82** G2
Logan Creek, NE **105** B8
Logansport, IN **93** C3
Lolo Pass, MT **144** D2
Lompoc, CA **137** G4
London, KY **69** D8
Londonderry, NH **43** I4
Lone Grove, OK **125** E8
Long Bay, NC, SC **75** E7
Long Beach, CA **137** H5
Long Beach, MS **73** I4
Long Beach, NY **47** H9
Long Beach Island, NJ **45** G5
Long Branch, NJ **45** D5
Long Island, NY **47** H9
Long Island Sound, NY **47** G9
Long Lake (lake), ME **37** A5
Long Lake (lake), ME **37** B4
Long Lake, ND **107** E6
Long Pond, MA **41** E7
Long Prairie, MN **101** E3
Long Trail, VT **53** D2
Longfellow Mountains, ME **37** F2
Longmont, CO **139** B5
Longview, TX **127** D8
Longview, WA **153** F3
Lonsdale, RI **51** B5
Looking Glass (river), MI **99** G6
Lookout Pass, ID **143** C2
Lookout, Cape, NC **75** D10
Lookout, Point, MD **39** F8
Lorain, OH **109** B5
Lordsburg, NM **123** G1
Loris, SC **77** D9
Los Alamos, NM **123** C4
Los Angeles, CA **137** H5
Los Lunas, NM **123** D4
Los Pinos (river), CO **139** F2
Lost River Range, ID **143** F3
Lostine N.W.&S.R., OR **149** B8
Loudonville, OH **109** C5
Louie B. Nunn Parkway, KY **69** E6
Louisiana, MO **103** B6
Louisville, CO **139** B5
Louisville, KY **69** B6
Louisville, MS **73** D4
Loup (river), NE **105** C7
Loup, Middle (river), NE **105** C5
Loup, North (river), NE **105** B5
Loup, South (river), NE **105** C5
Loveland, CO **139** B5
Lovell, WY **155** A5
Lovelock, NV **147** C3
Loving, NM **123** G7
Lovington, NM **123** G8
Lowell, IN **93** B2
Lowell, MA **41** A6
Lowell N.H.P., MA **41** A6
Lowell, Lake, ID **143** G1
Lower Bay, NJ **45** D5
Lower Peninsula, MI **99** F5
Lower Red Lake, MN **101** B3
Lowville, NY **47** C6
Loxahatchee N.W.&S.R., FL **65** F10
Lubbock, TX **127** C4
Lucedale, MS **73** H5
Ludington, MI **99** F4
Ludlow, MA **41** C3
Ludlow, VT **53** G3
Lufkin, TX **127** E8
Lumber (river), NC **75** D6
Lumber N.W.&S.R., NC **75** D6
Lumberton, NC **75** D7
Luray, VA **81** B8
Lusk, WY **155** D10
Luverne, MN **101** H2
Lyman, WY **154** G2
Lynchburg, TN **79** C5
Lynchburg, VA **81** D7
Lynches (river), SC **77** D8
Lynden, WA **153** A3
Lyndon B. Johnson N.H.P., TX **127** F6
Lyndonville, VT **53** C5
Lynn, MA **41** B7
Lyons, KS **97** D5

M

Machias, ME **37** F7
Machias (river), ME **37** F6
Machiasport, ME **37** F7
Mackinac Island, MI **99** D6
Mackinac, Straits of, MI **99** D5
Mackinaw (river), IL **91** D4
Macomb, IL **91** D2
Macon, GA **67** E3
Macon, MO **103** B4
Macon, Bayou (river), LA **71** B5
Macoupin Creek, IL **91** F2
Mad (river), VT **53** D3
Madawaska, ME **37** A5
Madeline Island, WI **113** A4
Madill, OK **125** E9
Madison, AL **61** A3
Madison, CT **33** E5
Madison, IN **93** G5
Madison, ME **37** F3
Madison, MN **101** F2
Madison, NE **105** C8
Madison, SD **111** D9
Madison, WI **113** G5
Madison, WV **82** G2
Madison (river), WY **154** A1
Madison (river), MT **145** E4
Madison Heights, VA **81** D7
Madisonville, KY **68** D3
Madras, OR **149** C4
Magazine Mountain (peak), AR **63** C2
Magee, MS **73** F3
Maggie L. Walker National Historic Site, VA **81** D9
Magic Reservoir, ID **143** H3
Magnolia, AR **63** G3
Mahoning (river), OH **109** B8
Maia, AS **157** I5
Maine, Gulf of, ME **37** H5
Makawao, HI **141** C7
Malad City, ID **143** I4
Malden, MA **41** B7
Malden, MO **103** G7
Malheur (river), OR **149** D8
Malheur Lake, OR **149** E7
Malheur N.W.&S.R., OR **149** D7
Malheur, North Fork (river), OR **149** D7
Malheur, North Fork N.W.&S.R., OR **149** D7
Malone, NY **47** A8
Malta, MT **145** B8
Malvern, AR **63** E3
Mammoth Cave N.P., KY **69** D5
Manalapan (river), NJ **45** D4
Manasquan, NJ **45** E5
Manassas, VA **81** B9
Manassas National Battlefield Park, VA **81** B9
Manchester, CT **33** B5
Manchester, IA **95** C8
Manchester, MD **39** A7
Manchester, NH **43** H4
Manchester, OH **109** G3
Manchester, TN **79** C6
Manchester Center, VT **53** H2
Mancos (river), CO **138** G1
Mandan, ND **107** E5
Mandeville, LA **71** F8
Mangum, OK **125** D6
Manhattan, KS **97** B7
Manila, AR **63** B8
Manistee, MI **99** F4
Manistee (river), MI **99** F5
Manistee N.W.&S.R., MI **99** F5
Manistique, MI **99** D4
Manitou Islands, MI **99** E4
Manitou Passage, MI **99** E5
Manitowoc, WI **113** E7
Mankato, MN **101** G4
Manning, SC **77** D7
Mannington, WV **83** C5
Mansfield, LA **70** C1
Mansfield, OH **109** C5
Mansfield, PA **49** B6
Mansfield Hollow Lake, CT **33** B7
Mansfield, Mount, VT **53** C2
Manti, UT **151** E4
Manua Islands (islands), AS **156** I3
Manville, RI **51** A4
Many, LA **70** D2
Manzanar National Historic Site, CA **137** F5
Maple (river), ND **107** E9
Maple (river), ND **107** F8
Maquoketa, IA **95** C9
Maquoketa (river), IA **95** C9
Marais des Cygnes (river), KS, MO **97** C10
Marathon, FL **65** I8
Marble Canyon, AZ **121** B5
Marblehead, MA **41** B8
Marcy, Mount, NY **47** B8
Marfa, TX **126** F2
Marianna, AR **63** D7
Marianna, FL **65** A3
Marias (river), MT **145** B4
Marietta, GA **67** C2
Marietta, OH **109** F7
Marinette, WI **113** D7
Marion, AL **61** E2
Marion, IA **95** C8
Marion, IL **91** H4
Marion, IN **93** C4
Marion, KY **68** D3
Marion, OH **109** D4
Marion, SC **77** C8
Marion, VA **80** E4
Marion Lake, KS **97** C7
Marion, Lake, SC **77** E6
Mark Twain Lake, MO **103** B5
Marked Tree, AR **63** C7
Marksville, LA **71** E4
Marlborough, CT **33** C6
Marlborough, MA **41** C6
Marlow, OK **125** E8
Maro Reef, HI **140** F2
Marquette, MI **99** C3
Mars Hill, ME **37** B6
Marsh Island, LA **71** H4
Marshall, MI **99** H6
Marshall, MN **101** G2
Marshall, MO **103** C4
Marshall, TX **127** D9
Marshallton, DE **35** B4
Marshalltown, IA **95** C6
Marsh-Billings-Rockefeller N.H.P., VT **53** F3
Marshfield, WI **113** D4
Marshyhope Creek, DE, MD **35** G4
Martha's Vineyard (island), MA **41** F8
Martin, SD **111** E4
Martin, TN **78** B2
Martin Luther King, Jr. National Historic Site, GA **67** C2
Martin Van Buren National Historic Site, NY **47** E8
Martin, Lake, AL **61** E5
Martins Ferry, OH **109** D8
Martinsburg, WV **83** C9
Martinsville, IN **93** F3
Martinsville, VA **81** E6
Marydel, DE **35** E4
Marys (river), NV **147** A6
Marysville, KS **97** A7
Marysville, OH **109** D3
Maryville, MO **103** A2
Maryville, TN **79** C8
Mascoma Lake, NH **43** F2
Mason, MI **99** H6
Mason, OH **109** F2
Mason City, IA **95** A6
Massabesic Lake, NH **43** H4
Massachusetts Bay, MA **41** B8
Massena, NY **47** A7
Massillon, OH **109** C6
Matagorda Bay, TX **116** F8
Matanuska (river), AK **135** E6
Mattawamkeag (river), ME **37** D6
Matthews, NC **75** C4
Mattoon, IL **91** F5
Maui (island), HI **141** C7
Mauldin, SC **77** B3
Maumee, OH **109** B3
Maumee (river), IN, OH **93** B6
Maumee Bay, OH **109** A3
Maumelle, AR **63** D4
Mauna Kea (peak), HI **141** E9
Mauna Loa (peak), HI **141** F9
Maurepas, Lake, LA **71** F7
Maurice (river), NJ **45** G2
Maurice N.W.&S.R., NJ **45** H2
May, Cape, NJ **45** I2
Mayagüez, PR **157** I9
Mayfield, KY **68** E2
Mayfield Creek, KY **68** E1
Mays Landing, NJ **45** H3
Maysville, KY **69** B9
Mayville, ND **107** C9
McAlester, OK **125** D10
McAllen, TX **127** I6
McCall, ID **143** F1
McCandless, PA **48** D2
McComb, MS **73** G2
McCook, NE **105** E4
McGee Creek Lake, OK **125** E10
McGehee, AR **63** F6
McGill, NV **147** D6
McIntosh, SD **111** A4
McKee Creek, IL **91** E2
McKeesport, PA **48** D2
McKenzie, TN **78** B3
McKenzie (river), OR **149** D2
McKenzie N.W.&S.R., OR **149** D3
McKinley, Mount (Denali), AK **135** D6
McLean, VA **81** A9
McLoughlin House National Historic Site, OR **149** B2
McMinnville, OR **149** B2
McMinnville, TN **79** C6
McPherson, KS **97** C6
Mead, Lake, AZ, NV **121** B2
Meade, KS **97** E3
Meade (river), AK **135** A5
Meadow Valley Wash (river), NV **147** G7
Meadville, PA **48** B2
Mechanicsburg, PA **49** E6
Mechanicsville, VA **81** D9
Medford, MA **41** B7
Medford, OR **149** G2
Medford, WI **113** D4
Medical Lake, WA **153** C9
Medicine Bow (river), WY **155** F7
Medicine Bow Mountains, CO **139** A4
Medicine Lodge (river), KS **97** E4
Medicine Lodge, KS **97** E5
Medina, NY **46** D3
Medina, OH **109** B6
Medora, ND **106** D2
Meeker, CO **139** B2
Meherrin (river), VA **81** E8
Melbourne, FL **65** D9
Melozitna (river), AK **135** C5
Memphis, TN **78** C1
Memphremagog, Lake, VT **53** A4
Mena, AR **63** D1
Menahga, MN **101** D3
Menasha, WI **113** E6
Mendota, IL **91** B4
Mendota, Lake, WI **113** G5
Menlo Park, NJ **45** D4
Menominee, MI **99** E3
Menominee (river), MI, WI **99** D3
Menomonee Falls, WI **113** G7
Menomonie, WI **113** D2
Mentor, OH **109** A7
Mequon, WI **113** G7
Merced, CA **137** E4
Merced N.W.&S.R., CA **137** E4
Mercersburg, PA **49** F5
Mercerville, NJ **45** E3
Meredith, NH **43** F3
Meredith, Lake, CO **139** E7
Meriden, CT **33** C4
Meridian, MS **73** E5
Merrill, WI **113** D5
Merrillville, IN **93** A2
Merrimack, NH **43** I3
Merrimack (river), MA, NH **41** A7
Merritt Island, FL **65** D9
Merrymeeting Lake, NH **43** G4
Mesa, AZ **121** F5
Mesa de Maya, CO **139** G7
Mesa Verde N.P., CO **138** G1
Mesabi Range, MN **101** C4
Mesquite, NV **147** G7
Metairie, LA **71** G8
Meteor Crater, AZ **121** D5
Methow (river), WA **153** B6
Methuen, MA **41** A7
Metolius N.W.&S.R., OR **149** D3
Metropolis, IL **91** I4
Mettawee (river), VT **53** G1
Mexico, ME **37** F2
Mexico, MO **103** C5
Mexico, Gulf of, **56** G3
Miami, FL **65** G9
Miami, OK **125** A11
Miami Beach, FL **65** G9
Miami Canal, FL **65** F9
Michigan City, IN **93** A2
Michigan, Lake, **86** D7
Middleboro, MA **41** D8
Middlebury, VT **53** E2
Middlesboro, KY **69** E9
Middleton, WI **113** G5
Middletown, CT **33** C5
Middletown, DE **35** C4
Middletown, NY **47** G8
Middletown, OH **109** F2
Middletown, RI **51** E5
Midland, MI **99** G6
Midland, TX **127** D3
Midway, DE **35** H7
Midway Islands (territory), US **156** D4
Milaca, MN **101** E4
Milan, NM **123** D2
Milan, TN **78** B2
Milbank, SD **111** B10
Miles City, MT **145** D10
Milford, CT **33** E3
Milford, DE **35** G6
Milford, MA **41** C6
Milford, NE **105** D8
Milford, NH **43** I3
Milford, UT **151** F2
Milford Lake, KS **97** B7
Mililani Town, HI **141** B4
Milk (river), MT **145** B8
Mill Creek, IN **93** F3
Millbrook, AL **61** E4
Millcreek, PA **48** A2
Mille Lacs Lake, MN **101** D4
Milledgeville, GA **67** D4
Millen, GA **67** E6
Miller, SD **111** C7
Millers (river), MA **41** A4
Millington, TN **78** C1
Millinocket, ME **37** D5
Millsboro, DE **35** I6
Millville, NJ **45** H2
Millwood Lake, AR **63** F2
Milo, ME **37** E4
Milton, DE **35** G6
Milton, MA **41** C7
Milton, NH **43** G5
Milton, VT **53** B2
Milton, Lake, OH **109** C7
Milton-Freewater, OR **149** A7
Milwaukee, WI **113** G7
Milwaukee (river), WI **113** F6
Minam N.W.&S.R., OR **149** B8
Minden, LA **70** B2
Minden, NE **105** D6
Mineral Wells, TX **127** D6
Minidoka Internment Camp Nat. Mon., ID **143** H3
Minneapolis, KS **97** B6
Minneapolis, MN **101** F4
Minnesota (river), MN **101** F2
Minot, ND **107** B4
Minute Man N.H.P., MA **41** B6
Minuteman Missile National Historic Site, SD **111** D3
Mio, MI **99** E6

Mishawaka — Odessa

Mishawaka, IN **93** A4
Mission, TX **127** I6
Mission Viejo, CA **137** H6
Missisquoi (river), VT **53** A2
Mississinewa (river), IN **93** D5
Mississinewa Lake, IN **93** C4
Mississippi (river), **56** B2
Mississippi National River and N.R.A., MN **101** F4
Mississippi Petrified Forest, MS **73** E2
Mississippi River Delta, LA **71** I10
Mississippi Sound, AL, MS **73** I5
Missoula, MT **144** C3
Missouri (river), **86** F5
Missouri N.W.&S.R., MT **145** B6
Missouri National Recreational River, NE, SD **105** A7
Misty Fiords Nat. Mon., AK **135** G11
Mitchell, SD **111** E8
Mitchell, Mount, NC **74** B3
Moab, UT **151** F6
Moberly, MO **103** B4
Mobile, AL **61** H1
Mobile (river), AL **61** H1
Mobile Bay, AL **61** I1
Mobridge, SD **111** B5
Modesto, CA **137** E3
Mogollon Rim, AZ **121** E6
Mohave, Lake, AZ, NV **121** C1
Mohawk (river), NY **47** D7
Mohican (river), OH **109** D5
Mojave Desert, CA, NV **130** F4
Mojave National Preserve, CA **137** G7
Moline, IL **91** C2
Moloka'i (island), HI **141** C6
Monadnock Mountain, NH **43** I2
Monahans, TX **127** E3
Moncks Corner, SC **77** F7
Monessen, PA **48** E2
Monett, MO **103** F3
Monhegan Island, ME **37** H4
Monitor Range, NV **147** E4
Monmouth, IL **91** C2
Monmouth, OR **149** C2
Mono Lake, CA **137** D5
Monocacy (river), MD **39** A6
Monocacy N.B., MD **39** B6
Monomoy Island, MA **41** E10
Monona, WI **113** G5
Monongahela (river), PA, WV **28** G1
Monroe, GA **67** C3
Monroe, LA **71** B4
Monroe, MI **99** I7
Monroe, NC **75** C5
Monroe, WI **113** H5
Monroe Lake, IN **93** G3
Monroeville, AL **61** G2
Montauk Point, NY **47** G11
Monte Vista, CO **139** F4
Monterey, CA **137** F2
Monterey Bay, CA **137** F2
Monterey Bay National Marine Sanctuary, CA **137** E2
Montevallo, AL **61** D3
Montevideo, MN **101** F2
Montezuma Castle Nat. Mon., AZ **121** D5
Montgomery, AL **61** E4
Montgomery, WV **83** F3
Montgomery Village, MD **39** B6
Monticello, AR **63** F5
Monticello, IA **95** C9
Monticello, IN **93** C3
Monticello, NY **47** F7
Monticello (site), VA **81** C8
Montpelier, ID **143** I6
Montpelier (site), VA **81** C8
Montpelier, VT **53** D3
Montrose, CO **139** E2
Monument Valley, AZ, UT **151** H6
Moodus, CT **33** D6
Moore, OK **125** D8
Moore Reservoir, NH, VT **53** C5
Moorefield, WV **83** D8
Moores Creek N.B., NC **75** D8
Moorhead, MN **101** D1
Moose (river), VT **53** C5
Moose (river), ME **37** D2
Moosehead Lake, ME **37** D4
Mooselookmeguntic Lake, ME **37** F2
Moosup, CT **33** B8
Moosup (river), RI **51** C2
Mora, MN **101** E4
Mora (river), NM **123** C6
Moreau (river), SD **111** B4
Morehead, KY **69** B9
Morehead City, NC **75** D9
Morgan City, LA **71** H6
Morgan Horse Farm (site), VT **53** D1
Morganfield, KY **68** C3
Morganton, NC **74** B3
Morgantown, WV **83** C6
Moriarty, NM **123** D4
Mormon Reservoir, ID **143** H3
Moroni, UT **151** D4
Morrilton, AR **63** C4
Morris, IL **91** C5
Morris, MN **101** E2
Morristown, NJ **45** C3
Morristown, TN **79** B9
Morristown N.H.P., NJ **45** C3
Morrisville, VT **53** B3
Morton, IL **91** D4
Moscow, ID **143** C1
Moses Lake, WA **153** D7
Mosquito Creek Lake, OH **109** B8
Moss Point, MS **73** I5
Mott, ND **107** E3
Moultrie, GA **67** H3
Moultrie, Lake, SC **77** E7
Moundsville, WV **83** B4
Mount Airy, NC **75** A5
Mount Desert Island, ME **37** G6
Mount Holly, NJ **45** F3
Mount Hope Bay, RI **51** D6
Mount Pleasant, IA **95** E8
Mount Pleasant, UT **151** D4
Mount Rainier N.P., WA **153** E4
Mount Rushmore Nat. Mon., SD **110** D2
Mount St. Helens National Volcanic Monument, WA **153** E4
Mount Vernon, IN **93** I1
Mount Vernon, KY **69** D8
Mount Vernon (site), VA **81** B10
Mount Vernon, WA **153** B4
Mountain Fork (river), OK **125** E12
Mountain Grove, MO **103** F5
Mountain Home, AR **63** A4
Mountain Home, ID **143** H2
Mountain View, AR **63** B5
Mountain View, HI **141** F9
Mountain Village, AK **134** D3
Mountainair, NM **123** D4
Mouse (river) *see* Souris, ND **107** B5
Mt. Carmel, IL **91** G5
Mt. Carmel, PA **49** D7
Mt. Pleasant, MI **99** G6
Mt. Pleasant, SC **77** G7
Mt. Pleasant, TX **127** C8
Mt. Sterling, KY **69** C8
Mt. Vernon, IL **91** G4
Mt. Vernon, OH **109** D5
Mud Lake, ID **143** G5
Mud Lake, MN **101** B2
Muddy Boggy Creek, OK **125** E10
Muir Woods Nat. Mon., CA **137** D2
Mulberry (river), AR **63** B2
Mulberry Fork (river), AL **61** B3
Mulberry N.W.&S.R., AR **63** B2
Mulchatna N.W.&S.R., AK **135** E5
Mullen, NE **105** B4
Mullens, WV **83** H3
Mullett Lake, MI **99** D6
Mullica (river), NJ **45** G3
Mullins, SC **77** C9
Mulvane, KS **97** E7
Muncie, IN **93** D5
Munising, MI **99** C4
Murdo, SD **111** D5
Murfreesboro, AR **63** E2
Murfreesboro, TN **79** B5
Murphysboro, IL **91** H4
Murray, KY **68** E2
Murray, UT **151** C4
Murray, Lake, SC **77** C4
Muscatatuck (river), IN **93** G4
Muscatine, IA **95** E9
Muscle Shoals, AL **61** A2
Musconetcong (river), NJ **45** C2
Muscongus Bay, ME **37** H4
Muskegon, MI **99** G4
Muskegon (river), MI **99** G5
Muskingum (river), OH **109** E6
Muskogee, OK **125** C11
Muskogee Turnpike, OK **125** C11
Musselshell (river), MT **145** D7
Myrtle Beach, SC **77** D9
Mystic, CT **33** D8
Mystic Island, NJ **45** G4
Mystic Seaport (site), CT **33** D8

N

Naches (river), WA **153** E5
Nacogdoches, TX **127** E9
Naknek, AK **135** F5
Namakan Lake, MN **101** B5
Namekagon (river), WI **113** B2
Nampa, ID **143** G1
Nanticoke (river), DE, MD **39** E9
Nantucket, MA **41** F10
Nantucket Island, MA **41** F10
Nantucket Sound, MA **41** F9
Napa, CA **137** D2
Napatree Point, RI **51** G1
Naperville, IL **91** B5
Naples, FL **65** G7
Napoleon, ND **107** E6
Napoleon, OH **109** B2
Nappanee, IN **93** B4
Narragansett Bay, RI **51** E5
Narragansett Pier, RI **51** F4
Nashua, NH **43** I4
Nashua (river), MA **41** B5
Nashville, AR **63** F2
Nashville, IL **91** G4
Nashville, TN **79** B5
Natchaug (river), CT **33** B7
Natchez, MS **73** G1
Natchez N.H.P., MS **73** F1
Natchez Trace Parkway, AL, MS **73** D4
Natchitoches, LA **70** C2
National Park of American Samoa, AS **156** I4
Natural Bridges Nat. Mon., UT **151** G6
Naugatuck, CT **33** D3
Naugatuck (river), CT **33** D3
Nauvoo, IL **91** D1
Navajo, NM **123** B1
Navajo Nat. Mon., AZ **121** B6
Navajo Reservoir, NM **123** A3
Navassa Island (territory), US **157** E11
Nazareth, PA **49** D9
Near Islands, AK **135** G5
Nebraska City, NE **105** D9
Neches (river), TX **127** E8
Necker Island, HI **141** F4
Needles, CA **137** G8
Neenah, WI **113** E6
Nehalem (river), OR **149** A2
Neligh, NE **105** B7
Nelson Island, AK **134** E3
Nelsonville, OH **109** F5
Neosho, MO **103** F2
Neosho (river), KS, OK **86** G4
Nepaug Reservoir, CT **33** B4
Nephi, UT **151** D4
Neptune, NJ **45** E5
Ness City, KS **97** C3
Neuse (river), NC **75** C8
Nevada, IA **95** D5
Nevada, MO **103** E2
New (river), VA **80** F4
New Albany, IN **93** H4
New Albany, MS **73** B4
New Bedford, MA **41** E7
New Bedford Whaling N.H.P., MA **41** E7
New Bern, NC **75** C9
New Braunfels, TX **127** F6
New Brunswick, NJ **45** D4
New Canaan, CT **33** E1
New Castle, DE **35** B5
New Castle, IN **93** E5
New Castle, PA **48** C1
New City, NY **47** G8
New Echota State Historic Site, GA **67** B2
New Fairfield, CT **33** D2
New Hampton, IA **95** B7
New Harmony State Historic Site, IN **93** H1
New Hartford, CT **33** B4
New Haven, CT **33** D4
New Iberia, LA **71** G5
New Ipswich, NH **43** I3
New Jersey Turnpike, NJ **45** E3
New Lexington, OH **109** E5
New London, CT **33** D7
New London, NH **43** G2
New London, WI **113** E6
New Madrid, MO **103** F8
New Martinsville, WV **83** C4
New Milford, CT **33** C2
New N.W.&S.R., NC **75** A4
New Orleans, LA **71** G8
New Paltz, NY **47** F8
New Philadelphia, OH **109** D6
New Richmond, WI **113** D1
New River Gorge Bridge, WV **83** F4
New River Gorge National River, WV **83** G4
New Rochelle, NY **47** H8
New Rockford, ND **107** C7
New Salem, ND **107** E4
New Smyrna Beach, FL **65** C8
New Town, ND **107** C3
New Ulm, MN **101** G3
New York, NY **47** H8
New York State Thruway, NY **47** D4
New, South Fork (river), NC **75** A4
Newark, DE **35** B4
Newark, NJ **45** C4
Newark, OH **109** E5
Newberry, SC **77** C4
Newberry National Volcanic Monument, OR **149** D4
Newburg, OR **149** B2
Newburgh, NY **47** G8
Newbury, VT **53** D5
Newburyport, MA **41** A8
Newcastle, WY **155** C10
Newfound Lake, NH **43** F3
Newfoundland Evaporation Basin (dry lake), UT **151** B2
Newington, CT **33** C5
Newmarket, NH **43** H5
Newnan, GA **67** D2
Newport, AR **63** B6
Newport, DE **35** B5
Newport, KY **69** A8
Newport, ME **37** F4
Newport, NH **43** G2
Newport, OR **148** C1
Newport, RI **51** F5
Newport, TN **79** B9
Newport, VT **53** A4
Newport News, VA **81** E11
Newton, IA **95** D6
Newton, KS **97** D7
Newton, MS **73** F4
Newton, NC **75** B4
Newton, NJ **45** B3
Newtown, CT **33** D2
Nez Perce N.H.P., ID **143** D1
Nez Perce Pass, MT **144** E2
Ni'ihau (island), HI **140** B1
Niagara, WI **113** C7
Niagara Falls, NY **46** D2
Niagara Falls (waterfall), NY **28** D2
Niagara River (river), NY **46** D2
Niangua (river), MO **103** E4
Niantic, CT **33** D7
Niceville, FL **64** A2
Nicodemus National Historic Site, KS **97** B4
Nihoa (island), HI **141** F4
Niles, MI **99** I4
Niles, OH **109** B8
Nine Mile Creek, UT **151** D5
Nine-Mile Prairie, NE **105** D8
Ninety Six National Historic Site, SC **77** C3
Ninigret Pond, RI **51** G3
Niobrara (river), NE, WY **105** A4
Niobrara National Scenic Riverway, NE **105** A5
Niskayuna, NY **47** E8
Nitro, WV **82** F2
Noatak N.W.&S.R., AK **135** B4
Noatak National Preserve, AK **135** B5
Noblesville, IN **93** D4
Nocona, TX **127** C6
Nodaway, East (river), IA **95** E3
Nogales, AZ **121** H6
Nolichucky (river), TN **79** B10
Nolin River Lake, KY **69** D5
Nomans Land (island), MA **41** F8
Nome, AK **134** C3
Nonquit Pond, RI **51** E6
Norfolk, CT **33** A3
Norfolk, NE **105** B8
Norfolk, VA **81** E11
Norfork Lake, AR **63** A5
Normal, IL **91** D4
Norman, OK **125** D8
Norman, Lake, NC **75** B4
Norris Lake, TN **79** B8
Norristown, PA **49** E9
North Adams, MA **40** A1
North Attleboro, MA **41** D6
North Augusta, SC **77** E3
North Bend, OH **109** F1
North Bend, OR **148** E1
North Bennington, VT **53** I1
North Branford, CT **33** D4
North Canton, OH **109** C7
North Cascades N.P., WA **153** A5
North Charleston, SC **77** F7
North Conway, NH **43** E4
North Fork Sprague N.W.&S.R., OR **149** F4
North Grosvenor Dale, CT **33** A8
North Haven, CT **33** D4
North Hero, VT **53** B1
North Hero Island, VT **53** A1
North Island, SC **77** E9
North Las Vegas, NV **147** G6
North Little Rock, AR **63** D4
North Manchester, IN **93** B4
North Myrtle Beach, SC **77** D10
North Ogden, UT **151** B4
North Olmsted, OH **109** B6
North Platte, NE **105** D4
North Pole, AK **135** D7
North Powder N.W.&S.R., OR **149** C7
North Providence, RI **51** B4
North Scituate, RI **51** B3
North Sioux City, SD **111** F10
North Slope, AK **135** B5
North Springfield, VT **53** G3
North Sterling Reservoir, CO **139** A8
North Stratford, NH **43** C3
North Sylamore Creek N.W.&S.R., AR **63** B4
North Troy, VT **53** A4
North Umpqua N.W.&S.R., OR **149** E2
North Vernon, IN **93** G5
North Walpole, NH **43** H1
North Wildwood, NJ **45** I3
Northampton, MA **41** C3
Northern Mariana Islands (territory), US **156** E1
Northfield, MN **101** G5
Northfield, NH **43** G3
Northfield, VT **53** D3
Northwestern Hawaiian Islands, HI **140** E1
Northwood, ND **107** C9
Norton, KS **97** A3
Norton, VA **80** E2
Norton Sound, AK **135** D4
Norwalk, CT **33** F2
Norwalk, OH **109** B5
Norway, ME **37** G2
Norwich, CT **33** C7
Norwich, NY **47** E6
Norwich, VT **53** F4
Norwood, MA **41** C7
Norwood, OH **109** F2
Nottoway (river), VA **81** E10
Nowitna N.W.&S.R., AK **135** D6
Nowood (river), WY **155** B5
Noxontown Pond, DE **35** C4
Noxubee (river), MS **73** D5
Nubanusit Lake, NH **43** H2
Nueces (river), TX **127** G6
Nunivak Island, AK **134** E3
Nuuuli, AS **156** I1

O

O'ahu (island), HI **141** B5
Oahe, Lake, ND, SD **111** B6
Oak Bluffs, MA **41** F9
Oak Harbor, WA **153** B3
Oak Hill, WV **83** G4
Oak Orchard, DE **35** H7
Oak Ridge, TN **79** B8
Oakdale, LA **71** E3
Oakes, ND **107** F8
Oakland, CA **137** E2
Oakland, MD **38** B1
Oakland, ME **37** F3
Oakley, KS **96** B2
Oakville, CT **33** C3
Obed (river), TN **79** B7
Obed N.W.&S.R., TN **79** B7
Oberlin, KS **97** A3
Obion (river), TN **78** B1
Ocala, FL **65** C7
Ocean City, MD **39** E11
Ocean City, NJ **45** H3
Ocean Lake, WY **155** D4
Ocean Pines, MD **39** E11
Ocean Shores, WA **152** D1
Ocean Springs, MS **73** I5
Ocean View, DE **35** I7
Oceanside, CA **137** I6
Ochlockonee (river), FL, GA **65** B4
Ochoco Mountains, OR **149** C5
Ocmulgee (river), GA **67** G4
Ocmulgee Nat. Mon., GA **67** E4
Oconee (river), GA **67** F5
Oconee, Lake, GA **67** D4
Oconto, WI **113** D7
Oconto (river), WI **113** D7
Ocracoke Island, NC **75** C10
Odessa, DE **35** C4

Odessa — Potomac

Odessa, TX **127** E3
Oelwein, IA **95** B8
Ofu (island), AS **156** I3
Ofu, AS **156** H3
Ogallala, NE **105** D3
Ogden, UT **151** B4
Ogdensburg, NY **47** A6
Ogeechee (river), GA **67** E6
Ogunquit, ME **37** I2
Ohio (river), **86** G7
Ohoopee (river), GA **67** F6
Oil City, PA **48** B2
Okanogan (river), WA **153** B7
Okatibbee Lake, MS **73** E5
Okeechobee, Lake, FL **65** F8
Okefenokee Swamp, GA **67** H5
Oklahoma City, OK **125** C8
Okmulgee, OK **125** C10
Okobojo Creek, SD **111** C5
Okolona, MS **73** C5
Olathe, KS **97** C10
Old Faithful (site), WY **154** B2
Old Hickory Lake, TN **79** B5
Old Oraibi (site), AZ **121** C6
Old Orchard Beach, ME **37** H2
Old Saybrook, CT **33** E6
Old Town, ME **37** F5
Olean, NY **46** F3
Olentangy (river), OH **109** D4
Oliver, Lake, GA **67** E1
Olivia, MN **101** G3
Olney, IL **91** G5
Olosega (island), AS **156** H3
Olosega, AS **156** H3
Olympia, WA **153** D3
Olympic Coast National Marine Sanctuary, WA **152** B1
Olympic Mountains, WA **152** C2
Olympic N.P., WA **152** C2
Olympus, Mount, WA **152** C2
Omaha, NE **105** C9
Omak, WA **153** B7
Onalaska, WI **113** F3
Onancock, VA **81** D12
Onawa, IA **94** C2
One Hundred and Two (river), MO **103** A2
Oneida, NY **47** D6
Oneida Lake, NY **47** D6
O'Neill, NE **105** B6
Oneonta, NY **47** E7
Onida, SD **111** C6
Onslow Bay, NC **75** D9
Ontario, OR **149** D9
Ontario, Lake, **28** D2
Ontonagon N.W.&S.R., MI **99** B2
Oologah Lake, OK **125** B10
Oostanaula (river), GA **67** B1
Opelika, AL **61** E5
Opelousas, LA **71** F4
Opp, AL **61** G4
Opportunity, WA **153** C10
Optima Lake, OK **124** B4
Orange, CT **33** E3
Orange, MA **41** B3
Orange, VA **81** C8
Orange City, IA **94** B2
Orangeburg, SC **77** E5
Orchard City, CO **139** D2
Ord, NE **105** C6
Ordway, CO **139** E7
Oreana, NV **147** C3
Oregon, OH **109** A3
Oregon Caves Nat. Mon., OR **149** G2
Oregon City, OR **149** B3
Oregon Dunes N.R.A., OR **148** D1
Orem, UT **151** C4
Orford, NH **43** E2
Organ Pipe Cactus Nat. Mon., AZ **121** G3
Orlando, FL **65** D8
Orleans, MA **41** E10
Orleans, VT **53** B4
Oro Valley, AZ **121** G6
Orofino, ID **143** D1
Orono, ME **37** F5
Oroville Dam, CA **137** C3
Orrville, OH **109** C6
Ortonville, MN **101** F1
Osage, IA **95** A6
Osage (river), MO **103** E3
Osage City, KS **97** C8
Osage Fork (river), MO **103** E4
Osawatomie, KS **97** C10
Osceola, AR **63** B8
Osceola, IA **95** E5
Osgood Mountains, NV **147** B4
Oshkosh, WI **113** F6
Oskaloosa, IA **95** E7
Ossabaw Island, GA **67** G7
Ossabaw Sound, GA **67** G7
Ossipee Lake, NH **43** F4
Oswego, NY **47** C5
Oswego (river), NY **47** D5
Othello, WA **153** E7
Otis Reservoir, MA **40** C1
Ottawa, IL **91** C4
Ottawa, KS **97** C9
Otter Creek (river), VT **53** E1
Otter Creek Reservoir, UT **151** F4
Otter Tail (river), MN **101** E1
Otter Tail Lake, MN **101** D2
Ottumwa, IA **95** E7
Ouachita (river), AR, LA **56** D2
Ouachita Mountains, AR, OK **63** D1
Ouachita, Lake, AR **63** D3
Outer Banks (islands), NC **75** C10
Overland Park, KS **97** B10
Overton, NV **147** G7
Owasso, OK **125** B10
Owatonna, MN **101** G4
Owensboro, KY **69** C4
Owl Creek, WY **155** C4
Owosso, MI **99** G6
Owyhee (river), OR **149** D8
Owyhee Mountains, ID **143** H1
Owyhee N.W.&S.R., OR **149** E8
Owyhee, Lake, OR **149** E8
Owyhee, North Fork N.W.&S.R., OR **149** F9
Owyhee, South Fork (river), ID, NV **143** I1
Oxford, MA **41** C5
Oxford, MS **73** B4
Oxford, NC **75** B7
Oxford, OH **109** F1
Oxnard, CA **137** H4
Oxon Cove Park and Oxon Hill Farm, MD **39** D6
Ozark, AL **61** G5
Ozark, AR **63** C2
Ozark National Scenic Riverways, MO **103** F6
Ozark Plateau, **86** G5
Ozarks, Lake of the, MO **103** D4
Ozona, TX **127** E4

P

Pachaug Pond, CT **33** C8
Pacific Crest National Scenic Trail, CA **137** G5
Paden City, WV **83** C4
Padre Island, TX **116** G8
Padre Island National Seashore, TX **127** H7
Paducah, KY **68** D2
Page, AZ **121** A5
Pago Pago, AS **156** I1
Pagosa Springs, CO **139** G3
Pahala, HI **141** F9
Pahranagat Range, NV **147** F6
Pahrump, NV **147** G5
Pahute Mesa, NV **147** F4
Painesville, OH **109** A7
Paint Creek, OH **109** F3
Paint N.W.&S.R., MI **99** C2
Painted Desert, AZ **121** B5
Palatka, FL **65** C7
Palestine, TX **127** E8
Palisades Reservoir, ID **143** H6
Palm Bay, FL **65** E9
Palm Coast, FL **65** C8
Palm Springs, CA **137** H7
Palmer, AK **135** E6
Palmer (river), RI **51** C5
Palmyra Atoll (territory), US **157** F5
Palo Alto, CA **137** E2
Palo Alto Battlefield National Historical Site, TX **127** I7
Palouse (river), WA **153** E9
Palouse Hills, WA **153** D9
Pamlico (river), NC **75** C9
Pamlico Sound, NC **75** C10
Pampa, TX **127** B4
Pana, IL **91** F4
Panama City, FL **65** B3
Pancake Range, NV **147** E5
Panguitch, UT **151** G3
Panorama Point (peak), NE **104** C1
Paola, KS **97** C10
Papillion, NE **105** C9
Paragould, AR **63** B7
Paramus, NJ **45** B5
Paria (river), AZ **121** A4
Paris, AR **63** C2
Paris, IL **91** E6
Paris, KY **69** B8
Paris, TN **78** B3
Paris, TX **127** C8
Park (river), ND **107** B9
Park Falls, WI **113** C4
Park Hills, MO **103** E6
Park Range, CO **139** A3
Park Rapids, MN **101** D3
Park River, ND **107** B9
Parker, AZ **121** E2
Parker, SD **111** E9
Parkersburg, WV **83** D3
Parkston, SD **111** E8
Parkville, MD **39** B8
Parma, OH **109** B6
Parris Island, SC **77** H6
Parsippany, NJ **45** C4
Parsons, KS **97** E9
Pasadena, CA **137** H5
Pascagoula, MS **73** I5
Pascagoula (river), MS **73** H5
Pasco, WA **153** F8
Pascoag, RI **51** A2
Pascoag Lake, RI **51** A2
Paso Robles, CA **137** G3
Passaic, NJ **45** C5
Passaic (river), NJ **45** C4
Passamaquoddy Bay, ME **37** E7
Passumpsic (river), VT **53** C5
Paterson, NJ **45** B4
Pathfinder Reservoir, WY **155** E6
Patoka (river), IN **93** H2
Patoka Lake, IN **93** H3
Patten, ME **37** C5
Patuxent (bay), MD **39** E7
Patuxent (river), MD **39** B6
Pauls Valley, OK **125** D9
Paulsboro, NJ **45** F1
Pawcatuck, CT **33** D8
Pawcatuck (river), CT, RI **33** D8
Pawhuska, OK **125** A10
Pawnee (river), KS **97** D3
Pawtucket, RI **51** B5
Pawtucket Reservoir, RI **51** A5
Pawtuxet (river), RI **51** C4
Payette, ID **143** G1
Payette (river), ID **143** G1
Payette, North Fork (river), ID **143** G1
Payette, South Fork (river), ID **143** G2
Payson, AZ **121** E5
Payson, UT **151** D4
Pea (river), AL **61** G4
Pea Patch Island, DE **35** B5
Pea Ridge N.M.P., AR **63** A1
Peabody, MA **41** B7
Peace (river), FL **65** F7
Peachtree City, GA **67** D2
Peaked Mountain, ME **37** B5
Pearl, MS **73** E3
Pearl (river), LA, MS **71** F9
Pearl and Hermes Atoll, HI **140** E1
Pearl City, HI **141** B4
Pearl Harbor, HI **141** C4
Pearsall, TX **127** G5
Pease (river), TX **127** C5
Pecatonica (river), WI **113** H4
Pecos, TX **126** E2
Pecos (river), NM, TX **116** E6
Pecos N.H.P., NM **123** C5
Pecos N.W.&S.R., NM **123** C5
Peekskill, NY **47** G8
Pekin, IL **91** D3
Pelican Rapids, MN **101** D2
Pell City, AL **61** C4
Pella, IA **95** E6
Pembina, ND **107** A9
Pembina (river), ND **107** A8
Pemigewasset (river), NH **43** E3
Peñasco, Rio (river), NM **123** G6
Pend Oreille (river), WA **153** B10
Pend Oreille Lake, ID **143** B1
Pender, NE **105** B8
Pendleton, OR **149** B7
Penn Hills, PA **48** D2
Penn Yan, NY **47** E4
Penns Grove, NJ **45** G1
Pennsauken, NJ **45** F2
Pennsville, NJ **45** G1
Pennsylvania Turnpike, PA **49** E3
Penobscot (river), ME **37** E5
Penobscot Bay, ME **37** G5
Penobscot, East Branch (river), ME **37** C5
Penobscot, West Branch (river), ME **37** D3
Pensacola, FL **64** B1
Peoria, IL **91** D3
Pepin, WI **113** E2
Pepin, Lake, MN **101** G5
Pequop Mountains, NV **147** B6
Perdido (river), AL, FL **61** H2
Pere Marquette N.W.&S.R., MI **99** F4
Perham, MN **101** D2
Perry, FL **65** B5
Perry, GA **67** F3
Perry, IA **95** D4
Perry, OK **125** B8
Perry Hall, MD **39** B8
Perry Lake, KS **97** B9
Perry's Victory and International Peace Memorial, OH **109** A4
Perrysburg, OH **109** B3
Perryton, TX **127** A4
Perryville, MO **103** E7
Perth Amboy, NJ **45** D4
Peru, IL **91** C4
Peru, IN **93** C4
Peshtigo (river), WI **113** C6
Petal, MS **73** G4
Petenwell Lake, WI **113** E5
Peterborough, NH **43** I2
Petersburg, AK **135** F10
Petersburg, VA **81** D9
Petersburg, WV **83** D7
Petersburg N.B., VA **81** E9
Petoskey, MI **99** D6
Petrified Forest N.P., AZ **121** D7
Petroglyph Nat. Mon., NM **123** D4
Phenix City, AL **61** E6
Philadelphia, MS **73** E4
Philadelphia, PA **49** E10
Philip, SD **111** D4
Philippi, WV **83** D6
Phillipsburg, KS **97** A4
Phillipsburg, NJ **45** C2
Phoenix, AZ **121** F4
Picayune, MS **73** I3
Pickwick Lake, AL, MS, TN **61** A1
Pictured Rocks National Lakeshore, MI **99** C4
Piedmont, AL **61** C5
Piedmont (region), **56** D5
Piedmont Lake, OH **109** D7
Piedra (river), CO **139** F3
Pierre, SD **111** D5
Pigeon (river), IN **93** A5
Pigeon (river), MI **99** D6
Pigeon (river), MN **101** B8
Pikes Peak, CO **139** D5
Pikeville, KY **69** D11
Pine (river), WI **113** C6
Pine Barrens (region), NJ **45** G3
Pine Bluff, AR **63** E5
Pine City, MN **101** E5
Pine Creek, NV **147** C5
Pine Creek, PA **49** B6
Pine Creek Gorge, PA **49** B6
Pine Hill, NJ **45** F2
Pine Mountain, KY **69** E9
Pine N.W.&S.R., MI **99** F5
Pine Ridge, NE **104** A2
Pine Ridge, SD **111** F3
Pinedale, WY **155** D3
Pinehurst, NC **75** C6
Pinelands National Reserve, NJ **45** F4
Pinetop-Lakeside, AZ **121** E7
Pineville, LA **71** D4
Pinnacles Nat. Mon., CA **137** F3
Pioche, NV **147** E7
Pioneer Valley, MA **41** B3
Pipe Spring Nat. Mon., AZ **121** A4
Pipestem Creek, ND **107** D7
Pipestone, MN **101** G2
Pipestone Nat. Mon., MN **101** G1
Piqua, OH **109** D2
Piscataqua (river), NH **43** H5
Piscataquis (river), ME **37** E4
Piscataway, NJ **45** D4
Piscataway Park, MD **39** D6
Pit (river), CA **137** B3
Pittsburg, KS **97** E10
Pittsburgh, PA **48** D2
Pittsfield, IL **91** E2
Pittsfield, MA **40** B1
Pittsfield, ME **37** F4
Pittsfield, NH **43** G4
Pittsford, VT **53** F2
Piute Reservior, UT **151** F3
Plainfield, CT **33** C8
Plainfield, IN **93** E3
Plainfield, NJ **45** C4
Plainfield, VT **53** D4
Plains, GA **67** F2
Plainview, TX **127** C4
Plainville, CT **33** C4
Plainville, KS **97** B4
Plaistow, NH **43** I5
Plankinton, SD **111** E8
Plano, TX **127** D7
Plaquemine, LA **71** F6
Platte (river), NE **105** D9
Platte, SD **111** E7
Platte, North (river), CO, NE, WY **130** D8
Platte, South (river), CO, NE **130** E8
Platteville, WI **113** H4
Plattsburgh, NY **47** A8
Plattsmouth, NE **105** D9
Playas Lake, NM **123** H2
Pleasant Grove, UT **151** C4
Pleasant Prairie, WI **113** H7
Pleasantville, NJ **45** H3
Pleasure Ridge Park, KY **69** C6
Plentywood, MT **145** A11
Plover, WI **113** E5
Plum, PA **48** D2
Plymouth, IN **93** B3
Plymouth, MA **41** D8
Plymouth, MN **101** F4
Plymouth, VT **53** F3
Pocahontas, AR **63** A6
Pocatello, ID **143** H5
Pocomoke (river), MD **39** F10
Pocomoke City, MD **39** F10
Pocono Mountains, PA **49** C9
Pocotopaug Lake, CT **33** C5
Poinsett, Lake, SD **111** C9
Point Hope, AK **135** B4
Point Judith, RI **51** G4
Point Judith Pond, RI **51** F4
Point Pleasant, NJ **45** E5
Point Pleasant, OH **109** G2
Point Pleasant, WV **82** E2
Point Reyes National Seashore, CA **137** D2
Polacca, AZ **121** C6
Polson, MT **144** C3
Pomeroy, WA **153** E9
Pompeys Pillar Nat. Mon., MT **145** E8
Ponaganset (river), RI **51** B2
Ponaganset Reservoir, RI **51** B2
Ponca City, OK **125** A9
Ponce, PR **157** I10
Pond (river), KY **69** D4
Pontchartrain, Lake, LA **71** G8
Pontiac, IL **91** C4
Pontiac, MI **99** H7
Pontoosuc Lake, MA **40** B1
Pontotoc, MS **73** B4
Poplar Bluff, MO **103** F7
Poplarville, MS **73** H4
Popple (river), WI **113** C6
Poquonock Bridge, CT **33** D7
Poquoson, VA **81** E11
Porcupine (river), AK **135** B8
Port Allen, LA **71** F6
Port Angeles, WA **152** B2
Port Arthur, TX **127** F9
Port Charlotte, FL **65** F7
Port Clinton, OH **109** B4
Port Huron, MI **99** G8
Port Jervis, NY **47** G7
Port Lavaca, TX **127** G7
Port Penn, DE **35** C5
Port Royal, SC **77** H6
Port Royal Sound (river), SC **77** H6
Port St. Lucie, FL **65** F9
Port Sulphur, LA **71** H8
Port Townsend, WA **153** B3
Port Washington, WI **113** G7
Portage, IN **93** A2
Portage, MI **99** H5
Portage, WI **113** F5
Portage (river), OH **109** B3
Portal, ND **107** A3
Portales, NM **123** E8
Portland, CT **33** C5
Portland, IN **93** D6
Portland, ME **37** H3
Portland, TN **79** A5
Portland, TX **127** H7
Portland, OR **149** B2
Portneuf Range, ID **143** H5
Portsmouth, NH **43** H5
Portsmouth, OH **109** G4
Portsmouth, RI **51** E6
Portsmouth, VA **81** E11
Post Falls, ID **143** B1
Poteau, OK **125** D12
Potholes Reservoir, WA **153** D7
Potlatch (river), ID **143** D1
Potomac, MD **39** C6
Potomac (river), MD, VA, WV **39** E7

Potomac — Sandstone

Potomac, North Branch (river), MD, WV **38** B2
Potomac, South Branch (river), WV **38** B2
Potsdam, NY **47** A7
Pottstown, PA **49** E9
Pottsville, PA **49** D8
Poughkeepsie, NY **47** F8
Poultney, VT **53** F1
Poultney (river), VT **53** F1
Poverty Point Nat. Mon., LA **71** B5
Powder (river), MT, WY **130** C7
Powder (river), OR **149** C8
Powder Wash, CO **139** A2
Powder, South Fork (river), WY **155** D6
Powell, WY **155** A4
Powell (river), TN, VA **79** A9
Powell, Lake, UT **151** H5
Pownal Center, VT **53** I1
Poygan, Lake, WI **113** E6
Prairie Dog Creek, KS **97** A3
Prairie du Chien, WI **113** G3
Pratt, KS **97** E5
Prattville, AL **61** E4
Prescott, AR **63** F3
Prescott, AZ **121** D4
Prescott Valley, AZ **121** D4
Presidential Range, NH **43** D4
Presidio, TX **126** F2
Presque Isle, ME **37** B6
Presque Isle N.W.&S.R., MI **99** C1
Preston, ID **143** I5
Preston, MN **101** H6
Prestonsburg, KY **69** C10
Pribilof Islands, AK **134** F2
Price (river), UT **151** E5
Price, UT **151** D5
Prichard, AL **61** H1
Priest (river), ID **143** B1
Priest Lake, ID **143** A1
Prince Frederick, MD **39** E7
Prince of Wales Island, AK **135** G10
Prince of Wales, Cape, AK **134** C2
Prince William Forest Park, VA **81** B9
Prince William Sound, AK **135** E7
Princeton, IN **93** H1
Princeton, KY **68** D3
Princeton, ME **37** E6
Princeton, NJ **45** D3
Princeton, WV **83** H4
Princeville, HI **140** A2
Prineville, OR **149** D4
Proctor, MN **101** D5
Proctor, VT **53** F2
Promontory, UT **151** A3
Prospect, CT **33** C4
Prosser, WA **153** F7
Providence, RI **51** B5
Providence, UT **151** A4
Providence (river), RI **51** C5
Provincetown, MA **41** D10
Provo, UT **151** C4
Prudence Island, RI **51** D5
Prudhoe Bay, AK **135** A6
Pryor, OK **125** B11
Pu'uhonua O Honaunau N.H.P., HI **141** F8
Pu'ukohola Heiau National Historic Site, HI **141** E8
Pu'uwai, HI **140** A1
Pueblo, CO **139** E6
Pueblo Bonito (site), NM **123** B2
Puerco (river), AZ **121** D7
Puerco, Rio (river), NM **123** D3
Puerto Rico (territory), US **157** E11
Puget Sound, WA **153** C3
Pukalani, HI **141** C7
Pulaski, TN **79** C4
Pulaski, VA **81** E5
Pullman, WA **153** E10
Pumpkin Creek, NE **104** C1
Punkin Center, CO **139** D7
Punta Gorda, FL **65** F7
Punxsutawney, PA **49** C3
Purcell, OK **125** D8
Purgatoire (river), CO **139** G7
Putnam, CT **33** A8
Putney, VT **53** H3
Puyallup, WA **153** D4
Pymatuning Reservoir, PA, OH **48** B1
Pyramid Lake (river), NV **147** C2

Q
Quabbin Reservoir, MA **41** B4
Quaddick Reservoir, CT **33** A8
Quaker Hill, CT **33** D7
Quakertown, PA **49** D9
Quartzsite, AZ **121** E2
Quartzville Creek N.W.&S.R., OR **149** C3
Queen (river), RI **51** E3
Queets (river), WA **152** C1
Questa, NM **123** A5
Quincy, IL **91** E1
Quincy, MA **41** C7
Quincy, WA **153** D7
Quinebaug (river), CT **33** C7
Quinn (river), NV **147** A3
Quinnipiac (river), CT **33** D4
Quinsigamond, Lake, MA **41** C5
Quitman, GA **67** H4
Quitman, MS **73** F5
Quonochontaug, RI **51** G2
Quonochontaug Pond, RI **51** G2

R
Rabun Gap, GA **67** A4
Raccoon (river), IA **95** C4
Raccoon Creek, OH **109** G5
Racine, WI **113** H7
Radcliff, KY **69** C6
Radford, VA **81** E5
Raft River Mountains, UT **151** A2
Rahway, NJ **45** C4
Rainbow Bridge Nat. Mon., UT **151** H5
Rainier, OR **149** A2
Rainier, Mount, WA **153** D4
Rainy (river), MN **101** B4
Rainy Lake, MN **101** A4
Raisin (river), MI **99** H6
Raleigh, NC **75** B7
Raleigh Bay, NC **75** D10
Rampart Range, CO **139** D5
Ramsey, NJ **45** B4
Randolph, MA **41** C7
Randolph, VT **53** E3
Randolph Center, VT **53** E3
Rangeley, ME **37** E2
Rangeley Lake, ME **37** F2
Rangely, CO **138** B1
Rantoul, IL **91** D5
Rapid City, SD **110** D2
Rapid N.W.&S.R., ID **143** E1
Rappahannock (river), VA **81** C10
Raquette (river), NY **47** B7
Raritan (river), NJ **45** D4
Rat Islands, AK **135** H7
Rathbun Lake, IA **95** F6
Raton, NM **123** A6
Ravenna, NE **105** D6
Ravenswood, WV **83** E3
Rawlins, WY **155** F6
Raymond, NH **43** H4
Raymond, WA **152** E2
Rayne, LA **71** G4
Raystown Lake, PA **49** E5
Rayville, LA **71** B5
Reading, PA **49** E8
Red (river), **116** C7
Red Bank, NJ **45** D5
Red Bank, TN **79** D7
Red Bay, AL **61** B1
Red Bluff Lake, TX **116** E5
Red Bud, IL **91** G3
Red Cedar (river), WI **113** D2
Red Cloud, NE **105** E7
Red Hills, KS **97** E3
Red Lake, AZ **121** C2
Red Lake, MN **101** C3
Red Lake (river), MN **101** B2
Red Lion, PA **49** E7
Red Lodge, MT **145** F7
Red N.W.&S.R., KY **69** C9
Red Oak, IA **95** E3
Red River of the North (river), MN, ND **86** A3
Red Rock, Lake, IA **95** E6
Red Willow Creek, NE **105** D4
Red Wing, MN **101** G5
Red, Elm Fork (river), OK **125** D5
Red, North Fork (river), OK **125** D5
Red, North Fork (river), TX **127** B4
Red, Prairie Dog Town Fork (river), OK, TX **125** E5
Red, Salt Fork (river), OK, TX **125** D5
Redding, CA **137** B2
Redfield, SD **111** C8
Redmond, OR **149** D4
Redmond, WA **153** C4
Redwood Falls, MN **101** G3
Redwood N.P., CA **137** A1
Reedsburg, WI **113** F4
Reedsport, OR **148** D1
Reedy Island, DE **35** C5
Reelfoot Lake, TN **78** B2
Reese (river), NV **147** C4
Rehoboth Bay, DE **35** H7
Rehoboth Beach, DE **35** H7
Reidsville, NC **75** A6
Reisterstown, MD **39** B7
Rend Lake, IL **91** H4
Reno, NV **147** D2
Rensselaer, IN **93** C2
Renton, WA **153** C4
Republic, MO **103** F3
Republic, WA **153** A8
Republican (river), KS, NE **86** F2
Republican, South Fork (river), KS, CO **96** A1
Reserve, NM **123** F1
Reston, VA **81** B9
Rexburg, ID **143** G5
Reynoldsburg, OH **109** E4
Rhinelander, WI **113** C5
Rhode Island (island), RI **51** E6
Rhode Island Sound, RI **51** G4
Rice City, RI **51** D2
Rice Lake, WI **113** C2
Richard B. Russell Lake, GA, SC **67** C5
Richardson lakes, ME **37** F2
Richfield, UT **151** E3
Richford, VT **53** A3
Richland, WA **153** E7
Richland Center, WI **113** G4
Richland Creek N.W.&S.R., AR **63** B3
Richlands, VA **80** E3
Richmond, IN **93** E6
Richmond, MO **103** C3
Richmond, VA **81** D9
Richmond, VT **53** C2
Richmond N.B. Park, VA **81** D9
Richwood, WV **83** F5
Ridgecrest, CA **137** G6
Ridgefield, CT **33** E2
Ridgeland, MS **73** E3
Ridgewood, NJ **45** B5
Ridgway, PA **49** B4
Rifle, CO **139** C2
Rifle (river), MI **99** F7
Rigby, ID **143** G5
Riggins, ID **143** E1
Ringwood, NJ **45** B4
Rio Chama N.W.&S.R., NM **123** B4
Rio Grande (river), CO, NM, TX **116** G7
Rio Grande City, TX **127** I6
Rio Grande N.W.&S.R., NM **123** A5
Rio Grande Wild and Scenic River, TX **127** F3
Rio Rancho, NM **123** D4
Ripley, MS **73** A4
Ripley, TN **78** C1
Ripley, WV **83** E3
Ripon, WI **113** F6
Ritzville, WA **153** D8
River Falls, WI **113** D1
Riverside, CA **137** H6
Riverton, UT **151** C4
Riverton, WY **155** D5
Roan Cliffs, UT **151** E6
Roan Mountain, TN **79** B11
Roan Plateau, CO **138** C1
Roanoke, AL **61** D5
Roanoke, VA **81** D6
Roanoke (river), NC, VA **56** C7
Roanoke (Staunton) (river), VA **81** E7
Roanoke Island, NC **75** B10
Roanoke Rapids, NC **75** A8
Roaring N.W.&S.R., OR **149** B3
Robert South Kerr Lake, OK **125** D12
Robinson, IL **91** F6
Robstown, TX **127** H6
Rochester, IN **93** B4
Rochester, MN **101** G5
Rochester, NH **43** G5
Rochester, NY **47** D4
Rock (river), IL, WI **91** B3
Rock Creek, NV **147** B5
Rock Creek, OK **125** B8
Rock Hill, SC **77** B5
Rock Island, IL **91** C2
Rock Springs, WY **155** G3
Rockcastle (river), KY **69** D8
Rockford, IL **91** A4
Rockingham, NC **75** D6
Rockland, MA **41** C8
Rockland, ME **37** G4
Rockport, ME **37** G4
Rockport, TX **127** H7
Rockville, MD **39** C6
Rocky Ford, CO **139** E7
Rocky Mount, NC **75** B8
Rocky Mount, VA **81** E6
Rocky Mountain N.P., CO **139** B5
Rocky Mountains, **130** A4
Rogers, AR **63** A1
Rogers City, MI **99** D7
Rogers, Mount, VA **80** F4
Rogue (river), OR **149** F2
Rogue N.W.&S.R., OR **148** F1
Rolla, MO **103** E5
Rolla, ND **107** A6
Rolling Fork (river), KY **69** D6
Rome, GA **67** B1
Rome, NY **47** D6
Romney, WV **83** D8
Roosevelt, UT **151** C6
Root (river), MN **101** H6
Roseau, MN **101** A2
Roseau (river), MN **101** A2
Rosebud, SD **111** E5
Roseburg, OR **149** E2
Rosepine, LA **70** E2
Ross Barnett Reservoir, MS **73** E3
Ross Lake, WA **153** A5
Ross Lake N.R.A., WA **153** A5
Roswell, GA **67** C2
Roswell, NM **123** F6
Rota Island, MP **156** D1
Rough (river), KY **69** D4
Rough River Lake, KY **69** C5
Round Rock, TX **127** F6
Round Valley Reservoir, NJ **45** C3
Roundup, MT **145** D7
Roxboro, NC **75** A7
Ruby Mountains, NV **147** C6
Rugby, ND **107** B6
Ruidoso, NM **123** F5
Ruleville, MS **73** C2
Rum (river), MN **101** E4
Rumford, ME **37** F2
Rupert, ID **143** I4
Rush Creek, CO **139** D8
Rushville, IN **93** E5
Rushville, NE **104** A2
Russell, KS **97** C5
Russell Cave Nat. Mon., AL **61** A5
Russellville, AL **61** B2
Russellville, AR **63** C3
Ruston, LA **71** B3
Rutland, VT **53** F2
Rye, NH **43** H5
Rye Patch Reservoir, NV **147** B3

S
Sabine (river), LA, TX **56** E2
Sabine Lake, LA **70** G1
Sable, Cape, FL **65** H8
Sac (river), MO **103** E3
Sacajawea, Lake, WA **153** E8
Saco, ME **37** H2
Saco (river), ME, NH **37** H2
Sacramento, CA **137** D3
Sacramento (river), CA **137** B2
Sacramento Mountains, NM **123** F5
Safford, AZ **121** F7
Sag Harbor, NY **47** G10
Sagamore Hill National Historic Site, NY **47** H9
Sagavanirktok (river), AK **135** B6
Saginaw, MI **99** G7
Saginaw Bay, MI **99** F7
Saguache Creek, CO **139** E3
Saguaro N.P., AZ **121** G5
Saint Albans, VT **53** B2
Saint John (river), ME **37** B4
Saint John, Baker Branch (river), ME **37** C3
Saint John, Northwest Branch (river), ME **37** B3
Saint John, Southwest Branch (river), ME **37** C3
Sainte Genevieve, MO **103** D7
Saint-Gaudens National Historic Site, NH **43** G1
Saipan (island), MP **156** C2
Sakakawea, Lake, ND **107** C3
Sakonnet Point, RI **51** F6
Sakonnet River, RI **51** E6
Salamanca, NY **46** F2
Salamonie (river), IN **93** C5
Salamonie Lake, IN **93** C4
Salem, IL **91** G4
Salem, IN **93** G4
Salem, MA **41** B8
Salem, MO **103** E5
Salem, NH **43** I4
Salem, NJ **45** G1
Salem, OH **109** C7
Salem, OR **149** C2
Salem, SD **111** E9
Salem, VA **81** D6
Salem, WV **83** D5
Salem (river), NJ **45** G1
Salem Maritime National Historic Site, MA **41** B8
Salida, CO **139** E4
Salina, KS **97** C6
Salinas, CA **137** F3
Salinas Pueblo Missions Nat. Mon., NM **123** E4
Saline (river), KS **97** C6
Saline (river), AR **63** E4
Saline (river), IL **91** H5
Saline Bayou (river), LA **71** B3
Saline Bayou N.W.&S.R., LA **71** C3
Salisbury, MD **39** E10
Salisbury, NC **75** B5
Salish Mountains, MT **144** A2
Sallisaw, OK **125** C12
Salmon, ID **143** E3
Salmon (river), CT **33** C6
Salmon (river), ID **143** F3
Salmon Falls (river), ME, NH **37** I2
Salmon Falls Creek Reservoir, ID **143** I3
Salmon N.W.&S.R., AK **135** B4
Salmon N.W.&S.R., ID **143** E2
Salmon N.W.&S.R., OR **149** B3
Salmon River Mountains, ID **143** F2
Salmon, Middle Fork (river), ID **143** F3
Salmon, Middle Fork N.W.&S.R., ID **143** E3
Salmon, South Fork (river), ID **143** F2
Salt (river), AZ **121** E6
Salt (river), KY **69** C6
Salt (river), MO **103** B5
Salt Creek (river), IN **93** G3
Salt Creek, IL **91** E4
Salt Fork Lake, OH **109** D7
Salt Lake City, UT **151** C4
Salt River Bay N.H.P. and Ecological Preserve, VI **157** I8
Salton Sea (lake), CA **137** I7
Saluda (river), SC **77** C4
Salvador, Lake, LA **71** H7
Sam Rayburn Reservoir, TX **127** E9
San Andres Mountains, NM **123** F5
San Angelo, TX **127** E4
San Antonio, TX **127** F6
San Antonio (river), TX **127** G6
San Antonio Missions N.H.P., TX **127** G6
San Bernardino, CA **137** H6
San Blas, Cape, FL **56** F5
San Carlos, AZ **121** F6
San Carlos Reservoir, AZ **121** F6
San Clemente (island), CA **137** I5
San Diego, CA **137** I6
San Francisco, CA **137** E2
San Francisco (river), NM **123** F1
San Francisco Maritime N.H.P., CA **137** E1
San Joaquin (river), CA **137** E4
San Jose, CA **137** E3
San Jose, MP **156** D1
San Jose, Rio (river), NM **123** D2
San Juan, PR **157** H11
San Juan (river), CO, NM, UT **116** B3
San Juan Island N.H.P., WA **153** B3
San Juan Islands, WA **153** B3
San Juan Mountains, CO **139** F2
San Juan National Historic Site, PR **157** H11
San Luis, AZ **121** G1
San Luis Creek, CO **139** E4
San Luis Lake, CO **139** F5
San Luis Obispo, CA **137** G3
San Luis Valley, CO **139** F4
San Manuel, AZ **121** G6
San Marcos, TX **127** F6
San Miguel (river), CO **138** E1
San Pedro (river), AZ **121** G6
San Rafael, CA **137** D2
San Rafael (river), UT **151** E5
Sanak Island, AK **134** H3
Sanbornville, NH **43** F5
Sand Arroyo (river), CO **139** F9
Sand Creek, IN **93** F4
Sand Creek, SD **111** D8
Sand Hills, NE **105** B3
Sand Springs, OK **125** B10
Sandersville, GA **67** E5
Sandpoint, ID **143** B1
Sandstone, MN **101** E5

Sandusky — Stilwell

Sandusky, MI **99** G8
Sandusky, OH **109** B4
Sandusky (river), OH **109** C4
Sandusky Bay, OH **109** B4
Sandwich, IL **91** B4
Sandwich, MA **41** E9
Sandy, UT **151** C4
Sandy Hook (point), NJ **45** D5
Sandy Hook Bay, NJ **45** D5
Sandy N.W.&S.R., OR **149** B3
Sandy Point, RI **51** H3
Sandy Springs, GA **67** C2
Sanford, FL **65** D8
Sanford, ME **37** I2
Sanford, NC **75** C6
Sangamon (river), IL **91** E4
Sangre de Cristo Mountains, CO, NM **130** F7
Sanibel Island, FL **65** G7
Sanpoil (river), WA **153** B8
Santa Ana, CA **137** H5
Santa Barbara, CA **137** H4
Santa Catalina (island), CA **137** I5
Santa Clara, UT **151** H2
Santa Claus, IN **93** H2
Santa Cruz (island), CA **137** H4
Santa Cruz, CA **137** E2
Santa Cruz (river), AZ **121** G5
Santa Fe, NM **123** C5
Santa Maria, CA **137** G4
Santa Monica, CA **137** H5
Santa Monica Mountains N.R.A., CA **137** H5
Santa Rita, GU **156** G1
Santa Rosa (island), CA **137** H3
Santa Rosa, CA **137** D2
Santa Rosa, NM **123** D6
Santa Rosa and San Jacinto Mountains Nat. Mon., CA **137** H7
Santa Rosa Lake, NM **123** D6
Santa Rosa Range, NV **147** A4
Santee (river), SC **77** E8
Santee Dam, SC **77** E7
Sapelo Island, GA **67** G7
Sapelo Sound, GA **67** G7
Sappa Creek, KS **96** A2
Sapulpa, OK **125** B10
Saraland, AL **61** H1
Saranac Lake, NY **47** B8
Sarasota, FL **65** F6
Saratoga, WY **155** G7
Saratoga N.H.P., NY **47** D8
Saratoga Springs, NY **47** D8
Sardis Lake, MS **73** B3
Sardis Lake, OK **125** D11
Sassafras (bay), MD **39** B9
Sassafras Mountain, SC **76** A2
Satilla (river), GA **67** H5
Saugatuck Reservoir, CT **33** E2
Saugus Iron Works National Historic Site, MA **41** B7
Sauk Centre, MN **101** E3
Sault Sainte Marie, MI **99** C6
Saunderstown, RI **51** E4
Savanna, IL **91** B3
Savannah, GA **67** F7
Savannah, MO **103** B2
Savannah, TN **78** C3
Savannah (river), GA, SC **56** D6
Sawtooth N.R.A., ID **143** G3
Sawtooth Range, ID **143** F2
Saylesville, RI **51** B5
Sayre, OK **125** D5
Sayre, PA **49** A7
Sayreville, NJ **45** D4
Scantic (river), CT **33** B5
Scappoose, OR **149** B2
Scarborough, ME **37** H2
Schaumburg, IL **91** B5
Schell Creek Range, NV **147** D6
Schenectady, NY **47** D8
Schuyler, NE **105** C8
Schuylkill (river), PA **49** D8
Scioto (river), OH **109** C3
Scituate Reservoir, RI **51** C3
Scobey, MT **145** A10
Scott City, KS **96** C2
Scotts Bluff Nat. Mon., NE **104** C1
Scottsbluff, NE **104** B1
Scottsboro, AL **61** A4
Scottsburg, IN **93** G4
Scottsdale, AZ **121** F4
Scranton, PA **49** B9
Sea Islands, GA, SC **56** E6
Sea Isle City, NJ **45** I3
Seaford, DE **35** H5
Seaman Range, NV **147** F6
Searcy, AR **63** C5
Searsport, ME **37** F5
Seaside, OR **148** A1
Seaside Heights, NJ **45** F5
Seattle, WA **153** C4
Sebago Lake, ME **37** H2
Sebec Lake, ME **37** E4
Sebring, FL **65** E8
Second Lake, NH **43** A4
Sedalia, MO **103** D3
Sedona, AZ **121** D5
Sedro Woolley, WA **153** B4
Seekonk, MA **41** E6
Seekonk (river), RI **51** B5
Seguam Island, AK **135** H10
Selawik N.W.&S.R., AK **135** C5
Selby, SD **111** B6
Selbyville, DE **35** I7
Seligman, AZ **121** C3
Selinsgrove, PA **49** D7
Selkirk Mountains, ID **143** B1
Sells, AZ **121** H5
Selma, AL **61** E3
Selway (river), ID **143** D2
Seminoe Reservoir, WY **155** F7
Seminole, OK **125** D9
Seminole, Lake, FL, GA **67** I2
Semisopochnoi Island, AK **135** H7
Senatobia, MS **73** B3
Seneca, KS **97** A8
Seneca, SC **76** B1
Seneca Falls, NY **47** D4
Seneca Lake, NY **47** E4
Senecaville Lake, OH **109** E7
Sequatchie (river), TN **79** C7
Sequoia N.P., CA **137** F5
Sespe Creek N.W.&S.R., CA **137** H5
Severn (river), MD **39** C7
Severna Park, MD **39** C8
Sevier (river), UT **151** G3
Sevier Desert, UT **151** D3
Sevier Lake (dry lake), UT **151** E2
Sevierville, TN **79** B9
Seward, NE **105** D8
Seward, AK **135** F6
Seward Peninsula, AK **135** C4
Seymour, CT **33** D3
Seymour, IN **93** G4
Seymour, MO **103** F4
Seymour Lake, VT **53** A5
Shafer, Lake, IN **93** C3
Shaker Heights, OH **109** B6
Shamokin, PA **49** D7
Shannock, RI **51** F3
Sharon, CT **33** B2
Sharon, PA **48** C1
Sharpe, Lake, SD **111** D6
Sharpsburg, MD **39** B4
Shasta Lake, CA **137** B3
Shasta, Mount, CA **137** A2
Shawano, WI **113** D6
Shawnee, OK **125** D9
Shawneetown, IL **91** H5
Sheboygan, WI **113** F7
Sheenjek N.W.&S.R., AK **135** B7
Sheep Range, NV **147** G6
Shelburne, VT **53** C1
Shelburne Falls, MA **40** B2
Shelby, MS **73** C2
Shelby, MT **145** B4
Shelby, OH **109** C5
Shelbyville, IN **93** F4
Shelbyville, KY **69** B7
Shelbyville, TN **79** C5
Shelbyville, Lake, IL **91** F4
Sheldon, IA **94** A2
Shell Creek, NE **105** C7
Shell Rock (river), IA **95** B6
Shelley, ID **143** H5
Shelton, CT **33** E3
Shelton, WA **153** D3
Shenandoah, IA **95** F3
Shenandoah (river), VA **81** A8
Shenandoah Mountain, VA **81** C7
Shenandoah N.P., VA **81** B8
Shenipsit Lake, CT **33** B6
Shepaug (river), CT **33** C2
Sheridan, AR **63** E4
Sheridan, OR **149** B2
Sheridan, WY **155** A6
Sherman, TX **127** C7
Sherman Mills, ME **37** D5
Shetucket (river), CT **33** C7
Sheyenne (river), ND **107** C6
Shiloh N.M.P., TN **78** C3
Shinapaaru, MP **156** D1
Shinnston, WV **83** D5
Ship Bottom, NJ **45** G4
Ship Rock (peak), NM **123** A1
Shippensburg, PA **49** E6
Shiprock, NM **123** A2
Shoshone, ID **143** H3
Shoshone (river), WY **155** B4
Shoshone Mountains, NV **147** D4
Shoshone Range, NV **147** C4
Shoshone, North Fork (river), WY **155** B3
Shoshone, South Fork (river), WY **155** B3
Show Low, AZ **121** E6
Shreveport, LA **70** B1
Shrewsbury, MA **41** C5
Sidney, MT **145** B11
Sidney, NE **104** C2
Sidney, NY **47** E6
Sidney, OH **109** D2
Sidney Lanier, Lake, GA **67** B3
Sierra Nevada, CA **137** C3
Sierra Vista, AZ **121** H6
Sikeston, MO **103** F8
Silicon Valley, CA **137** E2
Siloam Springs, AR **63** A1
Silver City, NM **123** G2
Silver Lake, MA **41** D8
Silver Spring, MD **39** C6
Silver Springs, NV **147** D2
Simi Valley, CA **137** H5
Simpsonville, SC **77** B3
Simsbury, CT **33** B4
Sinclair, Lake, GA **67** D4
Sioux Center, IA **94** A2
Sioux City, IA **94** C1
Sioux Falls, SD **111** E10
Sipsey (river), AL **61** D1
Sipsey Fork N.W.&S.R., AL **61** B2
Sisquoc N.W.&S.R., CA **137** G4
Sisseton, SD **111** A9
Sissonville, WV **83** E3
Sitka, AK **135** F10
Sitka N.H.P., AK **135** G10
Siufaga, AS **156** I4
Siuslaw (river), OR **149** D2
Skagit (river), WA **153** B4
Skagway, AK **135** E10
Skiatook Lake, OK **125** B10
Skillet Fork (river), IL **91** G4
Skowhegan, ME **37** F3
Skykomish (river), WA **153** C4
Skyline Drive, VA **81** C8
Slatersville, RI **51** A3
Slaughter Beach, DE **35** G6
Slayton, MN **101** G2
Sleeping Bear Dunes National Lakeshore, MI **99** E5
Slide Mountain, NY **47** F8
Slidell, LA **71** F8
Smackover, AR **63** G4
Smith Canyon, CO **139** F8
Smith Island, MD **39** F9
Smith Mountain Lake, VA **81** E6
Smith N.W.&S.R., CA **137** A1
Smith, North Fork N.W.&S.R., OR **148** G1
Smithfield, NC **75** C7
Smithfield, UT **151** A4
Smithfield, VA **81** E10
Smoke Creek Desert, NV **147** C2
Smoky Hill (river), KS **96** C1
Smoky Hills, KS **97** B4
Smoky Mountains, ID **143** G3
Smyrna, DE **35** D5
Smyrna, GA **67** C2
Smyrna, TN **79** B5
Smyrna (river), DE **35** D5
Snake (river), ID, OR, WA, WY **130** B3
Snake N.W.&S.R., ID, OR **143** D1
Snake River Plain, ID **143** H4
Snohomish, WA **153** C4
Snow Hill, MD **39** F10
Snow, Mount, VT **53** H2
Snowflake, AZ **121** D6
Snyder, TX **127** D4
Socastee, SC **77** D9
Socorro, NM **123** E3
Soda Springs, ID **143** H6
Soddy-Daisy, TN **79** C7
Sol Duc (river), WA **152** C1
Soledad, CA **137** F3
Solomon (river), KS **97** B6
Solomon, North Fork (river), KS **97** B3
Solomon, South Fork (river), KS **97** B4
Solomons, MD **39** E8
Somers Point, NJ **45** H3
Somerset, KY **69** D8
Somerset, MA **41** E7
Somerset, PA **49** E3
Somerset Reservoir, VT **53** H2
Somersworth, NH **43** G5
Somerville, NJ **45** D3
Songsong, MP **156** D1
Sonora, TX **127** F4
Sonoran Desert, AZ, CA **121** F3
Sooner Lake, OK **125** B9
Souhegan (river), NH **43** I3
Souris (Mouse) (river), ND **107** B5
South (river), NC **75** D7
South Bass Island, OH **109** A4
South Bend, IN **93** A3
South Berwick, ME **37** I2
South Boston, VA **81** E7
South Burlington, VT **53** C2
South Charleston, WV **83** F3
South Hadley, MA **41** C3
South Haven, MI **99** H4
South Hero Island, VT **53** B1
South Hill, VA **81** E8
South Lake Tahoe, CA **137** D4
South Milwaukee, WI **113** G7
South Paris, ME **37** G2
South Pass, WY **155** E4
South Point *see* Kalae, HI **141** G8
South Point, OH **109** H5
South Portland, ME **37** H3
South Sioux City, NE **105** B9
South Yarmouth, MA **41** E10
Southampton, NY **47** G10
Southaven, MS **73** A3
Southbridge, MA **41** D4
Southbury, CT **33** D3
Southern Pines, NC **75** C6
Southington, CT **33** C4
Southport, NC **75** E8
Southwest Harbor, ME **37** G5
Spanish Fork, UT **151** C4
Sparks, NV **147** D2
Sparta, NJ **45** B3
Sparta, TN **79** B6
Sparta, WI **113** F3
Spartanburg, SC **77** B3
Spearfish, SD **110** C1
Spencer, IA **95** A3
Spencer, MA **41** C4
Spencer, WV **83** E3
Spirit Lake, IA **95** A3
Spokane, WA **153** C9
Spokane (river), ID, WA **153** C9
Spoon (river), IL **91** D3
Spooner, WI **113** C2
Sprague (river), OR **149** F4
Spring (river), AR **63** A6
Spring Bay (dry lake), UT **151** A2
Spring Creek, NV **147** B6
Spring Hill, FL **65** D6
Spring Hill, TN **79** C5
Spring Lake, NC **75** C7
Spring Valley, NY **47** G8
Springdale, AR **63** A1
Springer, NM **123** B6
Springer Mountain, GA **67** B3
Springfield, CO **139** F9
Springfield, IL **91** E3
Springfield, MA **41** C3
Springfield, MO **103** F3
Springfield, OH **109** E3
Springfield, OR **149** D2
Springfield, TN **79** A5
Springfield, VT **53** G3
Springfield Armory National Historic Site, MA **41** D3
Springhill, LA **70** A2
Springvale, ME **37** H2
Springville, UT **151** C4
Spruce Knob (peak), WV **83** E7
Spruce Knob-Seneca Rocks N.R.A., WV **83** E7
Squam Lake, NH **43** F3
Squapan Lake, ME **37** C5
Square Lake, ME **37** A5
Squaw Creek N.W.&S.R., OR **149** D4
St. Albans, WV **82** F2
St. Andrew Sound, GA **67** H7
St. Anthony, ID **143** G5
St. Augustine, FL **65** B8
St. Catherine, Lake, VT **53** G1
St. Catherines Island, GA **67** G7
St. Catherines Sound, GA **67** G7
St. Charles, MD **39** D7
St. Charles, MO **103** C6
St. Charles (river), CO **139** E6
St. Clair, MI **99** H8
St. Clair Shores, MI **99** H8
St. Clair, Lake, MI **99** H8
St. Cloud, MN **101** E4
St. Croix (island), VI **157** I7
St. Croix (river), ME **37** D7
St. Croix (river), MN, WI **101** E5
St. Croix Falls, WI **113** C1
St. Croix Island International Historic Site, ME **37** E7
St. Croix N.W.&S.R., MN, WI **113** D1
St. Croix National Scenic Riverway, MN, WI **113** B2
St. Elias Mountains, AK **135** E8
St. Elias, Mount, AK **135** E8
St. Francis (river), ME **37** A4
St. Francis, ME **37** A4
St. Francis (river), AR, MO **63** A7
St. George, UT **151** H2
St. Georges, DE **35** C4
St. Helena Island, SC **77** H6
St. Helena Sound, SC **77** G6
St. Helens, OR **149** A2
St. Helens, Mount, WA **153** F4
St. Ignace, MI **99** D6
St. James, MN **101** G3
St. James, MO **103** D5
St. Joe (river), ID **143** C1
St. Joe N.W.&S.R., ID **143** C2
St. John (island), VI **157** G8
St. Johns, AZ **121** D7
St. Johns, MI **99** G6
St. Johns (river), FL **65** D8
St. Johnsbury, VT **53** C5
St. Jones (river), DE **35** E5
St. Joseph, MI **99** I4
St. Joseph, MO **103** B2
St. Joseph (river), IN, MI **93** A4
St. Joseph (river), IN, OH **93** B5
St. Lawrence (river), NY **47** A6
St. Lawrence Island, AK **134** D2
St. Louis, MO **103** D7
St. Louis (river), MN **101** D5
St. Lucie Canal, FL **65** F9
St. Maries, ID **143** C1
St. Maries (river), ID **143** C1
St. Marys, GA **67** I7
St. Marys, OH **109** D2
St. Marys, PA **49** B4
St. Marys, WV **83** D4
St. Marys (river), FL **65** B7
St. Marys (river), IN, OH **93** C5
St. Marys (river), MI **99** C6
St. Marys City, MD **39** F8
St. Marys Lake *see* Grand Lake, OH **109** D2
St. Matthew Island, AK **134** E1
St. Michaels, MD **39** D8
St. Paul, AK **134** F1
St. Paul, MN **101** F5
St. Paul, NE **105** C7
St. Paul's Church National Historic Site, NY **47** H8
St. Peter, MN **101** G4
St. Peters, MO **103** C6
St. Petersburg, FL **65** E6
St. Simons Island, GA **67** H7
St. Thomas (island), VI **157** G7
Stafford, CT **33** A6
Stafford Pond, RI **51** D6
Staffordville Reservoir, CT **33** A6
Stamford, CT **33** F1
Stamps, AR **63** G2
Stanley, ND **107** B3
Starkville, MS **73** C5
State College, PA **49** D5
Stateline, NV **147** D1
Staten Island, NY **47** H8
Statesboro, GA **67** F6
Statesville, NC **75** B4
Statue of Liberty Nat. Mon., NY **47** H8
Staunton (river) *see* Roanoke, VA **81** E7
Staunton, VA **81** C7
Stayton, OR **149** C2
Steamboat Springs, CO **139** B3
Steamtown National Historic Site, PA **49** B9
Steele, ND **107** E6
Steens Mountain, OR **149** F7
Stellwagen Bank National Marine Sanctuary, MA **41** B9
Stephenville, TX **127** D6
Sterling, CO **139** A8
Sterling, IL **91** B3
Steubenville, OH **109** D8
Stevens Point, WI **113** E5
Stillwater, MN **101** F5
Stillwater, OK **125** B9
Stillwater (river), OH **109** D1
Stillwater Range, NV **147** C3
Stilwell, OK **125** C12

Stockbridge — Waikoloa

Stockbridge, MA **40** C1
Stockton, CA **137** D3
Stockton Lake, MO **103** E3
Stone Mountain (site), GA **67** C3
Stones River N.B., TN **79** B5
Stonewall Jackson Lake, WV **83** D5
Stonington, ME **37** G5
Stony (river), AK **135** E5
Storm Lake, IA **95** B3
Storrs, CT **33** B6
Story City, IA **95** C5
Stoughton, MA **41** C7
Stoughton, WI **113** G5
Stowe, VT **53** C3
Stratford, CT **33** E3
Stratford Point, CT **33** E3
Stratton Mountain, VT **53** H2
Strawberry Reservoir, UT **151** C5
Streator, IL **91** C4
Strong (river), MS **73** F3
Strongsville, OH **109** B6
Stroudsburg, PA **49** C9
Stuarts Draft, VA **81** C7
Stump Lake, ND **107** C8
Sturbridge, MA **41** C4
Sturgeon Bay, WI **113** D8
Sturgeon N.W.&S.R., MI **99** D4
Sturgis, MI **99** I5
Sturgis, SD **110** C2
Stuttgart, AR **63** E5
Sudbury Reservoir, MA **41** C6
Sudbury, Assabet and Concord N.W.&S.R., MA **41** B6
Suffolk, VA **81** E11
Sugar (river), NH **43** G1
Sugar (river), WI **113** H5
Sugar Creek (creek), IN **93** E2
Sugar Creek (creek), IN **93** E4
Sugar Land, TX **127** F8
Sugarloaf Mountain, ME **37** E2
Suitland, MD **39** D7
Sullivan, MO **103** D6
Sullys Hill National Game Preserve, ND **107** C7
Sulphur, LA **70** G2
Sulphur, OK **125** E9
Sulphur Creek, SD **111** C3
Sulphur Springs, TX **127** C8
Summer Lake, OR **149** F5
Summersville, WV **83** F4
Summersville Lake, WV **83** F4
Summerville, SC **77** F7
Summit Lake, NV **147** A2
Sumner Lake, NM **123** D6
Sumter, SC **77** D6
Sun (river), MT **145** C4
Sun City, AZ **121** F4
Sun Prairie, WI **113** G5
Sunapee Lake, NH **43** G2
Sunapee, Mount, NH **43** G2
Sunbury, PA **49** C7
Suncook, NH **43** H4
Suncook (river), NH **43** H4
Suncook Lakes, NH **43** G4
Sundance, WY **155** B10
Sunflower, Mount, KS **96** B1
Sunland Park, NM **123** H4
Sunnyside, WA **153** E6
Sunnyvale, CA **137** E2
Sunset Crater Volcano Nat. Mon., AZ **121** C5
Superior, NE **105** E7
Superior, WI **113** A2
Superior, Lake, **86** B6
Surf City, NJ **45** G4
Surfside Beach, SC **77** E9
Surry Mountain Lake, NH **43** H1
Susanville, CA **137** B3
Susitna (river), AK **135** D6
Susquehanna (river), MD, NY, PA **39** A8
Susquehanna, West Branch (river), PA **49** C5
Susupe, MP **156** C2
Sutherlin, OR **149** E2
Sutton Lake, WV **83** E5
Suwannee (river), FL **65** C6
Swainsboro, GA **67** E5
Swanson Reservoir, NE **105** E4
Swanton, VT **53** A2
Sweet Home, OR **149** D2
Sweetwater, TN **79** C8
Sweetwater, TX **127** D4
Sweetwater (river), WY **155** E5
Sweetwater Lake, ND **107** B8
Swift (river), MA **41** C3
Sycamore, IL **91** B4
Sycan (river), OR **149** F4
Sycan N.W.&S.R., OR **149** F4
Sylacauga, AL **61** D4
Sylvania, OH **109** A3
Syracuse, NY **47** D5
Sysladobsis Lake, ME **37** E6

T

Table Rock Lake, MO **103** F3
Tacoma, WA **153** D3
Taconic Range, MA, NY, VT **47** F9
Tahlequah, OK **125** C11
Tahoe, Lake, CA, NV **137** C4
Tahquamenon (East Branch) N.W.&S.R., MI **99** C5
Taliesin (site), WI **113** G4
Talladega, AL **61** D4
Tallahala Creek, MS **73** G4
Tallahassee, FL **65** B4
Tallahatchie (river), MS **73** C3
Tallapoosa (river), AL **61** E4
Tallassee, AL **61** E5
Talleyville, DE **35** A5
Tallgrass Prairie National Preserve, KS **97** C7
Tallulah, LA **71** B6
Tamaqua, PA **49** D8
Tampa, FL **65** E6
Tampa Bay, FL **65** E6
Tampico, IL **91** B3
Tamuning, GU **156** F1
Tanaga Island, AK **135** H8
Tanana (river), AK **135** D7
Taneytown, MD **39** A6
Tangier Island, VA **81** C11
Tangier Sound, MD **39** F9
Tangipahoa (river), LA **71** E7
Taos, NM **123** B5
Tar (river), NC **75** B8
Tarboro, NC **75** B8
Tarpon Springs, FL **65** E6
Tarrytown, NY **47** G8
Tau (island), AS **157** I5
Tau, AS **156** I4
Taum Sauk Mountain, MO **103** E6
Taunton, MA **41** D7
Taunton (river), MA **41** E7
Tawas City, MI **99** F7
Taylors, SC **77** B3
Taylorville, IL **91** E4
Tazewell, VA **80** E4
Teche, Bayou (river), LA **71** G5
Tecumseh, MI **99** I7
Tecumseh, OK **125** D9
Tekamah, NE **105** C9
Tell City, IN **93** I3
Tellico Lake, TN **79** C8
Telluride, CO **139** F2
Telos Lake, ME **37** C4
Tempe, AZ **121** F4
Temperance, MI **99** I7
Temple, TX **127** E7
Ten Thousand Islands, FL **65** H8
Tenkiller Lake, OK **125** C11
Tennessee (river), AL, KY, MS, TN **56** C4
Tennessee-Tombigbee Waterway, AL, MS **73** B5
Tensas (river), LA **71** C5
Terre Haute, IN **93** F2
Terrebonne Bay, LA **71** I7
Terry, MT **145** D10
Terryville, CT **33** C3
Teton (river), MT **145** B5
Texarkana, AR **63** F1
Texarkana, TX **127** C9
Texoma, Lake, OK **125** F9
Thames (river), CT **33** D7
The Berkshires (hills), MA **40** C1
The Dalles, OR **149** B4
The Everglades, FL **65** H8
The Hermitage (site), TN **79** B5
Theodore Roosevelt Inaugural National Historic Site, NY **46** D1
Theodore Roosevelt Lake, AZ **121** E5
Theodore Roosevelt N.P. (Elkhorn Ranch Site), ND **106** D1
Theodore Roosevelt N.P. (South Unit), ND **106** D2
Thermopolis, WY **155** C5
Thibodaux, LA **71** G6
Thief River Falls, MN **101** B2
Third Lake, NH **43** A4
Thomas Stone National Historic Site, MD **39** D6
Thomaston, GA **67** E2
Thomaston, ME **37** G4
Thomasville, AL **61** F2
Thomasville, GA **67** H3
Thomasville, NC **75** B5
Thompson, CT **33** A8
Thompson (river), IA, MO **103** A3
Thompson Falls, MT **144** C1
Thomson, GA **67** D5
Thornton, CO **139** C6
Thousand Islands, NY **47** B5
Thousand Springs Creek, NV **147** A6
Three Mile Island, PA **49** E7
Three Rivers, MI **99** I5
Thunder Bay, MI **99** E7
Thunder Bay (river), MI **99** E6
Thunder Butte Creek (river), SD **111** B3
Thurmont, MD **39** A5
Ticonderoga, NY **47** C9
Tiffin, OH **109** B4
Tifton, GA **67** G4
Tillamook, OR **148** B1
Tillery, Lake, NC **75** C5
Tilton, NH **43** G3
Timbalier Bay, LA **71** I7
Timber Lake, SD **111** B4
Timberlake, VA **81** D7
Timms Hill (peak), WI **113** C4
Timpanogos Cave Nat. Mon., UT **151** C4
Tims Ford Lake, TN **79** C5
Timucuan Ecological and Historic Preserve, FL **65** A8
Tinayguk N.W.&S.R., AK **135** B6
Tinian (island), MP **156** D2
Tinton Falls, NJ **45** E5
Tioga, ND **106** B2
Tioga (river), PA **49** A6
Tiogue Lake, RI **51** D4
Tippecanoe (river), IN **93** B3
Tishomingo, OK **125** E9
Titusville, FL **65** D8
Titusville, PA **48** B2
Tiverton, RI **51** D6
Tlikakila N.W.&S.R., AK **135** E5
Toana Range, NV **147** B7
Toccoa, GA **67** B4
Toiyabe Range, NV **147** D4
Tok, AK **135** D8
Toledo, OH **109** A3
Toledo Bend Reservoir, LA, TX **70** D2
Tomah, WI **113** F4
Tomahawk, WI **113** C5
Tombigbee (river), MS **73** G6
Tombigee (river), AL **61** G1
Tombstone, AZ **121** H7
Toms (river), NJ **45** E4
Toms River, NJ **45** F4
Tonawanda, NY **46** D2
Tongue (river), MT **145** E9
Tonopah, NV **147** E4
Tonto Nat. Mon., AZ **121** F5
Tooele, UT **151** C3
Topeka, KS **97** B9
Toppenish, WA **153** E6
Toquima Range, NV **147** E4
Toronto, OH **109** D8
Torrington, CT **33** B3
Torrington, WY **155** F10
Touro Synagogue National Historic Site, RI **51** F5
Towanda, PA **49** B7
Towner, ND **107** B5
Townsend, DE **35** D4
Townsend, MT **145** D5
Towson, MD **39** B7
Tradewater (river), KY **68** D3
Trans-Alaska Pipeline, AK **135** C6
Trask (river), OR **148** B1
Traverse City, MI **99** E5
Traverse, Lake, MN, SD **101** E1
Tremonton, UT **151** A3
Trenton, MO **103** B3
Trenton, NJ **45** E3
Trenton, TN **78** B2
Trinidad, CO **139** G6
Trinity (river), TX **127** E8
Trinity Islands, AK **135** G5
Trinity N.W.&S.R., CA **137** B2
Trinity Site, NM **123** F4
Trotwood, OH **109** E2
Troy, AL **61** F5
Troy, MI **99** H7
Troy, NH **43** I2
Troy, NY **47** E8
Troy, OH **109** E2
Trujillo Alto, PR **157** H11
Trumann, AR **63** B7
Trumbull, CT **33** E3
Truro, MA **41** D10
Truth or Consequences, NM **123** F3
Tschida, Lake, ND **107** E3
Tuba City, AZ **121** B5
Tuckahoe (river), NJ **45** H3
Tuckerman, AR **63** B6
Tucson, AZ **121** G6
Tucumcari, NM **123** C7
Tug Fork (river), KY, WV **69** C11
Tugaloo (river), GA, SC **67** B4
Tulare, CA **137** F4
Tularosa, NM **123** F5
Tullahoma, TN **79** C5
Tulsa, OK **125** B10
Tumacacori N.H.P., AZ **121** H5
Tumwater, WA **153** D3
Tuolumne N.W.&S.R., CA **137** D4
Tupelo, MS **73** B5
Tupelo N.B., MS **73** B5
Turkey (river), IA **95** B8
Turlock, CA **137** E3
Turner Turnpike, OK **125** C9
Turners Falls, MA **41** B3
Turtle Mountains, ND **107** A6
Turtle-Flambeau Flowage, WI **113** B4
Tuscaloosa, AL **61** D2
Tuscarawas (river), OH **109** C6
Tuscarora Mountain, PA **49** E5
Tuscarora Mountains, NV **147** B5
Tuscola, IL **91** E5
Tuskegee, AL **61** E5
Tuskegee Institute National Historic Site, AL **61** F5
Tuttle Creek Lake, KS **97** B7
Tutuila (island), AS **156** I1
Tuxedo Park, NY **47** G8
Tuzigoot Nat. Mon., AZ **121** D4
Twin Falls, ID **143** I3
Twin Lakes, CT **33** A2
Two Butte Creek, CO **139** F9
Two Harbors, MN **101** D6
Two Rivers, WI **113** E7
Tybee Island, GA **67** F8
Tygart Lake, WV **83** D6
Tygart Valley (river), WV **83** E6
Tyler, TX **127** D8
Tyndall, SD **111** F9
Tyrone, PA **49** D4

U

U.S. Military Academy, NY **47** G8
U.S. Virgin Islands (territory), US **157** E12
Uhrichsville, OH **109** D7
Uinta Mountains, UT **151** C5
Ukiah, CA **137** C2
Ulysses, KS **96** E2
Ulysses S. Grant National Historic Site, MO **103** D7
Umbagog Lake, NH **43** B4
Umnak Island, AK **134** H1
Umpqua (river), OR **148** E1
Umpqua, North (river), OR **149** E2
Umpqua, South (river), OR **149** F2
Umsaskis Lake, ME **37** B4
Unalakleet, AK **135** D4
Unalakleet N.W.&S.R., AK **135** D4
Unalaska, AK **134** H2
Unalaska Island, AK **134** H2
Uncompahgre (river), CO **139** E2
Uncompahgre Plateau, CO **138** E1
Unimak Island, AK **134** G2
Union, MO **103** D6
Union, SC **77** B4
Union City, NJ **45** C5
Union City, TN **78** A2
Union Springs, AL **61** F5
Union Village, RI **51** A4
Uniontown, PA **48** E2
Unionville, CT **33** B4
University City, MO **103** D7
'Upolu Point, HI **141** D8
Upper Ammonoosuc (river), NH **43** C3
Upper Arlington, OH **109** E4
Upper Darby, PA **49** E9
Upper Delaware Scenic and Recreational River, PA, NY **49** B10
Upper Iowa (river), IA **95** A7
Upper Klamath Lake, OR **149** G3
Upper Mississippi River National Wildlife and Fish Refuge, IA, IL, MN, WI **101** G6
Upper Missouri River Breaks Nat. Mon., MT **145** B7
Upper Peninsula, MI **99** C3
Upper Red Lake, MN **101** B3
Upper Sandusky, OH **109** C4
Urbana, IL **91** E5
Urbana, OH **109** D3
Urbandale, IA **95** D5
USS Arizona Memorial, HI **141** C4
Utah Lake, UT **151** C4
Ute Creek, NM **123** B7
Utica, NY **47** D6
Utukok (river), AK **135** A4
Uvalde, TX **127** G5

V

Vail, CO **139** C4
Valdez, AK **135** E7
Valdosta, GA **67** H4
Valencia, NM **123** D4
Valentine, NE **105** A4
Vallejo, CA **137** D2
Valley, AL **61** E6
Valley City, ND **107** D8
Valley Falls, RI **51** B5
Valley Forge N.H.P., PA **49** E9
Valparaiso, IN **93** B2
Van Buren, AR **63** C1
Van Buren, ME **37** A6
Van Wert, OH **109** C2
Vanceburg, KY **69** B9
Vancouver, WA **153** G3
Vandalia, IL **91** F4
Vanderbilt Mansion National Historic Site, NY **47** F8
Vaughan, MS **73** E3
Vega Baja, PR **157** H10
Venice, FL **65** F6
Ventnor City, NJ **45** H4
Ventura, CA **137** H4
Verde (river), AZ **121** D4
Verde N.W.&S.R., AZ **121** E5
Verdigre Creek, NE **105** B7
Verdigris (river), KS, OK **125** A11
Vergennes, VT **53** D1
Vermilion (river), IL **91** C4
Vermilion (river), IL, IN **91** E6
Vermilion Cliffs Nat. Mon., AZ **121** A5
Vermilion Lake, MN **101** B5
Vermilion N.W.&S.R., IL **91** D5
Vermillion, SD **111** F10
Vermillion Creek, CO **138** A1
Vermillion, Middle Fork (river), IL **91** D5
Vernal, UT **151** C6
Vernon, CT **33** B6
Vernon, TX **127** C5
Vero Beach, FL **65** E9
Versailles, KY **69** C7
Vicksburg, MS **73** E2
Vicksburg N.M.P., MS **73** E2
Victoria, TX **127** G7
Vidalia, GA **67** F5
Vidalia, LA **71** D5
Vienna, WV **83** D3
Vieques Island, PR **157** I12
Villas, NJ **45** I2
Ville Platte, LA **71** F4
Vinalhaven, ME **37** G5
Vincennes, IN **93** G1
Vineland, NJ **45** G2
Vineyard Haven, MA **41** F8
Vineyard Sound, MA **41** F8
Vinita, OK **125** A11
Vinton, IA **95** C7
Virgin (river), AZ, NV, UT **147** G7
Virgin Islands N.P., VI **157** H8
Virginia, MN **101** C5
Virginia Beach, VA **81** E11
Virginia City, MT **145** E4
Virginia City, NV **147** D2
Viroqua, WI **113** F3
Visalia, CA **137** F4
Vivian, LA **70** A1
Volga, SD **111** D10
Voyageurs N.P., MN **101** B5

W

Wabash, IN **93** C4
Wabash (river), IL, IN **86** G7
Waccamaw (river), SC **77** E9
Waccamaw, Lake, NC **75** D7
Wachusett Reservoir, MA **41** B5
Waco, TX **127** E7
Waconda Lake, KS **97** B5
Wadena, MN **101** D3
Wagner, SD **111** F8
Wagoner, OK **125** C11
Wah Wah Mountains, UT **151** F2
Wahoo, NE **105** C9
Wahpeton, ND **107** E10
Wai'ale'ale (peak), HI **140** A2
Waialua, HI **141** B4
Waialua, HI **141** C6
Waikoloa, HI **141** E8

Wailuku, HI **141** C7
Waimea (Kamuela), HI **141** E8
Waipahu, HI **141** B4
Wake Island (territory), US **156** E2
WaKeeney, KS **97** B3
Wakefield, RI **51** F4
Walcott, Lake, ID **143** H4
Waldoboro, ME **37** G4
Waldorf, MD **39** D7
Waldron, AR **63** D1
Walhalla, ND **107** A9
Walker, MN **101** D3
Walker Lake, NV **147** E3
Walker, East (river), NV **147** D2
Walkersville, MD **39** B6
Wall, SD **111** D3
Walla Walla, WA **153** F9
Wallenpaupack, Lake, PA **49** B9
Wallingford, CT **33** D4
Wallingford, VT **53** G2
Wallkill (river), NJ **45** B3
Wallops Island, VA **81** C12
Wallowa (river), OR **149** B8
Wallowa N.W.&S.R., OR **149** B8
Wallula, Lake, WA **153** F8
Wallum Lake, RI **51** A2
Walnut (river), KS **97** E7
Walnut Canyon Nat. Mon., AZ **121** D5
Walnut Creek, KS **97** C4
Walnut Ridge, AR **63** B6
Walpole, NH **43** H1
Walsenburg, CO **139** F6
Walt Disney World and EPCOT Center, FL **65** D7
Walter F. George Reservoir, AL, GA **61** F6
Walterboro, SC **77** F6
Walters, OK **125** E7
Wamego, KS **97** B8
Wanaque, NJ **45** B4
Wanaque Reservoir, NJ **45** B4
Wapakoneta, OH **109** D2
Wapsipinicon (river), IA **95** A7
War in the Pacific N.H.P., GU **156** F1
Ware, MA **41** C4
Ware (river), MA **41** C4
Warner Robins, GA **67** E4
Warner Valley, OR **149** G5
Warren, AR **63** F5
Warren, MI **99** H8
Warren, MN **101** B1
Warren, NH **43** E2
Warren, OH **109** B8
Warren, PA **49** A3
Warren, RI **51** C5
Warrensburg, MO **103** C3
Warrensburg, NY **47** C8
Warrenton, VA **81** B9
Warrior, AL **61** C3
Warsaw, IN **93** B4
Warwick, RI **51** D5
Wasatch Range, UT **130** D5
Waseca, MN **101** G4
Washburn, ME **37** B6
Washburn, ND **107** D5
Washburn, WI **113** A3
Washington, GA **67** C5
Washington, IA **95** E8
Washington, IN **93** G2
Washington, KS **97** A7
Washington, MO **103** D6
Washington, NC **75** C9
Washington, NJ **45** C2
Washington, PA **48** E1
Washington Court House, OH **109** F3
Washington Island, WI **113** C8
Washington, Mount, NH **43** D4
Washita (river), OK **125** C6
Washita Battlefield National Historic Site, OK **125** C5
Wasilla, AK **135** E6
Wassuk Range, NV **147** D2
Watch Hill, RI **51** G1
Watchaug Pond, RI **51** F3
Water Valley, MS **73** B3
Waterbury, CT **33** C3
Waterbury, VT **53** C3
Wateree (river), SC **77** D6
Wateree Lake, SC **77** C6
Waterloo, IA **95** C7
Watertown, CT **33** C3
Watertown, NY **47** C6
Watertown, SD **111** C9
Watertown, WI **113** G6
Waterville, ME **37** F4
Watford City, ND **106** C2
Watkins Glen, NY **47** E4
Watonga, OK **125** C7
Watseka, IL **91** D6
Watts Bar Lake, TN **79** C7
Waubay Lake, SD **111** B9
Waukegan, IL **91** A5
Waukesha, WI **113** G6
Waukon, IA **95** A8
Waupaca, WI **113** E5
Waupun, WI **113** F6
Waurika Lake, OK **125** E7
Wausau, WI **113** D5
Wauseon, OH **109** B2
Wauwatosa, WI **113** G7
Waverly, IA **95** B7
Waverly, NE **105** D9
Waverly, OH **109** F4
Wawasee, Lake, IN **93** B4
Waycross, GA **67** H5
Wayne, NE **105** B8
Wayne, NJ **45** B4
Waynesboro, GA **67** D6
Waynesboro, MS **73** G5
Waynesboro, PA **49** F6
Waynesboro, VA **81** C7
Waynesburg, PA **48** E1
Waynesville, MO **103** E5
Waynesville, NC **74** C2
Weatherford, OK **125** C7
Webb City, MO **103** F2
Webster, MA **41** D5
Webster, SD **111** B9
Webster City, IA **95** C5
Weir Farm National Historic Site, CT **33** E2
Weirton, WV **83** A5
Weiser, ID **143** F1
Weiser (river), ID **143** F1
Weiss Lake, AL **61** B5
Welch, WV **83** H3
Weldon (river), MO **103** A3
Wellesley, MA **41** C6
Wellfleet, MA **41** D10
Wellington, KS **97** E6
Wells, ME **37** I2
Wells, NV **147** B6
Wells River, VT **53** D5
Wellsboro, PA **49** B6
Wellsburg, WV **83** B5
Wellston, OH **109** G5
Wellsville, NY **46** F3
Wellsville, UT **151** A4
Wellton, AZ **121** G2
Wenaha N.W.&S.R., OR **149** A8
Wenatchee, WA **153** D6
Wendell H. Ford Parkway, KY **69** D4
Wendover, UT **151** C1
Wentworth, Lake, NH **43** F4
Wessington Springs, SD **111** D8
West (river), VT **53** H3
West Allis, WI **113** G7
West Bend, WI **113** G7
West Chester, PA **49** E9
West Columbia, SC **77** D5
West Des Moines, IA **95** D5
West Fargo, ND **107** D10
West Frankfort, IL **91** H4
West Grand Lake, ME **37** E6
West Hartford, CT **33** B4
West Haven, CT **33** E4
West Helena, AR **63** D7
West Jordan, UT **151** C4
West Kingston, RI **51** F3
West Little Owyhee N.W.&S.R., OR **149** G8
West Memphis, AR **63** C8
West Milford, NJ **45** B4
West Monroe, LA **71** B4
West Okoboji Lake, IA **95** A3
West Palm Beach, FL **65** F9
West Plains, MO **103** F5
West Point, MS **73** C5
West Point, NE **105** B9
West Point, NY **47** G8
West Point, VA **81** D10
West Point Lake, AL, GA **67** D1
West Quoddy Head, ME **37** F8
West Rutland, VT **53** F2
West Seneca, NY **46** D2
West Warwick, RI **51** D4
West Wendover, NV **147** B7
West Yellowstone, MT **145** F5
Westbrook, CT **33** E6
Westbrook, ME **37** H2
Westerly, RI **51** G1
Westerville, OH **109** D4
Westfield, MA **40** C2
Westfield, NY **46** E1
Westfield (river), MA **40** C2
Westfield N.W.&S.R., MA **40** C2
Westfield, Middle Branch (river), MA **40** B2
Westfield, West Branch (river), MA **40** C1
Westminster, CO **139** C5
Westminster, MD **39** A6
Weston, WV **83** D5
Westport, CT **33** E2
Wet Mountains, CO **139** E5
Wethersfield, CT **33** B5
Wewoka, OK **125** D9
Weymouth, MA **41** C7
Wheatland, WY **155** F9
Wheaton, MN **101** E1
Wheeler Lake, AL **61** A3
Wheeler Peak, NM **123** B5
Wheelersburg, OH **109** G4
Wheeling, WV **83** B4
Whidbey Island, WA **153** B3
Whiskeytown-Shasta-Trinity N.R.A., CA **137** B2
White (river), CO, UT **151** D7
White (river), AR, MO **63** A2
White (river), AZ **121** E7
White (river), IN **93** D5
White (river), MI **99** G4
White (river), NE, SD **111** D5
White (river), OR **149** B4
White (river), VT **53** E3
White Butte (peak), ND **106** E2
White City, OR **149** F2
White Earth (river), ND **107** B3
White Hall, IL **91** F2
White Horse, NJ **45** E3
White Lake, LA **71** H3
White Mountains, NH **43** E2
White N.W.&S.R., OR **149** B4
White Oak Lake, AR **63** F3
White Plains, NY **47** G8
White River, SD **111** E5
White River Junction, VT **53** F4
White River Plateau, CO **139** C2
White Rocks N.R.A., VT **53** G2
White Salmon N.W.&S.R., WA **153** F5
White Sands Nat. Mon., NM **123** G4
White Sulphur Springs, WV **83** G5
White Woman Creek, KS **96** C1
White, East Fork (river), IN **93** G3
Whitefield, NH **43** D3
Whitefish, MT **144** B2
Whitefish Bay, MI **99** C6
Whitefish N.W.&S.R., MI **99** C4
Whiteriver, AZ **121** E7
Whiteville, NC **75** D7
Whitewater, WI **113** G6
Whitewater (river), IN **93** F6
Whitman, MA **41** D8
Whitman Mission National Historic Site, WA **153** F8
Whitney, Mount, CA **137** F5
Wibaux, MT **145** C11
Wichita, KS **97** E7
Wichita (river), TX **127** C6
Wichita Falls, TX **127** C6
Wichita Mountains, OK **125** D6
Wichita Mountains Wildlife Refuge, OK **125** D6
Wickenburg, AZ **121** E4
Wickford, RI **51** E4
Wiggins, MS **73** H4
Wilber, NE **105** D8
Wilburton, OK **125** D11
Wild Rice (river), MN **101** C1
Wild Rice (river), ND **107** F9
Wildcat Brook N.W.&S.R., NH **43** D4
Wildcat Creek, IN **93** D3
Wilder, VT **53** F4
Wildwood, NJ **45** I3
Wilkes-Barre, PA **49** C8
Will Rogers Turnpike, OK **125** B10
Willamette (river), OR **149** C2
Willamette N.W.&S.R., OR **149** D3
Willapa Bay, WA **152** E2
Willard, OH **109** C4
Willcox, AZ **121** G7
Willcox Playa (river), AZ **121** G7
William "Bill" Dannelly Reservoir, AL **61** F3
William H. Natcher Parkway, KY **69** D4
William Howard Taft National Historic Site, OH **109** G2
William Preston Lane Jr. Memorial Bridge (Chesapeake Bay Bridge), MD **39** C8
Williams, AZ **121** C4
Williamsburg, KY **69** E8
Williamsburg, VA **81** D10
Williamson, WV **82** G2
Williamsport, MD **39** A4
Williamsport, PA **49** C7
Williamston, NC **75** B9
Williamstown, KY **69** B8
Williamstown, NJ **45** G2
Williamstown, WV **83** C3
Willimantic, CT **33** B7
Willimantic (river), CT **33** B7
Willimantic Reservoir, CT **33** B7
Willingboro, NJ **45** E2
Williston, ND **106** B2
Williston, SC **77** E4
Willmar, MN **101** F3
Willoughby, Lake, VT **53** B5
Willow Creek, UT **151** D6
Wills Creek, OH **109** E6
Wilmington, DE **35** A5
Wilmington, NC **75** D8
Wilmington, OH **109** F3
Wilmington, VT **53** I3
Wilson, NC **75** B8
Wilson Creek Range, NV **147** E7
Wilson Lake, AL **61** A2
Wilson Lake, KS **97** B5
Wilson's Creek N.B., MO **103** F3
Wilton, CT **33** E2
Wilton, ME **37** F3
Wilton, NH **43** I3
Winchendon, MA **41** A4
Winchester, IN **93** D6
Winchester, KY **69** C8
Winchester, NH **43** I1
Winchester, TN **79** D6
Winchester, VA **81** A8
Wind (river), WY **155** C5
Wind Cave N.P., SD **110** E2
Wind N.W.&S.R., AK **135** B7
Wind River Range, WY **155** C3
Windber, PA **49** E4
Windom, MN **101** H3
Window Rock, AZ **121** C7
Windsor, CT **33** B5
Windsor, VT **53** F4
Windsor Heights, IA **95** D4
Windsor Locks, CT **33** A5
Winfield, AL **61** C2
Winfield, KS **97** E7
Winnebago, Lake, WI **113** F6
Winnebago (river), IA **95** A6
Winnemucca, NV **147** B4
Winnemucca Lake, NV **147** C2
Winner, SD **111** E6
Winnfield, LA **71** C3
Winnibigoshish, Lake, MN **101** C3
Winnipesaukee, Lake, NH **43** F4
Winnisquam Lake, NH **43** G3
Winnsboro, SC **77** C5
Winnsboro, LA **71** C5
Winona, MN **101** G6
Winona, MS **73** C3
Winooski (river), VT **53** C2
Winooski, VT **53** C2
Winslow, AZ **121** D6
Winslow, ME **37** F4
Winsted, CT **33** A3
Winston, OR **149** E2
Winston-Salem, NC **75** B5
Winter Haven, FL **65** E7
Winterset, IA **95** E5
Winterthur Museum and Gardens, DE **35** A5
Winthrop, ME **37** G3
Wiscasset, ME **37** G3
Wisconsin (river), WI **113** E5
Wisconsin Dells, WI **113** F5
Wisconsin Rapids, WI **113** E5
Wisconsin, Lake, WI **113** G5
Wishek, ND **107** F6
Wissota, Lake, WI **113** D3
Withlacoochee (river), GA **67** H4
Woburn, MA **41** B7
Wolf (river), WI **113** D6
Wolf Creek, OK **125** B5
Wolf N.W.&S.R., WI **113** D6
Wolf Point, MT **145** B10
Wolf Trap N.P. for the Performing Arts, VA **81** B9
Wolfeboro, NH **43** F4
Women's Rights N.H.P., NY **47** D5
Wood (river), RI **51** F2
Woodall Mountain, MS **73** A6
Woodbine, NJ **45** H3
Woodbridge, VA **81** B9
Woodburn, OR **149** B2
Woodbury, NJ **45** F2
Woodland, ME **37** E7
Woodland Park, CO **139** D5
Woods Hole, MA **41** F8
Woods, Lake of the, MN **101** A3
Woodstock, VT **53** F3
Woodstown, NJ **45** G1
Woodsville, NH **43** E2
Woodward, OK **125** B6
Woonasquatucket (river), RI **51** B4
Woonasquatucket Reservoir, RI **51** B3
Woonsocket, RI **51** A4
Woonsocket, SD **111** D8
Wooster, OH **109** C6
Worcester, MA **41** C5
Worden Pond, RI **51** F3
Worland, WY **155** B5
Worthington, MN **101** H2
Wounded Knee Massacre Site, SD **111** E3
Wrangell, AK **135** G11
Wrangell-St. Elias N.P. and Preserve, AK **135** E8
Wright, WY **155** C8
Wright Brothers National Memorial, NC **75** B10
Wrightsville Beach, NC **75** E8
Wupatki Nat. Mon., AZ **121** C5
Wyaconda (river), MO **103** A5
Wyandotte Cave, IN **93** H3
Wylie Lake, SC **77** A5
Wynne, AR **63** C7
Wyoming, RI **51** E2
Wyoming Range, WY **154** D2
Wytheville, VA **80** E4

X

Xenia, OH **109** E3

Y

Yadkin (river), NC **75** B4
Yakima, WA **153** E6
Yakima (river), WA **153** D6
Yalobusha (river), MS **73** C4
Yampa (river), CO **139** B2
Yankton, SD **111** F9
Yantic (river), CT **33** C7
Yarmouth, ME **37** H3
Yazoo (river), MS **73** E2
Yazoo City, MS **73** E2
Yellow (river), WI **113** D3
Yellow Dog N.W.&S.R., MI **99** C3
Yellowstone (river), MT, WY **145** C11
Yellowstone Lake, WY **154** A2
Yellowstone N.P., ID, MT, WY **154** A2
Yerington, NV **147** D2
Yoakum, TX **127** G7
Yocona (river), MS **73** B3
Yona, GU **156** F1
Yonkers, NY **47** G8
York, AL **61** E1
York, NE **105** D8
York, PA **49** E7
York, SC **77** A5
York (river), VA **81** D10
York Village, ME **37** I2
Yorktown, VA **81** D11
Yosemite N.P., CA **137** E4
Youghiogheny (river), PA **49** F3
Youngstown, OH **109** B8
Ypsilanti, MI **99** H7
Yreka, CA **137** A2
Yuba City, CA **137** C3
Yucca House Nat. Mon., CO **138** G1
Yukon, OK **125** C8
Yukon (river), AK **135** E4
Yukon Delta, AK **134** D3
Yukon-Charley Rivers National Preserve, AK **135** C8
Yuma, AZ **121** G2
Yuma, CO **139** B8
Yunaska Island, AK **135** G10

Z

Zachary, LA **71** F6
Zanesville, OH **109** E6
Zapata, TX **127** H5
Zeeland, MI **99** H5
Zion N.P., UT **151** G2
Zoar, Lake, CT **33** D3
Zuni, NM **123** D1
Zuni (river), AZ **121** D7

Published by the National Geographic Society

John M. Fahey, Jr.
Chairman of the Board and Chief Executive Officer

Timothy T. Kelly
President

Declan Moore
President, Publishing and Digital Media

Melina Gerosa Bellows
Executive Vice President; Chief Creative Officer,
Books, Kids, and Family

Prepared by the Book Division

Hector Sierra, Senior Vice President and General Manager

Nancy Laties Feresten,
Senior Vice President, Editor in Chief, Children's Books

Jonathan Halling, Design Director, Books and Children's Publishing

Jay Sumner, Director of Photography, Children's Publishing

Jennifer Emmett, Editorial Director, Children's Books

Eva Absher-Schantz, Managing Art Director, Children's Publishing

Carl Mehler, Director of Maps

R. Gary Colbert, Production Director

Jennifer A. Thornton, Director of Managing Editorial

Staff for this book

Priyanka Lamichhane, Project Editor

David Seager, Art Director

Sven M. Dolling, Laura McCormick, Thomas L. Gray,
Nicholas P. Rosenbach, Map Editors

Matt Chwastyk, Sven M. Dolling, Steven D. Gardner,
Michael McNey, Gregory Ugiansky, Mapping Specialists, and
XNR Productions, Map Research and Production

Tibor G. Tóth, Map Relief

Lori Epstein, Senior Illustrations Editor

Martha B. Sharma, Consultant

Martha B. Sharma, Timothy J. Hill, Writers

Stuart Armstrong, Graphics Illustrator

Michelle R. Harris, Researcher

Dan Sherman, Web Page Design

Jennifer Kirkpatrick, Web Page Editor

Kathryn Robbins, Design Production Assistant

Stacy Gold, Nadia Hughes, Illustrations Research Editors

Kate Olesin, Assistant Editor

Lewis R. Bassford, Production Manager

Grace Hill, Associate Managing Editor

Joan Gossett, Production Editor

Susan Borke, Legal and Business Affairs

Manufacturing and Quality Management

Christopher A. Liedel, Chief Financial Officer

Phillip L. Schlosser, Senior Vice President

Chris Brown, Vice President

Nicole Elliott, Manager

Rachel Faulise, Manager

Robert L. Barr, Manager

The National Geographic Society is one of the world's largest nonprofit scientific and educational organizations. Founded in 1888 to "increase and diffuse geographic knowledge," the Society works to inspire people to care about the planet. National Geographic reflects the world through its magazines, television programs, films, music and radio, books, DVDs, maps, exhibitions, live events, school publishing programs, interactive media and merchandise. National Geographic magazine, the Society's official journal, published in English and 33 local-language editions, is read by more than 38 million people each month. The National Geographic Channel reaches 320 million households in 34 languages in 166 countries. National Geographic Digital Media receives more than 15 million visitors a month. National Geographic has funded more than 9,400 scientific research, conservation and exploration projects and supports an education program promoting geography literacy. For more information, visit nationalgeographic.com.

For more information, please call 1-800-NGS LINE (647-5463) or write to the following address:

NATIONAL GEOGRAPHIC SOCIETY
1145 17th Street N.W., Washington, D.C. 20036-4688 U.S.A.

Visit us online at www.nationalgeographic.com/books

For teachers and librarians: ngchildrensbooks.org

For information about special discounts for bulk purchases, please contact National Geographic Books Special Sales: ngspecsales@ngs.org

For rights or permissions inquiries, please contact National Geographic Books Subsidiary Rights: ngbookrights@ngs.org

Printed in China

14/CCOS/4

Illustrations Credits

Abbreviations for terms appearing below: (t)-top; (b)-bottom; (l)-left; (r)-right; NGS = National Geographic Image Collection; iS = iStockphoto.com; SH = Shutterstock.com

Art for state flowers and state birds by Robert E. Hynes

Locator globe page 16 created by Theophilus Britt Griswold

Front cover, Tibor G. Tóth; (sunflower), Shutterstock; (Mt. Rushmore), Digital Stock; (Statue of Liberty), Punchstock; (eagle), Shutterstock

Back cover (t–b), FloridaStock/SH, Peder Digre/SH, Lou Ann M. Aepelbacher/SH, Olga Lyubkina/SH

Front of the Book
2 (l–r), Freerk Brouwer/SH; PhotoDisc; Brandon Laufenberg/iS; Richard Nowitz/NGS; 3 (l–r), Joel Sartore/NGS; Jeremy Edwards/iS; Eileen Hart/iS; PhotoDisc; 4 (l), PhotoDisc; 4 (r), Brian J. Skerry/NGS; 4–5, Lenice Harms/SH; 5 (l), italian-estro/SH; 5 (r), James Davis Photography/Alamy; 5 (b), Digital Stock; 11 (t–b), Lane V. Erickson/SH; Elena Elisseeva/SH; SNEHIT/SH; Nic Watson/SH; FloridaStock/SH; Sai Yeung Chan/SH; TTphoto/SH; 12 (l) Lowell Georgia/NGS; 12 (r), NASA; 14 (l–r), George F. Mobley/NGS; Skip Brown/NGS; Jan Brons/SH; Michelle Pacitto/SH; Tammy Bryngelson/iS; 15 (l–r), Carsten Peter/NGS; Mark Thiessen/NGS; Michael Nichols/NGS; Steven Collins/SH; Robert Madden/NGS; 18, Ira Block/NGS; 20 (t), Penny de los Santos; 20 (bl), Steven Clevenger/Corbis; 20–21, Sarah Leen/NGS; 22 (l), Marcelo Piotti/iS; 22–23, Jim Richardson/NGS; 23 (r), Sorin Alb/iS; 24, PhotoDisc; 24–25, PhotoDisc; 25 (t), L. Kragt Bakker/SH; 25 (b), Lori Epstein/National Geographic Stock.

The Northeast
30 (bl), Rudi Von Briel/Photo Edit; 30 (br), Les Byerley/SH; 30–31 (t), Michael Melford/NGS; 30–31 (b), Tim Laman/NGS; 31 (t), Donald Swartz/iS; 32 (both), David L. Arnold/NGS; 33, Catherine Karnow/NGS; 34 (bl), Kevin Fleming/NGS; 34 (br), Stephen R. Brown/NGS; 34–35, Stephen St. John/NGS; 36 (b), iS; 36–37, PhotoDisc; 37 (b), Roy Toft/NGS; 38 (t), Jeremy Edwards/iS; 38 (b), Justice Gecewicz/iS; 39, James L. Stanfield/NGS; 40 (t), Sarah Leen/NGS; 40 (b), Tim Laman/NGS; 41, Darlyne A. Murawski/NGS; 42 (t), Medford Taylor/NGS; 42–43, Steven Phraner/iS; 43 (t), Richard Nowitz/NGS; 44 (t), Richard Nowitz/NGS; 44 (b), Iconica/Getty Images; 44 (br), Matt Rainey/Star Ledger/Corbis; 44–45, Mike Derer/Associated Press; 46 (t), Glenn Taylor/iS; 46 (b), James P. Blair/NGS; 47, Kenneth Garrett/NGS; 48 (t), Kenneth Garrett/NGS; 48 (b), Jeremy Edwards/iS; 49, William Albert Allard/NGS; 50 (t), Todd Gipstein/NGS; 50 (b), Onne van der Wal/Corbis; 50–51, Ira Block/NGS; 52, Michael S. Yamashita/NGS; 52–53, David McLain/Aurora/Getty Images; 53, Daniel W. Slocum/SH.

The Southeast
58 (t), Klaus Nigge/NGS; 58 (bl), Tyrone Turner/NGS; 58 (br), Richard Nowitz/Corbis; 58–59, Skip Brown/NGS; 59 (t), Raymond Gehman/NGS; 59 (b), Robert Clark/NGS; 60 (t), Raymond Gehman/NGS; 60 (b), Richard Nowitz/NGS; 62 (t), Harrison Shull/Aurora/Getty Images; 62 (b), Joel Sartore/NGS; 63, Cary Wolinsky/NGS; 64 (t), David Burnett/NGS; 64 (b), Brian J. Skerry/NGS; 64–65, NASA; 66 (tl), NGS; 66 (tr), PhotoDisc; 66 (b), Michael Melford/NGS; 68, Melissa Farlow/NGS; 69, Randy Olson/NGS; 70 (t), Tyrone Turner/NGS; 70 (b), Jason Major/iS; 72 (t), William Albert Allard/NGS; 72 (b), Ira Block/NGS; 73, Elena Vdovina/iS; 74 (l), Jack Fletcher/NGS; 74 (r), Pete Souza/NGS; 75, Raymond Gehman/NGS; 76, Terry Healy/iS; 76–77, Annie Griffiths Belt/NGS; 77, Raymond Gehman/NGS; 78, Melissa Farlow/NGS; 79 (t), Dennis R. Dimick/NGS; 79 (b), Jodi Cobb/NGS; 80 (t), Robert Clark/NGS; 80 (b), Richard Nowitz/NGS; 80–81, Medford Taylor/NGS; 82 (t), James L. Stanfield/NGS; 82 (b), Joel Sartore/NGS; 83, Robert Pernell/SH.

The Midwest
88 (t), James L. Stanfield/NGS; 88 (b), Jim Richardson/NGS; 88–89, NGS; 89 (tl), Nadia M. B. Hughes/NGS; 89 (tr), Sean Martin/iS; 89 (b), Aga/SH; 90 (t), Chas/SH; 90 (b), Jenny Solomon/SH; 90–91 (t), Lenice Harms/SH; 92–93 (t), iS; 92–93 (b), Melissa Farlow/NGS; 94 (t), Joel Sartore/NGS; 94 (b), Madeleine Openshaw/SH; 95, Tom Bean/NGS; 96, Cotton Coulson/NGS; 97, Phil Schermeister/NGS; 98 (t), Kevin Fleming/Corbis; 98 (b), Vince Ruffa/SH; 99, Geoffrey Kuchera/SH; 100 (t), Joel Sartore/NGS; 100 (b), Medford Taylor/NGS; 101, Lawrence Sawyer/iS; 102, Phil Schermeister/NGS; 102–103 (b), PhotoDisc; 103, Sarah Leen/NGS; 104 (both), Joel Sartore/NGS; 105, Sarah Leen/NGS; 106 (t), Farrell Grehan/NGS; 106 (b), Beverley Vycital/iS; 107, Annie Griffiths Belt/NGS; 108 (t), PhotoDisc; 108 (bl), Weldon Schloneger/SH; 108 (br), Robert J. Daveant/SH; 110, Peter Digre/SH; 111, Dan Westergren/NGS; 112 (t), Paul Damien/NGS; 112 (b), PhotoDisc; 112–113 Medford Taylor/NGS.

The Southwest
118 (t), Joseph H. Bailey/NGS; 118 (b), Penny de los Santos; 118–119, Anton Folton/iS; 119 (t), Chih Hsueh Tseng/SH; 119 (b), Joel Sartore/NGS; 120 (t), Joel Sartore/NGS; 120 (b), George Burba/SH; 122 (tl), James P. Blair/NGS; 122 (tr), italian-estro/SH; 122 (b), Lynn Johnson/NGS; 124, Joel Sartore/NGS; 125, Annie Griffiths Belt/NGS; 126 (t), Sarah Leen/NGS; 126–127, Diane Cook & Len Jenshel/NGS.

The West
132 (both), PhotoDisc; 132–133, Digital Stock; 133 (t), Phillip Holland/SH; 133 (bl), Joel Sartore/NGS; 133 (br), Digital Stock; 134 (t), Joel Sartore/NGS; 134 (b), PhotoDisc; 136 (t), PhotoDisc; 136 (b), Randy Olson/NGS; 138 (both), PhotoDisc; 140, PhotoDisc; 141, Frans Lanting/NGS; 142 (b), Joel Sartore/NGS; 142–143, Michael Melford/NGS; 143 (r), J. Cameron Gull/SH; 144 (b), William Albert Allard/NGS; 145, SH; 146 (b), Sam Abell/NGS; 146–147, Andy Z./SH; 147 (b), Raymond Gehman/NGS; 148 (t), Jennifer Lynn Arnold/SH; 148 (b), Peter Kunasz/SH; 150 (b), Digital Stock; 150–151, PhotoDisc; 152 (l), PhotoDisc; 152 (r), Digital Stock; 154 (t), Michael Rubin/SH; 154 (b), Digital Stock; 155, PhotoDisc.

The Territories and Back of the Book
158 (l), Kendra Nielsam/SH; 158–159 (t), James Davis Photography/Alamy; 158–159 (b), Ira Block/NGS; 159 (t), VisionsofParadise.com/Alamy; 159 (b), Gerry Ellis/Minden/Getty Images; 160, SH.

Map Acknowledgments

2–3, 26–27, 54–55, 84–85, 114–115, 128–129, Blue Marble: Next Generation NASA Earth Observatory; 12–13, climate data adapted from Peel, M. C., Finlayson, B. L., and McMahon, T. A.: Updated world map of the Köppen-Geiger climate classification, Hydrol. Earth Syst. Sci., 11, 1633–1644, 2007; 14–15, data from Billion Dollar Weather Disasters 1980–2007 (map), NOAA's National Climatic Data Center (NCDC); 18–19, data from Center for International Earth Science Information Network (CIESIN), Columbia University, and Centro Internacional de Agricultura Tropical (CIAT), 2005. Gridded Population of the World Version 3 (GPWv3): Population Density Grids—World Population Density, 2005 (map). Palisades, New York: Socioeconomic Data and Applications Center (SEDAC), Columbia University. Accessed October 2007. Available at sedac.ciesin.columbia.edu/gpw; 20–21, United States Atlas of Renewable Resources, National Renewable Energy Laboratory; 22–23, U.S. Census Bureau, Census 2000 Redistricting Data (PL 94–171) Summary File, Population Division.

Paperback ISBN: 978-1-4263-1052-2
ISBNs for 2008 editions, titled United States Atlas for Young Explorers, 3rd ed.: 978-1-4263-0255-8 (hardcover); 978-1-4263-0271-8 (Direct Mail Expanded Edition); 978-1-4263-0272-5 (Deluxe Direct Mail Expanded Edition)